FROM THOUGHT TO THEME

A Rhetoric and Reader for College English
Eighth Edition

William F. Smith
Fullerton College

Raymond D. Liedlich
Columbia College

Harcourt Brace Jovanovich, Publishers

San Diego **New York** **Chicago** **Atlanta** **Washington, D.C.**
London **Sydney** **Toronto**

104946

ISBN: 0-15-529219-6
Printed in the United States of America

COPYRIGHTS AND ACKNOWLEDGMENTS

The authors wish to thank the following for permission to reprint the material listed:

AMERICAN PSYCHOLOGICAL ASSOCIATION   For Lois Timnick, "Electronic Bul-
lies." Reprinted with permission from *Psychology Today* Magazine. Copyright © 1982
American Psychological Association.
ATHENEUM   For Andrew A. Rooney, "A Rich Writer," from *Pieces of My Mind.* Copy-
right © 1984 Essay Productions, Inc. Reprinted with the permission of Atheneum
Publishers, Inc.
JAMES BALDWIN   For "On Being 'White' . . . and Other Lies." Originally published
in *Essence* Magazine. Copyright © 1984 by James Baldwin. Reprinted by permission
of the author.
CHRONICLE OF HIGHER EDUCATION   For Steven M. Weiss, "I Remember Max."
Copyright 1982 by *The Chronicle of Higher Education.* Reprinted with permission.
COWLES SYNDICATE, INC.   For Michael Gartner, "Words' Worth." Reprinted cour-
tesy Cowles Syndicate, Inc. All rights reserved.

Continued on page 468

PREFACE

Although this Eighth Edition is thoroughly revised and reorganized, the book's purpose and plan are essentially the same as in previous editions: to guide students from thought to theme—to show them, through both precept and practice, how they can shape the raw materials of personal experience, observation, and reflection into clear and convincing expository or argumentative prose.

The text is divided into two parts, rhetoric and readings. In this edition, Chapters 1 and 5 of Part One, the Rhetoric, have been most substantially modified. Chapter 1 presents a brief overview of the process of writing an expository theme, focusing on the important stages of that process. Chapter 5 provides a full, detailed discussion of these stages, giving more attention in this edition to prewriting and revision. Chapter 5 also contains a brief discussion of emphasis as a rhetorical principle, material on diction, a checklist of steps to follow in preparing the final draft of the theme, and a summary of the important points covered in the first five chapters.

Giving students a preliminary view of the entire expository writing process should help them to understand better the relevance of Chapters 2, 3, and 4. These middle chapters concentrate primarily on the paragraph, presenting it as a theme in miniature and providing explicit, detailed discussions of unity, development, and coherence as these principles relate to the expository paragraph and theme.

Chapter 6 introduces, in clear and simple terms, the fundamentals of sound thinking—and shows students how to apply them to their own

iii

writing. This chapter explains and illustrates how a deductive argument, in this case the categorical syllogism, can be used as the basis of an argumentative theme. Chapter 6 also presents another pattern of paragraph development—tracing cause and effect relationships—to supplement the discussion of that subject introduced in Chapter 3.

Nine sample themes and more than 70 sample paragraphs are used to illustrate the rhetorical principles presented in Part One. About 40 percent of the paragraphs are new to this edition. Most of these paragraphs are intrinsically interesting and are sufficiently self-contained to afford opportunities for discussion and writing. In addition to the illustrative paragraphs, more than 75 exercises on tear-out sheets encourage immediate application of the lessons as they are studied.

Part Two, the Reader, presents 36 essays arranged in nine groups of four selections each. For the first time, they are organized rhetorically rather than thematically, leading to an even closer connection between the two parts of the book. This new arrangement and the additional readings (four more than in previous editions) give the second half of the text a greater breadth of subject matter than ever before.

Seventeen of the selections are new to this edition; another seven are reintroduced from earlier editions because they are excellent examples of the forms they represent. Twelve essays are carried over from the Seventh Edition for the same reason. As in the past, two-thirds of the total have never before, to the best of our knowledge, been published in a college composition text. Authors appearing here for the first time are Jeffrey Cressy, Joan Didion, Roger Ebert, Peter Elbow, Ellen Goodman, Suzanne Britt Jordan, Manuel J. Martinez, N. Scott Momaday, Donald Murray, Jewell Parker Rhodes, William Stafford, Lewis Thomas, Alvin Toffler, Mark Twain, and Joel M. Vance.

The first three essays in each group are accompanied by headnotes that introduce each selection and point out rhetorical devices and techniques students should look for as they read; related questions on the author's use of language and the rhetorical principles and practices employed follow these selections, along with a list of vocabulary items. Additional questions and exercises designed to stimulate student discussion and writing complete the apparatus. Although some of these questions and exercises do not call explicitly for writing, most of them readily lend themselves to such assignments. The fourth and final selection in each group is presented without editorial apparatus in order to challenge students to evaluate their mastery of the material at hand. The guidelines provided through the headnotes and follow-up questions for the first three selections in each group should enable students to approach the final essay with a reasonable degree of confidence and to analyze it with a minium of additional assistance.

Three indexes are provided for Part Two—Index to Reading Selections by Subject Matter, Index to Reading Selections by Basic Rhetorical Type, and Index to Questions on Language and Rhetoric. The first index will help those who wish to utilize a thematic approach; the second and third should facilitate a closer integration of the study of rhetorical principles in Part One with the analysis of rhetorical models in Part Two.

Both the Rhetoric and the Reader concentrate on expository and argumentative prose, because these are the forms of writing that are most essential to success in college studies and because they contribute to the development of responsible critical thought as well as expression. We have, however, included readings and exercises in personal narrative and description because these forms are initially more accessible for beginning college students.

From Thought to Theme has been planned as a basic text to help students clarify, organize, and explain their thoughts and feelings. The rhetoric leads students through a sequence of lessons to an understanding and application of the principles that govern effective expository and argumentative prose. The readings have been selected and arranged to extend and expand these lessons. Although there is obviously more than one way to help students improve their writing, we believe that our emphasis on a sequential, structured approach is especially helpful to students with limited background or experience in writing. The response to the book in its previous editions has reinforced our confidence in the soundness of this approach.

Over the past twenty years we have been indebted to countless instructors and students in colleges and universities throughout the United States for their responses to, and recommendations for, the various editions of this book. We thank Professor Barry M. Maid of the University of Arkansas, Little Rock; Professor Janis Keller of State University Agricultural and Technical College, Farmingdale, New York; Professor Walt Klarner of Johnson City Community College; and Professor Joyce O. Jenkins of Alcorn State University for their suggestions for revision of this edition. We appreciate the editorial assistance we received from our publisher: in particular from Marlane Agriesti and Bill McLane for their helpful suggestions on the inclusion of new material as well as on organization and focus, and from Cate Safranek for her careful, patient supervision of the final preparation of the manuscript. And, as always, we are most deeply indebted to our wives, Dorothy and Martha.

W. F. S.
R. D. L.

CONTENTS

PART TWO

Reader

PART ONE
RHETORIC

CHAPTER ONE
AN OVERVIEW

The general purpose of this book is to help you to use and respond to language with greater assurance and skill. A more specific, practical purpose is to help you to write clear, coherent paragraphs and essays as well as to read and analyze expository prose more effectively. The discussion and writing assignments focus primarily on expository, persuasive prose, the kind of writing most frequently demanded of college students. As you develop greater skill in discovering, developing, and expressing your thoughts and feelings, you will also learn to think more clearly, more logically, since writing necessarily uses words, and most of our thinking is done with words. The ability to think and write clearly will be important to you in college because almost every subject you study will require writing in some form—essay examinations, laboratory reports, term papers, book reviews, and application forms of one kind or another. But the principles you will study, the skills you will acquire in reading, writing, and thinking more effectively, will have a broader relevance as well, for they will help you to function more successfully after college in your social, public, and professional life, as a citizen and human being in an increasingly sophisticated industrial society.

The first five chapters deal with rhetoric, the art of persuasive speech and writing. This subject has been studied by college students for hundreds of years; in fact, you have been using rhetoric in all your attempts at explanation or persuasion, in and out of school, whether you were aware of it or not. In these chapters we will concentrate on the basic principles of unity, development, coherence, and emphasis as they relate to the paragraph and essay. Chapter Six will take a brief look at some common problems of sentence construction beginning writers often encounter.

THE EXPOSITORY THEME

In your college classes you will frequently be asked to write papers of several hundred words, compositions consisting of several paragraphs linked together in support of one central idea. Since the paragraph is the basic unit of expository and persuasive writing, in the next three chapters we will concentrate primarily on the paragraph in illustrating the principles of unity, development, and coherence. But since the paragraphs you write will generally be a part of a longer paper, we will begin here by presenting a brief preview of the process of writing the longer paper and then return to this subject in greater depth and detail in Chapter Five.

Many students who have trouble with writing assignments think that writing is simply an intuitive, inherited aptitude; that those who write well simply have a natural facility for it; and that if one lacks this facility, there is little to be done about it. To these students writing is the product of unconscious inspiration, a "bolt from the blue," and if one isn't blessed, well . . . that's that. The ability to write is, of course, enhanced by a natural aptitude for words and their arrangement. Some persons do seem to have a gift for language, an intuitive grasp of what might be called the "art" of writing that teachers and texts can't impart. But good writing does not result from natural ability alone; it is the result of thoughtful planning, intelligently directed effort, and the practice of writing and rewriting. These are matters of the "craft" of writing, and they *can* be taught and learned. And even those who have language in their bones do not simply reach for a piece of paper, tune in to some creative instinct, and write lucid, polished prose. They must think about their subject, explore their memory, their feelings, plan what they want to say, and revise their work carefully. In short, good writing doesn't demand genius, but a willingness to learn and a steady application of what has been learned.

There are no simple mechanical rules to follow in writing a theme; a system that works well for one writer may not work well for another. There *is* a uniqueness, an intuitive aspect, to all writing; but by following a series of steps, moving through a number of closely related stages in the process of writing a theme, you should be able to avoid many of the frustrations and false starts that plague and panic students who have no plan of procedure. These steps include (1) selecting a subject, (2) focusing your subject, (3) exploring your subject and developing a thesis statement, (4) devising a plan, (5) writing the first draft, (6) revising the first draft, and (7) preparing the final copy. The first four stages involve important pre-writing activities, the last three the writing itself.

(1) Selecting a Subject

The problem of selecting a subject is simplified when you are asked to write an expository essay on an assigned, restricted subject. In this case make certain you understand precisely what the subject, or question as in an essay examination, calls for and organize your material to focus on that subject. When you are given greater latitude in choice of subject, as for example when you are writing about a personal experience and your own feelings, judgments, and attitudes are important, you will need to take more time to work up your subject, making certain it will have some interest and significance for your reader. When you have a choice, choose a subject you know something about or one you want to know more about. Don't undervalue the significance of your own experience, especially one that taught you something important about yourself or changed your life in some way.

(2) Focusing Your Subject

After you have decided upon a subject, you must limit it sufficiently so that you can deal with it satisfactorily within the length of the paper you intend to write. You could not write a 300–500 word paper on "The World of Work," but one aspect of it, the benefits college students gain by working while going to college, could serve as a more specific, interesting, and therefore more satisfactory topic for an audience of college students. Similarly, a loosely focused, autobiographical essay on your childhood, adolescence, and late teen years would be less successful than a paper limited to one experience that taught you something important.

(3) Exploring Your Subject and Developing a Thesis Statement

In this stage you begin to explore your subject, to think about what you want to accomplish in your paper, what effect you want to have on your reader. If, for example, you want to inform and persuade your readers of the benefits of foreign travel, you must ask yourself what information they'll need to understand and accept your ideas and opinions. Your own travel experience, your reading and observations, conversations with others—all will serve as sources of material. If your subject is a personal experience, you'll have to dig into your memory bank for material.

Formulate, at least tentatively, a thesis for your paper, one major point you want to get across, a central question you want to answer. Though you may change your thesis as your paper evolves, devising a thesis statement at this stage will give direction to your writing; it will provide a foundation upon which to build your detail. Purpose and thesis are related concepts, but they are not the same thing. Your purpose—what you want to do in a paper—provides an overall design, a basis for choosing the kind of detail and strategies you will use in organizing your paper. Your thesis statement, on the other hand, expresses your controlling idea, the point you want to make. It is useful to write them down at this stage so that you'll keep them in mind as you develop your ideas. For a paper on the benefit of foreign travel, they might look something like this:

PURPOSE   In this paper I want to inform and persuade my fellow students of the benefits I see in foreign travel.

THESIS   Foreign travel is an exciting, culturally enriching, and maturing experience for college students.

(4) Devising a Plan: The Scratch Outline

Having thought about your purpose and come up with a tentative thesis, you must now generate and organize ideas in support of that thesis. You must supply *enough* detail so that your readers fully understand your ideas and use the *appropriate* detail and strategies to persuade them of the validity of those ideas. The time you spend in pre-writing, in working up your detail—facts, illustrations, judgments—is time well spent, for it will make the later assembling of your sentences and paragraphs in their final form much easier.

As you think about your subject, jot down ideas that come to mind from your own experience and observations, and take notes on your reading as well. Then work up a brief scratch outline of your material, organizing the body of it around three or four main points that support your thesis. As you do this, *keep your readers in mind:* What do they already know about the subject? What do they need to know? What biases or prejudices might they possess that would shape their response to your subject? What do you expect them to learn from your paper? Such questions are important, for they will help you decide on the kinds of detail you'll include, the terms and concepts you'll have to define, the words you'll use, the tone you'll adopt, and so on. The more you know about your readers, the better you'll be able to stimulate their interests and satisfy their expectations.

A scratch outline for a five paragraph essay on why married women want to work outside the home might take this form:

1. Mental stimulation
    Keep mind active
    Break up monotony of housework, add spice to life
    Help to contribute to livelier, more stimulating conversation with husband, children, and friends
2. Financial benefits
    Help pay family expenses, fight inflation

Put away money for children's college education, family vaca-
tions, better house
Help protect family income if husband loses job, suffers disa-
bility, dies
3. Psychological benefits
Greater self-confidence and poise
Improve self-image
Open self to new experience because of greater self-confidence
Absorb energies, lessen problems of nervous depression with
departure of children

(5) Writing the First Draft

Your material sorted into a scratch outline, you are now ready to write
your first draft, to transform your notes into the sentences and paragraphs of your theme. The main headings of your outline will serve as
the topic sentences of your paragraphs, each paragraph advancing the
thought, supporting the thesis of your paper. Once you begin writing,
move steadily onward. Worry about grammar, spelling, word choice,
punctuation, and so on later when you revise. Remember, your outline
is simply a framework, not an irrevocable contract. You can change it,
adding or omitting detail, as your finished paper takes more definite
shape in your mind. The following draft develops the thesis that
emerges from the outline presented above: "Wives working outside the
home gain three major benefits: mental stimulation, financial gain, and
ego reinforcement."

Working Wives

The impact of the women's liberation movement, together
with the effects of inflation and the fact and threat of unemployment among male heads of households, has made the question of whether wives should work outside the home somewhat
academic, if not quaint. Many wives do not have a choice. They
must work if their families are to survive. Others, however, have
a choice. But whether a woman has to work or chooses to work,
the rewards are real enough.

Many wives, particularly those in their late thirties or forties,
take a job because they want a change from the boredom of
housework. They want relief from the deadly routine of dishes,
dusting, shopping, perhaps from the coffee klatches and bridge
games with neighbors. Being a housewife is, certainly, a lot of
hard work. It must be done, but it can be shared when the wife

works. Not all jobs are exciting, but many do provide some mental stimulation, a challenge, particularly for women with college degrees who feel their abilities, skills, and aptitudes have lain dormant during their childrearing years. In addition, women who work can often engage in more lively, interesting conversations about their work with their husbands and friends and so become more lively and interesting themselves.

Another obvious benefit is financial. As mentioned earlier, increasing costs of living have forced many women to work simply to keep their families afloat. And even in those families in which wives are not forced to work, the extra paycheck can ease the strain on their husbands in paying for college education expenses for their children or helping to pay for a long-delayed vacation or remodeling the home. And even when children have left the nest, their expense is frequently replaced by the expense of supporting aging parents with medical problems.

But perhaps the most significant benefit of working is psychological. Women who have spent their early married life wedded to their children and homes, as well as to their husbands, often feel at loose ends when their children are gone and their duties as cook, housemaid, chauffeur, teacher, and cheerleader are gone or greatly diminished. Working often gives such women something constructive to do outside the home, absorbing energies that if not constructively channeled can produce dissatisfaction, restlessness, and a nervous depression that weakens their ability to successfully cope with the extra time on their hands. Meeting new people on the job, putting long-neglected skills to work, competing successfully in the marketplace, bringing home a paycheck—all of these experiences will build her self-confidence and give her a sense of achievement. As she proves her worth on the job as well as in the kitchen, she will very likely open herself to new experiences generally. And as she takes on new interests, she will broaden her outlook and become a more vital person.

But, some will ask, won't this new maturity and self-confidence make her less dependent upon her husband? Mightn't they threaten his ego if he believes his wife's place is in the home? Won't there be problems in marriages in which the husband wants his wife tethered to the house, dependent upon him for all her needs? Yes, very likely. For some husbands the change will be painful, but all human growth involves pain. And, in the long run, it's an acceptable price to pay for the mental stimulation, personal growth, and sense of achievement his wife will gain.

(6) Revising the First Draft

Set aside your first draft for a day or two. Let it marinate. When you return to it, your mind will be fresher, and you'll be able to look at it more objectively. As you revise it, concentrate first on the substance of your paper—your ideas and their organization. Then go over it once more, this time checking grammar, punctuation, spelling, word choice.

As you reread your draft, keep your readers in mind. Ask yourself these questions: Is my thesis clear, well supported? Does each paragraph relate to the thesis, advance the thought? Does each paragraph have a topic sentence and sufficient detail to explain its controlling idea? Is the detail relevant, interesting, compelling? Are the judgments and generalizations anchored by specific facts, clarifying illustrations? Are the paragraphs arranged in the most effective order? Are they linked together so that readers can follow my train of thought?

Here is a second draft of "Working Wives." Read it carefully. Note the changes that have been made.

Working Wives

Should married women work outside the home? A serious question in the past, the question seems almost quaint today. More and more married women are working—51.2% of the female work force in 1982 contrasted with 14.7% in 1942—and for most of them the reason is obvious. They must work if their families are to survive. Inflation and the threat or fact of unemployment of their husbands have seen to that. But what about those who don't really have to work? Do the rewards justify their efforts? The anwser is pretty clearly yes.

The most obvious benefit is financial. As mentioned above, the rising costs of living have forced many women to work simply to keep their families afloat. And even in those families in which the wife has a choice, the extra paycheck eases the financial burden on her husband in paying for college for the children, remodeling the house, or taking a long-delayed vacation. For young couples the benefit is not being able to remodel a house, it's the possibility of buying one in the first place. Unless the wife works, buying a house is simply out of the question. Two other points merit consideration, too. Even when the children have left the nest, the reduction in family costs is frequently replaced by the cost of supporting aging parents. And second, a job provides a wife additional security, psychological as well as financial, in the event of the illness or death of her husband.

A second benefit, particularly for women in their late thirties or forties, is the relief from the boredom of housework. They want a change from the deadly routine of washing dishes, dusting, making beds, ironing shirts, polishing the furniture, and perhaps from the coffee klatches and bridge games with neighbors. Not all jobs are exciting, of course; but most provide some mental stimulation, a challenge, particularly for those with college degrees who feel their abilities and skills have lain dormant during their child-rearing years. In addition, women who work often have more to contribute to conversations with their husbands and friends. And as their conversation becomes livelier, more interesting, they become more lively and interesting themselves.

But perhaps the most significant benefit of working is psychological. Women who have spent their early married lives wedded to their homes and children, as well as to their husbands, often feel at loose ends when their children are gone and their duties as cook, housemaid, chauffeur, nurse, teacher, and guardian are eliminated or greatly diminished. Working gives them something constructive to do outside the home. It absorbs energies that, if not constructively channeled, can produce dissatisfaction, restlessness, nervous depression that weakens their capacity to cope with the extra time on their hands and, more important, the problems of aging. Meeting new people on the job, putting long-neglected skills to use, competing successfully in the marketplace—all of these experiences build self-confidence; they give a woman a sense of her own importance. As she proves to herself that she can bring home the bacon as well as cook it, she will open herself to new experience, broaden her interests, and so become a more vital, interesting person in her own right.

But traditionalists may ask, "Won't all this new maturity and self-confidence make a wife less dependent upon her husband? Mightn't they threaten his ego if he believes that his wife's place is in the home?" Yes, quite likely. Some husbands want their wives tethered to the home, dependent upon them for all their needs. But a truly happy, successful marriage means freedom as well as commitment, freedom for each partner to grow, develop, to satisfy a need for selfhood within the bonds of a loving relationship. Yes, for some husbands the change will be painful, but all growth involves pain. And, in the long run, it's an acceptable price to pay for the mental stimulation, personal growth, and sense of achievement his wife will gain.

The opening and closing parts of the first paragraph have been revised. A question has been added at the beginning to arouse reader interest; and the thesis, presented at the end, has been more narrowly focused on women who choose to work. Note also the inclusion of the statistic on the percentage of married women in the work force.

In the second paragraph the two sentences "Being a housewife . . . wife works," have been omitted because they introduce irrelevancies. The drudgery of housework and sharing its burdens don't support the topic sentence, which has to do with the mental stimulation provided by a job.

Two new sentences have been added to the third paragraph, which appears as the second paragraph in the revised version: one dealing with young married couples' purchasing a house, the second on the security provided by a job to a woman whose husband becomes ill or dies.

The last two paragraphs are basically unchanged. The phrase "bring home the bacon as well as cook it" has been added to the fourth paragraph to lighten the tone a bit. The term "traditionalists" has been substituted for "some" in the last paragraph to sharpen the reference a bit. Spelling, punctuation, and sentence structure have also been gone over. The sentences in the original version were somewhat longer; they have been shortened in places for emphasis.

(7) Preparing the Final Copy

Suggestions for making up the final copy are presented on page 223 of Chapter Five.

CHAPTER TWO
UNITY

An essential quality of all good writing is *unity,* or singleness of purpose. The paragraph is a unit of thought concerned with the exposition of a single idea, and if it is to communicate that idea clearly and concisely, it must possess oneness. That is, all the detail—the reasons, illustrations, facts—used to develop it must pertain to one controlling idea. Consider, for example, the following paragraph:

> I have an increasing admiration for the teacher in the country school where we have a third-grade scholar in attendance. She not only undertakes to instruct her charges in all the subjects of the first three grades, but she manages to function quietly and effectively as a guardian of their health, their clothes, their habits, their mothers, and their snowball engagements. She has been doing this sort of Augean task for twenty years, and is both kind and wise. She cooks for the children on the stove that heats the room, and she can cool their passions or warm their soup with equal competence. She conceives their costumes, cleans up their messes, and shares their confidences. My boy already regards his teacher as his great friend, and I think tells her a great deal more than he tells us. [From E. B. White, "Education," *One Man's Meat,* Harper & Row, 1939.]

The controlling idea of this paragraph is contained in the first sentence, "I have an increasing admiration for the teacher in the country school where we have a third-grade scholar in attendance," and the following sentences provide supporting detail. To explain his point, his admiration for his boy's teacher, the writer describes her quiet, effective performance in a variety of roles: as a teacher; as a guardian of the children's health, habits, clothing, and character development; and as a kind, wise, and good friend.

THE TOPIC SENTENCE

The sentence that expresses the controlling idea of a paragraph is called the *topic sentence*. In the paragraph above, it is the first sentence, the sentence on which the unity of the paragraph is based. An important first step in achieving paragraph unity is to express your thought in a topic sentence and place that sentence at the beginning of your paragraph. A beginning topic sentence provides an organizational focus, a guideline that will help you to stick to your subject. It will not guarantee paragraph unity, however. The following paragraph, for example, begins with a topic sentence, but it does not prevent the writer from wandering off the subject.

> Living in an apartment while attending college is not a bad idea. For one thing, it promotes self-reliance. To manage apartment living successfully, students have to do their own laundry, clean up their own messes, and buy and cook their own food. Since they are faced with expenditures they didn't have at home—such as rent, utility bills, food, and furniture—they must also learn to budget their money and spend it wisely. If they do, they will take an important step along the road to maturity. Those who can't manage their own finances should live at home or in a dormitory. Living in a dormitory, however, is not ideal for students who enjoy their privacy. And, finally, living in an apartment stimulates pride of ownership.

In the first five sentences of this paragraph, the writer stays on the subject. The first sentence presents the main point, and the second introduces the first supporting detail—students learn self-reliance. The third sentence clarifies the second by means of illustration, and the fourth and fifth sentences focus on a second benefit—students learn to manage their own finances. But the sixth and seventh sentences stray from the controlling idea. From a consideration of the benefits of apartment living for college students, the writer shifts his attention in these two sentences to living at home or in a dormitory. The last sentence returns to the main point—apartment living stimulates pride of ownership.

What has happened in this paragraph often happens in students' paragraphs. Although students place the topic sentence first and use it as a guide for supporting sentences, they may nevertheless insert irrelevant ideas. Why? One important reason is that they have not focused sharply enough on a controlling idea in the topic sentence. The topic sentence of the paragraph above seemed sufficiently broad to the writer to justify the comment on the connection between a lack of ability to manage money and the attraction of living at home or in a dormitory. Had the writer narrowed the topic in the topic sentence and made his controlling idea more precise, he would have been less likely to introduce extraneous ideas into the paragraph. Consider this revised version:

> Living in an apartment while attending college is advantageous for many students because it helps them to develop maturity. For one thing, it promotes self-reliance. To manage apartment living successfully, students have to do their own laundry, clean up their own messes, and buy and cook their own food. Since they are faced with expenditures they didn't have at home—such as rent, utility bills, food, and furniture—they must also learn to budget their money and spend it wisely. If they do, they will take an important step along the road to maturity. And, finally, living in an apartment stimulates pride of ownership. Decorating and furnishing an apartment, however simply, requires thought and taste in the purchase and arrangement of furniture and accessories. Those who have invested their time and energy in acquiring such possessions are apt to take care of them.

The topic of the revised version is more pointed. The original topic sentence has been modified by changing "is not a bad idea" to "is advantageous for many students because it helps them to develop maturity." The controlling idea is now more precise. It signals reader and writer alike that the paragraph will discuss why, in terms of the development of maturity, apartment living is advantageous for many students. Because he has now more tightly defined the subject, the writer is less likely to introduce irrelevant matter.

THE CONTROLLING IDEA

In the preceding section we have referred to and briefly explained the concept of the controlling idea in the topic sentence, but something more needs to be said about it. Like all normal sentences, a topic sentence has a subject and a predicate. In the sentence

> Traveling by train has several advantages over traveling by plane.

the controlling idea, *several advantages,* is part of the predicate. Most of the topic sentences you will write will follow this pattern, with the controlling idea in the predicate. The topic sentences that follow do so.

Occasionally, however, the controlling idea may be part of the subject of the topic sentence, as in the following:

> A number of methods for combating juvenile delinquency are now in use.

The controlling idea here is *number of methods*.

Whether you include your controlling idea in the subject or the predicate, make certain that every topic sentence you write does contain a key word or group of words that expresses a dominant idea. A controlling idea will help you to limit your subject to one that you can deal with more completely in a paragraph, and to avoid the kind of broad, general topic sentence that tempts students to include a variety of detail only loosely related to their central idea. Here are some examples of such broad, general topic sentences with their suggested revisions. Each revision sharpens the focus of the original sentence by stressing a more specific controlling idea.

ORIGINAL	REVISED
Professor Burkhardt is a fine teacher.	Professor Burkhardt is very successful in stimulating student interest in his subject.
Television soap operas are not dramatic masterpieces.	Television soap operas suffer from implausible, melodramatic plots.
Pollution presents a real problem today.	Air and water pollution threaten the health and safety of mankind today.
Maria Del Monte has a fabulous personality.	Maria Del Monte's wit, friendliness, and poise make her a popular girl.

The revised sentence about Maria Del Monte illustrates an important aspect of the controlling idea—it may contain more than one idea. Here is another example:

> The study of psychology is *interesting* and *useful*.

The two ideas in this topic sentence could be developed, although briefly of course, in a single paragraph. The controlling idea in this next sentence, however, is too comprehensive for development in one paragraph:

America is a *democratic society* based on a system of *free enterprise,* which emphasizes *individual initiative.*

Adequate development of the ideas in this sentence would require several paragraphs, for each of the italicized terms would have to be explained and illustrated. To attempt such a discussion in a single paragraph would create serious problems in unity, especially for an inexperienced writer.

EXERCISE 1

Underline the topic sentence and circle the controlling idea in the following paragraphs.

1. Good families are much to all their members, but everything to none. Good families are fortresses with many windows and doors to the outer world. The blood clans I feel most drawn to were founded by parents who are nearly as devoted to what they do outside as they are to each other and their children. Their curiosity and passion are contagious. Everybody, where they live, is busy. Paint is spattered on eyeglasses. Mud lurks under fingernails. Person-to-person calls come in the middle of the night from Tokyo and Brussels. Catcher's mitts, ballet slippers, overdue library books, and other signs of extrafamilial concerns are everywhere. [From Jane Howard, "All Happy Clans Are Alike," *The Atlantic Monthly,* May 1978.]

2. If we wish to hold on to the cultural heritage of the Southwest, we must preserve the Spanish language. If the language goes, the culture goes with it. This is precisely the spiritual crisis of the minorities of the United States. They are losing their native languages, and with the language they are losing a certain consciousness of their own existence. They are losing something of their vital polarity, something of their identity. They find themselves somewhat uprooted, somewhat disoriented. A manner of being, a way of life, forged slowly since the beginning of history, is lost with the loss of the language. Until a new consciousness, a new manner of being, is forged through and by the newly acquired language, these minorities will remain somewhat disoriented. [From Sabine R. Ulibarri, "The Education of Jose Perez," *We Are Chicanos: An Anthology of Chicano Literature,* ed. Phillip D. Ortega, Washington Square Press, 1973.]

3. The tensions and troubles of modern life often cause people, especially old people, to yearn for "the good old days," when life was simpler and therefore better. But was it? The truth is that life in America 150 years ago, before the beginning of the age of industrialization, was harsh for many people. Life expectancy was rather short, about 38 years for males and a few more for females. Farm labor was hard and never-ending, dawn to dusk, 72 hours and more per week for men; and women worked even longer hours cooking, scrubbing floors, feeding farm animals, making clothes, preserving food. And speaking of food, because of a lack of refrigeration there were no fresh vegetables in winter; as a result, vitamin deficiency diseases were common. In times of drought or insect invasions food supplies were scarce. Epidemics also caused heavy loss of life. Infant mortality was high and childbirth a serious business in isolated areas where doctors were few and midwives inadequately trained.

4. Our society is built on paper foundations. Every large building in a great metropolis existed first in hundreds of pages of closely written specifications. Every modern bridge, every highway, has emerged from the mind of man with the assistance of the written word. Millions of typewriters clatter from morning to night, creating the correspondence, the reports, the records upon which commerce, industry, and government depend for essential information. Forests fall to convey to modern man the news of this country and of the world. Constantly letters flow across the land, carrying messages of love and pain,

business and pleasure, to millions of readers. Even in the armed forces, thousands of messages are received and transmitted daily at any large base. It is said in the Navy that "communications cannot win a war, but they sure as hell can lose it." No American who wishes to hold a place of any significant responsibility can avoid the necessity of written communication. [From Donald R. Tuttle, "Composition," *The Case for Basic Education: A Program of Aims for Public Schools,* ed. James D. Koerner, Council for Basic Education, Little, Brown, 1959, p. 83.]

5. Yet, clearly, the family is the seedbed of economic skills, money habits, attitudes toward work, and the arts of financial independence. The family is a stronger agency of educational success than the school. The family is a stronger teacher of the religious imagination than the church. Political and social planning in a wise social order begin with the axiom *What strengthens the family strengthens society.* Highly paid, mobile, and restless professionals may disdain the family (having been nurtured by its strengths), but those whom other agencies desert have only one institution in which to find essential nourishment. [From Michael Novak, "The Family Out of Favor," *Harper's Magazine,* April 1976.]

EXERCISE 2

A. The controlling idea of a topic sentence, as explained earlier, is the key word or group of words that expresses its basic idea. In the following sentences circle the word or group of words that contains the controlling idea.

EXAMPLE   For most people regular exercise is (beneficial.)

1. The American boycott of the Olympic Games held in Moscow in 1980 and the Russian boycott of the Games held in Los Angeles in 1984 are likely to have serious effects on future Olympiads.

2. Divorce is a costly, traumatic experience for most couples.

3. Professor Chun is a lively, witty, well-informed lecturer.

4. Participation in sports can be a liberating, satisfying experience for a person.

5. A number of suggestions have been made by professional economists on reducing the budget deficit.

6. During the past thirty years travelling and living abroad have become very popular with Americans.

7. Getting an education is often a harrowing experience.

8. Michael Jackson is an enormously popular young singer.

9. The decline in the American steel industry over the past twenty years has many causes.

10. Surviving the first year of college requires hard work and endurance.

B. Revise the following topic sentences to narrow the focus on a more specific dominant idea.

EXAMPLE

ORIGINAL   The new Phaeton automobile is a fine car.

REVISION   Superior workmanship, beautiful design, and economical operation make the new Phaeton a fine automobile.

1. Claudia Cordovici is a swell girl.

_____

_____

2. The nuclear energy industry is in trouble.

_____

_____

3. Violence in motion pictures and on television is getting to be a real problem.

_____

_____

4. Computer science is a good college major.

_____

_____

5. Kathleen Russo is a marvelous singer.

_____

_____

6. Efforts by Third World nations and the Soviet bloc to regulate international news reporting are not a good idea.

_____

_____

7. Desmond Roberts is a super guy with a fabulous personality.

_____

_____

8. Albert Rubin, the current district attorney, would make a fantastic mayor.

_____

_____

9. Foreign students do not have an easy time at American universities.

_____

_____

10. The various ratings given American motion pictures don't really work.

_____

_____

EXERCISE 3

A. Compose a precise topic sentence on each of the following subjects. Focus on <u>one</u> idea in your controlling idea and underline that idea.

EXAMPLE

Subject—the American economy

Topic Sentence—High interest rates have a <u>destructive effect on the construction industry</u>.

1. A teacher who's made a strong impression on you

_____

_____

2. Owning a car

_____

_____

3. Popular music

_____

_____

4. Recreation

_____

_____

5. The Olympic Games

_____

_____

B. Revise each of the topic sentences in Exercise A above, this time including <u>two</u> ideas in your topic sentence. Again, underline your controlling idea.

EXAMPLE High interests rates have a <u>destructive effect on the construction and automobile industries</u>.

1. _____

_____

_____

2. _____

_____

_____

3. _____

_____

_____

4. _____

_____

_____

5. _____

_____

_____

C. Compose a paragraph using as your topic sentence one of the sentences you've written for A or B above. Work up a scratch outline for your paragraph, following the general procedure presented on pages 6–7 in Chapter One for developing a scratch outline for a theme. Below your topic sentence list the detail that might be used to develop your controlling idea. Make sure that your detail—your facts, judgments, illustrations—are clear, concrete, interesting. As you consider your material, you may wish to modify your topic sentence. Don't hesitate to do so. Check your detail once more to eliminate irrelevancies; then write your paragraph. Your plan might look something like this:

> *Topic*—Problems of college students
> *Topic sentence*—Beginning college students usually have to face three serious problems.
> 1. Financial
>   tuition, books, fees
>   housing, food
>   transportation
>   entertainment
> 2. Academic
>   deciding upon a major
>   scheduling important classes

3. Organizing their time
    for study
    for part-time job
    for recreation

The numbered items under the topic sentence represent primary support; the items below each number provide specific illustration of the more general primary items.

PRIMARY AND SECONDARY SUPPORTING DETAIL

When your topic sentence is somewhat complicated, you will often have to develop your paragraph more extensively than when your topic sentence is simple. In this case, some of your sentences will contain more important ideas than others. That is, the detail in some sentences will directly support the controlling idea, whereas the detail in other sentences will explain and clarify these direct supporting statements. We can thus conveniently distinguish between *primary* support—detail that relates directly to the main idea of the paragraph—and *secondary* support—detail that explains and clarifies primary support. In the following paragraph the topic idea is supported by a number of primary statements, each of which relates directly to the controlling idea of the topic sentence—the different ways the strength of alcoholic drinks is measured.

> The strength of alcoholic drinks is measured differently in Britain, the United States, and France. In Britain the concentration of alcohol is designated by its "proof," a rather quaint system involving gunpowder. In this system "proof" refers to the concentration of alcohol in gunpowder soaked with it that allows the powder to burn steadily—the higher the proof, the stronger the flame. In Britain 100 proof liquor contains, oddly enough, 57.1 percent alcohol. In the United States, however, 100 proof means a 50 percent concentration. That is, the percentage of alcohol in American liquor can be determined by dividing the proof figure in half; pure alcohol would be 200 proof. The French system is simpler and neater. The French measure percentage of alcohol by volume, as so many degrees Gay-Lussac: 100 degrees (100° Gay-Lussac) means 100 percent alcohol.

In this next paragraph the topic sentence is supported by one primary statement and three secondary statements.

> We can thus say that while the average human being is a mixture, some people are mainly "digestion-minded," some "muscle-minded," and some "brain-minded," and correspondingly digestion-bodied, muscle-bodied, or brain-bodied. The digestion-bodied people look thick; the muscle-bodied people look wide; and the brain-bodied people look long. This does not mean the taller a man is, the brainier he will be. It means that if a man, even a short man, looks long rather than wide or

thick, he will often be more concerned about what goes on in his mind than about what he does or what he eats; but the key factor is slenderness and not height. On the other hand, a man who gives the impression of being thick rather than long or wide will usually be more interested in a good steak than in a good idea or a good long walk. [From Eric Berne, "Can People Be Judged by Their Appearances?" *A Layman's Guide to Psychiatry and Psychoanalysis,* Simon and Schuster, 1947.]

An analysis of each of these two paragraphs illuminates this difference between primary and secondary supporting statements:

TOPIC SENTENCE   The strength of alcoholic drinks is measured differently in Britain, the United States, and France.

Primary Support
1.   In Britain the concentration of alcohol . . . involving gunpowder.

   Secondary Support
   In this system, "proof" . . . the flame.
   In Britain 100 proof . . . alcohol.

Primary Support
2.   In the United States, however . . . concentration.

   Secondary Support
   That is, the percentage of alcohol . . . 200 proof.

Primary Support
3.   The French system is simpler and neater.

   Secondary Support
   The French measure percentage of alcohol . . . alcohol.

TOPIC SENTENCE   We can thus say that while the average human being is a mixture, some people are mainly "digestion-minded," some "muscle-minded," and some "brain-minded," and correspondingly digestion-bodied, muscle-bodied, or brain-bodied.

Primary Support
The digestion-bodied people look . . . brain-bodied people.

Secondary Suport
This does not mean . . . he will be.
It means that if a man . . . not height.
On the other hand, a man who . . . . a good long walk.

When you have decided on a topic sentence, then examine its controlling idea carefully. If it is fairly complex, you will probably need both primary and secondary support to develop it adequately. The writer of the following paragraph uses both primary and secondary support in developing the controlling idea.

Automobile manufacturers have certainly catered to the public's love of comfort and convenience in designing the modern automobile. Ease of movement and relaxation of physical tension have been emphasized. Plush carpets, luxuriously padded seats curved to support the spine, and headrests enhance riding comfort. By simply touching a button, the driver can raise, lower, or tilt his seat forward or backward to obtain the most comfortable driving position. Tilt-away steering wheels also make it easier to get in and out of the car. Suspension systems have also been greatly improved to smooth out the bumps on the roughest of roads. Soft coil springs, heavy duty shock absorbers, gas and air-filled shocks, stabilizer bars—all of these options let buyers choose their level of comfort. Efficient air conditioning and heating systems let riders control the temperature. No longer must they freeze in winter nor roast in the summer. Visual and audio discomforts have also been reduced. Windows can be raised or lowered electrically to shut out external noise and tinted to cut down on glare. Stereophonic tape players and AM-FM radios provide listening pleasure to occupants as they glide along the highway. Even telephones can easily be installed to accommodate busy salespeople and executives who want to keep in touch with clients or the home office without having to waste time stopping the car to use a pay phone.

The controlling idea of this paragraph is contained in the first sentence: "Automobile manufacturers have certainly catered to the public's love of comfort in designing the modern automobile." Six primary statements support the controlling idea. What are they? Which sentences provide illustration and clarification of these primary statements? An understanding of the way this paragraph is assembled will provide practical guidance when you need more than primary support to develop the controlling idea of a paragraph.

This discussion of primary and secondary detail is intended to clarify a basic characteristic of the structure of the expository or argumentative paragraph. As you will discover in your reading and writing, however, this distinction is not precisely applicable to every paragraph of this type. That is, every sentence of such a paragraph does not necessarily add a new primary or secondary supporting detail. Occasionally, a writer begins a paragraph with one or more sentences that lead in to the topic sentence, as is the case with the paragraph on pages 36–37. And in a paragraph that is part of a longer composition, one or two sentences at the beginning may refer to an idea developed in a preceding paragraph. You will also discover that one sentence may simply repeat, as a means of emphasis, an idea in a preceding sentence of the same paragraph.

In the following excerpt from T. S. Matthews' "What Makes News," for example, the first three sentences of the second paragraph deal with one idea—the putative power of the press to influence public opinion. The first sentence, "In what way is the press supposed to be so powerful?" iterates the thought of the topic sentence of the preceding paragraph and thus serves to link these two paragraphs together. The next sentence, "The general notion is that the press can form, control, or at least strongly influence public opinion," expands upon the idea of the preceding sentence by elucidating the "way" in which the press is thought to exert its power. And the third sentence, "Can it really do any of these things?" contains the controlling idea that the following sentences develop.

Topic
Sentence   The biggest piece of claptrap about the press is that it deals exclusively, or even mainly, with news. *And the next biggest piece of claptrap is that the press has enormous power.* This delusion is persistent and widespread. It is taken for granted by the public-at-large, who are apt to be impressed by anything that is said three times; it is continually advertised by the press itself; and it is cherished by press lords, some of whom, at least, should know better.

Linking
Sentence   (1) In what way is the press supposed to be so powerful? (2) The general notion is that the press can form, control, or at least strongly influence public opinion.

Topic
Sentence   (3) *Can it really do any of these things?* Hugh Cudlipp, editorial director of the London *Daily Mirror,* and a man who should know something about the effect of newspapers on public opinion, doesn't share this general notion about their power. He thinks newspapers can echo and stimulate a wave of popular feeling, but that's all: "A newspaper may successfully accelerate but never reverse the popular attitude, which common sense has commended to the public." In short, it can jump aboard the bandwagon, once the bandwagon is under way, but it can't start the bandwagon rolling or change its direction once it has started. [From T. S. Matthews, "What Makes News," *The Atlantic Monthly,* December 1957, p. 82.]

EXERCISE 4

A. Read the following paragraph carefully and pick out the topic sentence, the primary sentences, and the secondary sentences. Write them in the blanks provided. Reread pages 27–28 and study the process presented on those pages.

Public transportation in the United States is in trouble, deep trouble. And the solution is not in sight. The most serious problem is funding. Mass transit is largely dependent upon government financing—local, state, and federal money provides 56 percent of current operating expenses—and that funding is being reduced in accord with the public demand to trim government spending. Equipment, fuel, and maintenance costs continue to rise; but raising fares is politically unpopular, so transit systems' woes increase. New York City, which has the largest system, needs more than $14 billion for repair and improvement of equipment. Mechanical failure also complicates the problem. *Newsweek* magazine reports that half of Houston's 760 buses are idled by breakdown and one quarter of New York's subway cars are out of commission at any one time.[1] The new Grumman Flexible bus, in use in more than 30 cities, was supposed to increase ridership with its modern innovations in comfort; but it has spent about as much time in the repair shop as on the road. But transit unions, in the opinion of many observers, represent the chief obstacle to progress. Big city transit workers are more generously paid than other government workers: in Chicago, for example, a bus driver can make $25,000 a year in 3½ years and in Boston the average salary is $33,000. Since unions resist attempts to lower operational costs by employing part-time drivers during rush hours, to eliminate unnecessary personnel, and to curb wage demands in troubled transit districts, the outlook for any improvement in the public transit system is bleak indeed.

TOPIC SENTENCE ———————————————————————

———————————————————————————————

CONTROLLING IDEA ———————————————————————

———————————————————————————————

Primary Support

1. ———————————————————————————————

———————————————————————————————

[1] "Can't Get There from Here," June 1, 1981, pp. 44–45.

Secondary Support

_____

_____

_____

Primary Support

2. _____

   Secondary Support

   _____

   _____

   _____

Primary Support

3. _____

   Secondary Support

   _____

   _____

   _____

B. In the following exercise a topic sentence and some supporting sentences
    provide the framework for a paragraph on sports fans. Supply the primary
    and secondary support needed to develop the controlling idea in the blanks
    provided.

   TOPIC SENTENCE   Scanning a crowded football stadium, one can quickly
                    distinguish three types of sports fans.

   Primary Support

   1. The true sports enthusiast is easily spotted.

      Secondary Support

      a. _____

      _____

      b. _____

      _____

Primary Support

2. The casual, mildly interested fan is also conspicuous.

Secondary Support

a. He is usually well dressed, accompanied by his wife or girlfriend and another couple.
b. He wants the home team to win, but he is not a fanatic, and he chats amiably with his companions during the course of the game.

c. _____

_____

Primary Support

3. _____

Secondary Support

a. _____

_____

b. _____

_____

C. Using the detail and framework you've developed for Exercise A, and any additional detail you wish to make it more interesting, colorful, and specific, compose a 100–150 word paragraph on sports fans.

PLACEMENT OF THE TOPIC SENTENCE

We have suggested that you place the topic sentence first. This advice is especially valid for inexperienced writers, for a beginning topic sentence provides the best guideline and the most effective check against irrelevant matter. However, as you gain skill and experience in writing lucid, well-developed paragraphs, you may occasionally wish to place the topic sentence elsewhere. For example, you may use it not to announce your controlling idea but to reinforce it at the conclusion of your paragraph. Presenting your evidence first lets your readers see the reasoning that supports your idea, in which case they would be more apt to accept it than if it were presented at the beginning of your paragraph. The following paragraph is from an article by Wayne Davis in which he argues that America has a more serious population problem than India because of the destructive effect of the American way of life on the land. The writer provides his evidence first and his conclusion in a topic sentence at the end.

> In his lifetime he will personally pollute three million gallons of water, and industry and agriculture will use ten times this much water in his behalf. To provide these needs the U.S. Army Corps of Engineers will build dams and flood farmland. He will also use 21,000 gallons of leaded gasoline containing boron, drink 28,000 pounds of milk and eat 10,000 pounds of meat. The latter is produced and squandered in a life pattern unknown to Asians. A steer on a Western range eats plants containing minerals necessary for plant life. Some of these are incorporated into the body of the steer which is later shipped for slaughter. After being eaten by man these nutrients are flushed down the toilet into the ocean or buried in the cemetery, the surface of which is cluttered with boulders called tombstones and has been removed from productivity. The result is a continual drain on the productivity of range land. Add to this the erosion of overgrazed lands, and the effects of the falling water table as we mine Pleistocene deposits of groundwater to irrigate to produce food for more people, and we can see why our land is dying more rapidly than did the great civilizations of the Middle East, which experienced the same cycle. The average Indian citizen, whose fecal material goes back to the land, has but a minute fraction of the destructive effect on the land that the affluent American does. [From Wayne H. Davis, "Overpopulated America," *The New Republic,* January 10, 1970.]

Another method is to begin and close with a topic sentence.

We have an image of what a leader ought to be. We even recognize the physical signs: leaders may not necessarily be tall, but they must have bigger-than-life features—LBJ's nose and ear lobes, Ike's broad grin. A trademark also comes in handy: Lincoln's stovepipe hat, JFK's rocker. We expect our leader to stand out a little, not to be like ordinary men. Half of President Ford's trouble lay in the fact that, if you closed your eyes for a moment, you couldn't remember his face, figure or clothes. A leader should have an unforgettable identity, instantly and permanently fixed in people's minds. [From Michael Korda, "What It Takes to Be a Leader," *Newsweek,* January 5, 1981.]

In some paragraphs you may need two sentences to express your central idea. In the paragraph below the first two sentences convey the main idea, that society's level of health is not simply a matter of medical treatment of the sick, of greater investment in medicine.

Many people believe that society's level of health depends primarily on medical treatment of the sick. But the relationship between increased investment in medicine and improvements in health is tenuous. Behavior usually has more to do with how long and healthily people live than does the soaring investment in medical treatments to restore health, or to slow its decline. Leon Kass of the University of Chicago notes that other animals "instinctively eat the right foods (when available) and act in such a way as to maintain their naturally given state of health and vigor. Other animals do not overeat, undersleep, knowingly ingest toxic substances, or permit their bodies to fall into disuse through sloth, watching television and riding in automobiles, transacting business or writing articles about health." For humans, health must be nurtured by "taming and moderating the admirable yet dangerous human desire to live better than sows and squirrels." So in one way, it makes little more sense to claim a right to health than to claim a right to wisdom or courage. [From George F. Will, "No Right to Health," *The Pursuit of Virtue and Other Tory Notions,* Simon and Schuster, 1982.]

The topic sentence of this next paragraph is the third sentence, "Such concern is justifiable, of course . . ." The first two sentences lead into this sentence, and the sentences following it develop its controlling idea—the increase in thievery and fraud in the United States.

Judging from the fervor with which candidates for public office ally themselves with efforts to reduce crime and punish criminals, Americans are deeply disturbed about the rising level of crime in this country. They want the Mafia exposed and destroyed; they want murderers, muggers, rapists, dope peddlers off the streets and into prison. Such concern is justifiable, of course; but other types of criminal activity, common thievery and fraud, are more common and ultimately more destructive. That many Americans routinely falsify their income tax reports is well established. Hundreds of millions of dollars earned by small business operators, self-employed workers, waiters, or taxi drivers, for example, go unreported. The General Services Administration, the agency that purchases supplies for the federal government, is being investigated because of reputed kickbacks and bribes in the awarding of contracts to suppliers. Investigations have also revealed chiseling by doctors, pharmacists, nursing home administrators, and laboratories in overbilling the government for services provided under the Medicaid program, fraud amounting to hundreds of millions of dollars. According to a governmental report, as of July 1977, 12 percent of college students who had obtained federally insured loans have defaulted on their loans, leaving the federal treasury $500 million poorer. And private industry suffers substantial losses every year, from executives who pad their expense accounts and use company cars and planes for their own use, from factory workers who steal tools and material, and from hotel and motel guests who pilfer towels and bedding. This decline in personal honesty is not yet epidemic, but it is growing. If it becomes the rule rather than the exception, if everyone cheats or steals because "everybody else is doing it," Americans will face a bleak future in moral and economic terms.

In some paragraphs, particulary narrative and descriptive paragraphs, the topic idea may be implied rather than explicity stated. The implied topic idea of the paragraph below is a description of a Hindu prisoner, who is being taken from his cell to be hanged. Notice how carefully George Orwell selects his details to render a unified impression of the scene.

One prisoner had been brought out of his cell. He was a Hindu, a puny wisp of a man, with a shaven head and vague liquid eyes. He had a thick sprouting moustache, absurdly too big for his body, rather like the moustache of a comic man on the films. Six tall Indian warders were guarding him and getting him ready for the gallows. Two of them stood by with rifles and fixed bayonets, while the others handcuffed him, passed a chain through his handcuffs and fixed it to their belts, and lashed his arms tight to his sides. They crowded very close about him, with their hands always on him in a careful, caressing grip, as though all the while feeling him to make sure he was there. It was like men handling a fish which is still alive and may jump back into the water. But he stood quite unresisting, yielding his arms limply to the ropes, as though he hardly noticed what was happening. [From George Orwell, *Shooting an Elephant and Other Essays,* Harcourt Brace Jovanovich, 1945.]

THE CONCLUDING SENTENCE

Be careful not to introduce a new idea or point of view at the end of your paragraph. Under pressure to develop an idea fully, students occasionally add in the final sentence an idea that is only loosely related to the controlling idea and so dissipate the unified impression they have labored to effect. Consider, for example, the following paragraph:

Travelling and living in Europe have become increasingly popular with Americans since the end of World War II. Some seek escape from the hurry and worry of contemporary American life, the rat race for material reward. They seek the more leisurely, culturally richer life, which they hope to find in such cities as Vienna, Paris, Rome, and Brussels. The increase in the number of American businesses and factories in Europe has dramatically increased the size of American "colonies" in foreign countries. In fact, American businessmen and their families comprise the largest group of Americans living in Europe. A third group consists of United States government employees, technical experts, researchers, and so forth, those sent to administer trade and aid programs. And, finally, college-age youths travel to Europe for study, fun, adventure, for a final fling before going to work. This influx of Americans, however, has not been universally welcomed by the people of the host countries. In fact, some European critics complain that this new American "invasion" is corrupting European life.

The writer's controlling idea, expressed in the first sentence, is that Americans are increasingly attracted to travelling and living in Europe. Four primary sentences provide basic support for this idea. In the last sentence, however, she disrupts the unity of the paragraph by adding a new idea, the feeling among some European critics that the American "invasion" is corrupting European life. These last two sentences should be omitted here and the idea they introduce reserved for another paragraph.

One final suggestion: if you are writing a single paragraph, especially one that is rather long or complex, you can improve its unity by reinforcing the controlling idea in your concluding sentence, as does the writer of the following paragraph:

> For a long time we have worked hard at isolating the individual family. This has increased the mobility of individuals; and by encouraging young families to break away from the older generation and the home community, we have been able to speed up the acceptance of change and the rapid spread of innovative behavior. But at the same time we have burdened every small family with tremendous responsibilities once shared within three generations and among a large number of people— the nurturing of small children, the emergence of adolescents into adulthood, the care of the sick and disabled and the protection of the aged. What we have failed to realize is that even as we have separated the single family from the larger society, we have expected each couple to take on a range of obligations that traditionally have been shared within a larger family and a wider community. [From Margaret Mead, "Can the American Family Survive?" *Redbook Magazine,* February 1977.]

EXERCISE 5

A. In the following exercise there are three topic sentences, accompanied by a number of supporting sentences. Most of the accompanying sentences directly support the controlling idea of the topic sentence; others are irrelevant. Eliminate the irrelevant sentences and organize those that remain into a paragraph, adding whatever detail may be necessary.

1. Stocks, municipal bonds, and real estate have been perennial favorites with investors for many years, but each has its drawbacks.
    a. Over the years stocks have proven a good investment for the wise investor.
    b. Investors have made money on dividends, stock splits (additional shares of stock given shareholders when profits are high), and sale of stock.
    c. Municipal bonds provide a good return for the long-term investor because the interest earned on them is tax-free, and this locked-in interest yield is a decided plus during periods of low inflation and low interest rates.
    d. Inflation, however, erodes the value of bond yields over the years; and though bonds can be sold, because of their long-term maturity, owners often lose money in such sales.
    e. But what goes up also comes down and shareholders lose money when the market falls or stagnates.
    f. Some critics complain that since municipal bonds are tax-free, they provide an unfair advantage for wealthy people who invest in them and thus pay no income tax at all.
    g. But this advantage must be weighed against the disadvantage that if this tax-free aspect of municipal bonds were eliminated, many cities, states, and school districts would have to pay more in interest to finance their various projects.
    h. And that's because interest rates on such bonds would have to be substantially increased to compensate for the tax loss potential buyers would sustain.
    i. But real estate requires maintenance, which can be a headache, and the money saved in tax deductions is not really voided, simply deferred.
    j. Real estate has attracted investors because of the steady appreciation in the value of such assets between the time of purchase and sale and the tax deductions owners can take.
    k. Moreover, real estate is not easy to sell in periods of recession or high-interest mortgages; and such investments often tie up money for extended periods of time.

2. Professor Todd is a lively, eccentric little man.
    a. He stands five feet five in his bare feet.
    b. When he smiles, his mouth stretches from ear to ear.
    c. When he lectures, he paces back and forth behind the lectern, his eyes glued to the floor or gazing out the window.
    d. His principal interest outside of school is bird watching.

e. In fact, he has published two books on the subject.

f. He seldom looks at the faces of his students when he lectures, but if a student asks what he considers an important question, his eyes light up and fasten intently on the questioner.

g. If a student asks him an interesting question after class, he grasps the student firmly by the elbow, knits his brow in furious concentration as he responds to the question, and then relaxes into that wide grin, eyes sparkling, as the student nods his head in understanding.

h. When, however, he is irritated or angry at student inattention to his lecture or lack of participation in class discussion, his lisp grows more pronounced, and he begins to stutter a bit.

i. He is genuinely concerned about students learning his subject, spending long hours in his office helping them to understand the material and offering wise counsel on other problems as well.

j. This is his last year, for he is now seventy and must retire.

k. His students will miss him; in fact, many have petitioned the Board of Trustees to allow him to continue teaching beyond seventy.

l. A professor's mental competence and teaching capability, not his age, should determine whether he should retire.

3. Classroom discussions evoke different responses from students.

a. Some students rarely contribute to the discussion, preferring to remain quietly on the sidelines letting classmates carry the load.

b. This lack of response may be caused by shyness, mental immaturity, or a lack of interest or preparation.

c. Students who don't participate, whatever the cause, put a greater burden on other students as well as on the instructor to make discussions lively and productive.

d. Anxious extroverts have their hands in the air constantly.

e. They are determined to add their thoughts, relevant or not.

f. Some students participate on occasion, when their interests are aroused, but instructors can't rely on them from day to day.

g. The mainstays of discussions are those students who neither hog the limelight nor wait silently in the wings offstage.

h. They take an interest in what is being said, and they contribute thoughtful, relevant ideas to keep the discussion moving forward.

i. Without a number of such students, class discussions frequently become boring and unproductive.

B. In the following paragraphs the beginning topic sentences have been omitted. Read each paragraph carefully, and then construct a sentence that conveys the main idea of the paragraph.

1. Wanderlust is an alien sentiment. The Taoist classic *Tao Te* captures the ideal of rootedness to place with these words: "Though there may be another country in the neighborhood so close that they are within sight of each other and the crowing of cocks and barking of dogs in one place can be heard in the other, yet there is no traffic between them; and throughout their lives the two peoples have nothing to do with each other." In theory if not in practice, farmers have ranked high in Chinese society. The reason is not only that they are

engaged in a "root" industry of producing food but that, unlike pecuniary merchants, they are tied to the land and do not abandon their country when it is in danger. [From Yi-Fu Tuan, "American Space, Chinese Place," *Harper's Magazine,* July 1974.]

_____

_____

2. Nevertheless, consider the average modern electrified house. If the current went off for a week during the winter, the oil furnace would fail to operate, water pumps would stop, lights would go out, cooking would cease, and the plumbing might burst. The house would be rendered unlivable unless it also contained an old-fashioned fireplace, a cookstove, and candles or kerosene lights. Consider a modern metropolis such as New York City. If it were completely shut off from outside territory, its food supplies would last only a matter of days, and starvation would overcome its population perhaps in one or two months. The ancient farmhouse, without plumbing but with a large woodpile and its own source of food, gave its owner a better sense of security than we might suppose. The smallest village with its own water-powered mills was actually more self-sufficient than the average metropolis of today! Progress and speed become more treacherous as they increase. [From Eric Sloane, "How Different Was Great-Grandfather?" *American Yesterday,* Funk and Wagnalls, 1956.]

_____

_____

3. In the Sahel region of Africa, for example, goats and sheep of nomadic tribes have overgrazed the land and trampled vegetation underfoot, vegetation sorely needed to anchor the soil. And when the surface soil is gone, the desert advances. To compensate for the loss of arable land, marginal lands are cultivated in a desperate attempt to produce food, a practice that further denudes the land in a vicious cycle. The need for wood as fuel for cooking and heating in Africa and India further aggravates the problem as trees are cut down and wooden plants demolished. Improper irrigation and poor farming practices in the United States have also contributed to the spread of the desert. In the Great Plains region millions of acres were cleared for farming in the mid-nineteenth century. The overuse of this land helped to create the dust bowl conditions in this area in the 1930s. The rapid depletion of ground water in the Southwest presents another problem since the lack of irrigation water will mean less vegetation and more sand and desert.

_____

_____

4. There is the meaning given to the word by the anthropologist, in which all social habits, techniques, religious practices, marriage customs, in fact everything—including the kitchen sink—is examined to throw light on how a particular society lives and moves, or just exists. Then there is "culture" in a narrower sense, in which we are concerned not with material techniques, not with the social organization that holds society together, but with the ideas, the aesthetic experiences and achievements, and the philosophical or religious ideas that affect and are affected by the aesthetic experiences and achievements of a given society. A special variant of the last sense of "culture" is the narrow identification of the word with the fine arts and the implicit relegation of the fine arts to the margin of life, to what is done in leisure or for leisure. [From D. W. Brogan, *America in the Modern World,* Rutgers University Press, 1960.]

_____

_____

C. Examine the following paragraphs for unity and be prepared to point out the specific weakness of those that lack unity and to explain how they might be improved. Check to see that each sentence in the paragraph supports a controlling idea in a topic sentence. As an aid here, enclose the topic sentence of each paragraph in brackets and underline its controlling idea. In those paragraphs that contain primary and secondary support, make certain that each primary statement directly develops the controlling idea and that each secondary statement provides a relevant explanation or clarification of each primary statement. Place a capital P before each primary statement and a capital S before each secondary statement. Before every irrelevant sentence place an I, and place an RTS before any statement that reinforces the topic sentence.

1. _____Americans' love affair with the automobile has been a costly romance. _____Perhaps the most obvious negative effect has been the pollution it has created. _____Of the 200 or more million tons of waste spewed into the air each year in the United States, automobiles contribute 94.6 million tons. _____Another problem is simply the space gobbled up by the automobile. _____In Los Angeles, a city that couldn't function without the automobile, 60 to 70 per cent of the space is devoted to cars in the form of streets, freeways, and parking lots. _____The citizens of that metropolis are hoping to ease the problem with an underground railway and perhaps a light-rail system. _____ These additions should help, but they won't alleviate the problem completely. _____Reliance on the automobile has also produced two other negative effects.

_____It has diminished people's desire to walk, reducing the opportunity for healthful exercise in this flabby age. _____And, by using up so much urban space, it has made it more difficult for people to find a place to walk. _____ This latter result is socially undesirable, for it reduces the opportunity for people to mingle, to get to know each other at least by sight.

2. _____Agricultural workers in England in the nineteenth century had a difficult life. _____Although they breathed purer air and ate better food than industrial workers, small farmers and agricultural laborers worked just as hard or harder. _____They worked from sunup to sundown, every hour of light, six days a week. _____Sunday was just a day of dull rest. _____Agricultural labor is still not easy in England, but today's farm worker can enjoy a pleasant evening in a rural ale house after a day's work. _____And he is able to enjoy many other forms of recreation denied his counterpart 100 years ago. _____ Although farm workers in the nineteenth century had access to a patch of ground upon which they could grow vegetables to supplement their income, their wages were generally so low that they could hardly afford to purchase enough flour or cheap clothing for their families. _____Meat, milk, or beer were out of the question. _____In addition to long hours and poor pay, they were rooted to the land with little chance of seeing the world beyond the horizon. _____Farmers' carts were seldom available for a Sunday trip to the village. _____No, farm workers' lives in the nineteenth century were not a romantic idyll. _____As Joseph McCabe tells us, "They poured into the world like mice, and they worked from the age of seven until they died."[2]

3. _____For many Americans freedom of choice is so closely associated with the pursuit of happiness that the two ideas are virtually identical. _____Yet freedom of choice can produce much unhappiness if pursued selfishly. _____ An increasing number of people apparently believe that happiness means "doing your own thing." _____If the result of "doing your own thing" means,

[2] *1825–1925: A Century of Stupendous Progress*, G. P. Putnam's Sons, New York and London, 1926.

however, that a married man leaves his wife and children to live a little, to break away from the burdens of married life, what then? _____Or if a married couple abandon their aging parents to rest homes and forget about them so that they can lead a freer life, is the sum of the happiness produced greater than the unhappiness? _____On the other hand, a person has a responsibility to himself, too. _____If he is so conditioned by the fear of upsetting others that he never really lives his own life, he may discover too late that life has passed him by. _____And, finally, we might consider the case of Richard Raskind—a Yale graduate, physician, and father who underwent a sex change. _____He decided, apparently, that his freedom of choice outweighed any consideration that his son would have a woman for a father. _____The decade of the 1970s was called the "Me Decade," when happiness seemed to consist of unlimited free choice. _____But as Ellen Goodman reminds us, "We may have to learn that the pursuit of happiness doesn't lie in rising expectations, but rather in realistic ones, and in a better understanding of the costs of our life's choices."

4. _____Not all thinking is of the same kind. _____Much of our thought consists simply of feelings and recollections, a free association of ideas concerned with the self in the form of reverie, daydreaming. _____It consists of hopes, fears, a remembrance of things past, perhaps a half-conscious sense of contentment. _____Walter Mitty, a character in one of James Thurber's stories, comes to mind. _____To cope with the dull routine of his life, he imagined himself in various dangerous situations in which his daring and ingenuity saved the day. _____He is one of Thurber's most successful creations. _____Rationalization defines a kind of thinking in which we seek reasons to justify our actions, to defend our beliefs when we feel ourselves challenged. _____Much of what passes for serious thinking, psychologists tell us, is of this type. _____Critical thinking, a third type, produces solutions to problems, for it has direction. _____It aims at truth, at an unbiased view of a problem and a sensible way of coping with it. _____Critical thinking deals realistically with facts to arrive at a conclusion to account for them.

5. _____The serious depletion of oil and natural gas reserves in the United States has prompted investigation of a number of new energy sources. _____ One of the most promising of these is the fast breeder nuclear reactor. _____ The conventional nuclear power plant taps only 1 percent of the energy produced by the splitting (fission) of uranium atoms; and uranium 235, the fuel used, is scarce. _____The fast breeder reactor, however, by a process of transforming uranium into plutonium, produces more fuel than it consumes and therefore virtually eliminates the problem of the scarcity of nuclear fuel. _____ An even more fantastic machine now being experimented with is the fusion reactor. _____It combines heavy hydrogen atoms to produce helium atoms, releasing nuclear energy that can be converted into electricity. _____Because the fusion reactor uses for fuel an element contained in sea water, the successful development of this device would solve humanity's energy problems for a long, long time. _____Other promising sources of energy are contained in sunlight, subsurface heat, ocean tides, and everyday trash. _____Various experiments are under way to trap sunlight to create heat energy that can be used in boiler turbines to produce electric currents. _____Geothermal power is produced by drilling holes into the earth and forcing cold water into one hole. _____As it comes into contact with hot rock four or five miles below the surface, the water is heated and fractures the rock. _____The hot water then rises to the surface in another hole and is used to drive a turbine to produce electricity. _____In several regions of the world, the ebb and flow of the tides could be harnessed to produce electrical power, as they are on the Rance River estuary in France. _____And, finally, the lowly trash Americans accumulate in ever-increasing quantities, about 2½ billions tons a year, should not be overlooked. _____ Experts estimate that if it were burned in power plants, enough electricity could be generated to take care of 50 percent of this country's current energy needs.

D. In the following short theme a student describes a crossing guard who, over a period of years, escorted her and her friends across a busy intersection as she walked to school. Read the composition at least twice, making certain you understand the dominant impression conveyed by the writer. Then read it over again, this time noting the specific details that communicate this impression.

Cliff

I remember vividly my first day of school, for on that day I met Cliff, the crossing guard at the intersection in front of Lincoln Elementary School. Cliff was an important part of my life for the next twelve years. He was sixty-one, gray-haired, with a mustache and a smile to warm the heart of any frightened five-year-old. No school ever had a more friendly, gracious host to welcome the pupils each morning and escort them safely across the busy boulevard every afternoon. Cliff invented a little hand-clapping game to greet his children. He would put out his right hand, palm up, and the children would laugh and clap his hand. Then they would put up their hands, and he would clap them resoundingly. All of us, big and small, enjoyed this greeting immensely.

Nine years and thousands of handclaps later when I was graduating from junior high school, Cliff decided to retire. He told us all that he was getting old and tired and wanted to do some fishing. One day in June at a flag ceremony in front of the school, the principal announced Cliff's decision. Many of us had moist eyes that day as Cliff walked up to thank the principal for his kind words. He waved to all of us and thanked us for being such good kids. And we all waved back, cheering lustily and clapping our hands furiously. We all loved Cliff and told ourselves that school just wouldn't be the same without him.

The summer passed all too quickly, and on my first day of high school I approached the crossing where Cliff had welcomed me my first day of elementary school nine years before. "It won't be the same with Cliff gone," I thought. But glancing up, I recognized that familiar yellow jacket, the wide smile, and the outstretched palm. Cliff hadn't retired after all. He couldn't, not while there were children to brighten his lonely days. He simply missed them too much.

Cliff is seventy-four now and still straight and tall. Last week I drove past my old friend at the old, familiar crossing. He was surrounded by his many new friends on their way to school. I honked my horn, and he waved his hand and gave me a smile that would warm the heart of any frightened eighteen-year-old on her way to her first day of college.

The central impression here is that of a friendly, gracious, warm-hearted older man. This controlling idea is expressed in the fourth sentence. The preceding three sentences provide background information. Succeeding sentences contain the details that convey the impression of a friendly, enthusiastic older man with a love for and need of children in his life. The writer tells us about his dignified, friendly appearance and manner, his hand-clapping game, his smile, his desire to retire, and the children's response to his friendliness. Think back over your own experiences, and select a person who has made a strong impression on you—a relative, a friend, a teacher, an employer. Write a short theme of one to three paragraphs in which you present a unified impression of that individual. Choose your details carefully, using only those that directly relate to the impression you wish to convey.

E.   Read the following poem carefully, at least twice. It is carefully constructed to present a dominant impression of a man, Richard Cory. Though he is shown to have several admirable qualities, they are all related to one overriding quality. What is that quality? What adjective best describes him? Bear in mind that you are not asked to relate the message of the poem, its central idea, but only the dominant quality of Richard Cory. Is the name Richard Cory well chosen? Why? How does it reinforce his dominant quality?

Richard Cory

Whenever Richard Cory went down town,
We people on the pavement looked at him:
He was a gentleman from sole to crown,
Clean favored, and imperially slim.

And he was always quietly arrayed,
And he was always human when he talked;
But still he fluttered pulses when he said,
"Good-morning," and he glittered when he walked.

And he was rich—yes, richer than a king—
And admirably schooled in every grace:
In fine, we thought that he was everything
To make us wish that we were in his place.

So on we worked, and waited for the light,
And went without the meat, and cursed the bread;
And Richard Cory, one calm summer night,
Went home and put a bullet through his head.

EDWIN ARLINGTON ROBINSON

SUMMARY

The most important quality of good writing is clarity. To achieve clarity and conciseness in your paragraphs, you must make sure they are unified. The following suggestions will help you write unified paragraphs:

1. Be sure that each paragraph has a controlling idea expressed in a topic sentence. As a check against irrelevancy, it is helpful to place this sentence at the beginning of a paragraph, but occasionally it may be placed elsewhere—at the end of a paragraph, for example, to summarize rather than to announce a topic.
2. Make certain that primary supporting detail focuses clearly on the controlling idea.
3. If the central idea requires more than primary support, make certain that secondary supporting detail explains and clarifies the primary detail.
4. Be especially careful to avoid inserting a new idea in the last sentence of the paragraph.

CHAPTER THREE

DEVELOPMENT

A second important quality of an effective paragraph is *completeness*. A major weakness in student writing is the underdevelopment of paragraphs, the failure to supply sufficient detail to clarify, illustrate, or support the controlling idea. Because the paragraph is an organic entity—a group of related sentences that develop a single idea—it must be reasonably complete if it is to communicate this idea satisfactorily. Consider, for example, the following paragraph:

> The notion that the only valuable knowledge to be acquired in college is that which can be put to some practical use is mistaken. Students who limit their choice of subjects to those emphasizing the acquisition of technical skill restrict their opportunities for intellectual growth and stimulation. College students should therefore not avoid the liberal arts in their choice of subjects.

This paragraph begins with a clear, concise topic sentence, but the paragraph is incomplete, for the topic sentence has not been fully developed. The only argument offered to support the idea that a concentration on practical subjects is mistaken is that such a focus inhibits intellectual growth and stimulation. Moreover, the argument is not substantiated. The writer should have explained how or why intellectual growth is inhibited and should have offered other arguments as well. The writer of this paragraph has simply not said enough about the controlling idea. By adding clarifying detail and supporting arguments, he or she could have developed the controlling idea more fully and made the thesis more persuasive. Here is a revised version:

> The notion that the only valuable knowledge to be acquired in college is that which can be put to some practical use is mistaken. Students who limit their choice of subjects to those emphasizing the acquisition of technical skill restrict their opportunities for intellectual growth and stimulation. Courses that

train students to build a computer, manage a business, or design a turbine engine are of course useful. Modern civilization would not be possible without them. But an exclusive concentration on utilitarian subjects narrows a student's range of interests and produces inward-looking individuals. Liberal studies—philosophy, art, literature, history, law—however, lead outward to the great network of ideas that have stimulated people's minds for centuries. They expose students to fundamental questions about the nature of humanity and society, about the ends of human life. They help students to learn to see themselves in their proper perspective apart from purely personal concerns. The liberal studies thus provide a balance to the technical studies. They also open avenues and outlets that students can pursue in later life apart from their work. The increasing productivity of machines promises a future of abundant leisure, but added leisure time will be tedious for those without a range of intelligent interests and activities.

This second version is more convincing because its controlling idea has been more fully developed. The original argument that a concentration on technical subjects inhibits intellectual growth has been clarified by contrasting the direction of liberal studies with that of technical studies. And a second argument has been added: nontechnical subjects stimulate interests that students can pursue later on in life during their leisure time.

The more fully developed the paragraph, the longer it will be, as in the example above; but there is no set length for a paragraph. In expository writing the majority of paragraphs consist of clusters of sentences that develop one idea. The writer, having finished with one aspect of the subject, moves on to another aspect in a new paragraph. Occasionally, however, factors other than thought movement influence paragraph length. Newspaper paragraphs, for example, often consist of only one sentence. The narrow-column format makes it necessary to reduce paragraph length to make it easier for the reader to digest information. Considerations of rhythm and emphasis may also dictate shorter paragraphs, particularly in the longer essay or article. In a term paper of fifteen to twenty paragraphs, for example, a short paragraph sandwiched between longer ones may provide a change of pace, a chance for readers to pause slightly and assimilate what they have read before continuing; or it may underscore an important point, the contrast in paragraph size focusing reader attention. And introductory or concluding paragraphs in an essay of five or six paragraphs may also be somewhat shorter for similar reasons. The kinds of expository paragraphs you will be required to write, however, usually demand 100 to

150 words (6 to 10 sentences) for adequate development. But regardless of paragraph length, your main concern will be to include sufficient detail so that your readers can comprehend your meaning without having to supply their own information.

The ability to write well-developed paragraphs requires a good deal of practice in thought development. The quality of your paragraphs will depend largely on your ability to think of effective ways to illustrate and support your ideas. A ready supply of ideas is therefore a basic asset to any writer. However, this supply is seldom available to the average college freshman. You are certainly not abnormal, therefore, if you have had trouble finding material to support your ideas in a written assignment. But you can do something about it. You can increase your stock of ideas and your fund of information and thereby facilitate your thinking and your writing.

One way of doing this is through reading—newspapers, weekly news magazines, books. Your studies will provide ample opportunity for improving your reading skills, but you will find that the news and editorial sections of first-rate newspapers and news magazines are especially valuable sources of ideas and information. When you need information on a specific subject, consult the *Readers' Guide to Periodical Literature,* a library reference work that alphabetically lists magazine articles by subject and by authors' last names. Listening to radio and television news commentators and conversing with persons knowledgeable in particular subjects will also provide information and insight.

Your choice of method in developing a paragraph will usually be determined by your topic sentence. That is, a well-written topic sentence generally implies a method of development. Consider the following topic sentence:

> Deficits in the federal budget of the United States have been increasing dramatically in recent years.

This statement obviously calls for factual detail to support it. The following sentence

> Slang is frequently vivid and expressive.

needs illustrative detail. The sentence

> The political labels "conservative" and "reactionary" are frequently confused in political discussions today.

clearly requires a combination of definition, comparison, and contrast for adequate development.

In the following pages you will be introduced to a variety of ways to develop the expository paragraph. The purpose of exposition is to explain the logical relationships between things, relationships involving the general and the specific, similarity and difference, the part and the whole. The patterns of development that will be discussed and illustrated—illustration, facts, judgments, comparison and contrast, analysis, definition, cause and effect, and combination of methods—all deal with these basic relationships. Illustration, facts, and judgments are the basic materials of which most expository paragraphs are constructed. The others represent common methods of organizing facts, judgments, and illustrations to construct a paragraph. Developing a paragraph by showing cause and effect relationships will be considered later in a discussion of the argumentative paragraph. This chapter does not include all the possible methods of developing paragraphs, but it does offer a variety of the most frequently used patterns.

1. ILLUSTRATION

An easy and effective way to support an idea is by the use of examples. In his topic sentence the writer makes a general statement and then clarifies it through specific illustrative detail: he points to a specific occurrence, condition, or fact that concretely illustrates his idea. A writer using this strategy often begins with a general statement, explains and elaborates upon that statement in a following sentence, and then provides examples and illustrations to support his controlling idea. The exemplification in such paragraphs may consist of one detailed example, as in the paragraph below:

> Work expands so as to fill the time available for its completion. General recognition of this fact is shown in the proverbial phrase "It is the busiest man who has time to spare." Thus, an elderly lady of leisure can spend the entire day in writing and dispatching a postcard to her niece at Bognor Regis. An hour will be spent in finding the postcard, another in hunting for spectacles, half an hour in a search for the address, an hour and a quarter in composition, and twenty minutes in deciding whether or not to take an umbrella when going to the mailbox in the next street. The total effort that would occupy a busy man for three minutes all told may in this fashion leave another person prostrate after a day of doubt, anxiety, and toil. [From C. Northcote Parkinson, *Parkinson's Law*, Houghton Mifflin, 1958.]

Or it may consist of several examples, as in the following paragraph about the occasionally humorous ambiguity of the English language:

> Isn't English wonderful? It is wonderfully confusing—and among the confusions is something called *amphiboly.* To quote *Webster's Third,* an amphiboly is an "ambiguity in language; a phrase or sentence susceptible of more than one interpretation by virtue of an ambiguous grammatical construction." Example: *Nothing is too good for my mother-in-law.* There's also the advertisement that tells us, presumably unintentionally, that *nothing is more effective than Esoterica.* A friend in Fort Lauderdale, Kathryn Passarelli, was impressed by the ad. "Naturally, I use nothing," she said. My own pet amphiboly became a popular song toward the end of the 1970s: *If I said you had a beautiful body, would you hold it against me?* An Indianapolis newspaper item reported that a suspect had been arrested "for entering a bedroom of the opposite sex." [From James Kilpatrick, "Fun and Games from the Watched Pot of Language," *Smithsonian,* April 1984.]

In general, several examples are more convincing than one. But a carefully chosen example, one that clearly illustrates and is honestly representative, is preferable to a series of superficial, atypical ones. If your controlling idea is fairly complex, it is probably better to use one extended example so that you have ample opportunity to develop your idea fully. In either case, the important point is that your examples be clear, relevant, and specific.

Narrative can also be used to illustrate a point. In the following short essay, the writer relates a personal incident that taught him a truth about racial prejudice—one isn't born with it.

> One of the significant, and encouraging, things about racial prejudice is that it is learned, absorbed, not inherited. People aren't born with a bias against minority groups. Whatever prejudice they have, they have acquired from those around them as they grew older. An incident from my own life made this fact clear to me.
>
> For the first seven years of my life, we lived next door to a Negro family, the Walkers. Mrs. Walker and my mother were especially good friends, helping each other in hundreds of ways the way good neighbors do. I often played with Marian, the Walkers' daughter, from the time I was two until I was seven, when we moved down to Pine Street into a better neighborhood. I liked Marian a lot; she taught me how to roller skate, to play marbles, and even how to read a little. Whenever my mother

was gone, Marian took care of me. As I've said, I liked Marian, and I don't remember ever being concerned with, or perhaps even aware of, the fact that she was black and I was white.

After we moved, I didn't see Marian again until the night I graduated from high school, ten years later. After the graduation ceremony that night, I hurried back to meet my mother and family friends with my girlfriend before we left for a party. Marian and Mrs. Walker were there with my mother, smiling and congratulating me. Marian gave me a present and a big hug, and I remember how embarrassed I was in front of my girlfriend and other friends who had come up to congratulate me for having won a scholarship award. I excused myself quickly, ignoring my mother's slightly pained expression, and hurried off with my friends on the way to the party.

The next morning at breakfast I began to think about the previous night, about graduation, the party, and then about the Walkers, Marian's present, and my mother's disappointed look. My thoughts wandered back to the time when Marian and I were children, and I began to feel ashamed, really ashamed, of the way I had acted the night before. I realized then what had happened to me. As a child I was free of prejudice; but as I'd grown older, I picked some up along the way.

The next two paragraphs use some form of illustration to develop their thought. The first, written by a student, is about the comforts of the modern automobile.

Until today I've never thought much about the many comforts and conveniences my new car provides. It's a scorching afternoon, 101 degrees in the shade, and yet I sit in comfort in a velour, cushioned, adjustable seat. I'm listening to the stereo sound of my own live orchestra while the air in my royal cocoon is automatically kept at a cool and refreshing 74 degrees. And it's all happening at 55 miles per hour in the fast lane of Interstate 5—amazing. As I whistle along in this almost surrealistic environment, I notice a hill ahead, and as I begin the ascent, the cruise control automatically maintains the speed uphill. As I glide on further down the road, the onboard computer reassures me that I have 85 miles left until I reach my destination and that with 10 gallons of fuel remaining, I will arrive home with a comfortable margin. Sure enough, here's my off ramp, and as I ease the car down my street and into the garage, I push one button, and all the doors unlock simultaneously, another and the antenna retracts. Ah yes, I wonder what it was like in the old days.

In this next paragraph the writer provides three examples to support her controlling idea. Note again the common pattern of paragraphs using examples to develop the main idea: the first sentence introduces the main point, that self-respect was a character trait familiar to our grandparents; the second sentence clarifies this idea—self-respect meant a willingness to accept responsibility for one's own life; and the remaining sentences contain the examples.

> Self-respect is something that our grandparents, whether or not they had it, knew all about. They had instilled in them, young, a certain discipline, the sense that one lives by doing things one does not particularly want to do, by putting fears and doubts to one side, by weighing immediate comforts against the possibility of larger, even intangible, comforts. It seemed to the nineteenth century admirable, but not remarkable, that Chinese Gordon put on a clean white suit and held Khartoum against the Mahdi; it did not seem unjust that the way to free land in California involved death and difficulty and dirt. In a diary kept during the winter of 1846, an emigrating twelve-year-old named Narcissa Cornwall noted coolly: "Father was busy reading and did not notice that the house was being filled with strange Indians until Mother spoke about it." Even lacking any clue as to what Mother said, one can scarcely fail to be impressed by the entire incident: the father reading, the Indians filing in, the mother choosing the words that would not alarm, the child duly recording the event and noting further that those particular Indians were not, "fortunately for us," hostile. Indians were simply part of the *donnée*. [From Joan Didion, "On Self-respect," *Slouching Toward Bethlehem,* Farrar, Straus, and Giroux, 1961.]

EXERCISE 6

A. Choose one of the following topics and write a paragraph or a short essay to develop it.

1. an incident that taught you something important (Use a narrative to illustrate your central idea, as in the short essay on pp. 57–58.)

2. different attitudes toward success, attending college

3. benefits of learning a second language

4. benefits of foreign travel, exercise, playing a musical instrument

5. architectural styles in your community (Focus on public buildings, residences, churches.)

6. the widespread use of computers

7. conserving energy in the United States

8. the dangers of pollution

9. the Olympic Games as a colorful spectacle

10. violence in professional sports, motion pictures, television

If you are planning to write a paragraph on one of these topics, transform the topic into a sharply defined, specific idea and express it as your topic sentence. Then list the examples that might be used to develop your controlling idea. After examining your supporting detail, you may wish to modify your original topic sentence. Do not hesitate to do so. Formulating a topic sentence at the beginning is simply a way of insuring unity. Eliminate the irrelevant items from your list; then write your paragraph, using examples from your list. Make sure your examples are clear, concrete, and interesting. After some time has elapsed, look over your paragraph and revise it if necessary, adding or deleting detail to insure unity and good development. Your preliminary plan might look something like this:

> *Topic*—The role of sex in selling
> *Topic sentence*—Sex plays an enormously important role in selling.
> 1. Men's and women's toiletries
>   aftershave lotion, men's cologne
>   perfume, lipstick, toothpaste, lingerie
> 2. Front pages of tabloid newspapers and magazine covers
>   *National Enquirer, Vogue, Cosmopolitan*
> 3. Sex in selling—cheesy but sleezy
>   Gross, crude
>   Too often too little subtlety

Here is a first draft:

It's no secret that sex plays an enormously important part in selling. Sometimes its use is obvious and explicit,

61

Add a transition here   at other times suggestive and symbolic. Sex is often used to promote the sale of men's and women's toiletries. Well-known athletes and handsome movie stars tout the sexually enhancing powers of aftershave lotions and colognes in television commercials. Joe Namath, for example,

Add a phrase here   speaks glowingly and knowingly of Brut cologne to enhance young men's sexual appeal. Perfume commercials put beautiful women in seductive poses wearing loose-fitting, suggestive clothing, while a voice in low, hushed tones suggests that love and romance await those who put

A transition here, too   just a dab behind the ears. Tabloid newspapers frequently feature racy headlines and sensational stories of love and

Needs examples here   lust on their front pages to catch the eyes of supermarket shoppers as they go out the checkout counter. And popular women's magazines—for example, *Cosmopolitan*, *Vogue*, *Mademoiselle*—display beautiful, scantily clad, well-nourished young women on their covers. The message is thus

Condense here
Too much comment   pretty clear. Sex sells. And what sells stays. One may, of course, deplore the crudity, the tastelessness of many sexually suggestive advertisements; but advertisers are not, in this day and age, going to give up a good thing to please the purists. Subtlety and discretion may be extolled as virtues in our private lives; they are seldom practiced in the market place, however.

This first draft is generally well organized and developed, but it needs some revision. A third example to support the controlling idea would flesh it out a bit; and the last few sentences, which present the writer's opinion of sex in selling, begin to shift the focus of the paragraph and need to be condensed. Some comment to conclude the paragraph would work, but it shouldn't be too involved, or it will weaken the unity of the paragraph. Note the changes made in the revision on pages 63–64.

First Primary Sentence

It's surely no secret that sex plays an important part in selling. Sometimes its use is obvious and explicit, at other times suggestive and symbolic. For instance, sex is often, if not invariably, used to promote the sale of men's and women's toiletries. In television commercials, well-known male professional athletes and handsome movie stars tout the sexually enhancing powers of aftershave lotion and men's cologne. Joe Namath, for example, speaks glowingly and knowingly of the potency of Brut cologne to lure the ladies. To promote the sale of perfume, television advertisers photograph beautiful women in seductive poses, wearing loose-fitting, suggestive clothing, while a voice in low, hushed tones suggests that love and romance await

Second Primary Sentence

those who put just a dab behind the ears. Sex is also used by tabloid newspapers, which frequently feature racy headlines and sensational stories of love and lust on their front pages to catch the eyes of supermarket shoppers as they scan the newspaper rack checking out. The *National Enquirer, Globe,* and the *Star Reporter* are good examples. And popular women's magazines—such as *Cosmopolitan, Vogue,* and *Mademoiselle*—display scantily clad, well-nourished,

Third Primary Sentence

beautiful women on their covers. But perhaps the most interesting use of sex in selling was evident in the introduction of the hardtop convertible a few decades back. A convertible in dealers' showrooms drew in male customers, but they usually bought a four-door sedan. The convertible, supposedly, had associations of youth, adventure—a mistress; but the sedan was the girl one married, one who would be a good wife and mother. To combine the appeal of mistress and wife, auto manufacturers brought out the

hardtop convertible. It was an instant success. The message
is, thus, pretty clear. Sex sells. And what sells, stays, regardless of its occasional tastelessness or lack of subtlety.

The plan for this paragraph could also serve as the foundation of a longer
essay. In this case each of the three primary supporting sentences in the revised
version could be transformed into a topic sentence for a full paragraph. (See
Chapter Five for a further discussion of the process for developing the multiparagraph essay.)

B.   The following quoted passages contain interesting subjects for paragraphs.
     Select one, explain its meaning, and provide illustrations to support your
     interpretation. Use your first sentence to introduce the passage, your second
     to explain its meaning, and the remainder of the sentences in the paragraph
     to provide needed exemplification.

1.   Learning should be a handshake instead of a kiss.   —Steven M. Weiss
2.   He that sups with the devil hath need of a long spoon.   —English proverb
3.   The man who marries for money will earn it.   —Jewish proverb
4.   Living well is the best revenge.   —Spanish proverb
5.   God is a busy worker, but He loves help.   —Basque proverb
6.   The world is a sure teacher, but it exacts a fat fee.   —Finnish proverb
7.   He who has come through fire will not fade in the sun.   —Hindu proverb
8.   The only one you should get even with is the one who has helped you.
     —Anonymous

2. FACTS AND JUDGMENTS

Factual detail is often used to support an idea. The writer may begin a paragraph with a topic statement and then support that statement with facts and statistics. Or the writer may present the details first and place the topic sentence at the end as the logical conclusion to be drawn from the evidence. The following paragraph is arranged with the topic idea at the beginning.

> Professional athletes are certainly well paid today, and in the case of the so-called superstars, earnings are simply incredible. The average income of the top twenty-five professional tennis players exceeds $100,000 a year. Bjorn Borg and John McEnroe, however, each earned over $1,000,000 in prize money in 1979, plus additional hundreds of thousands in endorsements. The average salary of big league baseball players exceeded $175,000 in 1981, and several players earned $1,000,000, such as Nolan Ryan, George Brett, and Phil Niekro. Dave Winfield of the Yankees has a contract that will pay him $20,000,000 over a 10-year period. Professional basketball players' salaries are equally high; the average salary of NBA players is more than $175,000, and one player, Magic Johnson of the Lakers, has a contract of $1,000,000 a year for a period of 25 years. Professional fighters, however, are in a class by themselves. Muhammad Ali and Sugar Ray Leonard have each earned $10,000,000 for a single fight.

Because both facts and judgments are useful in supporting topic sentences, and because confusion about them sometimes weakens student writing, a brief explanation of their differences should be instructive. A fact is a report, a statement of what has actually happened or of what actually exists. It can be verified: one can test the accuracy of the report through one's own observation or computation or by consulting a reliable source. For example, the following statement is factual:

Harry Truman defeated Thomas Dewey for the Presidency.

A judgment, on the other hand, records a personal opinion. It indicates approval or disapproval. Unlike a factual statement, it cannot be proven true or false. The following statement is judgmental:

Harry Truman was an effective president.

Many statements, however, cannot be so precisely differentiated as these two examples. The following statement involves both fact and judgment:

> Mountain climbing is an arduous activity.

It can be verified to an extent, and yet it clearly includes judgment.

In your writing make certain that your paragraphs do not consist solely of judgments unsupported by facts. Judgments can serve both as topic sentences and as supporting detail, but they need to be grounded in and illustrated by facts if they are to be convincing. The student who wrote the following paragraph, for example, relied too heavily on judgment unsupported by fact to prove his point.

> Plea bargaining, a negotiated agreement between the lawyer of the accused and the prosecuting attorney whereby the accused agrees to plead guilty to a lesser crime than the one he or she is charged with so as to avoid a possibly stiffer sentence, is corrupting the administration of criminal justice in the United States. Supporters of this practice claim that it is an efficient technique, saves the cost of a trial, and gives the defendant a break. In fact, however, it is simply a perversion of justice that puts criminals back on the streets to prey on society. The criminal justice system in the United States is in a mess because of plea bargaining. Those who defend the practice must bear a good share of the blame.

Such words and phrases as "corrupting," "perversion of justice," "prey on society," and "must bear a good share of the blame" express the writer's judgment. This judgment is not supported with facts, however. A revised version, with factual statements added, is more persuasive.

> I do not believe that plea bargaining represents a step forward for criminal justice in this country. This practice, whereby the accused agrees to plead guilty to a lesser crime than the one he or she is charged with so as to avoid a possibly stiffer sentence, has become an integral part of the administration of American criminal procedure. In 1974, for example, almost 68 percent of the criminal cases handled by the Los Angeles Supreme Court, 13,294 out of 19,608, were processed by means of plea bargaining.[1] Those who defend the practice—a group that includes

[1] Gene Blake, "Trial System Debate Is On in California," *Los Angeles Times,* November 9, 1975, Sec. VIII, p. 5.

numerous courts, the American Bar Association, and legal commissions—argue that plea bargaining is an efficient technique, saves court costs, and gives the defendant a break. It is true that eliminating plea bargaining would increase the cost of criminal justice: it has been estimated that the number of judges, prosecutors, public defenders—all those needed to try a defendant in a public trial—would have to be more than doubled.[2] The cost of such an increase, it must be admitted, would be substantial; but the present system, which puts criminals back on the street sooner, is, in the long run, far more costly to society. And this cost includes more than the loss or destruction of property. It includes the loss of innocent lives as well. The argument that plea bargaining gives the defendant a break is undeniable. But the "break" he or she gets in the form of more lenient treatment from prosecutors and judges is not a break for society, whose interests also deserve to be protected. And, finally, plea bargaining distorts justice because it is removed from public view in an open court where the interests of society and the rights of the defendant can be more effectively protected. "Too often," writes Gene Blake, a legal affairs writer for the *Los Angeles Times*, "some private defense lawyers who depend on a volume of small criminal cases for their livelihood and public defenders with too many cases to handle may urge guilty pleas which are not in the best interest of possibly innocent clients."[3] The best that can be said of plea bargaining is that it compensates for the failures of an inefficient criminal justice system. If this system is to function effectively in the future, however, other means must be found to sustain it.

The central proposition is more soundly argued in this revision, for several facts have been supplied to bolster the judgments of the original. Although readers may still reject the proposition, they are aware of the evidence that led the writer to his conclusion.

In the following three paragraphs facts and judgments support the controlling idea. In the first paragraph facts and judgments are combined.

A report prepared for President Carter by the State Department and the Council on Environmental Quality reveals that time is running out for action to prevent the world from becom-

[2] Blake, p. 5
[3] Blake, p. 5

ing unlivable by the year 2000.[4] Population pressures, dwindling food supplies, environmental pollution, and depleted natural resources will, according to the report, seriously diminish the quality of life on this planet. The world's population is expected to increase from 4 billion in 1980 to 6.35 billion in 2000. Mexico City, for example, will add 20 million inhabitants by 2000. World food production should increase about 90 percent in the next 20 years, but this increase will occur in countries whose diets are already good, not in the underdeveloped nations now suffering from malnutrition and starvation. In addition, the price of food will rise 100 percent in the next 20 years. Air and water pollution are likely to worsen as increasing quantities of coal and oil are burned. Deforestation of the world will continue, with stocks of wood throughout the world expected to decline by 47 percent by 2000. Fresh water shortages will increase also because of rising levels of human, agricultural, and industrial consumption. These gloomy forecasts may prove inaccurate if technological progress can solve some of these problems, but recent studies made by other agencies, American and international, reach similar conclusions.

In the next paragraph facts provide the sole support of the controlling idea.

In some ways illegal immigrants cost the government money; in other ways, they contribute to government coffers. Though some are indeed paid "off the books," a Labor Dapartment study in the 1970s found that 73 percent of working illegals had income taxes withheld from their paychecks, and 77 percent paid social security taxes. Fearing detection, however, few file for the income-tax refunds owed them, and the vast majority are too young to apply for social security benefits—even if they dared. The Social Security Administration thus reportedly nets an estimated $80 billion annually in payments that will never be collected. [From Melinda Beck, Christopher Ma, Diane Weathers, Nancy Cooper, and Daniel Pedersen, "Costs and Benefits," *Newsweek*, June 25, 1984.]

And in this last paragraph judgments provide the foundation for the writer's point.

[4] "Earth: Scarcely Livable by 2000?" *International Herald Tribune*, Paris, July 25, 1980, p. 1.

Marriages which have passed the test of time do not conform to the torrid specifications of romance. Wives are also mothers. Husbands go to work. Responsibilities permit them only a small fraction of the day with one another, and they do not pine away. They still love each other—but quietly. Their warmth is expressed in companionship, as for example, in revealing innermost thoughts to one another. Each has interests apart from the other. After all, marriage may be the most intimate human relationship; nevertheless two distinct personalities are involved. Probably there are activities each prefers to engage in without the other. The tendency is to be overly possessive when too many emotional eggs are in one basket. For example, a wife who has no friends or interests outside of her marriage hovers over her husband as she might over the Hope diamond. When he wants to go fishing in solitude or play poker with his cronies, her constant desire for his attention may constitute a "pain in the neck." [From Jackson Toby, "The Case Against Romance," in Harry C. Bredemeier and Jackson Toby, *Social Problems in America,* Wiley, 1960, p. 466.]

EXERCISE 7

A. The controlling idea in each of the following sentences could be developed by factual detail. Consult reference works in the library and supply four primary factual statements to support the controlling idea. List your data in the spaces provided.

1. Owning and operating a European sports car is costly.

    _____

    _____

    _____

    _____

2. During the Franklin Roosevelt administration several laws were enacted that changed the shape of American life.

    _____

    _____

    _____

    _____

3. Beginning salaries for those entering the various professions in the United States vary a good deal.

    _____

    _____

    _____

    _____

4. Wage rates and working conditions among Japanese and American workers contrast sharply.

    _____

    _____

    _____

    _____

B. Select one of the four topic sentences given in 7A, and, using the factual information you have listed, write a paragraph of 100 words or more.

C. The following subjects are often the bases of sharp differences of opinion. Select one and develop a paragraph in which you argue one side of the question. In your topic sentence make clear the position you favor, and then support your controlling idea with judgments.

    1. working wives
    2. rent controls
    3. health foods
    4. living at home or in an apartment while attending college
    5. building dams on wild rivers
    6. the American legal system
    7. hunting as a sport
    8. big-time college athletics
    9. liberal arts versus occupational education
   10. increasing import duties on foreign steel, autos, textiles to protect American industries

3. COMPARISON AND CONTRAST

In paragraphs of *comparison* writers point out similarities between two or more things. In paragraphs of *contrast* they point out the differences. As a student, you will frequently be asked to compare or contrast philosophical ideas, historical figures, characters in a novel, or political parties. By studying these two patterns carefully and by practicing the techniques involved, you can improve your ability to develop and communicate your thoughts clearly.

The supporting material for comparison or contrast frequently consists of factual details, judgments, or examples. In the following paragraph the writer contrasts the styles of two contemporary rock singers on the bases of the subject matter and quality of their music, their stage performance, and audience response. Factual and judgmental detail provide support for this contrast:

> Cat Stevens and Bruce Springsteen are both popular rock singers, but their styles contrast sharply. Cat Stevens sings of nature, of love lost and found, of peace. His music is soft, relaxing, suggesting vast forests and green meadows. On stage he plays the guitar or piano, with slides of trees and fields of flowers flashing on a bright screen behind him. He weaves a web of enchantment over silent, contented crowds. Bruce Springsteen's music, on the other hand, is hard-driving rock. Electric guitars, a solid drum beat, and a frenetic saxophone provide the background to his songs of city life, fast cars, and youths' dreams of freedom from parental control. At his concerts the crowds are not silent. They are constantly cheering, whistling, and clapping their hands to his pulsating rhythms until they're too tired to rock 'n' roll any longer and collapse in blissful exhaustion.

In this next paragraph the writer uses contrast to support his point that loose-fitting clothing is sexually appealing.

> As Herrick [an English poet] points out, looseness and disorder in dress are erotically appealing. Soft, flowing, warm-hued clothes traditionally suggest a warm, informal, affectionate personality, and the garment which is partially unfastened not only reveals more flesh but implies that total nakedness will be easily achieved. Excessive neatness, on the other hand, suggests an excessively well-controlled, possibly repressed personality. Tight, bundled-up or buttoned-up clothes (if not figure-revealing) are felt to contain a tight, erotically held-in person. Hard,

crisp fabrics—gabardines and starched cottons and stiff synthetics—also seem to deny sensuality, and so do grayed, dull colors. When drab-colored clothes are both unusually tight and unusually neat, observers will suspect not only sexual disinterest but impotence or frigidity. [From Alison Lurie, "Fabric, Fur, and Skin," *The Language of Clothes,* Random House, 1981.]

The pattern of development of the following paragraph includes both comparison and contrast. The writer discusses the similarities and contrasts of two of her teachers.

Two of my professors this semester, Dr. Henshaw and Mr. Johnson, are very different in personality and temperament but alike in love of their subject and concern for students. To begin with the differences: Dr. Henshaw is always well-organized and prepared. He arrives at class on time, impeccably dressed, eager to begin. His lectures are clear and coherent, and he speaks articulately. After lecturing, he probes student understanding with precise, well-focused questions. He is serious and intent, all business. Mr. Johnson, on the other hand, is more laid-back. He is often late to class, ambling in with books and papers jumbled together in general confusion. His clothes are a decade out of date. His lectures are rambling affairs, punctuated with jokes and anecdotes, as he paces behind the lectern mumbling. However, he encourages lively class discussions, occasionally interrupting them to emphasize a point. In spite of these differences, both teachers obviously love teaching and want their students to learn. Dr. Henshaw, though occasionally pained by poor performance, is quick to praise good work, reading well-written essays in class; and he spends a good deal of his time helping students in his office. Mr. Johnson is always chatting with students after class, lending them books from his own library, and encouraging and helping students who are having trouble in the course.

Arrangement of Supporting Material

You may arrange the supporting material for a paragraph based on comparison or contrast in a variety of ways. If you are comparing two persons, for example, you may present the information about the first person in the first four or five sentences and the information about the second person in the remaining sentences, as in the paragraph about Cat Stevens and Bruce Springsteen on page 73. Another method is to alternate between subjects in successive sentences, as does this writer, who illustrates the differences in current American and British English with reference to the automobile and related experiences:

Vocabulary differences in current American and British English can be illustrated by recounting the same experience as it happens on both sides of the Atlantic. An American driver pulls his *sedan* into a *gas station* to buy *gas,* get his *windshield* cleaned, and have the attendant look under the *hood* to check the electrical system. A British driver drives his *saloon car* into a *petrol station* to buy *petrol,* get his *windscreen* cleaned, and have the attendant look under the *bonnet* to check the electrical system. The American attendant *checks the battery,* tests the *generator,* and examines the *spark plugs* and the spare *tire* in the *trunk.* His British counterpart *tops off the accumulator,* tests the *dynamo,* examines the *sparking plugs,* and checks the spare *tyre* in the *boot.*

Before he leaves the station, the American driver takes a map from the *glove compartment* because he knows he has to take a *detour* at the next *corner* to get back to the *freeway.* Similarly, the British driver takes his map from the *cubby locker* because he knows he has to take the *road diversion* at the next *turning* to get back to the *motorway.* The American motorist looks for a *turnout* on the *divided highway* before the *overpass;* his British cousin looks for a *lay-by* on the *dual carriage way* before the *flyover.* On his way out of the station, the American sees other drivers *lining up* behind him, honking their *horns* for service; a *dump truck* leaking oil from its *pan;* a *station wagon* with a smashed *fender* and bent *bumper;* and a *convertible* with its *top* down and *muffler* dragging. As he leaves the station, the British driver observes other drivers *queuing up,* honking their *hooters* for service; a *tipping lorry* leaking oil from its *sump;* a *utility car* with a smashed *mudgard* and bent *overrider;* and a *drop head* with its *hood* down and its *silencer* dragging.

A third method is to alternate between subjects within the same sentence, as the writer of the following paragraph does in a contrast of Robert E. Lee and Ulysses S. Grant.

The two generals who led the Confederate and Union forces in the American Civil War, Robert E. Lee and Ulysses S. Grant, present a study in contrast. Though they were both strong men, their strengths represented two conflicting traditions in nineteenth-century American life. Lee was an aristocratic Virginian, Grant the son of a tanner on the Western frontier. Lee symbolized landed wealth, a privileged class at the top of a hierarchical social structure, Grant the self-reliance and rough-and-tumble democracy of frontier men. Lee stood for the noblest elements of a transplanted English aristocratic ideal—family, culture, a sense of obligation to one's community characteristic of the country squire; Grant embodied the frontier men for whom traditional forms and social patterns meant little. Whatever privileges a man might enjoy, he would have to earn them himself. Grant was, in the words of Bruce Catton, ". . . the modern man emerging . . . ," a precursor of "the great age of steel and machinery. . . . Lee might have ridden down from the old age of chivalry, lance in hand, silken banner fluttering over his head."

In a composition of several paragraphs, you will have a similar choice in arranging detail. For example, if you were contrasting liberal education with career education on the bases of purpose, historical development, and benefits, you might focus on liberal education in the first few paragraphs, each paragraph dealing with one of these three points, and then consider career education in the remaining paragraphs; or you might discuss purpose, historical development, and benefits in this order, shifting your focus between liberal education and career education as you progressed. In long compositions it is probably more effective to use this alternating focus. The steady comparison or contrast of detail keeps the purpose of the paper more clearly and forcefully in the reader's mind.

Analogy

A special kind of comparison is the *analogy*, a comparison of two things that are unlike but that have similar attributes. The paragraph that developed the likeness between Dr. Henshaw and Mr. Johnson (p. 74) is a straight comparison: both belong to the same class. However, a comparison of death and sleep is an analogy: they are not similar states, but they have similar attributes—the cessation of activity and the appearance of repose.

Carefully used, the analogy can be instructive. Alexander Pope, an eighteenth-century English poet known for his wit, uses a brief analogy to emphasize a truth about human egoism:

> 'Tis with our judgments as our watches, none
> Go just alike, yet each believes his own.

The analogy is especially helpful in explaining the unfamiliar in terms of the familiar. For example, a lecturer in physiology in a class of teenage boys might compare the heart with an automobile engine. Or a historian might compare the rise and fall of great civilizations with the life cycle of a human being. Thomas Huxley, a famous British biologist and defender of Charles Darwin's theory of evolution, uses analogy to enliven and clarify his idea that people tend to study the laws of nature in order to survive.

> Yet it is a very plain and elementary truth, that the life, the fortune and the happiness of every one of us, and, more or less, of those who are connected with us, do depend upon our knowing something of the rules of a game infinitely more difficult and complicated than chess. It is a game which has been played for untold ages, every man and woman of us being one of the two players in a game of his or her own. The chessboard is the world, the pieces are the phenomena of the universe, the rules of the game are what we call the laws of Nature. The player on the other side is hidden from us. We know that his play is always fair, just, and patient. But also we know, to our cost, that he never overlooks a mistake, or makes the smallest allowance for ignorance. To the man who plays well, the highest stakes are paid, with that sort of overflowing generosity with which the strong shows delight in strength. And one who plays ill is checkmated—without haste, but without remorse. [From Thomas Henry Huxley, "A Liberal Education," *Macmillan's Magazine*, 1868.]

In the following passage Robert Penn Warren uses analogy to characterize the law.

> "I'm not a lawyer. I know some law. In fact, I know a lot of law. And I made some money out of the law. But I'm not a lawyer. That's why I can see what the law is like. It's like a single-bed blanket on a double bed and three folks in the bed and a cold night. There ain't never enough blanket to cover the case, no matter how much pulling and hauling, and somebody is always going to nigh catch pneumonia. Hell, the law is like the pants you bought last year for a growing boy, but it is always THIS year and the seams are popped and the shankbones to the breeze. The law is always too short and too tight for growing mankind. The best you can do is do something and then make up some law to fit and by the time the law gets on the books you have done something different. . . ." [from Robert Penn Warren, *All the King's Men*, Harcourt Brace Jovanovich, 1946.]

An animal fable is a short narrative involving animals that act and talk like human beings from which a moral is drawn. A literary form that dates back hundreds of years, the fable is based on analogies between human beings and animals. Its primary purpose is to illustrate some human trait, to comment on human behavior. In the following fable, entitled "The Shrike and the Chipmunks," James Thurber provides a humorous comment on married life.

Once upon a time there were two chipmunks, a male and a female. The male chipmunk thought that arranging nuts in artistic patterns was more fun than just piling them up to see how many you could pile up. The female was all for piling up as many as you could. She told her husband that if he gave up making designs with the nuts there would be room in their large cave for a great many more and he would soon become the wealthiest chipmunk in the woods. But he would not let her interfere with his designs, so she flew into a rage and left him. "The shrike will get you," she said, "because you are helpless and cannot look after yourself." To be sure, the female chipmunk had not been gone three nights before the male had to dress for a banquet and could not find his studs or shirt or suspenders. So he couldn't go to the banquet, but that was just as well, because all the chipmunks who did go were attacked and killed by a weasel.

The next day the shrike began hanging around outside the chipmunk's cave, waiting to catch him. The shrike couldn't get in because the doorway was clogged up with soiled laundry and dirty dishes. "He will come out for a walk after breakfast and I will get him then," thought the shrike. But the chipmunk slept all day and did not get up and have breakfast until after dark. Then he came out for a breath of air before beginning work on a new design. The shrike swooped down to snatch up the chipmunk, but could not see very well on account of the dark, so he batted his head against an alder branch and was killed.

A few days later the female chipmunk returned and saw the awful mess the house was in. She went to the bed and shook her husband. "What would you do without me?" she demanded. "Just go on living, I guess," he said. "You wouldn't last five days," she told him. She swept the house and did the dishes and sent out the laundry, and then she made the chipmunk get up and wash and dress. "You can't be healthy if you lie in bed all day and never get any exercise," she told him. So she took him for a walk in the bright sunlight and they were both caught and killed by the shrike's brother, a shrike named Stoop.

Moral: Early to rise and early to bed makes a male healthy and wealthy and dead.
[From James Thurber, *Fables for Our Time*, Harper & Row, 1940. Originally printed in *The New Yorker*.]

EXERCISE 8

Write a paragraph of 100 to 150 words on one of the following topics, and develop it by means of comparison or contrast. Decide on the bases of your comparison or contrast before you begin to write, and keep these bases in mind as you write. For example, if you plan to contrast two political leaders, you might contrast their origins, personalities, and political and philosophical attitudes. If you plan to compare two automobiles, you might want to compare their design, performance, economy, and comfort. If you are writing an essay of several paragraphs, you may want to include both similarities and differences, a more difficult process in a single paragraph because of limitations of space.

1. a comparison or contrast of two well-known professional athletes, two political leaders, two musical groups, water skiing and snow skiing, men's and women's fashions in clothing, a fast food place and an expensive restaurant, two automobiles

2. a comparison or contrast between two sets of attitudes, two conflicting points of view, on one of the following subjects: success, sex education, professional boxing, abortion, big-time college athletics, rent controls, working wives, gun control, rearing children, premarital cohabitation

3. a contrast of the teaching styles of two teachers, the personalities of two friends

4. a contrast of the qualities of urban and rural living, of the benefits of general and career education, of the values in paying by cash and by installment

5. an analogy between a quarterback on a football team and a general of infantry, between an auto mechanic and a physician, a ship's captain and the President of the United States

6. a comparison or contrast between a conservative and a liberal, a neurotic and a psychotic, a socialist and a communist, a devout person and a pious person, a conservative and a reactionary

7. a contrast between two qualities: fame and celebrity, wit and humor, wisdom and intelligence, courage and rashness, tolerance and cowardice

8. a contrast between the appearance of a place (neighborhood, favorite recreational spot, home town, and so on) as you remember it from childhood and its appearance today

4. ANALYSIS (DIVISION AND CLASSIFICATION)

Analysis is the process of dividing a whole into its parts to provide better understanding of the whole. It serves a variety of purposes: to inform, persuade, amuse, and entertain. Sometimes it combines two or more of these purposes. A director of marketing, for example, may be given the task of analyzing the potential market for a new product his or her company is thinking of producing. Such an analysis would be intended not only to inform but also, very likely, to persuade the executive officers of the company to proceed with or abandon the project.

Analysis involves both *division,* the separation of a single concept (the American West, for example) into its subunits (geographical regions—Northwest, Southwest, Pacific Coast), and *classification,* the placing of examples of a subject (teachers) into categories that share common characteristics (scholars, entertainers, friendly philosophers). The subjects to be analyzed may be *entities,* that is, structurally complete units; *classes,* collections of things; and *processes* or *sequences of action.*

The writer of the paragraph below analyzes his subject, Hart's Island—Potter's Field for New York City, which is located in Long Island Sound—by showing us how the parts of the island relate to each other spatially.

> The island itself is bleak and unprepossessing. There are islands like this, serving all sorts of cheerless but necessary municipal functions, near every great city in the world—islands in the Thames and Danube and Seine, and in the yellow waters of the Tiber. This one, perhaps because it is American, seems more than necessarily dreary. No blade of grass grows here, only weeds. On the south end of the island stands a sewage disposal plant. North of this is a city detention home, a great mass of soot-stained brick and iron bars, where derelicts and drunks and the less-involved dope addicts are "rehabilitated." Moss and flakes of pale green lichen creep along the walls. In the treeless shade of the courtyards, flowering in crannies below shuttered windows, are chickweed and ghostly dandelions. Still farther north of this jail, separated by a quarter mile of dusty, weed-choked rising ground, is Potter's Field. The glens and willow-groves are gone, the picnickers and the slain deer; if you stand here on the hill beneath a dead, wind-twisted cedar, the island's only tree, you can get a good view of the land—the sewage plant and the prison and the burial ground, each a recipient, in its fashion, of waste and decay. [From William Styron, "Potter's Field," *Lie Down in Darkness,* Bobbs-Merrill, 1951.]

In the following paragraph the writer analyzes a digital computer, a structural whole, by dividing it into its three parts, subdividing the parts, and providing a brief explanation of the operational process as well.

Most digital computers are structurally organized into three parts: input and output elements, storage elements, and arithmetic and control elements. The input element transfers information external to the computer to the storage element. This information—which may be a program, that is, a predefined sequence of instructions, or data on which the program operates—is fed into the storage unit by means of a card or paper tape reader, a magnetic unit, a disc, or a video terminal. The storage element holds the input information and the intermediate and final results produced during execution of the program. The control element carries out the program instructions and controls the flow of information. All arithmetic and logical operations dictated by the program are performed by the arithmetic element under the supervision of the control element. The final results of these operations are presented through an output device—which may be a card or paper tape punch, a magnetic tape unit, a disc, a printer, or a video terminal.

In this paragraph the writer analyzes a class, offensive linemen in professional football, by dividing the class into its categories—centers, guards, tackles, and tight ends—and then classifying them in terms of their typical personalities.

Within the offensive line itself, the typical personalities of centers, guards, tackles, and tight ends are readily distinguishable. The center, who often has to call signals, is usually the brightest. His loquaciousness in relation to other members of the line reflects his leadership. The guard may be bright, and he is quicker than the center. He may also be more aggressive—in the violent, rather than the stubborn, sense—because on sweeps he may be called upon to block downfield. His assertiveness is more persistent; the center's is more volatile. The tackle is slower, more patient, and even more persistent than the guard. He is not called on to be as mobile as the guard, and he doesn't have to get the middle linebacker with an explosive block, as the center does. He maintains and sustains. Stubborn tenacity is prototypical of the offensive tackle; his loyalty and commitment to the welfare of the team know no match. [From Arnold J. Mandell, "In Pro Football, They Play Best Who Play What They Are," *Saturday Review/World,* October 5, 1974.]

An analysis of a process or a sequence of actions divides on the basis of time. A process is a series of actions repeated in chronological order for the purpose of producing a product or a desired result, as in the refining of crude oil to produce gasoline. Narrating the stages of a historical event or the incidents in a story involves an analysis of a sequence of actions. In the latter case the actions are not performed over again and are not intended to produce any product or result. The following paragraph is a process analysis that explains the steps a British student must follow in his quest for a university degree.

> Earning a university degree in Great Britain is a rigorous, competitive process. It commonly begins at the age of eleven, or thereabouts, when elementary children take the "eleven plus" examination to determine whether they will attend a secondary modern school, which provides a more comprehensive curriculum, or one of the more select private or public schools, which emphasize a more academic curriculum for those planning to enter the university. Between fourteen and sixteen years of age, students take another examination, a national, public, "O-level" examination, to earn a certificate that represents the terminal degree for most, since relatively few go on to the university. Those intent on university training spend the two years following successful performance on the O-level preparing for the "A-level" examination. Those passing this examination may enter the university. At the university the student must pass an examination at the end of his second year to continue on to his third year, at the end of which he takes a final examination to qualify for the bachelor's degree. This final examination at Cambridge and Oxford universities is rigorous indeed. In the arts section it usually consists of nine three-hour written examinations plus an oral. The English system, with its examination-oriented tracking process, may seen a bit rigid when compared with the more flexible American system; but it does assure quality in the final product.

The student who wrote the following paragraph analyzed Germany's military progress in the first year of the Second World War into three phases: the eastward thrust, the northern thrust, and the westward thrust.

> During the first year of the Second World War, German military forces thrust first to the east, then to the north, and finally to the west. Successful in his attempt to regain the Sudetenland from Czechoslovakia, Hitler demanded that Poland give up the

Polish Corridor and Danzig. When it became evident that Poland would not submit to his demand, German troops invaded Poland in September of 1939. German aircraft bombed and strafed Polish military formations and defenseless cities as well. Then mobile armored divisions drove through, encircled, and cut off enemy ground forces. After twenty-seven days Poland capitulated. In April of the following year, the German army occupied Denmark and Norway on the pretext that Britain and France were preparing to attack Russia, Germany's new ally, through the Scandinavian countries. On May 10, 1940, Germany's military juggernaut invaded the Netherlands and Belgium in its drive to conquer France. French defenses proved no match for Hitler's blitzkrieg tactics either, and on June 22, 1940, France was forced to sign an armistice with Germany.

These categories of analysis—the whole, the class, the process, and the sequence of actions—are not always exclusive. In some cases an analysis may involve more than one type of analysis, as in the analysis of the computer (p. 81), which involves both a structure and a process. When analyzing a class or group of things, however, you must make certain that your classification system is logical, that the categories do not overlap. Classifying college students under the headings of the *serious-minded,* the *moderately interested,* the *indifferent,* and the *athlete* is obviously illogical since a student could be classified as an athlete and as serious-minded as well.

Here are additional examples of paragraphs developed by analysis.

Schizophrenia can be divided into four major subgroups. The *paranoid* group includes those whose evaluation of reality is seriously affected. Paranoids become suspicious of others, misinterpreting their actions and intentions. They feel they are being persecuted and usually develop hallucinations, imagining they hear voices, smell odors, and see things. A second type, the *hebrenic,* suffers a disintegration of normal behavior patterns, acting silly and engaging in other bizarre mannerisms. The *catatonic* withdraws almost completely from reality. He may become very excited or aggressive or remain in a state of stupor, showing little, if any, reaction to the world outside himself. Many are completely mute. The fourth category, *simple* schizophrenia, includes those who lack interest in the world around them and who show a steady decline in intelligence and emotional response.

In this next paragraph the writer uses judgment, comparison, and contrast in her analysis of college students.

In terms of their general attitude toward politics and the world around them, many students can be placed in one of four basic groups: the contented, the rebels, the escapists, and the reformers. Those in the first group pretty much accept their lot. They don't seriously question the political, economic, social, and educational institutions that govern their lives. Of course, they may occasionally complain about the President, a boring part-time job, or a graduation requirement, but they don't worry about changing much. On the other end of the continuum are the rebels. They think the world's a hopeless mess and the only solution a radical restructuring of society. In their view politicians, business leaders, their teachers and parents—the establishment—conspire to prevent a free expression of humanity's inherent goodness; and the solution to all this is a big bonfire. Their motto is "Up against the wall for the oppressors." The third group includes students who want to escape the system. Though they may, and often do, agree with the rebels that the system is hopelessly corrupt, their reaction is flight, not fight— a retreat into an isolated and insulated world of their own pleasures. And, finally, there are those who are concerned about contemporary social issues, who seek change, but who favor evolutionary rather than revolutionary solutions. They sense that civilized life is not assured, that human beings and their institutions, though capable of change, are not changed quickly nor painlessly.

EXERCISE 9

Write a paragraph of 100 to 150 words, or a three paragraph essay, developing by means of analysis one of the following topics. If you are analyzing a class, remember to divide your subject into three or four subclasses; then describe and differentiate each subclass from the others and, especially if you're writing a multiparagraph essay, present vivid examples. One more point: make certain your subclasses don't overlap.

1. a *process* analysis of any of the following: producing oil from shale; producing electricity from nuclear energy; diamond cutting; sky diving; making a good impression upon a boyfriend or girlfriend or his or her parents; operation of a jet engine or a laser beam; reading a textbook or a newspaper; scuba diving; tuning a motorcycle or automobile; making gasohol

2.   a *class* analysis of any of the following: teachers, sports fans, wines, restaurants, recreational activities, women on the basis of their attitude toward the women's liberation movement, neighborhoods, drugs, college courses, cigarette smokers, bores, campus Romeos, rock singers, athletes, automobile drivers, comedians, parents, coaches, politicians

3.   an analysis of a *whole,* a structure: a modern windmill; a diesel engine; a modern tank; a character sketch of a friend, describing briefly those characteristics that distinguish him/her as an individual; a limited geographical area—such as a stretch of beach, a mountain scene, a desert scene, a campsite, a boulevard scene (Select a specific scene and describe what you see from left to right, right to left, near to far, or far to near.)

4.   an analysis of a *sequence of actions,* such as a narrative of something of interest or importance that happened to you, an important battle of the Revolutionary War, Civil War, World War I or II (In the latter consider El Alamein, Bastogne, Guadalcanal, the Coral Sea, the D-Day invasion.)

5. DEFINITION

Definition serves a number of purposes. By identifying precisely the special characteristics of an idea, an institution, or a group, you can fix their meaning and significance more firmly in your mind as well as communicate them to another person. Definition thus serves to promote clear thinking and writing on the one hand and to facilitate explanation and persuasion on the other. Many disagreements would never occur if disputants took care to define their terms adequately. Learning to define will also be of practical value to you, since you are likely to be asked to define terms from a variety of disciplines: *capitalism, naturalism, monetarism, osmosis, plasticity, symbolism,* and so forth.

You can define in a number of ways. One is to use *examples,* illustrative instances:

> An example of a primate is a gorilla.

This method is useful when writers can assume that readers know something of the meaning of the term: the examples simply provide further clarification. But when the reader lacks this knowledge, this method is rather confusing.

A second method defines by means of a *synonym,* a word with a similar meaning:

> To denigrate means to defame, sully, or disparage. An efflux is an emanation.

This method is helpful if the synonym clarifies the original term, but not if the synonym is likely to be more abstract or general than the original term, as for example:

Flagitious means heinous.

A third method, the *historical* or *etymological* method of definition, clarifies the meaning of a word by revealing its origin and the changes in meaning it has undergone. The following extract from *Webster's Third New International Dictionary* illustrates this type of definition.

> *Sinister* . . . [Middle English *sinistre,* from the Latin *sinister* left, on the left side, . . . evil, unlucky, inauspicious] . . . (2) *obsolete:* conveying misleading or detrimental opinion or advice (the sinister application of the malicious, ignorant, and base interpreter—Ben Jonson) . . . (4) evil or productive of evil: BAD, CORRUPTIVE (the sinister character of the early factory system—Walter Lippmann) . . . (5) . . . b: of ill omen by reason of being on the left (the victor eagle, whose sinister flight retards our host—Alexander Pope) . . . [By permission. From *Webster's Third New International Dictionary.* © 1981 by Merriam-Webster Inc., publishers of the Merriam-Webster® Dictionaries.]

Another method, the *formal* definition, defines a term by placing its referent in a general class and then differentiating it from other members of the same class:

TERM		CLASS	DIFFERENTIATING DETAIL
A marsupial	*is*	an animal	that shelters its young in an external abdominal pouch containing mammary glands.
A hypothesis	*is*	an inference	that accounts, within the framework of a theory, for a set of facts and that can be used as the basis of action or further investigation.
Serendipity	*is*	the faculty	of stumbling upon fortunate, unexpected discoveries.

Defining formally is an exacting process. You must observe several precautions to avoid inadequate and fallacious definitions:

1. The term to be defined should be specially placed in a class. Statements that appear to be analytic definitions are sometimes simply descriptions of the object:

> A steel mill is a noisy, smoky place with tall chimneys.

and sometimes they are interpretations of it:

> Home is where the heart is.

In classifying an object, avoid using "is where" or "is when." *Where* signifies location, *when* signifies time, and neither represents a class of things:

> ORIGINAL   Democracy is when the people rule themselves.
> REVISION   Democracy is a form of government in which the people rule themselves.

2. The general class into which the term is placed should not be too extensive. Defining a telescope as something that helps the eye to see distant objects is not very helpful: the class of things is simply too broad. It could include, for example, binoculars, eyeglasses, magnifying glasses, and many others. In general, the narrower the classification, the clearer the definition. A telescope would thus be more precisely defined as an optical instrument, consisting of parts that fit and slide one within another, that enlarges the image of a distant object.

3. The definition should not repeat the name of the thing to be defined or a derivative of it:

> Certified mail is mail that has been certified.

This definition still leaves the reader uninformed as to what "certified mail" means. Definitions that repeat the term to be defined, as in the example above, are called *circular* definitions, for they lead the reader back to where he started. A better definition would be:

> Certified mail is first class mail for which proof of delivery is secured but for which no indemnity value is claimed.

4. The differentiation should be sufficient to distinguish the term clearly from other members of the class:

> Buddhism is a religion of Asia.

This definition does not supply enough information to distinguish Buddhism from Mohammedanism, Hinduism, or Christianity, all religions of Asia. With the necessary information added, the meaning is clearer:

> Buddhism is a religion of central and eastern Asia derived from the teachings of Gautama Buddha, who taught that suffering is inherent in life and that one can escape from it into *nirvana*— a state of spiritual peace—through mental and moral self-purification.

5. The definition should not be expressed in highly technical, obscure language. Dr. Samuel Johnson's definition of *network* as "anything reticulated or decussated, at equal distances with interstices between the intersections" is accurate but complex. The definition of *network* as a fabric or structure of threads, cords, or wires that cross each other at regular intervals and are knotted or secured at the crossings, as defined in *Webster's Third International Dictionary,* is much simpler and clearer.

Observing these precautions will improve the clarity and precision of your formal definitions. There are times, however, when you will have to write more than a single sentence, a *minimum* definition, to define a term adequately. An explanation of Mohammedanism, freedom, or liberalism would obviously require more than one sentence. In developing a paragraph by means of definition, it is a good idea to start with a minimum definition as a basis and then use examples, comparisons, contrasts, historical information, and so forth, to support and extend your definition. Definitions that are developed in one or more paragraphs are called *extended* definitions.

The following paragraph offers a definition of a hypochondriac.

Minimum Definition   A hypochondriac is a person who is preoccupied with his imaginary ill health. He is constantly fearful of developing some dreadful disease, or he is convinced he already has one, though medical examination reveals his fears to *Differentiating Detail* be groundless. A typical hypochondriac does not suffer from deep dejection, from melancholia. He doesn't try to hide his concern. On the contrary, he loves to talk about his diseases, his colds, the gory details of an operation, his close calls with death. My uncle Cedric is a perfect exam- *Use of Example* ple. No conversation with him is complete without a detailed description of his past illnesses, an analysis of some new pills he is taking, and an update of his current condition. His physical ailments are clearly very dear to his heart, his traumatic experiences almost sacred. He derives his deepest pleasure, however, when his listeners catch their breath when he starts slumping in his easy chair and sliding to the floor in an apparent physical collapse.

Russell Nye tries his hand at defining the essay, a difficult genre to define. Note that he presents his formal definition near the end of the paragraph to summarize the characteristics of the form he has presented earlier.

Differen-
tiating
Detail

Minimum
Definition

But an essay, difficult as it is to define, is nevertheless marked by certain characteristics. To varying degrees, it is personal, establishing a more or less direct relationship between writer and reader. Its purpose is primarily to stimulate interest, thought, and attention for a relatively brief period of time; secondarily, it may amuse, instruct, prove, convince, narrate, or explain. The essay style is individualized and subjective, attempting to say in prose what it has to say in the best possible manner and the most personal way. Its scope is elastic, adjustable to the topic and its treatment; it need not be complete, usually treating one or more facets of a subject with some sense of finish, or perhaps only suggesting a treatment. Structurally the essay has no set form; its arrangement and emphasis are governed by the internal requirements of the subject matter and the logic of the topic itself. Its organization may vary from the formal on one extreme to the casual and accidental on the other. The essay may be loosely defined as a short prose form, dealing with its subject in a more or less limited manner from a more or less personal viewpoint, with considerable latitude as to style, method, organization, and scope. Or as one essayist remarked succinctly, "I doubt if anyone could define the essay, but I see no reason why anybody should be afraid to write one if he has anything to say worth saying." [From Russell Nye, "On the Reading of Essays"]

E. M. Forster, an English novelist, defines plot in this paragraph. A minimum definition of the term appears in the third sentence.

Minimum
Definition

Let us define a plot. We have defined a story as a narrative of events arranged in their time-sequence. A plot is also a narrative of events, the emphasis falling on causality.

Use of
Example

Differen-
tiating
Detail

"The king died and then the queen died," is a story. "The king died, and then the queen died of grief," is a plot. The time sequence is preserved, but the sense of causality overshadows it. Or again: "The queen died, no one knew why, until it was discovered that it was through death of the king." This is a plot with a mystery in it, a form capable of high development. It suspends the time sequence, it moves as far away from the story as its limitations will allow. Consider the death of the queen. If it is in a story we say "and then?" If it is in a plot we ask "why?" That is the fundamental difference between these two aspects of the novel. A plot cannot be told to a gaping audience of cave men or to a tyrannical sultan or to their modern descendant the movie-public. They can only be kept awake by "and then—and then." They can only supply curiosity. But a plot demands intelligence and memory also. [From E. M. Forster, *Aspects of the Novel*, Harcourt Brace Jovanovich, 1927.]

In this paragraph the author defines *euphemism*. His first sentence provides a minimum definition, which he amplifies by historical reference, judgment, and example in the sentences that follow.

Minimum
Definition

Historical
Reference

Judgment

Example

From a Greek word meaning "to use words of good omen," euphemism is the substitution of a pleasant term for a blunt one—telling it like it isn't. Euphemism has probably existed since the beginning of language. As long as there have been things of which men thought the less said the better, there have been better ways of saying less. In everyday conversation the euphemism is, at worst, a necessary evil; at its best, it is a handy verbal tool to avoid making enemies needlessly, or shocking friends. Language purists and the blunt-spoken may wince when a young woman at a party coyly asks for direction to "the powder room," but to most people this kind of familiar euphemism is probably no more harmful or annoying than, say, a split infinitive. [From "Euphemism," *Time, The Weekly Newsmagazine*, 1969.]

EXERCISE 10

A. In the blanks below indicate which of the following methods is used to define: (1) example, (2) synonym, or (3) formal. Write the number of your answer in the blank to the right of the sentence.

1. The monkey, ape, and man are examples of primates. ———

2. A headland is a point of land, usually in the form of a cliff, extending out into a body of water. ———

3. Bucolic means pastoral, sylvan. ———

4. *Huckleberry Finn* illustrates the picaresque novel. ———

5. Platonic love is a spiritual attraction between persons that is divorced from physical desire and derived from the philosophy of the Greak Plato. ———

B. Some of the definitions given below violate the conditions necessary for a minimum formal definition. Mark the definitions as follows: (1) if the term has not been specifically placed in a class, (2) if the class into which the term has been placed is too large, (3) if the term is not sufficiently differentiated from other members of the same class, (4) if the term to be defined, or a derivative of it, is repeated in the definition, (5) if the definition is expressed in highly technical language, (6) if the definition seems clear and sound.

1. A *democracy* is a form of government based upon democratic principles. ———

2. *Botany* is a fascinating study. ———

3. A *Molotov cocktail* is a makeshift incendiary bomb made of a breakable container, usually a glass bottle, filled with flammable liquid, and provided with a rag wick. ———

4. A *carpetbagger* went to the South after the Civil War to seek his own political or financial advantage. ———

5. A *winch* is a gadget that employs a drum around which a rope or chain winds as the load is lifted. ———

6. The psychological novel is a work of prose fiction that places more than the usual amount of emphasis on interior characterization, on the mental states, motives, and circumstances of characters, which result from and develop the external action.

7. A *computer* is composed of three parts: an input device, a memory unit, and an output device. ———

8. A *stoic* is a person who believes that men and women should stoically accept whatever fate puts in their path. ———

9. A *raphe* is the part of the funiculus of an anatropous ovule adnate to the integument, forming a ridge along the body of the ovule that provides a diagnostic character in the various seeds. _____

10. *Cant* is a special language peculiar to a specific group of speakers. _____

C. Rewrite each of the following definitions in one sentence making them more precise or more informative. Be prepared to explain why the original version is inadequate.

1. Pragmatists are very practical in coping with problems they face.

_____

_____

_____

2. Louisiana Cajun is a unique and amusing American dialect.

_____

_____

_____

3. A good sport is not the same thing as a sports enthusiast.

_____

_____

_____

D. Reread the three paragraphs dealing with the terms *hypochondriac, plot,* and *essay* (pp. 88–90). For each definition list (1) the *general class* into which the term has been placed and (2) the *differentiating detail* that distinguishes the term from other members of the class.

TERM	CLASS	DIFFERENTIATING DETAIL
1. A hypochondriac is	_____	_____
		_____
		_____

2. A plot is ——————————— ———————————

———————————

———————————

3. An essay is ——————————— ———————————

———————————

———————————

E. Write a paragraph definition of any of the following terms. Begin with a minimum definition (term, class, differentiating detail) as your topic sentence and use whatever kind of support you wish—facts, analysis, illustration, analogy, judgment—to develop your definition.

1. a classic

2. a klutz, a mature person, a successful person

3. a particular breed of animal—Arabian horse, Hungarian puli dog, river otter, and so on

4. a neurotic, a psychotic, a paranoiac

5. a liberal, a conservative, a reactionary, a fundamentalist

6. prejudice, fanaticism, sentimentality

7. a gourmet, a gourmand, a glutton

8. an idealist, a pragmatist, a fatalist, a stoic, a cynic, an existentialist

9. a boor, a bore

10. a connoisseur, a dilettante

11. a male chauvinist, a *macho* man

12. a demagogue, a patriot, a racist

13. wisdom, intelligence, wit, humor

14. civil disobedience, charity

15. a sportsman, an amateur

16. a communist, a socialist

17. a liberated woman

18. a scholar, a swinger, an intellectual

19. chutzpah, pizzazz

20. a snob

F. Write a paragraph definition of one of the following terms using the historical or etymological method:

1. villain   2. vulgar   3. assassin   4. yahoo
5. limousine   6. boycott   7. mistress   8. maverick
9. liberal   10. serendipity

G. Write a three-paragraph definition of one of the following words. In your opening paragraph provide a formal definition of the term and some mention of origin and historical background. In your second and third paragraphs use contrast (with a term similar in meaning), analysis, exemplification, or analogy to provide further development.

1. fanaticism   2. charity   3. liberal   4. agnostic
5. patriotism   6. puritanical   7. devout   8. charisma
9. success   10. classic

6. COMBINATION OF METHODS

A good many, if not most, of the paragraphs you write will use a combination of the methods of paragraph development that have been explained and illustrated in this chapter. If you are developing a paragraph by means of examples, then statistics and other factual detail may strengthen your point. If your controlling idea requires definition for support, you will probably find comparison and contrast useful in providing additional clarification.

Here are two paragraphs that combine several methods in their development. In the first Michael Korda offers an opinion on the pleasures of life. He uses judgments, comparison, and illustration in support of his main idea.

Judgment

Illustration

Comparison

> Personally, I don't believe that this simple-minded denial of pleasure constitutes a positive social virtue. The world is not going to be made a better place by our refusing to enjoy ourselves—let alone by our refusing to *admit* we are. It is a fallacy to assume that the social forces behind the French Revolution would have been held in check if only Marie Antoinette had given up eating cake. On the contrary, the worse things get, the more sensible it is to take what pleasure one can before it's too late. The dollar may be falling, but the pleasures of life, whatever yours happen to be, hold their value steadily. The warm glow of a good meal or a bottle of wine does not depreciate. It may be temporary, but then so is life. [From Michael Korda, "Hooray for Hedonism," *Newsweek*, November 26, 1979, p. 29.]

This next selection uses definition, exemplification, and anecdote:

Definition

Example

> Blue is the color of royalty and quality. A *blueblood* is a person of noble or aristocratic descent. A *blue chip* is the poker chip of highest value, the stock that is the safest investment. The *blue ribbon* is the prize given the winner of the horse race, the dog show, the pie-baking contest.
>
> In England, the blue ribbon is worn by members of the Order of the Garter, the highest order of knighthood. In France, it is worn by Knights of the Holy Ghost. In France, of course, a blue ribbon is not called a blue ribbon. It's a *cordon bleu,* which gets us, in a roundabout way, to a question posed by a reader: "Why is a great chef known as a *cordon bleu?*"

Anecdote   One story has it that in days gone by those Knights of the Holy Ghost were fellows who loved to eat. If they were served a wonderful meal, so the story goes, they told the chef that it was a blue-ribbon meal, *un repas de cordon bleu.* At any rate, *cordon bleu* eventually attached itself to chefs, first in a jocular way and later in quite a serious way. So today, a distinguished chef is known as a *cordon bleu* or a *cordon bleu* chef. . . . [From Michael Gartner, "Words' Worth," *Los Angeles Times,* May 10, 1981.]

EXERCISE 11

A. In the space provided indicate a suitable method, or methods, of developing the controlling idea in each of the following topic sentences.

1. One sees a variety of beachwear on a public beach. _____

    _____

2. Providing a college education for their children imposes a financial burden

    on parents today. _____

    _____

3. The one abiding truth about the stock market is that it will fluctuate. _____

    _____

4. Shelby Van Heusen is a popular man on campus. _____

    _____

5. The United States is both a democracy and a republic. _____

    _____

6. Joggers exhibit a variety of motivations. _____

7. Investing in the commodities market is like shooting dice. _____

    _____

8. Ernest Hemingway's novels and short stories reveal several existential prin-

    ciples. _____

9. The Rose Parade is a colorful spectacle. _____

10. Pornography is not easy to define or identify. _____

    _____

11. Bull McCrunch and Slats Donahue differed in their approach to women.

    _____

12. Exploring for oil in the ocean is an expensive operation. _____

    _____

13. Snorkling in the South Pacific lagoons is an exhilarating pastime. _____

_____

14. Nikolai Lenin and William Gladstone had much in common. _____

_____

15. The law is like a single-bed blanket on a double bed. _____

_____

16. Souping up a stock car is an expensive process. _____

_____

17. If carried to the extreme, tolerance can become cowardice. _____

_____

18. My first date with Hermione was a disastrous experience. _____

_____

19. The structure of an atom is like a miniscule solar system. _____

_____

20. There are four common types of fishermen. _____

B. For each of the five topics listed below, write five topic sentences that could be used as the basis of a paragraph.

1. popular music in the United States

_____

_____

_____

_____

_____

2. autointoxication—Americans' love affair with the automobile

_____

_____

—————————————————————————————

—————————————————————————————

—————————————————————————————

3. genetic engineering and the curing of disease

—————————————————————————————

—————————————————————————————

—————————————————————————————

—————————————————————————————

—————————————————————————————

4. a friend with an unusual trait(s)

—————————————————————————————

—————————————————————————————

—————————————————————————————

—————————————————————————————

—————————————————————————————

5. the growing interest in health and physical fitness in the United States

—————————————————————————————

—————————————————————————————

—————————————————————————————

—————————————————————————————

—————————————————————————————

C. Use the following sentences to compose a paragraph on gobbledygook. Do not begin with the topic sentence, but lead into it. (See pp. 36–37.)

1. Governmental gobbledygook describes poor and ill-fed people as having "inadequate financial resources to purchase the products of agricultural communities and industrial establishments . . ."

2. In simpler terms, you can charge your dental bills to the Public Health Service.

3. Those who wish to communicate with others should aim to express, not impress.

4. It seems to be especially difficult for Washington bureaucrats.

5. Interoffice memos, particularly in the defense industries, are loaded with phrases like "balanced logistical contingency," "integrated organizational mobility," and "parallel policy options."

6. Legal documents are larded with such phrases as "party of the first part," "cease and desist," "give and convey," "irrelevant, incompetent, and immaterial."

7. The following is fairly typical of insurance policy prose: "This policy is issued in consideration of the statements in the application of this policy and the payment in advance of the first premium stated in the schedule which includes premiums for attached riders, if any, . . ."

8. The ability to write clear, concise, uncluttered prose is not common.

9. Maury Maverick, a Congressman from Texas, invented a term, "gobbledygook," to describe the kind of pretentious, long-winded, polysyllabic language found in government documents and memos.

10. Stuart Chase cites another instance, a government department announcement on dental bills: "Voucherable expenditures necessary to provide adequate dental treatment required as adjunct to medical treatment being rendered a pay patient in in-patient status may be incurred at the expense of the Public Health Service."[5]

11. Gobbledygook also flourishes in law, business, and industry.

12. Though gobbledygook is a pervasive disease of language, it can, fortunately, be eradicated by careful elimination of the excess baggage, the clutter, the pretense of long-winded prose.

D. Analyze the following paragraphs for fullness of development. Explain how those paragraphs you believe to be underdeveloped could be improved.

1. Illegal immigration into the United States poses serious political and economic problems. Illegal aliens commonly do the more physically demanding, tedious jobs that native workers shun, as in farming and the manufacture of clothing. Their willingness to do such work without complaint, however, invites their exploitation; and their generally low wages illustrate the point. Such exploitation not only hurts them, of course, it also depresses wages for native workers in related industries since employers prefer docile, less expensive workers. Because undocumented aliens often live in crowded, somewhat unsanitary living quarters and lack the means to pay for private medical care, they must depend on public health services. But providing such care adds a burden to

[5] *The Power of Words,* Harcourt Brace Jovanovich, 1953.

local, county, and state governments, whose budgets are already tight because of the cutbacks in grants from the federal government. Americans have taken pride in their willingness to accept the homeless, "huddled masses" of the world who have sought the friendly shores of America, but they are beginning to discover that they no longer have the financial resources to continue to do so for all who want to come.

2. After years of neglect, the study of foreign languages is beginning to gain more attention again, and a good thing, too. To begin with, anyone wishing to work abroad for an American company should know more than a smattering of phrases if he hopes to communicate successfully with foreigners in a business or social context. German, Dutch, or French businessmen may speak English, but they are more responsive to Americans who can readily communicate with them in their own language. Travelers will also benefit from language study.

3. I have been observing cigarette smokers for some time now, and I have tried to classify the different types. First, there is the puffer. By holding the cigarette between the forefinger and the thumb, he avoids nicotine stains on his hands. His little finger is usually crooked, and the hand is held perfectly still to avoid dropping hot ashes on himself or the floor. Next is the dragon. This smoker is completely different from the puffer. He has no particular grip for holding the cigarette. He takes large drags, one after another, which tend to form a rather long hot ash on the end of the cigarette. He then inhales deep into the lungs and exhales quietly and quickly through his nostrils, giving the impression of a fire-breathing dragon. Last, there is the whoosher. He has, essentially, the same characteristics as the dragon, except that the whoosher spews smoke out in all directions, the sound reminiscent of wind escaping from a wind tunnel. These three types, and others, should quit smoking before they impair their health. They would probably enjoy life more—and longer.

4. The rising divorce statistics of recent years have prompted the suggestion that the traditional lifetime marriage contract be replaced by a short-term, renewable contract. This solution would, however, aggravate, not improve the situation, for it would create serious complications in the lives of the children of such a marriage and undermine the emotional relationship of the husband and wife. Those who support renewable, short-term marriages claim that traditional marriage ties are unrealistic because they seek to bind a couple together for life, a chancey proposition in a fast-moving world. But loosening those ties through short-term marriages will simply increase marital instability. In a successful marriage there must be time for the partners to adjust to each other's temperament. A short-term marriage decreases the chance of a husband and wife's working out difficult problems by giving each partner an easy way out. Moreover, a happy marriage is not likely to result if one partner worries about whether the other will renew the contract.

5. Putting aside, for the moment, what the men say and feel, and looking at what they actually do and the choices they make, getting a job, keeping a job, and doing well at it is clearly of low priority. Arthur will not take a job at all. Leroy is supposed to be on his job at 4:00 P.M. but it is already 4:10 and he still cannot bring himself to leave the free games he has accumulated on the pinball machine in the Carry-out. Tonk started a construction job on Wednesday, worked Thursday and Friday, then didn't go back again. On the same kind of

job, Sea Cat quit in the second week. Sweets had been working three months as a busboy in a restaurant, then quit without notice, not sure himself why he did so. A real estate agent, saying he was more interested in getting the job done than in the cost, asked Richard to give him an estimate on repairing and painting the inside of a house, but Richard, after looking over the job, somehow never got around to submitting an estimate. During one period, Tonk would not leave the corner to take a job because his wife might prove unfaithful; Stanton would not take a job because his woman had been unfaithful. [From Elliot Lebow, "Penny Capitalism on an Urban Streetcorner," Little, Brown, 1967.]

E. As a preliminary suggestion to help you develop a paragraph by means of examples (pp. 56–59), you were advised to work up an outline, transforming the topic into a specific topic sentence, jotting down details as they entered your mind, eliminating irrelevant items, and so forth. This procedure is helpful, for it demands that you think about your subject and get your thoughts in order before you begin to write, thus ensuring a more unified paragraph. Another useful technique, one proposed by Robert Louis Stevenson, involves imitation. Stevenson urged the young writer to imitate a variety of writing styles. Through such imitation, he argued, the writer would gradually begin to develop a richer style of his own. One advantage of this method is that it offers the writer a model, a standard for comparison—a decided asset to an inexperienced writer, who, though he may have a fairly good idea of what he wants to say, begins to flounder because he cannot find the right words, phrases, or sentences in which to express it.

After selecting a passage to imitate, Stevenson read the selection carefully, concentrating on its rhythm and structure. When he had fixed this movement and pattern in his mind, he selected an appropriate subject and tried to express his own thoughts in a similar style. Apply this procedure in this exercise. Read the model paragraph carefully, noting the placement of the topic sentence, the kinds of detail used to support the controlling idea, and the wording and sentence structure. Then choose one of the topics listed and compose your own paragraph, imitating the general pattern and style of the model.

The topic sentence in this paragraph is the first sentence. The second sentence comments on the controlling idea in the topic sentence—the attraction of board surfing—and informs the reader that the primary detail will consist of reasons. Sentences 3, 6, 8, and 10 supply these reasons. Sentences 4, 5, 7, 9, and 11 provide secondary support. You need not try to imitate the exact structure or wording of each sentence, but copy the general plan of the paragraph and use expressions such as *in recent years, but reasons for this attitude, for one thing, another reason, a third appeal,* and *but perhaps* to introduce your reasons. Round off your paragraphs with an appropriate quoted passage.

(1) *In recent years* an increasing number of young men who live in southern California, Florida, and Hawaii have come to regard board surfing not simply as a sport but almost as a way of life. (2) This intense

love of surfing may seem excessive, a youthful fad, *but reasons for this attitude are not hard to find.* (3) *For one thing,* surfing is challenging and exciting. (4) When a curling wave lifts the surfer and propels him swiftly toward the beach, the sense of speed, power, danger, and surprise he experiences stimulates the emotions. (5) Surfers often use the term "stoked" to describe the experience. (6) *Another reason* is that surfing develops coordination and control of the body. (7) It develops grace and self-confidence in the face of danger, not unlike gymnastics, or perhaps bullfighting. (8) *A third appeal* of surfing is that it inspires the surfer to develop his own style of performance. (9) He can, in a sense, create his own art form, a kind of aquatic dance, as he confronts and masters the wave. (10) *But perhaps* it is simply the aesthetic experience—the beauty of the sea, of the rolling surf and the curving beach, the feel of the water and the board under him—that attracts surfers like lemmings in the spring and summer months. (11) The surfer's world, writes John Costello, is "sometimes soft and gentle, sometimes wild and rough, the same only in that it is always challenging and seductive, a siren whose song can never be naysaid."[6]

TOPICS

1. the value of a college education, of studying a foreign language, of general education, of career education, of bilingual education

2. protecting the whale or seal pup against commercial hunters

3. reinstating the draft

4. restricting foreign imports of steel, textiles, or automobiles to protect American industry

5. the value of owning a personal computer

6. the nuclear freeze proposal, developing satellite space weapons to destroy enemy missiles

7. alternative sources of energy—thermonuclear fusion, solar energy, subsurface heat, tidal power, windmills

8. violence in motion pictures, television programs, professional sports

9. a favorite recreational activity—sky diving, hang gliding, motorcycling, scuba diving, snow or water skiing, tennis, racketball; driving a sports car, van, camper, pickup truck

10. salaries of professional athletes, taking steroids to improve athletic performance, football scholarships

---

[6] "Surfers: Riding a Ten-Foot Wave Is Only for the Brave," *Nation's Business,* April 1980, p. 81.

Bear in mind that this assignment asks you to provide *reasons* to support your controlling idea. You must explain *why* reinstating the draft is beneficial or harmful, *why* one should or should not own a computer, *why* the whale needs to be protected. Reasons are judgments, opinions. (See pp. 65–69). Although you may already have opinions on the subject you select, investigate your subject further by consulting a reference book, for example. This research will strengthen your understanding of the subject, give additional supporting reasons for your controlling idea, and, of course, provide a quoted passage to reinforce your final reason. It will also provide relevant secondary detail—facts and illustrations—to support your primary reasons.

In connection with your library research, fill in the reference sheet. It will serve as a rudimentary outline for your paragraph. The topic sentence on this sheet is the tentative topic sentence for the paragraph you will write. Make certain that each of the four items is a reason that directly supports the controlling idea. The fourth item should contain a quoted passage.

Reference Sheet for Exercise 11E

Author _____

Title of magazine article or book chapter _____

_____

Title of magazine or book _____

Date of publication _____ Volume _____ Page numbers _____

Tentative topic sentence:_____

_____

_____

Reasons:

1. _____

_____

2. _____

_____

3. _____

_____

4. (Include a quoted passage) _____

_____

SUMMARY

Good paragraphs must be adequately developed. You should therefore take special care to see that your paragraphs contain sufficient supporting material to explain clearly and fully your topic statement. There are a number of ways to do this: (1) use *illustrative detail*—examples, illustrations, anecdotes—when you can clarify by pointing to a particular incident, a concrete phenomenon; (2) use *facts* and *statistics* when verifiable detail is required to substantiate your point; (3) use *comparison* and *contrast* when you can explain your subject best by noting how it is similar to or different from another object or situation; (4) use *analysis* when your subject lends itself naturally to subdivision; (5) use *definition* when your purpose requires the establishment of the meaning of a term; and (6) use a *combination* of any of these methods whenever you need or desire a variety of supporting material.

CHAPTER FOUR

COHERENCE

Clear, readable paragraphs must be coherent as well as unified and well developed. Their sentences must not only adequately develop a controlling idea but they also must link together smoothly. Each sentence should lead into the next so that the reader can easily follow the progression of thought. To achieve this orderly progression, you must arrange your material in some logical sequence and provide connecting links between sentences.

To help your reader understand your meaning quickly and easily, you must take special care with this first task, the proper ordering of ideas. In the following paragraph, for example, the lack of an orderly grouping of the sentences disrupts the continuity.

(1) The dramatic increase in violent crime in southern California in recent years—in particular the senseless, random killings that have occurred in broad daylight in affluent communities—has angered citizens and government officials alike. (2) Everyone wants the slaughter stopped, but before solutions can be found and implemented, the nature of the violence must be understood. (3) A recent California Department of Justice study provides this kind of information in its analysis of the victims, the perpetrators of violence, the weapons used, and the judicial treatment of criminal defendants.[1] (4) These facts do not by themselves point the way to a solution, but any proposed solution that ignores, for example, the prominence of the handgun or the violence from which minorities suffer, is bound to fail. (5) The perpetrators of the violence also are likely to come from minority communities: of those arrested for murder, 71 percent were from minority groups; 29 percent were white. (6) Though members of minorities are often thought to suffer most in the dispensation of criminal justice, the report reveals that race is

[1] John Van de Kamp, "The Slaughter Statistics: Working Together for a Better Tomorrow," *Los Angeles Times*, December 31, 1980.

not a significant factor. (7) Of those charged in court with murder, 77 percent of the whites charged were convicted, blacks at a rate of 76 percent, Mexican-Americans at a rate of 74 percent. (8) The majority of the victims were from minority communities: 62 percent were black, Mexican-American, or from other nonwhite minorities; 38 percent were white. (9) The most commonly used weapon in killings was the gun, the handgun in particular, which was used in about 75 percent of the murders committed by firearms.

This paragraph contains enough detail to support its controlling idea, but the sentences are not well ordered. The first sentence provides an introduction to the controlling idea, which is expressed in the next two sentences: the nature of criminal violence must be understood—in terms of its victims, the perpetrators, the weapons used, and the judicial treatment of those charged—before solutions can be implemented. The fourth sentence, however, is a conclusion, a summing up, and should be placed at the end of the paragraph. The fifth sentence begins the analysis, but it focuses on perpetrators rather than victims, as it should, because of the order of items in the topic sentence. The subjects of the succeeding sentences are also not presented in the order in which they were originally presented. The paragraph would have been more coherent if the detail had been discussed in the proper order. In particular, the judicial treatment of criminal defendants should be left to the end since it is the most emotionally charged of the four subjects and deserves such emphasis. As mentioned, the fourth sentence rounds out the paragraph and should appear last. Notice how the coherence of the paragraph is strengthened when the sentences are grouped more logically.

The dramatic increase in violent crime in southern California in recent years—in particular the senseless, random killings that have occurred in broad daylight in affluent communities—has angered citizens and government officials alike. Everyone wants the slaughter stopped, but before solutions can be found and implemented, the nature of the violence must be understood. A recent California Department of Justice study provides this kind of information in its analysis of the victims, the perpetrators of violence, the weapons used, and the judicial treatment of criminal defendants. The majority of the victims were from minority communities: 62 percent were black, Mexican-American, or from other nonwhite minorities; 38 percent were white. The perpetrators of the violence also are likely to come from minority communities: of those arrested for murder, 71 percent were from minority groups; 29 percent were white. The most commonly used weapon in killings was the gun, the handgun in particular, which was used in about 75 percent of the murders committed by firearms. Though members of minorities are often thought to suffer most in the dispensation of criminal justice, the report reveals that race is not a significant factor. Of those charged in court with murder, 77 percent of the whites charged were convicted, blacks at a rate of 76 percent, Mexican-Americans at a rate of 74 percent. These facts do not by themselves point the way to a solution, but any proposed solution that ignores, for example, the prominence of the handgun or the violence from which minorities suffer is bound to fail.

ORDERING DETAIL

If your paragraphs are to be coherent, you must first arrange your materials in a reasonable, consistent order. The kind of order you use will depend on your purpose and the nature of your materials. When you wish to narrate an experience, describe an event, or present the steps of a process, you should normally order your detail on the basis of time. When you wish to describe something other than a process or an event—a landscape, a person, the structure of an atom, for example—you should organize your detail in terms of its spatial relationships. And when you wish to explain an idea or defend an opinion, you should arrange your detail in a logical order that effectively presents the continuity of ideas from sentence to sentence. These three methods of ordering detail are somewhat arbitrary. The controlling idea of a paragraph explaining or defending an idea, for example, may employ a spatial or chronological analysis. A narrative paragraph may include a description of items in terms of their spatial relationships as well as their occurrence in time. Nonetheless, these methods do provide a convenient illustration of common patterns of ordering sentences in a paragraph. In the discussion that follows we shall explain and illustrate these methods in greater detail.

Time

Arranging the detail of a paragraph in chronological order is a natural and effective method of describing a personal experience. In the paragraph below, Mason Williams, an American writer and singer, groups his detail in this manner as he recalls his first experience driving a car.

I had started watching people drive to learn how myself, and one day while everybody was gone, I thought I'd sneak a try. I got in the car and started it up. The engine seemed to be running fast, but I thought it would probably slow down after I put it in gear. I pushed in the clutch, put it in reverse and let the clutch out. The gear grabbed and the car took off backwards all the way across the yard and crashed into a tree. It knocked off the trunk lid, broke the back window and bent up a bunch of other stuff underneath. I found out later that my stepfather had been working on it and had left the dashboard throttle out all the way. I spent the afternoon staring at what I'd done, walking off and coming back. I must have looked at it 40 times from 40 different angles, trying to see it so it didn't look so bad. There was just no way to glue it back and hide it.

Space

The details of a paragraph describing an object are arranged spatially to give the reader a clear picture of the object described. In this paragraph Isak Dinesen describes a stretch of African landscape seen from the Ngong Hills, first to the south, then to the east and north, and finally to the west.

> From the Ngong Hills you have a unique view, you see to the South the vast plains of the great game-country that stretches all the way to Kilimanjaro; to the East and North the park-like country of the foot-hills with the forest behind them, and the undulating land of the Kikuyu-Reserve, which extends to Mount Kenya a hundred miles away—a mosaic of little square maize-fields, banana-groves and grass-land, with here and there the blue smoke from a native village, a small cluster of peaked mole-casts. But towards the West, deep down, lies the dry, moon-like landscape of the African low country. The brown desert is ir-regularly dotted with the little marks of the thornbushes, the winding river-beds are drawn up with crooked dark-green trails; those are the woods of the mighty, wide-branching Mimosa-trees, with thorns like spikes; the cactus grows here, and here is the home of the Giraffe and the Rhino. [*Out of Africa,* Random House, 1937, 1952, pp. 5–6.]

Continuity of Idea

The details of a paragraph intended to explain or persuade can be grouped in a number of patterns. The most frequently used are the *inductive,* the *deductive,* and the *climactic.* Induction is a process of rea-soning in which one proceeds from an examination of particular facts to the formulation of an inference to account for them. An inductive paragraph often ends with a topic sentence. When writers think their readers may resist the point they wish to make, they often use an inductive order to present their facts, illustrations, and definitions before their conclusion.

In the following paragraph Francis Parkman reserves his main point for the last sentence after he has presented the concrete detail that illustrates it.

> The face of the country was dotted far and wide with countless hundreds of buffalo. They trooped along in files and columns, bulls, cows, and calves, on the green faces of the declivities in front. They scrambled away over the hills to the right and left; and far off, the pale blue swells in the extreme distance were dotted with innumerable specks. Sometimes I surprised shaggy old bulls grazing alone, or sleeping behind the ridges I ascended. They would leap up at my approach, stare stupidly at me through their tangled manes, and then gallop heavily away. The antelope were very numerous; and as they are always bold when in the neighborhood of buffalo, they would approach to look at me, gaze intently with their great round eyes, then suddenly leap aside, and stretch lightly away over the prairie, as swiftly as a racehorse. Squalid, ruffian-like wolves sneaked through the hollows and sandy ravines. Several times I passed through villages of prairie dogs, who sat, each at the mouth of his burrow, holding his paws before him in a supplicating attitude, and yelping away most vehemently, whisking his little tail with every squeaking cry he uttered. Prairie dogs are not fastidious in their choice of companions; various long checkered snakes were sunning themselves in the midst of the village, and demure little gray owls, with a large white ring around each eye, were perched side by side with the rightful inhabitants. The prairie teemed with life.

Deduction is a process of reasoning that proceeds from a generalization to a conclusion derived from that generalization. A paragraph in which the materials have been arranged deductively thus begins with the topic statement followed by the detail in support of this statement. The following paragraph illustrates the deductive order of development:

> Expressing one's thoughts is one skill that the school can easily teach, especially to people born without natural writing or speaking talent. Many other skills can be learned later—in this country there are literally thousands of places that offer training

to adult people at work. But the foundations for skill in expression have to be laid early: an interest in and an ear for language; experience in organizing ideas and data, in brushing aside the irrelevant, in wedding outward form and inner content into one structure; and above all, the habit of verbal expression. If you do not lay these foundations during your school years, you may never have an opportunity again. [From Peter Drucker, "How to Be an Employee," *Fortune,* May 1952, p. 127.]

Readers are apt to remember best what they read last. Therefore, writers frequently organize their detail in an order of climax, beginning with the least important detail and closing with the most important. This pattern is effective when one of the facts, examples, or judgments used to develop a paragraph is especially relevant and impressive. In the following sentences the ideas are arranged in an order of climax.

1. In 1984 Antonia graduated from college, was accepted at Stanford law school, and married her childhood sweetheart.

2. Emily is witty, sophisticated, and beautiful, but much too imperious.

3. This past year has been a disaster for me: in April I had to pay $10,000 in back taxes to the IRS, in June I lost my job, and in September my wife divorced me.

The following paragraph is arranged in an order of climax:

Our primary focus has been on the launching of a new business, which is in many ways a most extraordinary kind of undertaking. When you go into business for yourself you trade off the familiar and the safe for the unknown and the risky. The business is the only source of support for you and your family. You take on long-term financial obligations with money that belongs to relatives, friends, strangers, and institutions. You have to work 14 hours a day, seven days a week, for the foreseeable future. And, after all that, the odds are you'll fail; although there are no reliable data, conventional wisdom says that two thirds of new businesses go under by the fifth year. [From Albert Shapero, "The Displaced, Uncomfortable Entrepreneur," *Psychology Today,* November 1975, p. 83.]

Three other possibilities for the ordering of detail in an expository paragraph are the orders of *familiarity, complexity,* and *cause and effect.* Writers attempting to explain a difficult subject frequently arrange detail in an order of familiarity, proceeding from the known to the unknown. For example, if a writer were explaining the principle of jet propulsion, he or she might begin with a reference to the flight of a balloon from which the air had suddenly been released. In the order of complexity, simpler details are presented first and are followed by more complicated ones. And in the order of cause and effect, the writer organizes the material to trace the relationship between a cause and its resulting effect. The cause-and-effect order is quite similar to the narrative order, but it has a causal rather than a chronological emphasis.

EXERCISE 12

A. The sentences in the following paragraphs have been scrambled so that they are improperly ordered. Rearrange the sentences to form a more coherent paragraph and indicate the new order by writing the numbers of the sentences in their proper sequence in the blanks following each paragraph. Indicate also the type of order each writer has used: *time, space,* or *continuity of idea.*

1. (1) There is no doubt that "Sport for All" is a twentieth-century movement of real significance. (2) Other mass movements have oppressed where they intended to liberate. (3) The choice of speed, route, distance, or company is entirely yours. (4) Whatever the choice, it rests in freedom, echoing passion and needs that have primitive, evolutionary significance and which to our peril we have too often dismissed as uncivilized and immature. (5) This augurs well for the future. (6) This movement liberates because it has an essentially individual basis. (7) The experience of the past 25 years has only served to reinforce my belief in the courage and infinite resourcefulness of athletes the world over. [From (rearranged) Sir Roger Bannister, "The Pursuit of Excellence," *The Four Minute Mile,* Dodd, Mead, 1955, 1981.]

Proper Sequence _____

Type of Order _____

2. (1) Scott was a man then who looked like a boy with a face between handsome and pretty. (2) His chin was well built and he had good ears and a handsome, almost beautiful, unmarked nose. (3) The mouth worried you until you knew him and then it worried you more. (4) He had very fair wavy hair, a high forehead, excited and friendly eyes and a delicate long-lipped Irish mouth that, on a girl, would have been the mouth of a beauty. (5) This should not have added up to a pretty face, but that came from the coloring, the very fair hair and the mouth. [From (rearranged) Ernest Hemingway, *A Moveable Feast,* Bantam Books, 1965, p. 147.]

Proper Sequence _____

Type of Order _____

3. (1) *Spinster,* according to dictionaries, originally and sensibly meant nothing more than a woman who spins. (2) Poor degenerate word! (3) By Elizabethan times it was restricted to refer to an unmarried woman of "gentle" birth. (4) Finally, perhaps in the patriarchal prime of the Victorian period, it acquired its classic—to us—significance: unattractive, elderly, unmarried female. (5) In the seventeenth century it lost this aura of aristocracy and designated any unmarried woman. (6) Era by era it has been stripped linguistically of 1) occupation, 2) husband, 3) social status, 4) youth and beauty—and now of any viable meaning

whatever . . . [From (rearranged) Audrey C. Foote, "Notes on the Distaff Side," *The Atlantic Monthly,* January 1977.]

Proper Sequence —————————————————————————————————

Type of Order —————————————————————————————————

B. Leaf through a magazine, newspaper, or book to find an example of a paragraph organized in each of the following patterns: (1) chronological sequence, (2) spatial relationships, and (3) continuity of idea. Be prepared to explain which of the various types of patterns is used in the paragraph arranged on the basis of continuity of idea.

C. Using a climactic order, write a paragraph or a three-paragraph theme on one of the following subjects. (If you write the longer composition, review the procedure presented on pp. 61–64.)

1. how to survive during the first year of college

2. things my parents never told me

3. the value of competing on an intercollegiate athletic team

4. a disastrous or unexpectedly fortunate experience

5. television soap operas as a reflection of contemporary values

6. the impact of inflation on the housing market

7. the dangers of drug abuse

8. the importance of maintaining wilderness areas

9. disposing of dangerous industrial wastes

10. sports heroes as role models for the young in modern America.

D. Select an interesting object, scene, or person, and write a paragraph or longer composition describing your subject. Focus on one or two prominent features if you're writing a single paragraph, no more than three if you're writing a longer paper. Select significant detail. Do not attempt a complete rendering.

DEVICES FOR ENSURING COHERENCE

Coherence in a paragraph depends basically on an orderly arrangement of the ideas. If readers cannot follow the direction of thought, they are apt to become confused and puzzled, to feel that the parts of the paragraph do not cohere. But coherence is not solely a matter of logical sequence. It depends also on the use of explicit connecting links between sentences. Consider, for example, the following adaptation of a paragraph about the capacity of words to wound as well as to heal.

> In our personal lives, surely each of us must have ample evidence by now that the capacity of words to exacerbate, wound, and destroy is at least as great as their capacity to clarify, heal, and organize. There is no good reason for parents always to be honest with their children (or their children always to be honest with them). The goal of parenthood is not to be honest. It is to raise children to be loving, generous, confident, and competent human beings. Where full and open revelation helps to further that end, it is "good." Where it would defeat it, it is stupid talk. There is no good reason why your boss always needs to know what you are thinking. It might scare him out of his wits and you out of a job. Many of the problems you and he have do not arise from lack of communication, but from the nature of the employer-employee relationship, which sometimes means that the less money you make, the more he does. This is a "problem" for a labor organizer, not a communication specialist.

The continuity of thought in this paragraph is obstructed by the lack of explicit connecting links between sentences. As a result, the writer's thought does not flow smoothly from sentence to sentence. When the links (shown in italics) are provided, notice how much more coherent the paragraph becomes.

> In our personal lives, surely each of us must have ample evidence by now that the capacity of words to exacerbate, wound, and destroy is at least as great as their capacity to clarify, heal, and organize. There is no good reason, *for example,* for parents always to be honest with their children (or their children always to be honest with them). The goal of parenthood is not to be honest, *but* to raise children to be loving, generous, confident, and competent human beings. Where full and open revelation helps to further that end, it is "good." Where it would defeat it, it is stupid talk. *Similarly,* there is no good reason why

your boss always needs to know what you are thinking. It might, *in the first place,* scare him out of his wits and you out of a job. *Then, too,* many of the problems you and he have do not arise from lack of communication, but from the nature of the employer-employee relationship, which sometimes means that the less money you make, the more he does. This is a "problem" for a labor organizer, not a communication specialist. [From Neil Postman, "The Communication Panacea," *Crazy Talk, Stupid Talk,* Delacorte, 1976.]

Transitional Words and Phrases

The words and phrases italicized in the preceding paragraph act as bridges between the sentences. *For example, but, in the first place,* and similar expressions provide transitions between sentences to make it easier for the reader to follow the writer's thought. Although overuse of such expressions as *therefore, however,* and *in the last analysis* can make writing awkward and mechanical, used moderately and with variety they can improve paragraph coherence. Beginning writers should try to develop skill in the use of these expressions.

The following is a list of words and phrases commonly used to provide continuity between sentences or within the sentence itself.

RELATIONSHIP	EXPRESSION
addition, sequence	and, also, in addition, moreover, furthermore, first, second, again
contrast	but, however, nevertheless, notwithstanding, on the other hand, yet, still
similarity	similarly, likewise, in a like manner, in the same way, in a similar case
exemplification, illustration	for example, as an illustration, for instance, as an example
restatement, clarification	in other words, that is, in particular, in simpler terms
concession	though, although, even though, granted that, it may be true that, admittedly
emphasis	most important, indeed, in fact, I repeat, certainly, truly
conclusion, result	therefore, consequently, thus, as a consequence, hence, as a result
summation	to sum up, in conclusion, finally, in short, in sum, in summary

Repetition of Key Terms

The repetition of key words and phrases provides another way to connect sentences within a paragraph. The deliberate repetition of words that carry the basic meaning emphasizes them in the reader's mind and thus serves to weave together the sentences that contain them. Students are frequently advised to avoid repeating words, and such advice is often valid. The frequent recurrence of unimportant words can make writing mechanical and monotonous, thus dulling reader interest. A haphazard use of synonyms for the sake of variety may simply confuse your reader and defeat your purpose. But do not be afraid to repeat important words to explain your thought clearly.

The paragraph below provides a pattern of linkage through the repetition of such words as *Bushmen, farmers, labor.* These words have been italicized.

> Besides the fact that *Bushmen* alone can live in the land they occupy, there is another reason for their remoteness and shyness. They are in many instances exploited by the Bantu *farmers,* and by a few of the European *farmers,* usually those who need free or almost free *labor.* Many Bantu farms and households have *Bushman* servants, or serfs, rather, as they usually come from the land on or near the farm, and when working they are paid nothing, but are given food, tobacco, and sometimes cast-off clothing as wages. Some European farms in Bechuanaland and some in South-West Africa have *Bushman laborers* too, though most European *farmers* do not depend on *Bushman labor.* Those European *farmers* who do employ *Bushmen* usually pay wages, about ten shillings a month, plus a ration of food to each *Bushman* who is working, though not necessarily to his family, consisting of about a pound of cornmeal and a quart of milk a day, meat occasionally, and weekly a ration of tobacco. Perhaps the employer will add a set of clothing—that is, a pair of cast-off pants and a shirt—and perhaps a blanket every year, but occasionally they pay their *labor* in cast-off clothing and omit the ten shillings altogether. [From Elizabeth Marshall Thomas, *The Harmless People*, Knopf, 1958.]

In the following paragraph the writer ties his sentences together through a repetition of the words *thinking, thought, writing, written,* and *words,* which we have emphasized with italics.

> It is surely no accident that greater lucidity and accuracy in *thinking* should result from the study of clarity and precision in

writing. For *writing* necessarily uses *words,* and almost all *thinking* is done with *words.* One cannot even decide what to have for dinner, or whether to cross town by bus or taxi, without expressing the alternatives to oneself in *words.* My experience is, and the point of my whole course is, that the discipline of marshaling *words* into formal sentences, *writing* them down, and examining the *written* statement is bound to clarify *thought.* Once ideas have been *written* down, they can be analyzed critically and dispassionately; they can be examined at another time, in another mood, by another expert. *Thoughts* can therefore be developed, and if they are not precise at the first *written* formulation, they can be made so at a second attempt. [From F. Peter Woodford, "Sounder Thinking Through Clearer Writing," *Science,* Vol. 156, May 12, 1967, pp. 743–45.]

Parallelism

A third way to ensure continuity within a paragraph is to phrase important ideas in the same grammatical structures. The recurrence of similar grammatical forms and the consequent repetition of rhythmic patterns tends to make writing concise, emphatic, and easy to follow. Recurring patterns of expressions are effective in speech as well as writing, as the examples below illustrate. The parallel repetitions in each passage have been italicized.

1. . . . "We must get the American people to look *past the glitter, beyond the showmanship,* to the reality, the hard substance of things. And we will do that *not so much with speeches that sound good as with speeches that are good and sound, not so much with speeches that bring people to their feet as with speeches that bring people to their senses.*" [From Governor Cuomo's address to the Democratic National Convention, 1984.]

2. "There is a strong view that holds that success is a myth, and ambition therefore a sham. Does this mean *that success does not really exist? That achievement is at bottom empty? That the efforts of men and women are of no significance alongside the forces of movements and events? . . .*" [From Joseph Epstein, "The Virtues of Ambition," *Ambition,* E. P. Dutton, 1980.]

3. "So long as I remain alive and well I shall continue *to feel* strongly about prose style, *to love* the surface of the earth, and *to take* a pleasure in solid objects and scraps of useless information." [From George Orwell, "Why I Write," Volume 1, *The Collected Essays, Journalism and Letters of George Orwell*, ed. Sonia Orwell and Ian Angus, Harcourt Brace Jovanovich, 1968, p. 6.]

Gilbert Highet uses parallel repetition to order his ideas and give them balance and emphasis. Again, the parallel elements have been italicized.

That is why teaching is such a wonderful profession. *Doctors make* sick people well again. *Lawyers reconcile* people's differences. *Clergymen make* people better in spirit. But *teachers make* children and youngsters, *half-animal* and *half-savage*, into human beings. Even that would not be possible unless they wanted to become human. *Every child, every boy, every youth,* in his heart wants *to learn* and *to grow* in mind, to the fullest powers of which he feels himself capable. The best teacher in the world cannot force him to do so. All that he can do is *to help* and *to encourage.* His best reward is to see, not a "product," but a free and independent human being who can think. [From Gilbert Highet, "Teaching Not Facts But How to Think," *New York Times Magazine*, New York Times, February 25, 1961.]

Pronoun Reference

Another way to establish continuity between sentences is through the use of pronouns. Using a pronoun in one sentence to repeat a noun in the same or in a previous sentence provides an effective link between these sentences. In the following paragraph, lines have been drawn connecting pronouns with their antecedents to indicate graphically how the reader's attention is naturally directed back to the antecedent of a pronoun. This repetition of key words through the use of pronouns ties these sentences together.

We might call this the right of curiosity, the right to ask whatever questions are most important to us. As adults, we assume that we have the right to decide what does or does not interest us, what we will look into and what we will leave alone. We take this right for granted, cannot imagine that it might be taken away from us. Indeed, as far as I know, it has never been written into any body of law. Even the writers of the Constitution did not mention it. They thought it was enough to guarantee citizens the freedom of speech and the freedom to spread their ideas as widely as they wished and could. It did not occur to them that even the most tyrannical government would try to control people's minds, what they thought and knew. That idea was to come later, under the benevolent guise of compulsory universal education. [From John Holt, "The Right to Control One's Learning," *Escape from Childhood,* E. P. Dutton, 1974.]

In the next example the writer repeats *he* and *his* to carry his thought throughout the paragraph.

Just under three hundred years ago, the Lucasian Professor of Mathematics at Cambridge did a distinctly unusual thing. *He* decided that one of *his* pupils was a much better mathematician than *he* was, and in all respects more fitted for *his* job. *He* wasn't content with this exercise in self-criticism. *He* promptly resigned *his* Chair, on condition that *his* pupil be immediately appointed. In the light of history, no one can say that *his* judgment was wrong. For the Professor's name was Barrow, and *he* was a very good mathematician by seventeenth-century standards; but *his* pupil was Isaac Newton. [From C. P. Snow, "On Magnanimity," *Harper's Magazine,* July 1962, p. 37.]

Beginning writers frequently have trouble in using the demonstrative pronouns *this* and *that* as a means of transition. When *this* or *that* is placed on the beginning of one sentence to refer to something in a previous sentence, ambiguity can result if the pronoun is not followed by a noun. Consider, for example, the following sentence:

> Father could get angry, all right, but he had a sense of humor,
> too. This used to upset Mother, however, for. . . .

It is not clear from reading this sentence whether *this* refers to Father's anger or to his sense of humor. This ambiguity is easily avoided by placing a noun immediately after *this*, specifying to what it refers.

> Father could get angry, all right, but he had a sense of humor,
> too. This sense of humor (or this anger) used to upset Mother,
> however, for. . . .

Ambiguity does not, however, always result when *this* appears by itself at the beginning of a sentence. So long as the writer's meaning is clear—an important "if"—there is no reason *this* or *that* may not refer to a larger element than a single antecedent, to a clause, or even to the general idea of a preceding sentence.

> Occasionally, of course, a senator or a congressman becomes
> involved in a dishonest business affair. This does not mean that
> politicians are crooks. On the contrary. . . .

EXERCISE 13

A. Underline the transitional expressions in the following paragraphs and indicate in the blanks at the end of each paragraph the relationship that each expression shows.

1. The slaughter of baby harp seals in Newfoundland, Canada, is arousing the anger of increasing numbers of people throughout the world, and for good reason, too; for it is a cruel waste of precious life. For example, in killing them, hunters club these one- to six-week old pups over the head with a blunt or spiked bat, sometimes a dozen times. And the murder takes place right in front of the pup's helpless mother. Moreover, about fourteen percent of the seal pups are not completely dead when their furry white coats are stripped from their still warm bodies. Another argument frequently raised against the hunt is that stopping it would not seriously affect the economy of Newfoundland since only two percent of the province's income is derived from the seal skins and only one tenth of one percent of the population is actually employed in the hunt, and for only four to six weeks. But perhaps the most persuasive argument against killing the seal pups is that it may well lead to the extinction of the harp seal. Since 1960, for instance, the harp seal population has declined sixty percent to a current population of about one million. But in 1900, it is estimated, there were more than ten million harp seals, a decline in eighty years of ninety percent.

_____

_____

_____

2. Unfortunately, some instances of epping [literary plagiarism] have been nothing more than fraudulent attempts to garner publicity and communicate publicly with famous authors. For instance, a struggling New York writer of pornographic novels named Ava Michaels admitted before the camera of a local network affiliate that she had cribbed parts of *Hot to the Touch* and *Tex-Mex Sex Kitten* from the works of Louis Auchincloss. Under questioning, however, it came out that Michaels had only stolen several subjunctive clauses and the description of a tax lawyer's bedroom. At this point, Michaels broke down, whimpering, "I'm sorry, I know it's not much, but I was on a tight deadline." A similar case of false epping involved Priscilla Fuente's assertion, imprudently printed by a New Jersey paper, that in her volume *Secrets of Mulching*, she had plagiarized freely from Clifford Irving's biography of Howard Hughes, Reporters who rushed to the library to verify the claim quickly discovered that it was a lie, and consequently her newly released biography of Greta Garbo is still doing poorly in the bookstores. [From R. D. Rosen, "Epping," *The New Republic*, November 15, 1980.]

_____

_____

_____

B. What device or devices does the writer of the following paragraph use to provide coherence? Write your answers in the blanks following the paragraph.

The Greeks held that the free man, the real man, the complete man, must be something more than a mere breadwinner, and must have something besides the knowledge necessary to earn his living. He must have also the education which will give him the chance of developing the gifts and faculties of human nature and becoming a full human being. They saw clearly that men were breadwinners but also that they were, or ought to be, something more: that a man might be a doctor or a lawyer or a shopkeeper or an artisan or a clerk, but that he was also a man, and that education should recognize this and help each individual to become, so far as his capacities allowed, what a man ought to be. That was the meaning of a liberal education, and that is its aim—the making of men; and clearly it is different from a technical education which simply enables us to earn our bread, but does not make us complete human beings. [From Sir Richard Livingstone, "A Complete Human Being," *The Future in Education,* Cambridge University Press, 1954.]

_____

_____

_____

_____

C. The transitional expressions in the following paragraphs have been omitted. Read the paragraph carefully. Determine the relationship between the ideas in the sentences to be connected and select an appropriate word or phrase that expresses this relationship.

1. Because of the development of new electronic machines for recording, duplicating, and transmitting the human voice and the written word, many students seem to think that there is no compelling need for them to know how to write well. _____ this notion that only newspaper workers, novelists, scholars, researchers, and the like have to know how to write is foolish. Students majoring in business, _____, think their secretaries will do their writing for them, _____ this belief reveals a rather

naive faith in the competency of secretaries. _____ young business men and women seldom have their own secretaries. Students going into science and engineering _____ believe that writing is something they will seldom have to do, _____ scientists and engineers say they spend almost half their time writing letters and reports. _____, those persons who can express themselves well in writing are sure to succeed more rapidly than those whose command of language is minimal.

2. The term "Third World" is frequently used to refer to the 130 or more underdeveloped nations of the world as if they were a cohesive entity sharing the same interests and ideologies. _____ they do share certain attitudes such as an intense nationalism and a hypersensitivity to foreign criticism of their internal affairs, _____ they have not formed a tightly knit alliance by any means. _____, this group contains oil exporters and oil importers, nations with healthy growing economies and others whose economies are stagnating, and nations with centrally planned economies as well as those with market economies. _____ myth is that achieving economic development in the Third World is almost impossible, owing to the rigidity of the world economic order and the lack of concern of the capitalistic nations of the West. Achieving rapid development is, _____, not easy; _____ several Third World nations—Brazil, Korea, Taiwan, Singapore—have achieved solid growth rates of 9 percent annually in the last decade. Much of their economic success can be attributed to three conditions: a stable government, an economic climate hospitable to foreign investment, and a reasonably controlled rate of inflation. A _____ myth is that the most important objective of Third World leaders is to modernize their economies. _____ many, if not most, have other goals: achieving recognition and prestige in the international community, pursuing their own political aims, and acquiring modern military equipment. _____, if Third World leaders truly want to develop and modernize their economies, they are not doomed to

failure. As Charles Wolf, Jr., of the Rand Corporation writes, "If development is accorded primary emphasis among national objectives, success seems to depend on imposing limits on the scope and character of government intervention. Few Third World leaders are willing to let go the reins of control and unleash the market forces that can help their economies grow."[2]

D. In the following pairs of sentences the flow of thought between sentences is somewhat obstructed. Rewrite the sentences to make this connection smoother, using the specific devices indicated in parentheses.

1. Some special interest groups support limitation of free speech on behalf of what they conceive to be noble goals. Limitation of free speech, whatever the rationale, is still censorship, with all its attendant evils. (transition word)

    _____

    _____

    _____

2. Great minds discuss ideas; average minds discuss events. People are the subject discussed by people with small minds. (parallel repetition)

    _____

    _____

    _____

3. A good teacher must not only know his subject. A good teacher must also love it and be able to share his knowledge and love. (pronoun reference)

    _____

    _____

    _____

4. The Bow Wow theory of human speech asserts that language grew out of primitive man's imitations of natural sounds. This theory overlooks the fact that the same natural noise is apparently heard differently by different people: what is "cock-a-doodle-do" to an Englishman is "cocorico" to a Frenchman and "chicchirichi" to an Italian. (transition word)

[2] "Third World—Myths and Realities," *Los Angeles Times,* January 27, 1981.

_____

_____

_____

5. An eighty-year national trend may be reversing as more and more young people drop out of school. Young people drop out for a variety of reasons: boredom, economic necessity, pregnancy, and mobility of population. (pronoun reference)

_____

_____

_____

6. Martina Navratilova is a great tennis player. She dominates women's tennis. She has won the U.S. Open, Wimbledon, and the French and Australian Open tournaments. She hasn't lost an individual match in over twelve months and has the talent and desire to continue her dominance for several years. Some tennis historians consider her the greatest women's tennis player who ever lived. (transition word)

_____

_____

_____

7. To develop a more effective, sensible transportation system in this country, we will have to change several long-held American attitudes. Americans want to drive their automobiles whenever and wherever they please, to park them close to their work in the city, and to ride on freeways uncluttered by traffic. (repetition of key term)

_____

_____

_____

8. Breakfast cereal makers are trying hard to appeal to adults in the 18- to 45-year-old age bracket who want nutritional value. Kellogg Company, the

number one cereal maker in the United States, is spending $50 million to market a new natural cereal called "Nutri-Grain." (transition word)

_____

_____

_____

9. Terrorist groups that kidnap people for use as pawns to gain political concessions from hostile governments have created difficulties for law enforcement authorities. Protecting innocent lives and preventing further kidnappings presents the police authorities with a dilemma. (repetition of key term)

_____

_____

_____

10. Leon Trotsky was a difficult man to please. He didn't like the Czar, so he murdered him. He didn't like the Imperial Government, so he blew it up. His attitude toward the moderate views of Kerensky and Savinkov was negative, and they were removed from their positions in the Social Revolutionary party. (parallel repetition)

_____

_____

_____

E. Construct a coherent paragraph using the following notes and any pertinent information you wish to add. Use at least two of the devices for ensuring continuity discussed in this chapter: transitional words, pronoun references, parallelism, and repetition of word and phrase. Underline whatever transition words you use. The notes are not now listed in a logical order.

1. High interest rates justified as a means of controlling inflation

2. Dampening effect on housing market

3. Increase cost of doing business generally

4. Cost of borrowing up—hurts builders and buyers alike

5. Increase cost of buying new car

6. Aggravate woes of auto industry, already hurt by foreign competition

7. High interest rates have disruptive effect on American economy

8. People with modest incomes priced out of market

9. Little businessmen especially hurt because cost of borrowing money increases

10. Higher business costs passed on to consumer in form of higher prices for goods and services—hence more inflation

11. Strengthen dollar abroad, but this effect harmful—prices of American exports rise

POINT OF VIEW

Point of view defines the position, the point of focus, that a writer assumes in relation to the subject. It embraces matters of tone, person, tense, number, and voice. Maintaining a consistent point of view is essential to paragraph coherence. If, for example, you are discussing a subject in the third person, you should stay in the third person unless you have a good reason for shifting to first or second person. The same principle applies to tense, number, tone, and voice. A reader is likely to become confused if you change from the past to the present tense, from a singular to a plural noun, from an objective, matter-of-fact tone to a subjective one, or from the active to the passive voice of the verb.

Tone

Tone refers to the attitude a writer takes toward his subject and reader. It can vary widely, depending on his purpose, subject, audience, and interests. A student writing about her roommate might assume an informal, personal, even whimsical tone. If she were discussing the advisability of tax reform, however, her tone would probably be more serious and objective.

The problem of tone is complex, but a knowledge of the distinctive qualities of the formal and the informal tone should be helpful. Formal writing uses a more extensive and exact vocabulary. It may allude to historical and literary events; its sentences are usually longer and more carefully constructed than those used in informal writing; and it follows the traditional conventions of English grammar carefully, avoiding contractions, omissions, and abbreviations. Informal writing permits the use of colloquial words and phrases. Its vocabulary is less extensive and its sentences less elaborate, with a more conversational rhythm. Informal writing also permits the use of first- and second-person personal pronouns (I, you, we) and contractions (I'm, you're, he's).

The following student essay is written in an informal style. The tone is chatty, conversational, good-humored. The writer uses many colloquial words and phrases ("sandbagger," "pretty sly," "a lot of," "drops on you like a load of bricks"), the second-person pronoun *you,* and contractions ("should've," "he's," "don't"). The sentences and paragraphs are also not very long. The style and tone are appropriate here because the writer is addressing his fellow students on a topic of common, lively interest; and he wants to convey his feelings and attitudes in a friendly, lively manner.

Pals, Preachers, and Mr. Sly

My advisor told me that to succeed in any class, you had to study your teacher first. She was right. But she should've added,

"Be especially careful if you get a sandbagger, a friendly philosopher, or a true believer." The first type, the sandbagger, is
pretty sly. At the beginning of the semester, he's nice and easy—
reasonable assignments, a lot of smiles, a few jokes, all sweetness
and light. But after the withdrawal deadline, look out! He drops
on you like a load of bricks, with lots of homework, weekly
quizzes, and a term paper he neglected to tell you about. He
figures you're committed to the course now, and he lets you
have it.

By contrast, the friendly philosopher is a pussycat. He loves
to rap with students, whom he calls by their first name, to share
experiences with them, to meet them on their own level. Unfortunately, his class discussions often degenerate into free-
wheeling bull sessions on the lawn in the quad. Students often
like him, for he's a nice guy and an easy grader, but by the end
of the semester they haven't learned much.

Unlike the friendly philosopher, the true believer doesn't want
pals. She wants converts, followers, apostles. Serious and intent,
she prefers preaching to teaching. She may be a very stimulating
lecturer—she often is—but don't cross her if you're looking for
a good grade. For there is but one truth, and she has it. The
sandbagger, the friendly philosopher, and the true believer do
make college life more interesting. But pray to the gods you
don't get all three in the same semester.

This next paragraph is more formal. It is taken from an essay on the
American intellectual that appeared in a magazine whose readers are
typically intelligent, well-educated, and seriously interested in ideas. Its
tone is, appropriately, more serious, its sentences are longer, its diction
("partisan involvement," "impinge with any force," "a measure of resentment," "presumption," "alienation") is more formal.

The second rule of behavior for the intellectual, comparable
in importance to the one which limits his partisan involvement
in affairs, is that he cannot demand that society love him without
reservation. A certain hostility is part of the tribute paid to
distinction. Intellectuals are not alone in provoking it. Businessmen, lawyers, doctors, public officials, army officers, clergymen, even people who are just good-looking or quick witted—
all who impinge with any force upon their fellow men receive
a measure of resentment. The distrust which intellectuals generate is not only natural but, provided always that it does not
turn morbid, it is also desirable. It is a necessary defense of the
population against an elite group which, being human as well

as elite, is subject to error, presumption, and impatience, and is no more to be followed blindly than are priests or politicians. The country protects itself against Wall Street bankers in the same way; so much so, in fact, that a public statement in actual praise of them is almost unheard of. This natural hostility towards the intellectual, together with his own need to maintain an intellectual's distance, means that he need never give up a claim to that lovely word *alienation.* [From Morton Cronin, "The American Intellectual," *AAUP Bulletin,* Summer 1958.]

The style and tone of your writing should, as mentioned earlier, be appropriate to your subject and audience. While you are in college, your audience will usually be your teacher or your fellow students; and unless, like the student who wrote the essay on professors, you wish to assume a light-hearted tone for the purpose of humor, you will need to master the more formal style and tone used in the discussion of serious issues. But whatever tone you adopt, be careful not to shift from an impersonal, serious treatment of your subject to a breezy, colloquial tone, and vice versa, unless there is good reason for doing so and your reader has been adequately prepared for the shift.

INCONSISTENT	CONSISTENT
In the treatment of serious psychological disorders, the therapist seeks to establish rapport with her patient so that he can be induced to take it easy and discuss his problems freely.	In the treatment of serious psychological disorders, the therapist seeks to establish rapport with her patient so that he can be induced to relieve his tensions and discuss his problems freely.
Rocko McNally was a gutty fighter. He could take it as well as dish it out. His capacity for absorbing punishment was, however, exceeded during a match with Kid McGuff. In that contest, he was rendered unconscious in the sixth round by his opponent's right fist.	Rocko McNally was a gutty fighter. He could take it as well as dish it out. His ability to take a punch was, however, exceeded in his match with Kid McGuff, who flattened him with a right in the sixth round.

Person

Pronouns and verbs can be classified according to person, a form whose change indicates whether a person is speaking (first person), is being spoken to (second person), or is being spoken about (third person). A shift in person, as indicated earlier, disrupts continuity. Be careful, therefore, not to change person carelessly from sentence to sentence as you develop your paragraph. Whether you decide to use the informal first or second person (*I, we, you*) or the more formal third person (*he, she, they*), maintain a consistent point of view throughout.

INCONSISTENT	CONSISTENT
To get the most from a lecture, a student should listen carefully and take notes. You should not, however, try to record everything your instructor says. Limit your notes to the important points of the discussion.	To get the most from a lecture, listen carefully and take notes. Don't try to record everything your instructor says, however. Limit your notes to the important points of the discussion.

Tense

A verb undergoes changes in form to show the time of its action or state of being—the past, present, or future. These changes in verb forms are called tenses. Once you have determined the tense you will use in developing your topic, avoid shifting this tense unless you have prepared your reader for the change.

INCONSISTENT	CONSISTENT
After a delay of thirty minutes, the curtain came down, and the orchestra begins to play. Then the house lights dim, and the audience grows quiet.	After a delay of thirty minutes, the curtain came down, and the orchestra began to play. Then the house lights dimmed, and the audience grew quiet.

As noted above, if tense changes occur, the reader must be prepared for them. When he is, they do not violate the principle of consistency. In the following passage the writer maintains a consistent point of view with regard to time even though she changes tense.

> The original settlement of Paris *was founded* by a Gallic tribe in the first century B.C. Paris *is* thus about 2000 years old. During these years it *has become* perhaps the most beautiful and cultured city in Europe. In fact, in the opinion of many travelers, it *is* the most beautiful city in the world.

The writer begins in the past tense to establish a point of reference for her remarks. In the second sentence she moves into the present tense to state a fact about Paris at the present time. In the third sentence she shifts to the present perfect tense with *has become,* but this shift does not violate consistency of tense either, for the verb reports a condition— the beauty and sophistication of Paris—that began in the past and continues into the present. And in the last sentence the writer returns to the present tense, again to express a current opinion about her subject.

Number

Number refers to the changes in a word that indicate whether its meaning is singular or plural. As you read over your writing, make certain that you have not shifted number needlessly. In particular, make certain that your pronouns agree in number, as well as in person, with their antecedents, the things or persons to which they refer.

INCONSISTENT	CONSISTENT
The student who wants to improve his writing can, in the majority of cases, do so if he puts his mind seriously to it. If they are not willing to make this effort, however, the results will be minimal.	The student who wants to improve his writing can, in the majority of cases, do so if he puts his mind seriously to it. If he is not willing to make this effort, however, the results will be minimal.

Voice

Voice refers to the form of the verb that indicates whether its subject acts or is acted upon. If the subject of the verb acts, the verb is said to be in the *active* voice:

Guillermo won the election.

If the subject is acted upon, the verb is said to be in the *passive* voice:

The election was won by Guillermo.

The active voice is used more often than the passive voice, the latter being reserved for occasions when the doer of the action is either unknown or unimportant or when the writer wishes to stress the importance of the receiver of the action. Examine your sentences carefully to make certain that you have used the appropriate voice.

INCONSISTENT

In September of his freshman year, Harvey decided to work thirty hours a week in order to buy a car. After conferring with his counselor about his program, however, the plan was abandoned by him.

CONSISTENT

In September of his freshman year, Harvey decided to work thirty hours a week in order to buy a car. After conferring with his counselor about his program, however, he abandoned the plan.

EXERCISE 14

A. Read each of these paragraphs carefully, and in the blanks provided describe (1) the writer's tone, (2) the linguistic elements (vocabulary, sentence length, allusions, grammatical conventions) that create the tone, and (3) the audience for whom the passage was likely intended. (Review pp. 135–37 on tone.)

1. Genius was a word loosely used by expatriated Americans in Paris and Rome, between the Versailles peace treaty and the Depression, to cover all varieties of artistic, literary and musical experimentalism. A useful and readable history of the literary Twenties is *Being Geniuses Together* by Robert McAlmon and Kay Boyle—Joyce, Hemingway, Scott Fitzgerald, Pound, Eliot and the rest. They all became famous figures, but too many of them developed defects of character—ambition, meanness, boastfulness, cowardice or inhumanity—that defrauded their early genius. Experimentalism is a quality alien to genius. It implies doubt, hope, uncertainty, the need for group reassurance; whereas genius works alone, in confidence of a foreknown result. Experiments are useful as a demonstration of how not to write, paint or compose if one's interest lies in durable rather than fashionable results; but since far more self-styled artists are interested in *frissons à la mode* rather than in truth, it is foolish to protest. Experimentalism means variation on the theme of other people's uncertainties. [From Robert Graves, "Genius," *Playboy*, December 16, 1969.]

Tone _____

Linguistic elements _____

_____

Audience _____

2. Some professional athletes really give their sport a bad name, and they give me a pain in the neck, too. Take tennis, for instance. The way some topflight players chew out line judges, shout at the referee, and badger the fans you'd think the game owes them a living—a very good one at that—and that spectators are privileged to see them play. And, of course, baseball has its egomaniacs, too, guys who hit .265 and demand a long-term, no-cut contract in the millions of dollars or they'll quit. I suppose if baseball club owners want to shell out millions of bucks to some players, that's their business. Paying such players more than four or five times as much as the President earns in a year may make economic sense, but I wish these superstars would quit bellyaching about their contract disputes to sports reporters. And, finally, what about ice hockey! It's always been a tough game involving a lot of body contact; but what was only a part of the game, the violence, is now the main point. The stick-swinging goons, the flying elbows and fists, the brawls—they make me sick.

Tone _____

Linguistic elements _____

Audience _____

B. In the following paragraph underline the words and phrases that reveal an inconsistency in point of view. In the blanks following the paragraph, identify the error more specifically as an inconsistency of tone, person, number, tense, or voice.

Though many drivers must buy a used car at one time or another, surprisingly few of them approach this matter in a prudent, systematic way. Actually, the process is kind of simple. One should first examine the engine carefully, for engine repairs can be costly and inconvenient. Blue exhaust smoke usually meant worn piston rings. You should check the dip stick, too, for the previous owner may have put in heavy oil to make a mechanically defective engine run more smoothly, or they may want to make it more difficult to detect water in the oil, often an indication of a blown gasket. After examining the engine, inspect the body. Dents, scrapes, and rusted metal should be looked for, and add the cost of such repair to the selling price. Open and close the doors to determine whether the body is aligned. The frame of a car that has been seriously banged around in an accident may be bent out of shape; if such is the case, the doors may not hang or shut properly. Next look at the interior of the car for evidence of the kind of care the car has received. Inexpensive seat covers may hide grubby upholstery and broken springs. Finally, the make and model of the car should be considered. Popular makes and models have a higher resale value. One further word, if you don't know diddly about automobiles, take along someone who does, a friend or a mechanic, to advise you. If one doesn't want to get taken, you should be alert and cautious.

_____

_____

_____

_____

C. In each of the following passages the point of view is inconsistent because of a shift in *tone, tense, number, person,* or *voice.* Indicate the particular error in each passage and correct it in the blanks provided.

1. An alcoholic usually tries to hide his addiction from his family and friends. More significantly, they try to hide it from themselves as well.

   Error _____

   _____

   _____

   _____

2. One who wants to maintain friendly relations with others should not speak the truth unseasonably. If you do, you're apt to hurt people's feelings and find yourself *persona non grata*.

   Error _____

   _____

   _____

   _____

3. My economics professor is knowledgeable, articulate, and witty. She is also a skillful lecturer with a store of relevant, clarifying anecdotes and examples. But when she gets her dander up, she's a pistol. When she doesn't like an answer or thinks it stupid, she bawls you out in front of the class. I mean, she really reads you the riot act.

   Error _____

   _____

   _____

   _____

4. A well-known American columnist said that millions of Americans resent the rich but aspired to join their ranks.

   Error _____

   _____

   _____

   _____

5. Sometimes those who are bored with life are really bored with themselves. They desire a change of scene; whereas what's really needed is a change of self.

   Error _____

   _____

   _____

   _____

6. A limerick is a form of light, nonsense verse containing five lines, of which the first, second, and fifth rhyme. Its subject matter has dealt with the

manners, morals, and peculiarities of people. It has tended to be somewhat bawdy, laced with earthy humor.

Error _____

_____

_____

_____

7. Getting a college education is a harrowing experience. It requires self-discipline, tenacity, and an intelligent use of time and resources. If one is not willing to give it a shot, he ought to chuck it up and move on.

Error _____

_____

_____

_____

8. Investing in commodities is a risky business. Before one commits funds to such a venture, they ought to obtain expert advice from an investment counselor.

Error _____

_____

_____

_____

9. If you want to persuade others of the soundness of your arguments, listen to theirs carefully, attentively. An attitude of contempt for their point of view should be avoided.

Error _____

_____

_____

_____

10. When one considers the magnitude and complexity of the political, social, and economic problems facing world leaders today, you sometimes wish you could turn back the clock a hundred years or so to a simpler, less troubled world.

Error _____

_____

_____

_____

SUMMARY

Coherence is a third quality of good writing. To make your writing coherent, be sure that your material is organized in some logical order, that your sentences are tied together smoothly, and that your point of view is consistent throughout. The most important quality is the first, for if your thought is developed in an orderly way, you have the basis of a coherent paragraph. Continuity between sentences and point of view are then less of a problem. If your thought lacks logical progression, the addition of transitional expressions and the maintenance of a consistent point of view cannot by themselves supply coherence.

Coherence is the result of careful planning and organization. Therefore, think through what you want to say before you begin to write, and keep your reader in mind as you write. If you build your paragraph as a unit of thought and help your reader to move smoothly from sentence to sentence as you develop that thought, your reader will have no trouble grasping the meaning of your paragraph.

CHAPTER FIVE

THE EXPOSITORY THEME

The general process of writing the longer theme has been presented in Chapter One. In this chapter we will review and elaborate upon that discussion, developing in greater detail many of the suggestions.

1. GETTING STARTED—SELECTING A SUBJECT

Selecting a topic for a theme is directly related to your purpose in writing. At times a specific subject will be assigned, as, for example, on an essay examination, and your response, the essay you write, will be governed by the terms of the question. In this instance, your purpose will be to demonstrate your knowledge of the subject in an essay that is well focused; supported with facts, judgments, and examples; and clear and coherent. At other times you will have greater latitude, often a choice among a number of topics, or perhaps complete freedom. When you have a measure of choice, take time to think about your subject, to talk to yourself and explore your thoughts and feelings about it: Does the subject interest you? Would your readers find it interesting? Is it significant? What would you try to accomplish in a paper on the subject? Fixing upon a purpose is not necessary at this time. In fact, many times your purpose will gradually evolve as you work up your material.

For example, if your subject is a public issue, a current controversy, you may simply want to inform your reader about an important aspect of the subject that has been neglected or take a stand on the issue or refute an opinion you think wrongheaded. With this kind of subject, you will want to investigate what others have to say about the issue in books, journals, magazines, and newspapers to buttress your own ideas on the subject. If, on the other hand, your subject is more personal, one derived from your own experience, your basic source of material will be your memory bank, as well as your current observations, feelings, attitudes, and opinions. As mentioned earlier, you may underrate the value of your own experience, but a personal experience that clarified something for you, changed the way you thought or acted, can make an interesting subject for an essay. It need not be an earthshaking event, one that illuminated a profound idea, but simply an experience that had meaning for you and that you would like to share with a reader.

Freewriting

Selecting a subject and getting started can be exasperating. Many writers, professionals as well as beginners, have trouble getting out of the starting blocks. They steam and fret, pace the room, scribble words on a sheet and then throw it away. If you have experienced writer's block, you might want to try freewriting to help you choose a subject. Simply sit down and begin writing whatever comes into your head. Don't worry about punctuation, perfect sentences, unity, coherence, spelling—just write for ten or fifteen minutes without stopping. Focus on one topic or shift back and forth among several. The important thing is to get on with it. The activity of putting ideas on paper in a free association process, forgetting your critical sense for the moment, will help relieve tensions and fears and release creative energy to help focus your thoughts. After you have written for a while, look over what you have written. Very likely you will discover a topic that can be developed into a theme. Of course, much will be confused, repetitive, and incoherent; that's not important here. If you find a topic, you can use whatever ideas seem relevant and discard the rest.

Here is a sample of a student's freewriting exercise.

"Seems like a waste of time . . . putting down what's in my head. That's the problem, I guess, nothing in my head. Depressing . . . a beautiful day out there, and I'm in here racking my brain for something to say on this stupid theme. Maybe I ought to write on why I can't write. Yeah, that'd be great. Kind of funny. Probably come up with something lively . . . some pizzazz. Don't bore us to death. I wonder how he is, old Jonesy, a nice guy. Wanted to be a writer, he said . . . good class that senior English class. I'm getting nowhere. Remember how his eyes sparkled when he read a favorite passage from Hemingway. *The Sun Also Rises* and the lost generation. I'm getting lost . . . and depressed. Wonder what it's like to face a bull, two tons of pot roast coming at you . . . only a piece of cloth between you and death in the afternoon. Hemingway was depressed. Couldn't lick it. Depressed. Many people depressed these days . . . hot lines, drugs, liquor. Wonder why. I suppose the fast pace of twentieth century. Travel . . . Pamplona, Paris, Serengetti

Plain, Africa. Maybe I should learn to box. Old Jonesy would chuckle at that."

This bit of rambling freewriting may seem unpromising at first glance, but a closer reading suggests at least two topics: Mr. Jones, his high school English teacher or, perhaps, depression, the blues, and what to do about them.

EXERCISE 15

A. List five topics of current public interest that have generated lively controversy. Select subjects you'd like to learn more about or ones you already know something about and on which you have an opinion to express.

1. _____

2. _____

3. _____

4. _____

5. _____

B. The following subjects should bring to mind specific experiences that taught you something worth sharing with a reader. For each area provide a more specific subject.

EXAMPLE   School—My Favorite High School Teacher

1. Family _____

2. Friends _____

3. Work _____

4. Disappointments _____

5. School _____

6. Happy times _____

7. First love _____

8. Cars _____

9. Vacations _____

10. Hopes, fears _____

C. In the space on page 154, or on a separate sheet, try your hand at freewriting. For ten or fifteen minutes write down anything that comes into your mind. Don't worry about perfect sentences, spelling, and so on; just keep writing uninterruptedly. Then look over what you've written, and list one or more topics that suggest themselves as possible subjects for a theme.

Topics ————————————————————

————————————————————

————————————————————

EXERCISE 16

A. Select a subject from the following list, and split it up into four or five more specific subjects:

1. Pollution

2. Jogging

3. Intercollegiate sports

4. American education

5. Television advertising

6. Newspaper cartoons or comic strips

7. Popular music

8. New sources of energy

9. Technology and modern life

10. The Olympic Games

General Subject ————————————————————————

Specific Subjects ————————————————————————

————————————————————————————————————

————————————————————————————————————

————————————————————————————————————

B. Select one of the general categories of Exercise 15B, narrow it down, and then divide that less general subject into four specific subjects.

EXAMPLE   *General Category*—Disappointments
                 Less General—Learning from Mistakes
                 Specific—Dating My Best Friend's Girl
                         Lending My Car to Crazy Al
                         Taking Boxing Lessons
                         Backpacking in the Sierras in Late Fall

General Category _____

Less General _____

Specific _____

_____

_____

_____

2. LIMITING YOUR SUBJECT

Limiting your subject is not so crucial if you have been assigned a specific topic to begin with. If you are allowed to choose your topic, or if the assigned topic is rather broad, restrict it to one you can deal with effectively within the length of the paper you intend to write. The subject of a 300-word theme to be written in class needs to be more narrowly restricted than a 700-word paper written out of class. This stipulation of length is not designed to make you produce an exact number of words: it is meant to define the scope of your subject. The shorter your paper, the more you will have to restrict your focus.

The degree to which a large, general subject is to be narrowed depends, as we said above, on the length of the paper to be written. A subject such as Sports in America can be restricted to yield subjects for a medium-sized paper, 500–700 words, or a shorter paper, 300–500 words:

GENERAL SUBJECT	Sports in America
MEDIUM-SIZED PAPER	Salaries of Professional Athletes
	Upgrading Intercollegiate Sports for Women
	Banning Professional Boxing
	Steroids and Sports
	Violence in Professional Sports
SHORT PAPER	Football Fans
	Synthetic versus Natural Turf
	Jaguar versus Porsche
	Hang Gliding

Like these subjects of public concern, topics drawn from personal experience must also be limited. For example, should you decide to write about Mr. Jones, your high school English teacher, you would be wise to concentrate on a few dominant traits or qualities rather than attempt a comprehensive treatment covering many aspects of his character and personality, a paper that would likely be more superficial and therefore less convincing.

GENERAL SUBJECT	Mr. Jones and Senior English
RESTRICTED FOCUS	Mr. Jones: Teacher, Philosopher, Ham
	Ol' Jonesy: Humor, Humanity, and Homework
	Mr. Jones: Firm, Fair, and Friendly
	Mr. Jones: No Pal, But a Fine Friend

Again, keep your audience in mind when selecting and narrowing your subject. You can expect an audience of your classmates to understand and respond to a lively discussion of some topic of current public interest or an account of a personal experience. But they would not likely respond to a technical explanation of some complicated engineering process. A paper on the possibilities of solar energy would be more suitable than a technical, detailed discussion of a particular solar heating device.

3. GENERATING IDEAS ABOUT A TOPIC

Having chosen your topic and limited it, you must now generate ideas about it. Sometimes, as we've noted earlier, you will have a fairly definite idea of what you want to do in a paper—for example, to inform your audience on some aspect of a general subject that is not commonly known or understood, or to persuade your audience to follow a course of action. In this case you can explore your subject systematically. At other times your subject will require you to probe your memory for ideas, and, usually, you will not be able to formulate your purpose until you have generated and organized your material in some detail. A good method of generating ideas about a subject based upon personal experience is to brainstorm it.

Brainstorming: Probing Your Memory

Brainstorming is like freewriting: both strategies are designed to help you overcome inertia and get moving. Both involve a free association of ideas and feelings in which you write down quickly what comes into your head without regard to order, precision of thought, punctuation, and so on. There is a slight difference in that when freewriting you write out your thoughts and feelings in longer phrases and in full sentences. When brainstorming you simply jot down these ideas and feelings in single words, phrases, bits of sentences. Brainstorming about Mr. Jones, a high school English teacher mentioned earlier, might look something like this:

Ol' Jonesy

1. heavy rimmed glasses, blue eyes
2. tall, slender, slight roll to walk
3. gray hair, thinning on top
4. pacing behind lectern, eyes on floor, lost in thought at times
5. cardigan sweaters, windbreaker jackets, always a tie
6. friendly, courteous, somewhat formal, the old school
7. frequent jokes to lighten mood
8. laughed at his own jokes, sometimes subtle
9. everpresent tie, usually solid color
10. loafers, slacks, never jeans
11. not serious about self, but serious about subject
12. mid forties, maybe older, laugh wrinkles
13. tough-minded about good work, tender-minded in personal contacts

14. a good listener
15. firm, fair, friendly—his code
16. lots of homework, too much
17. Socratic method—lots of questions—no place to hide
18. nailed you for lack of preparation, goofing off
19. pop quizzes, essays
20. simplicity, clarity, write to express, not to impress
21. eyes sparkled, laughed at his own jokes
22. occasional stories, family, friends
23. loved his subject . . . cummings, Hemingway, Fitzgerald . . . literature
24. liked students, attended games, dances, senior picnic
25. somewhat formal with students, Mr. this, Miss that, friendly, but no pal
26. praised good work, smiled, a wink for excellence
27. popular with students, but no nonsense
28. tough but fair
29. an existentialist of sorts
30. brought in books, loaned his own, always reading and recommending books
31. some teacher, knew his subject, loved it, shared it
32. open-minded about politics, religion

The Less Personal Paper

Material for papers on the more impersonal public issue topic, like the one on whether married women should work presented in Chapter One, is derived from a variety of sources: your own observations of the current scene—people, ideas, events; lecture notes; class discussions, conversations with friends; investigations of the opinions of authorities in books, magazines, newspapers; your own research on the subject—public records, documents, and so on. Working with this kind of subject, you may have a tentative idea of what you want to accomplish in the paper, the point you want to make, before you begin collecting your data and going over your notes. It's wiser, however, not to decide upon a purpose and thesis until you've assembled your material, thought about it, and put it in some sort of order since your preliminary ideas may change as you proceed.

Let's assumed that you've decided to write on population growth in a paper of 300 to 500 words. You would want to know the answers to such questions as the following: Is there really a problem? If so, what is it, and what information will my reader need to know to understand it? What are the causes of the problem and the consequences if it is not solved? And, finally, what are some possible solutions to the problem?

Such questions do not exhaust the possibilities. Others may suggest themselves as you proceed. After you have done some reading and thinking on your subject, jot down in a list the ideas that come to mind. Your list will contain irrelevant and awkwardly phrased items, but, like the process of brainstorming a personal subject, the important thing is to get your ideas down on paper so that they don't get away from you. A preliminary listing on population growth might develop in this manner:

1. population growth doubling in fewer years
2. food, starvation a problem
3. Green Revolution has helped, but still serious problem of feeding people
4. air pollution, smog
5. adding 80,000,000 people each year, particularly in Asia, Latin America, Africa
6. death rate declining, birth rate up
7. epidemic diseases checked
8. contamination of environment
9. automobile exhausts, factory smoke, chemical wastes in rivers
10. limitation of space . . . people jammed together
11. more food needed to feed existing population—cereal grains, vegetables, fruits
12. psychological problem due to crowding of living space—tensions, irritability
13. tankers at sea polluting oceans, killing sealife
14. more housing developments, more super highways to gobble up land
15. destruction of land . . . strip mining
16. crowded recreational areas—beaches, ski resorts, national parks
17. pollution of water
18. rapid depletion of natural resources—forests, fossil fuels, minerals
19. famine, starvation in Africa especially, also Latin America, Asia
20. educate people about danger of growing population
21. destruction of phytoplankton in sea
22. more people, less food, more political instability, authoritarian governments to maintain order
23. distribution of food not basic problem
24. gray haze in cities
25. dissemination of birth control information needed
26. family planning needed, limitation of family size, birth control

EXERCISE 17

A. Select a subject from one of the exercises indicated below, and provide additional details—facts, judgments, examples—about the subject to serve as the basis of an essay of 300 to 500 words. Choose your subject from one of the following exercises: 6A; 6B; 8; 9; 10E, F, G; 11E; 15A; 16A, B.

TOPIC _____

Detail   1. _____

2. _____

3. _____

4. _____

5. _____

6. _____

7. _____

8. _____

9. _____

10. _____

11. _____

12. _____

13. _____

14. _____

15. _____

B. Select one of the subjects dealing with a personal experience in Exercise 15B, limit it, and, in the spaces provided on the following page, list detail that can be organized and developed into a theme.

GENERAL TOPIC _____

SPECIFIC TOPIC _____

Detail   1. _____

2. _____

3. _____

4. _____

5. _____

6. _____

7. _____

8. _____

9. _____

10. _____

11. _____

12. _____

13. _____

14. _____

15. _____

4. PURPOSE AND AUDIENCE

The process of generating ideas about your subject, the mental activity involved in writing down ideas, will help to clarify your subject as well as your purpose. Looking over your list of items, you will begin to see more clearly what your subject is and what you want to accomplish in your paper, what effect you want to have on your reader. It is important at this stage to think more precisely about your purpose because your purpose will determine the kind of information you'll want to include and exclude, your strategies for organizing and developing the ideas, as well as matters of tone, style, and length.

In deciding upon a purpose, you must also give serious thought to your audience, for your readers' knowledge of your subject, their attitudes and biases, interests, and level of sophistication will affect the choices you make about detail, strategies of organization and development, tone, style, and so on. For the papers you write in college, your audience will usually be your classmates and instructor, and, to be sure, yourself as well.

As you read over what you've written, ask yourself, as a representative of your audience, whether what you've written is clear, informative, timely, and persuasive to you. You can't give it a completely objective reading because of your own bias, the effort and time you've invested, and your natural desire to succeed in achieving your purpose. But you can pretty well determine if what you've written is not working. If your paper seems vague, poorly focused, and dull, your readers are likely to have the same reaction. After you have considered your own response, think about your fellow students, or the general reader. How much do they know about the subject? What ideas and images do they have in their heads about the subject? Do they have special interests you can appeal to? If their ideas about the subject differ from yours, you must consider your tone, style, and supporting detail carefully so that you can change their ideas and images to those you want them to have. Speaking of tone and style, the kinds of words you use, the length of your sentences and paragraphs, and similar matters will be affected by your audience. If that audience is your fellow students and your subject not too serious, you would want to adopt a lighter tone, a more informal style. If your audience is your instructor and your subject more serious, you would want to adopt a more serious, objective tone and a more formal style.

How a consideration of purpose and audience affects, and is affected by, the shaping of material for an essay can be illustrated by reviewing the detail about Mr. Jones (pp. 161–62) and population growth (pp. 162–63). The items about Mr. Jones, for example, focus on his appearance, his personality, his relations with students, and his teaching methods. Though his teaching methods are described, the primary emphasis here is on Mr. Jones as a person—a friendly, sensitive, concerned human being, enthusiastic about his subject and eager to share his knowledge and enthusiasm with his students. A paper concentrating on his personal qualities would very likely appeal to an audience of college students, most of whom probably remember a favorite high school teacher and whose remembered impressions are likely to be about the person who taught the class rather than about the subject matter. A personal emphasis would warrant a lighter tone, a less formal style, and the writer's purpose would be to amuse and entertain as well as to inform and persuade.

Examining the ideas generated on the subject of population growth (pp. 162–63), one can see how an initial purpose may change in the process of developing the material for an essay. The items on this list cover a range of ideas: the problem itself, causes of the problem, consequences, and solution. These are important matters to consider in a paper on population growth, but most of the items deal with consequences, the results of rapid population growth. Since there appears to be sufficient detail on this aspect of the subject and since a paper including all of these aspects would require more than three to five paragraphs, it would make sense to limit the initial purpose and concentrate on this one area. This limited subject would, moreover, find a response in college students, most of whom would have read or heard about or experienced firsthand the consequences of rapid population growth.

5. FORMULATING A THESIS STATEMENT

Your thesis is the one major point you want to drive home, the controlling idea of the essay. An examination of the ideas you have jotted down about your subject will give you a clearer idea of your thesis as well as your purpose. It is important in this stage to formulate your main point in a thesis statement, for it will provide a point of reference for organizing and unifying the materials you have developed. The thesis statement for an essay thus performs the same function as the controlling idea of a paragraph—to keep out irrelevant ideas.

A thesis statement, as we have mentioned earlier, is not a statement of purpose: "In this paper I want to inform and persuade my reader of the admirable human qualities of Mr. Jones, my senior English teacher," nor is it a statement of the topic: "In this paper I want to talk about Mr. Jones, my senior English teacher." A thesis statement *neither states an intention nor announces a topic.* It *expresses an attitude* toward the topic in a complete sentence. It makes a *judgment* about it: "Mr. Jones, my senior English teacher in high school, is a friendly, sensitive, concerned human being; enthusiastic about his subject; and eager and able to share his enthusiasm and knowledge."

One other point, a corollary of the one just made (see also pp. 15–17, Chapter Two): if the thesis statement is to be judgmental, *it should not be a factual statement.*

> John Steinbeck was born in Salinas, California.
> Banks now charge 15% on home loans.

These statements would not work as thesis statements because they lead nowhere. They're self-contained. They could serve as supporting detail but not as unifying generalizations that other sentences could support because they need no support. The fact that John Steinbeck was born in Salinas, California, could be used to support the thesis that John Steinbeck's work reflects his California roots, but it would not work as the thesis itself.

What was said about the controlling idea of a paragraph also applies to thesis statements: they need to be *limited, specific.* A broad, general thesis statement simply covers too much territory; it justifies the inclusion of such a range and variety of detail that any essay based on it would be superficial, vague, poorly focused.

GENERAL	BETTER
A well-educated person is a combination of many qualities.	A well-educated person is a harmonious blend of intellectual, moral, and emotional capacities.
A checking account is a good idea.	A checking account is useful because it provides convenience, safety, and a record of payment.
Emily Brett is a great girl.	Because of her wit, charm, and sophistication, Emily Brett is very popular.
The Bugliachi straight-eight roadster is a fine car.	The Bugliachi straight-eight roadster has beautiful lines, superior workmanship, and durability.

EXERCISE 18

A. Choose two of the subjects listed in Exercise 15B and make up a purpose and a thesis statement for each.

EXAMPLE

Subject   My First Date with Monica

PURPOSE STATEMENT   I want to describe my first date with Monica, to make my reader understand the anticipation and anxiety I felt, the pleasure, and the panic and pain of that rainy evening.

THESIS STATEMENT   An experience that begins in eager anticipation and proceeds smoothly may still end in disaster but nonetheless teach you something useful about human beings and human relationships.

1. *Subject* ————————————————————————

PURPOSE STATEMENT ——————————————————————

—————————————————————————————

—————————————————————————————

THESIS STATEMENT ——————————————————————

—————————————————————————————

—————————————————————————————

2. *Subject* ————————————————————————

PURPOSE STATEMENT ——————————————————————

—————————————————————————————

—————————————————————————————

THESIS STATEMENT ——————————————————————

—————————————————————————————

—————————————————————————————

B. Choose two of the specific topics you split off from a general subject in Exercise 16A and provide a thesis statement about each. Your thesis sentence, remember, should be a full sentence, not a phrase. It should be limited and specific, not general and vague.

171

EXAMPLE

Subject   Running for political office

THESIS STATEMENT   Running for political office is physically exhausting, emotionally depleting, and, at times, spiritually demoralizing.

1. *Subject* _____

   THESIS STATEMENT _____

   _____

   _____

2. *Subject* _____

   THESIS STATEMENT _____

   _____

   _____

C. Using the detail in the following groups of sentences, phrase a concise, comprehensive thesis statement for an outline on the subject. Write your thesis statement in the blanks provided.

1. (1) Over the eighty years of its history, winners of the Nobel Prize have been recognized as international leaders in their fields. (2) The Nobel award amounts to about $200,000 for the winner, or winners if more than one is chosen in a field. (3) Award winners receive additional honors and rewards: honorary degrees, higher salaries, large lecture fees, consulting fees, and membership on boards of corporations. (4) These extras can amount to several times the amount of the award itself. (5) There is a prestige connected with the award that can elevate an unknown researcher into prominence overnight.

   THESIS STATEMENT _____

   _____

2. (1) Women who work in clerical jobs and sales occupations have coronary disease rates twice that of other women. (2) Women clerical workers often have husbands and children, and family problems frequently aggravate their situation. (3) Clerical workers' jobs are demanding less skill because of new office equipment—word processors, data processors, microprocessors. (4) Work on computers is often reduced to monotonous, repetitive tasks, which are not satisfying. (5) The accompanying frustration increases stress and the chances of heart problems.

THESIS STATEMENT _____

_____

3. (1) Japan's Black Emperors are the young counterparts of America's Hell's Angels. (2) Police estimate that there are 1,730 juvenile gangs across the country. (3) In 1981, 44 percent of all felony arrests involved juveniles. (4) Japan's highly competitive educational system produces frustration and anger among those who can't keep up and who resort to violence to assert themselves. (5) A breakdown in traditional family patterns caused by Japan's increasingly industrialized society is thought to be the primary cause of this rise in delinquency and the popularity of youth gangs. (6) Japanese police are worried about this problem, and they don't expect it to diminish for several years.

THESIS STATEMENT _____

_____

4. (1) Businesslike style of recruiting suggests that serving in the armed forces is just another job. (2) The emphasis is not on patriotic duty, obligation to serve one's country, but on self-interest. (3) A completely voluntary military service draws heavily upon minorities. (4) It thus places an unfair burden on youth from poor, underprivileged families to defend the country. (5) The mental aptitude of recruits in a purely voluntary program is lower than it would be if all youth were required to fulfill a military obligation. (6) And sophisticated new weapons and weapon systems require more intelligence and mental alertness than was required of servicemen two to three decades ago.

THESIS STATEMENT _____

_____

5. (1) Students learn to organize their time more effectively. (2) They learn to make better use of study time since it is limited. (3) They develop and strengthen character traits such as responsibility, self-discipline, punctuality. (4) They learn to work harmoniously with others, to accept direction, to endure demanding bosses. (5) They learn to manage money more effectively. (6) A part-time job usually forces them to budget their income and spend it wisely.

THESIS STATEMENT _____

_____

6. ORGANIZING DETAIL

The Scratch Outline

The ideas and impressions you have generated in support of a limited topic in the preceding pre-writing activities must now be organized and developed to carry out your purpose and support your thesis. They must be transformed into the sentences and paragraphs of a first draft of your theme. A scratch outline is an effective tool to help you sort through the material you have accumulated—ideas from brainstorming and freewriting, notes from readings and lectures, remembered experiences, conversations, and so on—to see if you can discover some pattern in your detail and establish relationships among the items. Consider, for example, the detail developed about Mr. Jones (pp. 161–62). Sorting through the detail, we can see that it can be organized into three main groups: those items dealing with his appearance, others with his personality and attitude toward students, and a third group with his teaching techniques. Grouping related items under these three headings produces this preliminary outline.

1. appearance
   - #1   heavy rimmed glasses, blue eyes
   - #2   tall, slender, slight roll to walk
   - #3   gray hair, thinning on top
   - #5   cardigan sweaters, windbreaker jackets, always a tie
   - #10   loafers, slacks, never jeans
   - #12   mid forties, maybe older, laugh wrinkles
2. personality
   - #6   friendly, courteous, somewhat formal in class
   - #7   jokes to lighten the mood
   - #8   laughed at his own jokes—make sure we knew it was a joke, he said
   - #11   not serious about self, but serious about subject
   - #13   tough-minded about good work, tender-minded in personal contacts
   - #14   a good listener
   - #15   firm, fair, friendly—his code
   - #25   somewhat formal with students, Mr. this, Miss that, friendly, but no pal
   - #27   popular with students, but no nonsense
   - #28   tough but fair
3. teaching methods
   - #4   pacing behind lectern, eyes on floor, lost in thought at times
   - #16   lots of homework, too much

#17 Socratic method—lots of questions, no place to hide

#18 nailed you for lack of preparation, goofing off

#19 pop quizzes, essays

#20 simplicity, clarity, write to express, not to impress

#22 occasional stories, family, friends

#23 loved his subject . . . cummings, Hemingway, Fitzgerald . . . literature

#30 brought in books, loaned his own, always reading and recommending books

As you look over your groupings, you may discover that one heading contains more items than any other. The second and third groupings of this outline contain about twice as many items as the first. When this occurs, you may decide to change your subject to one of the main headings. Shifting your attention to your new subject, you could then supply additional detail and organize it in the same manner as you did the original topic. With a few more details a short theme of 300 words could be developed on Mr. Jones' personality. This possibility illustrates an important fact about a scratch outline: it is simply a tool, a means to an end. It's not inviolable. When you modify your purpose, modify your outline accordingly.

The initial grouping completed, you must now arrange your major and minor ideas in some effective order. The order you use will depend on the nature of your material and on your purpose. The order of detail about Mr. Jones focuses first on his appearance, then on his personality, then on his teaching methods. This order is reasonable since the first impression students usually form of instructors is of their general appearance. If readers get a strong image of Mr. Jones in their minds at the outset, they are more likely to understand more clearly and visualize more precisely his personality and teaching methods as they are presented.

Here is a revised version of the first outline. The order of the minor items under the main headings has been rearranged a bit to put closely related items together, and some new items have been added. Note also that a thesis statement has been added to serve as a visible guide to minimize the possibility of irrelevant material creeping in.

Ol' Jonesy: Firm, Fair, and Friendly

1. appearance
   tall, slender, with a roll to his walk
   mid forties or so
   gray hair, thinning on top
   great smile: face lights up, eyes sparkle

    cardigan sweaters, windbreaker jackets, slacks
    always a tie—solid color
    loafers
2. personality—relations with others
    friendly but a bit formal in class, courteous
    addressed students as Mr. or Miss
    jokes to lighten mood
    laughed at his own jokes—to make sure we knew it was a joke, he
      said
    not serious about self, but serious about subject
    tough-minded about good work, tender-minded in personal contacts
    liked students, a good listener, generous with time in office
    popular with students—attended games, dances, senior picnic
    respected, popular with faculty
3. teaching methods
    lots of homework—too much
    Socratic method—questions, lots of questions, no place to hide
    pop quizzes, essays, seldom objective tests
    paced behind lectern at times, eyes on floor, lost in thought
    occasional stories about family, friends, college days
    loved his subject. . . cummings, Hemingway, Fitzgerald. . . literature,
      slides of Paris, Montparnasse
    brought in books, loaned his own, always reading and recommend-
      ing books
    tough but fair
    praised good work, smiled at a good response, a wink for excellence
    nailed you for lack of preparation, goofing off, slipshod work

With this rough outline as a framework for your theme, you can begin the first draft. You may still want to supply additional clarifying and supporting detail, but this plan will provide sufficient direction for a theme of 500 words.

Before moving on to the formal outline, we should mention one other use of the scratch outline. Besides helping you discover the pattern in a list of details, a scratch outline is useful for organizing ideas on essays and examinations written in class. In this instance, begin with the major ideas, the ideas that will serve as the topic sentences of your paragraphs, and then jot down a few supporting details under each of the main ideas. The time it takes to develop a brief outline is time well spent, for your essay will be more unified and coherent than it would otherwise be. A scratch outline on the advantages of urban life might look like the following:

    nearness of essential services
      grocery and drug stores, shopping malls

hospitals
police substation, post office

convenience and economy of public transportation
  good bus system
  no need to fight freeway traffic
  less dependence upon automobile, less expense for car

variety of recreational and cultural activities
  movie theatres, stage plays, museums
  nearby parks, musicals in summer
  little cafes and restaurants

EXERCISE 19

A. Work up a scratch outline of the detail you listed on a subject for Exercise 17A or B. Present three or four main headings and arrange your minor detail under the appropriate heading. Compose a purpose statement and a thesis statement and write them in the blanks provided.

Title _____

PURPOSE STATEMENT _____

_____

_____

THESIS STATEMENT _____

_____

_____

1. _____

_____

_____

_____

_____

2. _____

_____

_____

_____

_____

3. _____

_____

_____

_____

_____

B.   In each of the following groups, one idea could serve as a major heading for the other ideas. Identify the heading and write it in the blank space provided.

1.   the world not running out of mineral resources; production of chromite, essential to metals industry, increased 248 percent in last decade; 200 years worth of land-reserve supply of manganese on hand at current use levels; American industry not threatened by lack of mineral resources; embargoes of vital mineral imports not likely; U.S. has large, untapped reserves and stockpiles of most minerals; U.S. imports 20 percent of minerals needed— much less than other industrial nations; large reserves of cobalt and manganese in seabed nodules

     Main Heading _____

2.   grade point average all-important for many students, so fewer solid academic subjects taken; state legislature and colleges and universities reduced requirements for high school graduation; demand for "relevant" courses increases range of choices available; decline in value of high school diploma in job market; decline in funding of public education; easier grading practices

     Main Heading _____

3.   waste products include strontium 90 and plutonium 239, both deadly; strontium is carcinogenic and plutonium can poison all vegetation; plutonium 239 needs to be isolated for more than 250,000 years, strontium for 600 years; no container yet devised is foolproof even for decades, let alone for thousands of years; dumping nuclear wastes in the ocean creates problems because containers corrode; serious weakness of nuclear power is disposal of wastes; problem of corrosion and cracking in underground salt bed storage sites; by 2000 A.D. millions of gallons of wastes will have to be disposed of

     Main Heading _____

4.   variety of recreational and cultural activities available; proximity of supermarkets, shopping malls, drugstores; nearby parks; benefits of urban living; economy and convenience of bus transportation; intimacy and emotional involvement in chats with neighbors at block parties; sidewalk cafes, good restaurants

     Main Heading _____

5.   command of language; interesting lectures, illuminated by relevant anecdotes and pointed examples; well prepared; a good teacher; patient but not a patsy; praises good work; stimulates student interest in subject by his or her enthusiasm and love of the subject; sense of humor

     Main Heading _____

C.   Arrange the following items under three main headings. One of the items will serve as a title, another as a thesis statement (the statement that expresses the main point). Place the number of the item in the appropriate blank.

1. An educated person should know a little about everything and a lot about something.

2. A vision of the good life is needed.

3. An educated person has the ability to recognize specious reasoning, phony arguments.

4. Reinforcement of moral virtues—courage, integrity, compassion, honor—is provided by a good education.

5. The qualities of an educated person.

6. The corruption of personal honor ultimately corrupts society.

7. A well-educated person is a harmonious blend of intellectual, moral, and emotional capacities.

8. Mastery of self-expression is basic in speaking and in writing.

9. When uncontrolled, emotions can paralyze, disorient, and isolate people.

10. Knowledge in the major categories of learning is required—humanities, social sciences, natural sciences.

11. An educated person is not only willing to listen to others but is also willing to take a stand.

12. An understanding of the disruptive power of the emotions is needed.

13. To think clearly requires the ability to formulate a persuasive argument and to follow one presented by someone else.

14. A good education gives one knowledge about and experience in controlling one's emotions.

15. Intellectual capacity means a well-stocked, flexible mind as well as a mind capable of thinking clearly and expressing itself clearly.

16. Development of emotional stability is a third requirement.

17. A well-educated person is less a victim of uncontrolled passions.

18. A human being is more an emotional than a rational animal.

Title _____

THESIS STATEMENT _____

_____

a. First main heading _____

_____

_____

_____

_____

_____

b. Second main heading _____

_____

_____

_____

_____

c. Third main heading _____

_____

_____

_____

_____

The Formal Outline

The kind of scratch outline described in the preceding section is usually sufficient for a theme of 300 to 500 words. For a longer, more intricate writing assignment, however, you will find it helpful to make a more detailed, formal outline. The longer paper requires more careful preparation; it requires you to work out the relationships and the development of your thought more thoroughly. And a formal outline forces you to do just this. Beginning writers sometimes neglect the outline because of the time required to prepare it. But, as you will discover, the more time you spend in carefully preparing your outline, the less time you will waste when you begin to write. With a clearly detailed plan of your theme before you, you will not have to grope for ideas to clarify and develop your thesis. Properly used, an outline will give your writing a sense of proportion and direction. It should not, however, be thought of as a sacred covenant, an inflexible contract that must be adhered to at all costs. You should depart from it by adding an idea or illustration whenever you can move your thought forward more smoothly.

An outline has three parts: the *title,* the *thesis statement,* and the *body.* The body consists of the major and minor ideas that develop the main idea of the outline expressed in the thesis statement. The main ideas are represented by Roman numerals, minor ideas by capital letters, Arabic numerals, and lowercase letters, as illustrated in the following system:

> I.
> > A.
> > > 1.
> > > > a.
> > > > > (1)
> > > > > > (a)

Each main heading (I, II, and so on) need not be developed in as much detail as this illustration. An outline for a theme of 300 to 500 words usually does not require subdivision beyond the first Arabic numerals.

> I.
> > A.
> > > 1.
> > > 2.
> > B.
> II.

Capitalize the first word of each heading, and if the heading is a sentence place a period at the end. Occasionally the entries on a sentence outline may extend to two or three lines. When they do, make certain that your left-hand margin does not extend to the left of the period after the topic symbol, as illustrated below.

I. _____

  A. _____

     _____

     _____

The thesis statement appears between the title and the first Roman numeral.

Title

THESIS STATEMENT _____

_____

I. _____

The most frequently used forms of the outline are the *topic outline* and the *sentence outline*. The entries on a topic outline are made up of short phrases or single words. The following exemplifies a topic outline:

Violence in School: A Growing Problem in the United States

THESIS STATEMENT The increase in violence in American schools is creating serious financial and educational problems for school districts.

  I. Nature of problem
    A. Abuse of students
      1. Physical assaults
        a. Beatings
        b. Rape
        c. Murder
      2. Mental and emotional harassment
    B. Attacks on teachers and school board members
    C. Vandalism of school property
  II. Response by school authorities
    A. Increased use of armed guards
      1. Off-duty policemen in Chicago
      2. District-employed patrols in Los Angeles

      B. Increased use of hardware
          1. Laser-beam alarm signals
          2. Walkie-talkies for teachers
          3. Police helicopters
III. Consequences of increasing violence
      A. Depletion of school budgets
          1. Less money for supplies and facilities
          2. Less money for maintenance
          3. Less money for teaching staff
      B. Adverse effect on student learning
      C. Community anger at lack of safety in schools
          1. Attacks on school board members
          2. Lack of financial support for school bonds
IV. Solutions to problem
      A. Hard-line approach
          1. Increased use of armed guards and police
          2. Swift apprehension of offenders
          3. Jail and prison sentences for juveniles
      B. Long-term approach
          1. Reduction of violence in mass media
          2. Improvement in lives of underprivileged
          3. Restructuring of schools to ease competition and tensions
      C. Other approaches
          1. More vocational education
          2. Reductions in class size
          3. Release of unmotivated students
          4. Alternative of community service instead of jail for offenders
          5. New rights and responsibilities for students to aid in control of violence

In a sentence outline each entry is a sentence.

The Ecological Importance of Open Space

THESIS STATEMENT Open space is essential to the maintenance of a healthful, life-supporting environment.

   I. Open space plays a vital role in maintaining breathable air.
      A. Open space vegetation filters particles from the air.
      B. It produces oxygen through the process of photosynthesis.
      C. Automobiles and factories in urban areas produce smog.

II. Intelligent use of open space can help to maintain a healthful climate.
  A. Open space dissipates islands of heat produced in urban areas.
    1. Covered surfaces, such as asphalt, absorb heat.
    2. Urban areas produce heat through combustion.
  B. Native vegetation of open space helps to reduce humidity produced by evaporation of water used to irrigate exotic plants in cities and suburbs.
III. Invasion of open space by urban and suburban sprawl impairs its recreational use.
  A. Open space surrounding cities is often used by city-dwelling hikers and cyclists.
  B. Housing tracts and shopping centers occupy space that could be better used for public parks and campgrounds near densely populated cities.
  C. Empty beach land should be purchased by a state or the federal government and preserved for recreational use.
IV. Wildlife, essential to a healthful ecological system, is threatened by the elimination of open space.

Of the two forms, the topic outline is generally easier to manage, but because the theme itself will be composed of sentences, the sentence outline provides a more convenient basis than the topic outline for the translation of thought from outline to theme.

If you are to do an effective job of outlining, you must know something of the principles that govern the construction of an outline, as well as its format. These concern (1) logic subordination of ideas, (2) parallel structure, (3) single subdivisions, and (4) specific, meaningful headings. The most important of these principles is the first, for the main purpose of your outline is to give you a logical, well-organized structure for your composition. Examine your outline first to be sure that your main headings are logical divisions of the subject expressed in the title and thesis statement. Make certain that the subheadings are logical divisions of the headings under which they are listed. In the outlines on school violence and open space presented above, the main and subheadings are logically subordinate to the thesis and main headings respectively.

The principle of parallelism, which requires that ideas of equal importance in a sentence be expressed in the same grammatical form, applies to the construction of outlines. An outline is parallel when the headings designated by the same kind of letter or numeral are phrased in parallel form. That is, if Roman numeral I is a prepositional phrase, the other Roman numerals should be prepositional phrases also. If A and B under I are nouns, so must be the other capital letters under II, III, and so on. A sentence outline is automatically parallel, for each entry is a sentence and hence parallel. In the topic outline on school violence, each main heading—"Nature of problems," "Response by school authorities," and so on—is a noun followed by a prepositional phrase.

The third and fourth criteria—single subdivisions and specific, meaningful headings—follow logically from the process and purpose of outlining. The basis of outlining, as we have seen, is the division of larger topics into smaller ones. When you divide a topic into its parts, you must, logically, have at least two parts. In constructing an outline, therefore, avoid the single subdivision. If you divide a Roman numeral heading, you must have at least an A and a B under it. If you divide a capital letter heading, you must provide at least a 1 and a 2 under it, and so on through each successive stage of the outline.

Since the purpose of an outline is to provide a framework, a concise structure of the thought of a composition, make certain your headings convey specific, meaningful ideas. General headings such as "Introduction," "Body," "Conclusion," or "Examples," "Functions," "Types," and the like do not represent the subject matter of an outline very clearly and therefore provide little guidance when you translate the ideas from your outline to the essay itself.

After you have completed your outline, examine it carefully to see that its format is correct and that the organization of its ideas is logical and consistent. Be sure that you have included a title and a thesis statement and that you have used symbols correctly and consistently. As you check the body of the outline, make certain that you have avoided single subdivisions and vague, meaningless headings and that entries of the same rank are expressed in parallel structure. If your outline meets these tests, you are ready to begin your first draft.

EXERCISE 20

A. Compose a formal outline sentence on population growth, using the detail presented on page 163. Arrange the detail under three main headings, and provide a title and thesis statement. Eliminate any items that don't fit under any of the three headings, and make certain minor items are placed under the appropriate heading. Order the main headings in a sequence of importance, the last being the one you consider most important.

Title ⎯⎯⎯⎯⎯⎯⎯⎯⎯⎯⎯⎯

THESIS STATEMENT ⎯⎯⎯⎯⎯⎯⎯⎯⎯⎯⎯⎯⎯⎯

⎯⎯⎯⎯⎯⎯⎯⎯⎯⎯⎯⎯⎯⎯⎯⎯⎯⎯⎯

⎯⎯⎯⎯⎯⎯⎯⎯⎯⎯⎯⎯⎯⎯⎯⎯⎯⎯⎯

I. ⎯⎯⎯⎯⎯⎯⎯⎯⎯⎯⎯⎯⎯⎯⎯

⎯⎯⎯⎯⎯⎯⎯⎯⎯⎯⎯⎯⎯⎯⎯⎯⎯

A. ⎯⎯⎯⎯⎯⎯⎯⎯⎯⎯⎯⎯⎯

⎯⎯⎯⎯⎯⎯⎯⎯⎯⎯⎯⎯⎯⎯⎯

1. ⎯⎯⎯⎯⎯⎯⎯⎯⎯⎯⎯⎯⎯

⎯⎯⎯⎯⎯⎯⎯⎯⎯⎯⎯⎯⎯⎯

2. ⎯⎯⎯⎯⎯⎯⎯⎯⎯⎯⎯⎯⎯

⎯⎯⎯⎯⎯⎯⎯⎯⎯⎯⎯⎯⎯⎯

3. ⎯⎯⎯⎯⎯⎯⎯⎯⎯⎯⎯⎯⎯

⎯⎯⎯⎯⎯⎯⎯⎯⎯⎯⎯⎯⎯⎯

B. ⎯⎯⎯⎯⎯⎯⎯⎯⎯⎯⎯⎯⎯

⎯⎯⎯⎯⎯⎯⎯⎯⎯⎯⎯⎯⎯⎯⎯

C. ⎯⎯⎯⎯⎯⎯⎯⎯⎯⎯⎯⎯⎯

⎯⎯⎯⎯⎯⎯⎯⎯⎯⎯⎯⎯⎯⎯⎯

II. ⎯⎯⎯⎯⎯⎯⎯⎯⎯⎯⎯⎯⎯⎯

⎯⎯⎯⎯⎯⎯⎯⎯⎯⎯⎯⎯⎯⎯

A. _____

    1. _____

    _____

    2. _____

    _____

B. _____

_____

    1. _____

    _____

    2. _____

    _____

C. _____

_____

    1. _____

    _____

    2. _____

    _____

III. _____

_____

A. _____

_____

B. _____

_____

C. _____

_____

B. List below the numbers of the items you omitted from the original list of detail on population growth, page 163, in making up your outline for 20A above and briefly explain why.

	DETAIL OMITTED	REASON
1.	_____	_____
2.	_____	_____
3.	_____	_____
4.	_____	_____
5.	_____	_____
6.	_____	_____
7.	_____	_____
8.	_____	_____
9.	_____	_____

7. THE FIRST DRAFT

The scratch or formal outline completed, you are now ready to write the first draft of your paper. Your outline provides the framework; now you must transform this plan into the sentences and paragraphs of your theme.

The major headings of your outline will become the topic sentences of your paragraphs, though the correspondence is not always exact. That is, a major heading may occasionally require more than one paragraph to develop it, depending upon the amount of supporting material it encompasses. The first main heading of the outline "Violence in School: A Growing Problem in the United States" (pp. 183–85):

I. Nature of problem
  A. Abuse of students
  B. Attacks on teachers and school board members
  C. Vandalism of school property

would require at least a paragraph and possibly two or three for full development. Conversely, in a short composition, two Roman numeral headings might be included in one paragraph.

Plan your time so that you can revise your first draft carefully. Concentrate on the body of your paper, the major points of your outline. You can work on your opening and closing later. Once you begin, move steadily forward. Do not worry about perfection at this stage. The important thing is to get your ideas on paper. You can correct errors in spelling, punctuation, and grammar; make improvements in wording; and add, delete, or reorder material later when you revise this draft. If you stop to check these items now, you may lose your train of thought.

Here is a first draft of a theme developed from the scratch outline on Mr. Jones, pp. 175–77.

Firm, Fair, and Friendly

In my senior year in high school, I had Mr. Jones for English, one of the best teachers I've ever had. He was a tall, slender man in his late forties with gray, thinning hair. Heavy rimmed glasses perched precariously on his nose, which he was always taking off and polishing or sticking in his mouth while he mulled over a response to a student's question. When he walked into class, he always carried two or three books under his arm with strips of paper dangling from them, marking passages he planned to read. I remember, too, the cardigan sweaters—he must have had a dozen of them—neatly pressed slacks, Oxford loafers, and a tie, always a tie. On rainy days he wore a navy blue windbreaker jacket, but that was the only time he was without a sweater. He was always carefully dressed, but he was no dandy. But perhaps the thing I remember best was his smile. When he smiled, his blue eyes sparkled and crinkled at the corners. His smile made you feel good, at ease, somehow reassured.

But though he was friendly and naturally at ease in company with others, he was a bit formal in class. He never called us by our first names. It was always Mr. Weaver or Miss Powers, never Brad nor Marie. He obviously loved his work and liked his students, but he kept his distance somehow. Yet though he never deliberately embarrassed a student in front of the class with a sarcastic remark, he could communicate his displeasure all right. He'd look steadily at the offending student for a few seconds, his lips firming slightly shut. That was usually enough, but if it didn't work, he'd say something in a lowered tone of voice. He didn't have to do this often because students liked and respected him and wanted to please him. I suppose because he liked and respected us and was so obviously serious about his subject and intent on our learning it and sharing his enthusiasm. He was serious about his subject, his teaching, but not about himself. He always had a witty comment or a joke to lighten the mood when necessary. He'd laugh harder than anyone else, to make sure we knew it was a joke he said. His friendliness, his enthusiasm, his wit attracted students wherever he was. Students were always waiting to talk to him in his office, to ask advice about college, for a letter of recommendation, or just to chat a bit. I don't think he ever missed a football game or the senior dance or picnic, for that matter.

Jonesy had personality, integrity, vitality—all of which made him popular, as I said; but what I liked most about him was that he was a fine teacher. Yes, he cared about students, but he cared more about teaching them his subject. And that meant homework, lots of it, and pop quizzes now and then to keep them current on the reading. He lectured occasionally, to provide background whenever we moved on to a new period in American literature. After a brief glance at his notes, he'd begin to move around—to the blackboard, to the windows, back to the lectern—as he talked; but he preferred discussion, a Socratic dialogue. He'd write several questions on the board for the next day's discussion, and he'd expect you to be prepared to discuss them. He directed the discussion, but he didn't dominate it; for he was a good listener and made sure every student had a chance to respond, whether he or she wanted to or not. If he were pleased with a response, he'd nod his head and smile. Occasionally he'd also read a good essay from a student, praising its good points and then winking at the writer when he handed it back. But he was tough-minded, too. He really nailed you for sloppy work or inattention. When you got an A from him, you really felt good, for he wasn't an easy grader. We used to moan about his grading standards, usually to no avail, though he would change a grade if after rereading a student's paper he thought he had been unfair.

We had many interesting discussions on Twain, Crane, and Dreiser, as I recall, but his favorite period was the 1920's. He loved the expatriates: Anderson, cummings, Hemingway, Fitzgerald. He was always bringing in books for us to read, as I said; but when he got to this period, he was a walking library. I think he'd read every book written by or about Hemingway and Fitzgerald, or about Paris in the twenties. He must have seen the films and slides he showed us about the expatriates and Paris dozens of times, but his enthusiasm never flagged when he discussed them. I can still see him, and hear him, reading and chuckling over some passage from *The Sun Also Rises* or *A Moveable Feast.* Yes, I can still see him.

EXERCISE 21

Write a first draft of a theme based on the outline you prepared for 17A or B.

8. REVISING THE FIRST DRAFT

Revision is the final stage in the process of composition, and it is an important one. Revision means to see again, and that's what you must do now: look again at what you've written to see what changes need to be made in the content and organization and how you might polish and refine the writing itself. Actually, you have been revising at every stage along the way—selecting and revising your subject, revising your scratch outline, rethinking your purpose and thesis, and so on. This final revision, is, however, more than just a brief last look to correct some spelling or grammatical errors. It requires a serious reexamination of your first draft to make sure it does what you want it to do.

As we have suggested earlier, don't begin to revise your first draft immediately after you have completed it. Don't think about it for at least a day or two. When you look at it again, you will be able to view it more objectively, to discover more clearly what you must do to give it its final shape.

First Stage

In the first stage of your revision, reexamine the *content* and *organization* of your paper. Put yourself in the mind of your reader as you take a fresh, objective look at your paper. Have you ordered your paragraphs in an effective sequence so that your reader can easily follow the progress of your thought? Do your paragraphs support your thesis and advance the thought logically, compellingly? Have you provided enough detail, enough evidence and illustration of your ideas? Do any parts need to be rewritten to add or delete material? Have you defined important terms and concepts? Is your tone appropriate, consistent?

After you have looked at the structure of the whole paper, concentrate on your paragraphs. Read them carefully to see that they are unified, well developed, and coherent.

Unity   The controlling idea of each paragraph should be clearly and concisely stated in a topic statement. Each sentence of the paragraph should support this idea.

Development   Each paragraph should contain enough detail—enough facts, illustrations, comparisons, judgments—to explain the controlling idea adequately. The supporting detail should be concrete and specific. Every generalization should be supported by sufficient evidence to persuade a fair-minded reader.

Coherence   The ideas in each paragraph should be arranged in a logical sequence and the sentences linked together smoothly with transitional expressions, repetition of key terms, parallel structure, and pronoun reference.

The last suggestion regarding coherence needs further comment. Our previous discussion of coherence concentrated on coherence *within* the paragraph. When you write a longer composition, you must make certain that the thought flows smoothly *between* paragraphs as well as between sentences. If you have organized your paper carefully, there should be a steady development of thought from paragraph to paragraph, but you can accentuate this continuity through judicious use of transitional expressions and through repetition of key words. In the following passage, for example, the writer uses both these devices to ensure continuity between paragraphs.

Even the shift in the kind of curriculum is upsetting. The students are used to having the day arranged for them from, say, nine to three, high-school fashion. They now find themselves attending classes for only fifteen hours or so a week. The concentration in depth on a few subjects is a new idea to them. The requisite self-discipline is often something they learn only after painful experience.

Furthermore, college is the students' first encounter with live intellectuals. They meet individual members of the faculty who have written important books or completed important pieces of research. The various intellectual fields become matters of personal experience. The students learn that work does not just happen to get done. They find that the productive intellectual is not a superman but an everyday figure. They will also make the discovery that there are those who consider intellectual pursuits reason enough for an entire life. Students are nearly always surprised to find such pursuits valued so highly.

Students are surprised, too, at their first meeting with really violent political opinion. . . . [From James K. Feibleman, "What Happens in College," *Saturday Review,* October 20, 1962.]

Furthermore, the first word of the second paragraph, informs us that the writer is adding another illustration of the idea he has been developing in the preceding paragraph. The transition between the second and third paragraphs is especially smooth.

. . . Students are nearly always surprised to find such pursuits valued so highly.

Students are surprised, too, at their first meeting . . .

The repetition of the word *students* in the latter sentence plus the use of the transitional *too,* which signals an additional illustration of the author's point in the preceding two paragraphs, provides an uninterrupted bridge of thought as we move from one paragraph to the next. The repetition of key words such as *students* and its pronoun *they* throughout the passage also ties the paragraphs together.

Emphasis

After you have tested your paper for unity, development, and coherence, examine it once more to make certain you have given your most important ideas the proper emphasis. To make your reader receptive to the effect you wish to create, you must communicate your thoughts clearly and forcefully. The most emphatic positions in a composition are the beginning and the end. Reread your opening and closing sentences. Now is the time to revise and polish these sentences. What you say in the opening sentence often determines the kind of reading your paper will receive. If your first sentence successfully arouses the interest and curiosity of your readers, they will probably give your paper a sympathetic reading. If it is rather dull and colorless, their reading will probably be more perfunctory. The first few sentences are especially important if the purpose of your paper is to argue a point. In this case you must establish yourself as a reasonable individual, not a fanatic. If your introduction makes the readers suspicious or uneasy about your motives, it will be difficult to persuade them of anything.

What you say in the closing sentence is even more important. You can regain your readers' interest after an uninspiring introduction with lively material in the body of the paper, but you have no second chance after they have finished reading. What your readers read last, they usually remember best. If your last sentence is vague and inconclusive, their final impression is not apt to be favorable. Read over your first draft carefully, therefore, and revise your opening and closing sentences to make them as effective as possible. The following discussion will provide some specific suggestions for opening and closing sentences.

Beginning the Paper

The beginning of an essay must do three things: it must engage the reader's attention, introduce the subject, and set an appropriate tone for the essay. We have considered tone in a previous chapter. Tone, we said, defines your attitude toward your subject, the stance you take toward your readers. If your purpose is humor or autobiography, a light, playful tone is in order. But if you are dealing with a serious subject, as you will be in much of your college writing, you should adopt a more straightforward, serious tone. Above all, you should establish yourself as a reasonable, trustworthy person. If your readers conclude at the outset that you are a hothead or a bigot, they will simply tune you out.

A paper of 500 words or longer may require an introductory paragraph, but for most short themes of 300 words or less the first paragraph can introduce the subject, set the tone, and begin the first main idea. Whether your introduction is a single sentence or a whole paragraph, however, begin with a sentence that is interesting and says something important about the subject.

You may use a number of ways to gain your reader's attention at the beginning of an essay:

1. An *unusual comparison* may stimulate reader interest:

> Prime Minister Trudeau has observed that, for Canada, coexisting with the United States is like sleeping with an elephant. No matter

how friendly the animal, every grunt and twitch shakes the smaller partner. [From Henry C. Wallich, "The Elephant in Bed," *Newsweek*, September 22, 1969, p. 94.]

2. Or a slightly barbed, *provocative statement:*

Tis nearly autumn, season of mists and mellow fruitfulness, and God as a punishment has sent another football season. [From George F. Will, "Is That a Red Dog in the Seam?" *Newsweek*, September 6, 1976, p. 72.]

3. A *simple, direct statement* of the main idea can be effective:

It is not enough these days to guard against those who would make us believe new myths. We must also guard against those who would make us believe our old ones are dead. [From Jack Smith, "Dream a Little Dream of Me," *Los Angeles Times*, November 12, 1980.]

Good teachers are those who know their subject, love their subject, and are willing and able to share it.

4. An *appropriate quoted passage* may attract reader attention:

Oscar Wilde's description of a cynic as one "who knows the price of everything and the value of nothing" might well be applied to those who argue that the Alaskan wilderness ought to be commercially exploited to yield its mineral riches.

Courage and fear are often thought of as mutually exclusive states of mind, one admirable, the other shameful. Mark Twain knew better. "Courage," he said, "is resistance to fear, mastery of fear— not absence of fear. Except a creature be part coward it is not a compliment to say it is brave; it is merely a loose misapplication of the word. Consider the flea!—incomparably the bravest of all the creatures of God, if ignorance of fear were courage."[1]

5. The writer may use a *startling statistic:*

Harry is one of 5,000 young Americans a year who commit suicide—a near epidemic average of thirteen a day. Suicide is now the third leading cause of death for 15- to 24-year-olds, after accidents and homicides." [From "Teen-Age Suicide," *Newsweek*, August 28, 1978, p. 74.]

---

[1] From *Pudd'nhead Wilson.*

6. A *personal experience* can be effective in catching reader interest, particularly when you are writing about yourself:

> I'll never forget one Saturday night when I was a junior in high school and my pals decided to take me to my first burlesque show in downtown Los Angeles. They were all older and taller than I, and I had always felt a bit self-conscious with them, as if I somehow had to prove my manhood to be worthy of their friendship. I wanted to go, but I was a bit nervous for fear I'd reveal my naiveté, my innocence. On the way they decided to stop for a beer, and of course I had to drink one, too. As a matter of fact, I drank two, to fortify myself, I suppose. . . .

These suggestions do not exhaust the possibilities, of course. As you gain experience, you will discover other effective ways to introduce your subject and to elicit reader interest at the same time. As you experiment with various openers, keep the following points in mind.

First, limit your introduction to one or two sentences and get directly into your subject unless you are writing a paper of 400 words or longer. Wandering, irrelevant introductions like the following are deadening:

Why I Want to Be a Doctor

> I guess I've always wanted to be a doctor. My grandfather on my mother's side was a doctor, and I was very fond of Grand-dad. He used to take me with him on his house calls. . . .

Next, avoid apologizing. A theme that begins "I am not an expert on politics, but . . ." is not likely to arouse much interest.

Third, avoid the kind of provocative, intimidating statement that forces a response from your reader. "We've had enough of politicians who promise fiscal responsibility and then saddle hardworking Americans with backbreaking taxes." Such a beginning suggests anger and narrow-mindedness. It will cause a thoughtful reader to lose interest quickly.

Be wary also of the broad generalization as an opener. Statements like "Americans have always envied the Europeans' cultural sophistication" are simply too comprehensive to be supportable. They will not impress an intelligent reader.

Finally, make certain that your first sentence is easily understood without reference to the title. For a theme entitled "Tobacco and the Teen-ager," the following beginning sentence would only confuse the reader: "I guess everybody has tried it at least once by the time he or she is seventeen."

Ending the Paper

For the short theme of 300 to 400 words a special summarizing paragraph is not necessary. A sentence or two is usually sufficient. If your paper is well organized and coherent,

1. A *final detail* will often provide a satisfactory conclusion:

> And, finally, boxing should be banned because of the severe physical damage inflicted on the fighter himself. This result is not surprising, for in no other sport is it the primary purpose of one contestant to knock his opponent senseless, and it is a rare fighter who can absorb such punishment without suffering serious after-effects. If it does not kill him—and the possibility is not remote—it may well leave him with the characteristic stumbling shuffle, the thick tongue, the battered face, and the impaired vision of the punch-drunk ex-fighter.

2. An *apt quotation* may conclude as well as begin an essay:

> Personal success is not really a matter of money, celebrity, youth, and good looks. It is a matter of commitment, of effort in the pursuit of some life-enhancing activity. Oliver Wendell Holmes, Jr., wrote: "Whether a man accepts from Fortune her spade and will look downward and dig, or from Aspiration her axe and cord, and will scale the ice, the one and only success which is his to command is to bring to his work a mighty heart."

3. If you have focused on a problem in your essay, you may conclude with a *call for action:*

> The American government must cut off all imports of Libyan oil. Continuing such imports, however economically expedient they may be, will simply dramatize the hypocrisy of the American government's fervent opposition to Colonel Kadafi's support of international terrorism, political assassination, and military involvement in neighboring African states. Morality should not be sacrificed to expediency; principles should not be subverted for profits.

4. A conclusion that *repeats an idea expressed in the opening paragraph* may provide an effective finishing touch. Henry Wallich provides an illustration as he summarizes his thesis about American economic relations with foreign countries (see p. 198, number 1, "The Elephant in Bed"):

It is good to know that, in a pinch, we could go it alone. It adds to our bargaining power. But we must remember that the final result of isolationism is isolation. If the U.S. cannot be a comfortable sleeping partner, at least it can try to be a considerate one.

5. And you may refresh your reader's mind by *enumerating the main points* of your paper:

The United States needs a more coherent, efficient mass transit system in order to 1) reduce its dependence on imported oil, 2) reduce traffic congestion in urban areas, 3) reduce air pollution, and 4) insure a satisfactory means of transportation for all citizens lacking access to automobiles.

Study the final paragraph of your first draft. If you think a special concluding sentence would give emphasis to your paper, add one. But do not tack on unneeded sentences after you have completed your thought, especially if they contain apology. An apology at the end of your paper is just as ineffectual as one at the beginning. And do not inject a new idea into your final sentences. A paper that concludes

Increased pollution, rapid depletion of vital natural resources, increased world hunger and starvation—all these await us if world population continues its rapid expansion. And yet one wonders if such dire predictions will really come to pass, for if human beings can split the atom and land a man on the moon, surely they can defuse the population bomb.

makes a reader wonder whether the writer had second thoughts about the validity of his own conclusions.

Proportion

The preceding discussion has stressed the importance of *position* in achieving emphasis. Of equal importance is *proportion,* or balance. In a well-proportioned essay the more important points are given more space; they are developed at greater length. Minor ideas and illustrative detail are not allowed to overshadow or obscure the central thesis. The following essay, based on the outline in Exercise 25A, illustrates this principle.

The Population Problem: Everybody's Baby

Introduction   Throughout history population growth has proceeded at a rather leisurely pace, from approximately 250 million people in A.D. 1 to 500 million people by 1650. Within the past 300 years, however, our numbers have increased dramatically, doubling in ever-shortening cycles, so that by 1930 world population stood at 2 billion and a brief 48 *First Topic* years later at over 4 billion. If population growth continues *Sentence* at its present rate, it will put enormous pressure on world food supplies, making it difficult, if not impossible, to avoid hunger and starvation on a massive scale. Despite all the triumphs of agriculture in the twentieth century, population growth is outstripping the gains in food production. For example, if all the food in the world were equally distributed with each person receiving the same share, we would all still be undernourished. And food is not equally distributed. Hundreds of millions of people in Africa, Asia, and South America lead lives dominated by hunger and malnutrition, and we are adding 75 million people to the world each year. To provide reasonable diets for the world's people by the year 2000, according to one expert, the production of cereal grains must be doubled, animal products quadrupled, and fruits and vegetables tripled.[2] The probability of accomplishing such goals is not high, given the vagaries of weather and the difficulty of raising sufficient capital to finance such efforts.

Second   In addition to food shortages, rapid population growth *Topic* will increase the contamination of the environment. The *Sentence* air over many large cities has become a grayish haze because of automobile exhaust and industrial pollutants; and as population grows, so will the number of automobiles and factories—and people suffering from respiratory diseases. Americans alone add more than 140 million tons of smoke and fumes to their air each year. And pollution of our water and land grows apace. Monstrous oil tankers now spill millions of gallons of oil into the oceans each year; factories and municipalities pour chemical and human waste into rivers, lakes, and streams. This pollution could have catastrophic effects if phytoplankton—minute, floating aquatic plants—are destroyed, since they provide 70 percent of the earth's oxygen. Destruction of the land will increase as it becomes covered with asphalt for more

[2] Carl Bakal, "The Mathematics of Hunger," *Saturday Review*, April 27, 1963.

roads and highways, as it becomes despoiled by giant strip-mining machines in search of more coal, and as its natural vegetation is removed to make room for more houses and refuse dumping sites. The solution to hunger and famine obviously depends on the intelligent use of the land. If we do not cherish and protect it, it will not support our current population, to say nothing of billions more.

Third Topic Sentence   People also have a need for space, for room to live and play. Though we might be able to feed, clothe, and house more billions, we cannot create more space for them; and limitations of space will create serious psychological problems for humanity. Because humans are adaptive animals, they have been able to adjust to crowded living conditions in huge metropolises, but they have paid a price in increasing irritability and feelings of alienation. Like other animals, they need a territory of their own, a home commodious enough for them to relax and restore their energies. The more people are jammed together, the more hostile and irrational they become. Such irrationality is evidenced in the higher crime rates, the more frequently disrupted public services, and the general impersonality and lack of community in large cities. And people need recreational space, too, especially if they live and work in cramped quarters. Yet recreational areas—beaches, camping grounds, national parks, ski resorts, and the like—are already inundated with people. What will conditions be like by the year 2000 when world population reaches 6 or 7 billion? One doesn't need a crystal ball to find the answer. To sum up, unchecked population growth is not merely an annoying problem exaggerated by pessimists who always worry about the future. It is, on the contrary, the most serious problem humanity faces today. Hunger and starvation, environmental destruction, and increasing human tensions and irritability—these are the certain results if we are not able to solve it.

Conclusion

Second Stage

In the second stage of your revision, you must edit the writing itself: the sentence structure, diction, mechanics, and punctuation.

Sentence Structure, Diction, Mechanics, and Punctuation

If your ideas are to have force and significance, to arouse the interest of your reader, they must be expressed in sentences that are clear, grammatical, and forceful. Clarity is primary. If your sentences are vague, awkward, or imprecise, you will not communicate your ideas effectively. Reread your essays carefully, then, to make certain that

1. each sentence is clear, without dangling or misplaced modifiers, ambiguous pronoun reference, or shifts in point of view;
2. each sentence is grammatically complete, not a fragment;
3. you have avoided fused sentences and comma splices.

The *sentence fragment,* the *fused sentence,* and the *comma splice* need special attention since they confuse readers about the beginnings and endings of sentences. The *sentence fragment,* as its name implies, is not a complete sentence. Though it begins with a capital letter and ends with a period, the group of words does not form an independent clause that makes sense by itself. Sometimes the group lacks a subject and/or a predicate:

A night on the town.

My favorite singer.

Sometimes a dependent clause in punctuated as if it were a complete sentence:

Even though the doctor had explained in great detail the seriousness of his illness.

In the fragment above the subordinating conjunction *even though* renders the clause that follows it subordinate, and so incomplete as a sentence. Without the conjunction, the clause would be independent and able to stand as a full sentence:

The doctor had explained in great detail the seriousness of his illness.

To qualify as a complete sentence, a group of words must have a subject and a predicate, and the subject-predicate construction must not be preceded by a subordinating conjunction.

Fragments also occur when *verbals* are confused with verbs. A verbal is a word (or words), derived from a verb, but which does not function as a verb. Instead, verbals function as modifiers or nouns. One type of verbal, the *participle,* commonly ends in *ing, ed, t,* or *en.* It is used as an adjective to modify (or describe) nouns and pronouns:

The waves *pounding* the shore damaged the beach houses.

The runner, *exhausted* by the race, fell to the ground.

The participle *pounding* in the first sentence modifies the noun *waves;* in the second the participle *exhausted* modifies the noun *runner.*

Another type of verbal, the *infinitive,* consists of the word *to* plus a verb form: *to read, to write, to sleep.* The infinitive functions as a noun or modifier:

To *ski* well requires concentration, patience, and courage.

Don has the desire to *succeed.*

Dorothy plays *to win.*

In the first sentence above, the infinitive *to ski* functions as a noun, as the subject of the verb *requires;* in the second, *to succeed* functions as a modifier of the noun *desire;* in the third, *to win* functions as a modifier of the verb *plays.*

A third type of verbal is the *gerund.* Like one form of the participle, the gerund ends in *ing,* but it functions as a noun, frequently as the subject or object of the verb, and as the object of a preposition:

Living well is the best revenge.

Coaches discourage *smoking.*

The fireman died from *inhaling* smoke.

In the first sentence, the gerund *living* is the subject of the verb *is;* in the second sentence, *smoking* is the object of the verb *discourage;* and in the third sentence, *inhaling* is the object of the preposition *from.*

To reiterate, *verbals are not verbs.* If the only verb form in a sentence is a verbal, the sentence is a fragment.

Fragments sometimes result from a lack of understanding of the fundamentals of sentence construction, sometimes from carelessness and haste. Though permissible in certain circumstances, as will be explained below, you should avoid them, for they are confusing and indicative of sloppy thought. As you read over your sentences, keep in mind what you have learned about verbals, subordinate or dependent clauses, and independent clauses.

In other words, never punctuate as complete sentences any of the following:

1. a group of words lacking a subject and/or a predicate, like "Along the beach near the jetty"

2. a dependent clause preceded by a relative pronoun, like "Who turned out to be my best friend"

3. a dependent clause preceded by a subordinating conjunction, like "Although I had learned a good deal"

4. an infinitive construction, like "To ensure the success of our venture"

5. a gerund construction, like "From a love of swimming"

6. a participial construction, like "Believing he had won the race"

The simplest way to eliminate fragments like these is to tie them to independent clauses: "Believing he had won the race, Leonard raised his arms and waved to the crowd." Or, as illustrated earlier, simply add a subject and/or a predicate to complete the thought of a phrase: "Dave jogged along the beach near the jetty." It is also helpful to read your sentences aloud, for the pitch of your voice drops more sharply at the end of a sentence than it does at the end of a phrase or subordinate clause. If your ear does not detect such a drop at the end of a word group you have punctuated as a sentence, your sentence may be a fragment.

The warning against the use of fragments is important advice, but since you will occasionally find them used by experienced writers, we should explain the circumstances that permit them. A nonsentence, for example, may be used for emphasis:

> Young writers are advised to be true to themselves, to be honest. They are told to respect their readers, to be clear. And they are told to be brief, not to waste their readers' time. *All good advice, but hard to follow.*

Or it may be used to present a number of separate, distinct impressions in a passage of description:

> The road curved to the left around the hill. The desert heat beat down on us after we abandoned the car and started walking north. *Nothing but cactus and sand. Drifting tumbleweed. Swirls of dust.*

And it is often used in dialogue or in answers to questions:

Where did you go with Karen? *To the dance.*

Should we be persuaded on such flimsy evidence as the testimony of a convicted perjurer? *Certainly not.*

A *fused sentence* results when two independent clauses come together with no punctuation between them.

> Many edible fish have unappetizing names the ratfish, the dog-fish, the gagfish, and the grunt are among them.

The lack of punctuation or a conjunction after *names* produces a confusing sentence. You should be able to detect fused sentences like this one by simply listening to your voice as you read your sentences aloud. When reading this one aloud, you will observe the pause and drop in voice after *names,* evidence of the end of one independent clause and so requiring a period, a semicolon, or a comma with a coordinating conjunction before the beginning of the next independent clause.

> Many edible fish have unappetizing names; the ratfish, the dog-fish, the gagfish, and the grunt are among them.

A *comma splice* results when two independent clauses are joined by only a comma:

> Parents who indulge their children's every whim don't help them, children need to know how to handle disappointment.

The comma after *them* does not clearly reveal the relationship between the two ideas, that each is a self-contained thought. A period, a semi-colon, or a coordinating conjunction is needed:

> Parents who indulge their children's every whim don't help them. Children need to know how to handle disappointment.

> Parents who indulge their children's every whim don't help them; children need to know how to handle disappointment.

> Parents who indulge their children's every whim don't help them, for children need to know how to handle disappointment.

When you are satisfied with the content and clarity of your sentences, examine them for *variety of length and pattern.* The length of your sentences should vary. A continuous use of short sentences will make your writing choppy and prevent a smooth flow of thought. On the other hand, a succession of long sentences often weakens the interest and tires the patience of readers as they seek to keep important ideas in mind and distinguish major from minor points.

Remember to vary the order of your sentences as well. Normally, the subject precedes the verb in a sentence.

> The English coffeehouse was a meeting place for men with similar interests in the eighteenth century.

But an essay composed entirely of sentences that begin with the subject is less interesting, and therefore less effective, than one that contains variety in sentence order. Experienced writers put something before the subject in almost half of their sentences.

One of the simplest ways to vary sentence order is to place a *prepositional phrase* before the subject. *Prepositions* are words like *in, on, around, above, below,* that connect a following noun or pronoun to the rest of the sentence. A preposition plus the following noun or pronoun is called a prepositional phrase: *over the river, through the woods, to Grandmother's house.* The sentence about the English coffeehouse would be more emphatic if the prepositional phrase ending the sentence were placed at the beginning.

> In the eigtheenth century the English coffeehouse was a meeting place for men with similar interests.

Adverbs modify the meaning of verbs, adjectives, or other adverbs. They commonly answer such questions as how, when, where, or why:

> The soldier strode *energetically* up the street.
>
> She seemed *somewhat* frightened.
>
> They scampered *very* quickly across the field.

An *adverb clause* is simply a dependent clause that functions as an adverb:

> Vivian worked on her needlepoint *while her husband dozed in his chair.*

Though they commonly appear after the subject, adverbs and adverbial clauses may also be placed before the subject for purposes of variety and emphasis:

> *Eventually,* Mother Nature punishes those who do not learn her lessons.
>
> *Again and again* we learn that human desires are infinite and insatiable.
>
> *Although he is irascible and moody,* he is a good public administrator.

And you may begin a sentence with a *verbal phrase:*

To increase circulation, some newspapers focus on crime, scandal, and corruption on the front page.

After winning his tennis match, Jim shook hands with his opponent.

Pushing her way through the crowd, Marilyn approached the speaker's platform.

The methods of altering sentence order described above are those most commonly used, but occasionally you may also want to begin with the *object of the verb* or with one or more *adjectives*. In most senences the object comes after the verb, as in the sentence "Frank detests self-pity." Placing the object before the subject makes the sentence more emphatic: "Self-pity Frank detests." Adjectives frequently occur between *a, an,* and *the* and a following noun or nouns:

The *beautiful, airy* patio provided a cool retreat from the heat of the sun.

Placing them at the very beginning of a sentence or between the subject and the verb, as in the following instances, often makes for a more interesting, graceful sentence:

Beautiful and *airy,* the patio provided a cool retreat from the heat of the sun.

The patio, *beautiful* and *airy,* provided a cool retreat from the heat of the sun.

To recapitulate, look over your sentences to make sure

1. that you have used at least some of the grammatical elements described above—prepositional phrase, verbal phrase, adjective, adverb, adverbial clause, direct object—to vary sentence order;
2. that you have also varied the length of your sentences.

Diction   As you read over your sentences, make certain also that the words and phrases you have used are accurate, specific, and vigorous. In particular, limit the use of *passive verbs* and eliminate *clichés* and *deadwood.*

Passive verbs, those which act upon the subject, often produce wordy sentences and colorless writing:

The assault on the fortress was considered risky by the general.

This sentence is more concise and pointed without the passive verb construction *was considered:*

The general considered the assault on the fortress risky.

Clichés are expressions so overused that they have lost whatever vigor and freshness they originally possessed. Instead of communicating thought they block it, for the reader becomes bored and irritated by the writer's inability or unwillingness to suit word to thought. Here is a brief list:

trials and tribulations	few and far between
in the last analysis	foot loose and fancy free
last but not least	in the same boat
sight for sore eyes	light as a feather

Deadwood is superfluous language. It is a roundabout language that blurs rather than focuses meaning, diffuses rather than concentrates thought. It often occurs in short phrases involving direct duplication: *the modern woman of today, a mistaken fallacy, in close proximity, utmost peak, a total of ten, an extra added attraction, a miserly attitude toward money.* The expressions *there is* and *there are* often produce wordy sentences. They can often be removed with a resultant gain in conciseness and emphasis.

There are many historians who believe that Lincoln was America's greatest President.

There is one thing that I know.

Revised:

Many historians believe that Lincoln was America's greatest President.

One thing I know.

And a final suggestion: check your spelling carefully, especially with a word that has the same sound as another word but a different spelling and meaning. Their differing meanings may provide a bit of unintended humor for your reader and embarrassment for you.

American military forces were stymied by the stealth of the Vietnamese gorillas.

In the 1930s Britain's Lord Keynes was hailed as the profit of a new era of responsible capitalism.

Harvey asked his boss to except his apologies for being late.

Mechanics, Spelling, Punctuation   Look over your mechanics, spelling, and punctuation to see to it that

1. sentences are correctly punctuated and paragraphs properly indented
2. words are correctly spelled, apostrophes are in the right place
3. verbs agree with their subjects and pronouns with their antecedents

Here is a revision of the first draft of the theme on Mr. Jones presented on pages 193–95. Note the changes that have been made in organization as well as language.

Firm, Fair, and Friendly

I liked most of my teachers in high school. They were, for the most part, friendly and competent, willing to help students who showed the faintest flicker of interest in their subjects. I liked them—but I don't remember them very well, except for Mr. Jones, my senior English teacher. He was a friendly, enthusiastic, sensitive man, who knew his subject and was determined that we would learn it and love it, too.

Mr. Jones was a tall, slender man in his mid forties with gray, thinning hair. Perched precariously on his nose, his glasses gave him a serious, studious look. But they didn't remain there long, for he was always taking them off and polishing them and putting them in his mouth when he mulled over a response to a student's question. When he walked into class, he was always carrying two or three books with strips of paper sticking out of them, marking passages he planned to read. I remember, too, the cardigan sweaters—he must have had a dozen of them—the neatly pressed slacks, Oxford loafers, the tie, always a tie. On rainy days he substituted a navy blue windbreaker for the sweater. He was no dandy, but he was always carefully dressed. He was definitely not the Levis-and-tennis-shoe type. But what I remember best was his smile. When he smiled, his whole face lit up; his eyes sparkled. His smile made you feel good, at ease, somehow reassured.

Yet though he was friendly and naturally at ease with people, he was a bit formal in class, and he could be stern on occasion. He never called us by our first names. It was always "Mr. Weaver" or "Miss Powers," never "Brad" nor "Marie." He obviously loved his work and liked his students, but he kept his distance. He never deliberately embarrassed a student in front of the class with a sarcastic remark, but he could communicate his displeasure all right. He'd look steadily at the offending student for a few seconds, his lips firming slightly shut. That was usually enough, but if it didn't work, he'd say something to the student in a lowered tone of voice. He didn't do this often. He didn't have to, because we liked and respected him and wanted to please him. And the reason was that he respected us and was serious about his subject and intent on our learning it and sharing his enthusiasm.

He *was* serious about his subject, his teaching, but not about himself. He could always come up with a witty comment or a joke to lighten the mood when necessary. He'd laugh harder than anyone else, to make sure we knew it was a joke, he said. His friendliness, his enthusiasm, his wit attracted students wherever he was. Students were always waiting to talk to him in his office, to ask his advice about college, to request a letter of recommendation, or just to chat a bit. I don't think he ever missed a football game, or the senior dance or picnic, for that matter. And wherever he was, in the stands or on the dance floor, students gathered around him.

Jonesy had personality, integrity, vitality—all of which made him popular, as I said; but what I liked most about him was that he was a fine teacher. Yes, he cared about students, but he cared more about teaching them his subject. And that meant homework, lots of it, and pop quizzes now and then to keep them current on the reading. He lectured occasionally, to provide background information whenever we moved on to a new literary period. After a brief glance at his notes, he'd begin to move around as he talked—to the blackboard, to the window, back to the lectern. But he preferred discussion, a Socratic dialogue. He'd write several questions on the board for the next day's discussion, and he'd expect you to be prepared to discuss them. He directed the discussion, but he didn't dominate it; for he was a good listener and made sure we all had a chance to respond, whether we wanted to or not. If he were pleased with a response, he'd nod his head and smile. Occasionally he'd read a student's essay, praising its good points and then winking at the writer as he passed it back. But he was tough-minded, too, as I suggested before. He really nailed you for sloppy work or inattention. When you got an A from him, you really felt good, for he wasn't an easy grader. We used to moan about his grading standards, usually to no avail, though he would change a grade if he thought he had been unfair.

We had many interesting discussions on Twain, Crane, and Dreiser, as I recall, but his favorite period was the 1920's. He loved the expatriates: Anderson, cummings, Hemingway, Fitzgerald. He was always bringing in books for us to read, but when he got to this period, he was a walking library. I think he'd read every book ever written by or about Hemingway and Fitzgerald, or about Paris in the twenties. He must have seen the films and slides he showed us about Paris and the expatriates dozens of times, but his enthusiasm never flagged when he discussed them. I can still see him, and hear him, reading and chuckling over some passage from *The Sun Also Rises* or *A Moveable Feast*. Yes, Jonesy was a fine teacher all right: he knew his subject, and he could teach it. But more than that, he made us love it, too. He made us want to continue to read it and study it on our own.

The first paragraph has been divided into two paragraphs. The original paragraph is rather long for an opening paragraph, and it provides no unifying idea for the essay. The last sentence of the revised opening paragraph, "He was a friendly, enthusiastic man . . . too," supplies a thesis. It introduces the reader to the traits of character and personality—friendliness, enthusiasm, sensitivity, forcefulness—that will be described in the essay. The introduction has also been changed: the original one-sentence lead-in is a bit prosaic, lackluster. The revised opening is sharper, shorter, more direct. And the friendly tone ("I liked most of my teachers in high school. . . .") is appropriate. It suggests an amiable, fair-minded individual whose impressions and judgments would not be biased. The second paragraph of the revised version includes all the details of the original first paragraph that concern the subject's appearance, focusing first on his head and eyes, then clothing, then back to his eyes, the feature the writer remembers most vividly and therefore logically placed at the end of this paragraph. The sentence "He was definitely not the Levis-and-tennis-shoe type" has been added after "He was no dandy" for emphasis.

The second paragraph of the first draft has also been divided into two paragraphs. It is a long paragraph, fifteen sentences; but, more important, it presents two ideas: his formal manner in class and his friendliness and wit. In the revised draft a paragraph is devoted to each idea. And the topic sentence of the paragraph dealing with his formality has been altered to mention his sternness since the paragraph discusses the latter idea as well as formality.

The last two paragraphs have not been changed. They describe Mr. Jones's classroom teaching and make up about half of the essay. This proportion is reasonable since the writer admired most this aspect of his subject. The conclusion has been changed: the final sentence "I can still see him" has been enlarged upon to reinforce the ideas mentioned in the thesis in the first paragraph and provide an effective conclusion to the theme.

Some changes have been made in word choice, but the diction remains essentially the same. And a few sentences have been reconstructed to begin with something other than the subject. In the first draft fifteen sentences vary the normal subject-verb pattern, in the second draft nineteen.

EXERCISE 22

A. The following paragraph communicates the writer's idea clearly and forcefully. Examine the opening and closing sentences in particular. What devices
does he use to arouse reader interest and to stress his main idea?

Is the sport of hunting, simply as such, a man-worthy thing or isn't it? Let it
be supposed that all hunters obey all regulations. Let it be supposed that no
whiskey bottle is dropped to pollute any glen or dingle, no fence is broken, no
fawn is shot, no forest is set afire, no robins are massacred in mistake for
pheasants and no deer-hunters in mistake for porcupines (or possible chipmunks), and no meditative philosopher, out to enjoy the loveliness of autumn,
is ever plugged through the pericardium. The question persists: Is it a spectacle
of manhood (which is to say of our distinctive humanness), when on a bracing
morning we look out upon the autumn, draw an exhilarating breath, and cry
"What a glorious day! How golden is the light of the sun, how merry the
caperings of creatures; *Gloria in excelsis Deo!* I will go out and kill something"?
[From Alan Devoe, "On Hunting," *American Mercury,* February 1951.]

B. The following essay by George F. Will is about fishing for the rainbow trout.
The author's tone blends humor with serious, though not solemn, reflection. Read the composition twice, and on the second reading observe the
devices used to connect the paragraphs, in particular the repetition of key
words, transitional expressions, and pronoun reference. Are the opening
and closing paragraphs effective? If so, why? What ideas introduced in the
opening paragraph are developed in the body of the essay? The writer's
thesis concerns fishing and children. Comment. As mentioned, the tone
blends humor with reflection. At what point in the essay does the tone
become more serious?

Getting a Hook Into the Meaning of Life

The scene was sublime. The occasion was, occasionally, ridiculous. It was at
Maroon Lake, a kind of reflecting pool for the twin peaks of the mountains
known as the Maroon Bells and known to millions through one of Ansel Adams'
most famous photographs. The hills were alive with the sound of children in
pursuit of the elusive rainbow trout.

The Will boys, now 9 and 7, caught their first fish (bluegills) a few years ago
at Eric Sevareid's pond in rural Virginia. They caught them the way first fish
ought to be caught, with bamboo poles and worms.

But as Eric, a passionate fisherman, would be the first to insist, there are fish
and then there are trout, and there is fishing and then there is fishing with
flies. A mature rainbow, dancing its tail on the surface of the water to express
the prejudice of its species against hooks in the mouth, is an almost perfect
embodiment of the components of life: earth, air, fire and water.

The Will boys were across the lake when my soulmate from Denver, Michael
Shaffer, 6, made his first cast of the morning and instantly hooked something

217

big. From Michael's father came, instantly, four carefully measured but heartfelt words—a plea, not advice—"DON'T REEL IT IN!" The "it" was Michael's father, in whose thigh the fly was implanted.

Michael's father has a lawyer's job but a mountain man's soul, so he fished all morning with the fly in his thigh. Then we made our regular stop at one of Aspen's laid-back doctors, who removed part of the hook and suggested that Michael's father think of the rest of the hook as shrapnel.

Fishing with the children is more dangerous to parents than to fish, but there is a bigger danger. It is that too many people will reach adulthood without experiencing the instruction of time spent with nature. Such time is important to the development of something without which we cannot live well: piety.

"Piety," says James M. Gustafson of the University of Chicago Divinity School, "is a fundamental stance toward what is given in the world and human life: It is an attitude or disposition of respect, awe and even devotion that is evoked by human experience of dependence on powers we do not create and cannot fully master."

By piety, Gustafson means neither piousness (pretentious display of religiosity) nor pietism (the religious movement that strives to engender a high pitch of emotion) nor the "fleeting emotions evoked by the glory of a sunset over New Mexican mesas."

Rather, he means "a profound sense of dependence that comes with the recognition that, for all our human achievements, the world was brought into being by powers long before the emergence of our species; that the continuation of life relies upon powers that are not fully in human control, and that the destiny of the universe is not in human hands."

Most of us, most of the time, lead lives that narrow our minds to a small gauge appropriate to our daily purposes. But, mysteriously, it is somehow enlarging to focus all one's being on the task of tricking a trout into striking a tiny bit of metal and feather and thread.

Fishing is a way of turning one's back on "the world"—that being, as Charles Dickens said, "a conventional phrase which signifieth all the rascals in it."

Fishing in the shadow of great mountains and in running water is a sweet reminder that man is but a shadow and that nations are but bubbles on the river of time. Fishing for trout in clear water is among life's most frustrating experiences. You can see your fly, and can see trout following your fly and disdainfully curling their lips at it.

Fishing is especially good for the unformed souls of children, who are never too young to learn what trout-fishing teaches—the lesson that there is generally a considerable gap between one's inclinations and the world's willingness to see them realized.

Trout are much like children. They are often willful, capricious and maddeningly disinclined to eat what is put in front of them. [From George F. Will, "Getting A Hook Into the Meaning of Life," *Los Angeles Times*, August 27, 1981.]

C. Construct three effective opening sentences for each of the following topics. Use any of the methods illustrated on pages 198–200 or any of your own invention.

1. professional boxing—should it be banned?

    a. _____

        _____

    b. _____

        _____

    c. _____

        _____

2. the Olympic Games—sport or spectacle?

    a. _____

        _____

    b. _____

        _____

    c. _____

        _____

3. a remembered pet

    a. _____

        _____

    b. _____

        _____

    c. _____

        _____

D. Find three examples of good concluding sentences in recent magazine or newspaper articles, and write them in the appropriate spaces below. Be prepared to tell why you think the conclusion is successful.

1. SUBJECT MATTER _____

Concluding Sentence _____

_____

_____

2. SUBJECT MATTER _____

Concluding Sentence _____

_____

_____

3. SUBJECT MATTER _____

Concluding Sentence _____

_____

_____

E. The paragraph below illustrates a monotony of sentence pattern, an excess of deadwood, and an occasional poor choice of words. Revise it by varying sentence order, eliminating the deadwood, and improving word choice where warranted. Some of the short sentences should also be joined to provide a smoother transition of thought.

The prison has been considered a place for rehabilitation and punishment of the criminal for the past 200 years in America. Today, however, there are many persons who are connected with the criminal justice system—lawyers, judges, wardens, criminologists, and even convicts themselves—who are now beginning to believe that rehabilitation in correctional institutions doesn't work. The United States spends more than $1 billion each year to confine and rehabilitate criminals. Over 65 percent of those released are returned to prison within five years. Inmates have been encouraged to study while in prison and learn a trade that will sustain them when they get out. Parole boards commonly reduce length of confinement for prisoners who accept therapy and job training. Many inmates have undertaken such treatment and training, wishing to reduce their time in prison. Many criminals have thus been released earlier than warranted as a result. A number of criminologists still favor rehabilitation. They think it should not reduce sentences so as to eliminate fakirs who pretend interest in order to impress prison officials with their change in outlook. The growing feeling among prison professionals today is that the primary function of a penal system is to punish the criminal by incarceration and to protect society. In the last analysis, it is the certainty of punishment, not the acquisition of vocational skills, that will prevent criminals from preying upon society.

F.   Revise the draft of the paper you prepared for Exercise 21.

9. PREPARING THE FINAL COPY

Before you prepare your final copy, read your essay aloud to yourself (or to a friend) to test once more its clarity, unity, and coherence, and to catch any omission of words or punctuation errors. Examine your title in this reading also. Is it brief, accurate, and consistent with the tone of the paper? Will it catch the reader's attention and stimulate interest? Remember that the title is not part of the composition itself. As mentioned earlier, the first sentence of the essay should not depend on the title for its meaning.

If possible, type your final copy on $8\frac{1}{2} \times 11$-inch unlined white paper. Double space so that your instructor can insert comments between the lines when necessary. Double spacing also makes for easier reading. If you must write your final copy, use ink and write on only one side of the paper. The other side may be required for later revisions when your theme is returned to you. Next, space the body of your composition evenly on the page with suitable margins on each side and at the top and bottom. Center your title and place it a few spaces above the first sentence of your text. Capitalize the first word and all other words in the title except articles, conjunctions, and short prepositions. Number your pages and endorse your paper in the manner prescribed by your instructor. The endorsement usually includes your name, the title of your paper, and the date.

EXERCISE 23

Turn in a final copy of the theme you revised for Exercise 22F.

SUMMARY

Like the paragraph, the theme requires careful attention to unity, development, coherence, and emphasis. Because of its increased length and complexity, however, you must plan its construction in greater detail. To help you with this planning, we have suggested the following steps:

1. Limit your topic in accordance with the length of your paper and the interests and background of your reader.

2. Think through your subject.

3. Gather and organize your material; group major and minor ideas, and arrange them in a logical sequence to effect your purpose.

4. Outline your theme. For a short paper, especially one written in class, a rough outline will suffice. For a longer paper the formal outline is almost essential.

5. Write your first draft as rapidly as possible, using your outline as a guide. Put the first draft aside for a few hours, and do not think about it.

6. After you have been away from your first draft for awhile, revise it, giving close scrutiny to content and organization as well as to mechanics. In particular, check opening and closing sentences and the continuity of thought between paragraphs.

7. Prepare a final copy, observing the conventions for preparing a manuscript prescribed by your instructor.

CHAPTER SIX

ARGUMENTATION

The preceding chapters have concentrated on exposition, the kind of writing that explains and clarifies. At times, however, you will want to persuade your reader of the soundness of a judgment, to convince him or her of the appropriateness of a course of action. On such occasions you will have need of the skills of *argumentation*. Exposition and argumentation are not, to be sure, mutually exclusive categories. Writers of expository essays hope to persuade the reader that their explanations are informative and reasonable. The characteristics of good exposition—unity, adequate development, coherence—apply as well to argumentation. But in writing devoted to argument, writers make clear the logic behind the positions they take. They spell out the logical steps that led them to their conclusions. Specific knowledge of the processes of logical reasoning will help you to think more clearly, to construct logical arguments, and to follow and analyze arguments of other writers and speakers. Combined with facility in the arts of persuasion, it will make your writing more thoughtful and convincing.

Simply defined, argumentation is a process of reasoning in which a coherent series of facts and judgments is arranged to establish a conclusion. A discussion of argumentation can be complex, for there are many ways of arranging these facts and judgments. However, the discussion that follows will be a simple one, for what is important here is not that you gain a precise knowledge of the variety and complexity of argumentation, but rather that you understand the basic pattern of all arguments and, more important, that you learn to use sound, logical arguments in your own writing.

Any argument, however complex, expresses a relationship between one assertion and another. The first assertion serves as the reason for the second. For example, if you say "Professor Sanderson's exams are difficult. Therefore, I'll have to study hard this weekend," you are making an argument. The second statment is a conclusion based on the first statement.

The first part of an argument may consist of a series of statements:

In the presidential election of 1976, 56.5 percent of those Americans eligible to vote actually voted. In the election of 1980, the percentage was 54. And in 1984 it was 53. As these statistics reveal, a sizable segment of the American electorate does not take its voting privilege seriously.

In this example, the *conclusion*, the last sentence, follows a series of factual statements. This kind of argument, which proceeds from a study of particulars to the making of a generalization or hypothesis based on those particulars, is called an *inductive argument;* and the supporting particulars that precede the conclusion are called the *evidence*.

The other basic form of argument is called *deduction*. The *deductive argument* has more than one form. A common type, the *categorical syllogism*, begins with a general statement and closes with a particular statement. The supporting reasons in this type of argument are called the *premises*. In the following categorical syllogism the premises provide the basis for the conclusion:

PREMISES   All Americans are freedom-loving.
            George is an American.
CONCLUSION George is freedom-loving.

THE INDUCTIVE ARGUMENT

As mentioned above, the inductive argument has two forms: one concluding with a *generalization*, the other with a *hypothesis*. In an inductive argument ending in a generalization, the generalization makes a statement about a class or group of things or people, and the evidence consists of statements about individual members of that class. The inductive argument about American voters (see above) is of this type. The evidence consists of three statements, each one a particular factual observation about members of the same class, American voters. And the conclusion, ". . . the American electorate does not take its voting privilege seriously," is a more general statement, covering more ground than any of the particular facts that preceded it. This conclusion is an inference about American voters' attitude toward voting; the evidence consists of observations about their behavior at the polls in 1976, 1980, and 1984.

Here is another example:

EVIDENCE   1. Professor Rodriguez is witty and perceptive.
            2. Professor Armstrong is witty and perceptive.
            3. Professor Weiss is witty and perceptive.
CONCLUSION All professors are witty and perceptive.

The conclusion of an inductive argument is a hypothesis when it deals not with a class but with an individual object or situation. In this case the hypothesis attempts to account for the set of facts that preceded it.

EVIDENCE
1. The Hawkins' front lawn across the street is getting long.
2. It is getting brown in spots.
3. Newspapers have been accumulating on the front porch.
4. The drapes have been pulled across the living room windows.
5. Today is August 15.

CONCLUSION   The Hawkins are on vacation.

The conclusion of this argument does not concern a class of things, but rather one particular situation. It is not a generalization, but an inference that attempts to account for the five preceding observations. Each item of the evidence is not a member of a class or group mentioned in the conclusion, as is true of the previous arguments about professors and American voters, but is a description of a different aspect of the appearance of a house on a summer day.

To sum up then, an inductive argument begins with a look at the evidence and ends with a conclusion based on that evidence. It moves from the particular to the general, from fact to conclusion. The distinguishing quality of the inductive argument, however, the characteristic that differentiates it from the deductive argument, is not this movement, but the degree of certainty of the conclusion. The conclusion of an inductive argument *does not necessarily follow* from the evidence. The concluding hypothesis or generalization is only a probability: other conclusions are possible. The conclusion that American voters do not take their voting seriously, because of their failure to turn out in great numbers on three consecutive national elections, may be erroneous. The voters may have been essentially satisfied with the candidates running for election at the time and did not vote because of general contentment rather than indifference. And another hypothesis is possible to explain the appearance of the Hawkins' house—the family could be away on an emergency visit to a disabled relative.

Evaluating the Evidence of an Inductive Argument

The conclusion of an inductive argument will be sound if there is a logical connection between the evidence and the conclusion. If the connection is missing, the conclusion will not be valid even though it may satisfy the person making the argument. In the following discussion we will examine several general principles that will help you to determine whether the arguments you construct or encounter are sound.

Supporting a Generalization

The conclusion that any researcher draws from the study of specific cases is necessarily tentative. As you would expect, a generalization based on many samples is more reliable than one based on few. A large sampling, however, does not guarantee a sound generalization. The sampling must be representative as well. For example, to ensure the reliability of his conclusions regarding the popularity of political figures, Dr. Gallup, as well as other professional pollsters, makes certain to poll a sufficient number of voters from a broad cross section of American life. To insure the soundness of the generalizations you use, follow this important principle:

1.   Support your generalizations firmly with an *adequate, representative*, and *relevant* sampling of evidence.

The generalization on page 228 that all professors are witty and perceptive is clearly not justified by the evidence presented. More than three professors must be observed before a valid generalization about the wit and perceptivity of all professors can be made. A more accurate generalization would result if a more specific poll of student opinion of professorial wit and perceptivity were conducted. A professional pollster such as Dr. Gallup would have to poll at least several hundred students on campuses throughout the country before reaching a conclusion. But even this kind of poll would not support the original conclusion that *all* professors are witty and perceptive. It might reveal, however, that 34.6 percent, or 41.3 percent, or 61.7 percent, or some other proportion of the group, are witty and perceptive.

But the point here is not that you should generalize about a group of people or any group of objects only if you have made a scientific study of the subject. We all live and work by generalizations, and common-sense generalizations based on previous experience are ordinarily trustworthy in everyday life. Persons who have enjoyed reliable service from automobiles manufactured by one company will likely consider the same make of automobile when they are ready to purchase a new one. Investors consistently disappointed by the performance of stock they have purchased on the advice of a broker are not likely to continue following that advice. Nonetheless, though scientific precision is not essential in formulating useful generalizations, a generalization based on many samples is obviously more dependable than one based on just a few.

The following paragraph is interesting and lively. The evidence is relevant, but there is not enough of it, and what there is, is not sufficiently representative to justify the sweeping generalization in the opening sentence.

> You can't trust politicians. Whenever I receive a progress report in the mail from Assemblyman Parker, I wince. During his campaign he lambasted his incumbent opponent for refusing to support legislation restricting campaign contributions. Yet he is now under investigation for diverting money from his campaign funds to redecorate his summer cottage at Blue Lake. It's just as bad at City Hall. Councilman Bertoli has been extolled for years as the pride of our fair city, the symbol of clean, honest, responsible government. But according to yesterday's paper he has been indicted by the Grand Jury for soliciting a bribe from a builder whose proposal to construct a condominium at Third and Fairhaven had been rejected by the Council. And then, of course, there's Watergate.

Inexperienced writers who base their conclusions on atypical evidence frequently do so through ignorance of the complexity of their subjects. However, well-informed, experienced writers who select only those facts that support their positions and ignore others that do not are guilty of *stacking the cards*. Writers who stack the cards may cite an impressive body of facts and maintain a fairly objective tone, yet create a false impression of their subjects in the reader's mind because of the facts that they have omitted. Consider, for instance, this argument concerning the desirability of abandoning nuclear power as a source of energy.

> Although opponents of nuclear power have become more militant in recent years, Americans simply cannot do without nuclear energy at this time. To begin with, no truly satisfactory alternative power source is available. America has abundant supplies of coal, but it is hazardous to mine. Thousands of miners have lost their lives, and more will die in the future as demand for coal continues. But coal is not only hazardous to mine, it is hazardous to burn as well, for coal plants emit dangerous elements into the atmosphere. Some of them combine with other elements in the air to produce acid rain; some are radioactive and can cause premature deaths. Studies comparing the health hazards of coal plants and nuclear plants, for example, reveal coal plants to be 100 times as dangerous in causing such deaths.[1] Solar energy is still in its infancy, and it will be

[1] George F. Will, "As I Was Saying," *Newsweek,* April 16, 1979, p. 100.

many years, perhaps decades, before it can make a serious dent in America's energy needs. Though oil shale is abundant, the cost of converting it to oil is high and the ecological problems formidable. At this time it does not represent a viable option. And, finally, the increase in current oil consumption that would result if nuclear energy were abandoned would present serious problems. For one thing, the supply of oil is limited, and as world demand grows in the years ahead, it will become much more expensive and less available. Secondly, as a National Academy of Science study reveals, the cumulative effect of burning fossil fuel could produce disastrous climatic changes that would seriously disrupt agriculture throughout the world.

And other arguments apply. Nuclear power is a reasonably safe, assured, inexpensive means of providing energy. To date no one has been killed by a nuclear power plant failure, a rather remarkable record for a new industry. Airplane crashes, train wrecks, and automobile accidents, on the other hand, have killed hundreds of thousands. Automobiles alone account for about 45,000 deaths each year. Moreover, the United States has adequate supplies of nuclear fuel within its borders, supplies that are not apt to be disrupted by unfriendly foreign governments. And electricity generated by nuclear plants is reasonably priced. According to a recent analysis of United States electrical generating costs, electricity produced by nuclear plants cost 11.4 mills per kilowatt-hour, by coal-fired plants 14.71 mills, and by oil-fired plants 32.73 mills.[2] To sum up, nuclear power should not be abandoned at this time, because alternative choices are simply not that attractive.

Although the writer presents several important and relevant facts and judgments to bolster his contention that nuclear power should not be abandoned, his presentation is one-sided. He does not, for example, consider the problem of the disposal of nuclear wastes, a serious matter since these wastes will continue to be radioactive for thousands of years. And although it is true that no one has yet been killed by a nuclear power plant failure, the possibility of widespread death and destruction from such a failure is, nonetheless, uncomfortably real. The writer's comment on the relative reasonableness of the current cost of producing nuclear power is valid, but he does not mention the fact that future costs are likely to be much higher because of construction delays and the rapidly escalating costs of building new nuclear power plants. A more reliable judgment of the need for nuclear energy would consider

[2] Robert L. Loftness, *Energy Handbook,* Van Nostrand, 1978, p. 605.

facts and judgments on both sides of the question. In your own attempts at persuasive writing, be sure that you have not omitted important facts that do not support your argument. If you have, revise your paper to present a more balanced view. A balanced view may not be as bold or dramatic as a one-sided view, but it is more effective with informed readers.

2. Back up your generalizations with *accurate, verifiable* evidence.

The following paragraph illustrates a common failing in the writing of persons who feel so strongly about an issue that they fail to provide any factual detail to anchor their generalizations.

Americans need not worry about the gloomy predictions of pessimists that disaster awaits us because of population growth and pollution. For example, reports indicate that city air is getting cleaner, not dirtier. One hundred years ago the air over large eastern cities was filled with smoke so thick it could be cut with a knife. Yet today coal smoke has been largely eliminated. Our rivers, lakes, and oceans may not be as pure as they once were, but the amount of water pollution has been grossly exaggerated. Alarmists point to mercury contamination of fish caused by industrial wastes as proof of contamination; yet, as scientists know, the amount of mercury in the oceans today is not significantly higher than it was fifty years ago. Doom sayers predict that world population growth represents a time bomb that will explode and destroy us if population is not curtailed. But according to government reports, the birth rate in the United States has been dropping since 1955. Moreover, demographic experts believe that if the trend is not reversed, the United States will be faced with a serious shortage of people. An objective assessment of these facts invalidates the assumption that pollution and population growth pose a serious threat to the American people.

This paragraph appears to contain a good deal of factual information to support its thesis, but a careful reading reveals that the evidence is tenuous and vague, incapable of justifying the assertion made in the first sentence. Such phrases as "reports indicate," "as scientists know," "according to government reports," and "demographic experts believe" purport to introduce concrete, factual detail. But what specific reports contain information of the quality of city air? What scientists say that mercury contamination of the oceans has not increased? And what demographic experts believe that population growth is not a serious problem? Unless such particulars are supplied, thoughtful readers are justified in withholding their assent to the writer's conclusion.

3.   Make certain that the *opinions or testimony* of authorities you use to buttress your arguments are those of a qualified observer.

A "qualified observer" is one who is competent in his or her field and able to report observations accurately and objectively. We all tend to believe in those who share our opinions and to seek out evidence that confirms these opinions, but it is a tendency that can be fatal to persuasive writing—and to truth. The president of a tobacco company is hardly an unbiased source of information on the health hazards of cigarettes. A chief of police may not be qualified to determine satisfactorily the difference between pornography and literary art. And a retired physicist, however famous for research done in the past, may not be able to speak authoritatively on recent scientific developments.

The preceding discussion has emphasized the need to supply sufficient evidence for generalizations. We have said that the evidence must not be one-sided, that it should be grounded in fact, and that if "experts" are quoted, they must be legitimate authorities. When evidence supporting generalizations meets these tests, a thoughtful reader is likely to consider them carefully.

Common Inductive Fallacies

A *fallacy* is an error in reasoning. It refers to an argument that violates a principle of logical inference. In the following discussion we will examine briefly a few common types of faulty induction.

A writer who makes a *hasty generalization* fails to supply enough evidence to support the generalization. The writer "jumps to a conclusion." The author of the paragraph on politicians (p. 231) is guilty of this error.

A *sweeping generalization* results when the writer provides no evidence at all to support an assertion: "Economists know that government spending simply produces inflation." Modified, this statement is much more defensible: "Many economists fear that continued high levels of deficit government spending will produce a dangerous increase in inflation." The point is not to avoid generalizations for fear they might be exaggerated, but to make certain your generalizations are justified by the supporting evidence. Reread your papers carefully, therefore, and avoid extravagant, unsupported statements.

No one can say precisely how much evidence is needed to produce a reliable generalization, but common sense would suggest these simple precautions:

1. Do not generalize too quickly.

2. Modify sweeping generalizations, the generalization that covers all the members of a class. Use such words as *all, every, no one, always, never, average, typical,* and the like, cautiously.

3. Consult the judgments of recognized authorities when you are uncertain about the adequacy or accuracy of your own data and opinions.

4. To measure the soundness of your evidence supporting a generalization, ask yourself whether that generalization has proven a reliable basis for action over a period of time. Students entering college soon discover that success in their studies demands hard work, self-discipline, and perseverance. Such a generalization is clearly dependable. It has been proven true, painfully true, for many generations of students in the past.

A second common fallacy is the generalization based on *deceptive statistics.* Generalizations drawn from statistical data need to be examined carefully because statistics can be manipulated to yield a variety of interpretations. For example, if a man increases his contribution to a charitable organization from five dollars to ten dollars a year, he can legitimately claim to have increased his contribution 100 percent, an impressive figure to one not aware of the actual amount involved. Or suppose that a report of the income of individuals working in a small business firm indicates that the average annual salary of the employees is $22,000. This information by itself might lead you to the conclusion that these employees were well paid and that the owners of the firm were justified in refusing to consider salary increases. Upon closer examination, however, you discover that, of the ten persons working in the firm, five earn $10,000 annually, three $15,000, one $25,000, and one $100,000. The average annual salary of this group is in fact $22,000, but for most people *average* connotes *typical;* yet only two of the ten persons actually earns $22,000 or more in a year. The typical salary in this case would be closer to $12,000 than $22,000. Be careful, then, when you use statistics to establish or reinforce a generalization. If one figure in a set of figures is considerably larger or smaller than the others (for example, the $100,000 salary in the case cited above), taking an average of them will distort their relationship. In such cases it would be more informative to report the *median* value (the middle figure in an odd number of figures) or the *mode* value (the figure that appears most frequently). In short, use statistics as honestly and informatively as you can, lest your reader suspect that you have manipulated them to suit your purpose.

The *post hoc fallacy*, a third type of faulty induction, occurs when we assert that one event caused another because it preceded it. If one thing occurs before another, it does not *necessarily* cause the latter. This kind of inference is known technically as the *post hoc, ergo propter hoc fallacy* ("after this, therefore because of this"), or more simply, the post hoc fallacy. That one political administration was in office when war broke out, for example, does not mean that that administration brought on the war. The fact that the number of capital crimes committed in a state decreased the year after capital punishment was abolished does not prove that the change in punishment caused this decrease.

It frequently happens, of course, that one event *is* the cause of another. When a person collapses after being struck a blow on the head, it is fairly clear that the first event, the blow, caused the second, the collapse. But establishing a causal relation between two events is often more difficult. It is especially difficult in the field of economics. Here is an example:

> The recent tax cut passed by Congress was obviously warranted. The American economy was given the shot in the arm it needed. Retail sales and business profits have gone up, the rate of unemployment has gone down, and our foreign trade has expanded.

To prove that the tax cut specifically caused the improvement in retail sales, business profits, and foreign trade would necessitate the examination of a considerable body of facts. An economist, or an experienced reader, would want to know, for example, the effect of seasonal variation in consumer and government spending, the business community's confidence in the economy, and the actions of foreign governments in reducing tariffs before accepting such an explanation.

One of the methods of paragraph development presented in Chapter Two was the *analogy*, a comparison of two things that are unlike but that have similar attributes. Analogy is frequently used as evidence to support an argument.

> Recently *The New York Times* reported an address by Supreme Court Justice Powell in which he deplored the deterioration of the nation's moral fiber and cited, as an example, the open selling of student themes and term papers to college and university undergraduates.
>
> It seemed to me a rather feeble for instance, and one which

a politician (and let's not pretend the Supreme Court isn't a political as well as a judicial body) might well eschew. If it's all right for the President of the United States to hire people to write his speeches on which the fate of nations may rest, why isn't it equally acceptable for a college student to hire someone to write his term papers, on which nobody's fate rests but his own! [From Ed Zern, "Exit Laughing," *Field and Stream*, December 1972, p. 160.]

The argument contained in this passage is a *false analogy,* another common inductive fallacy. Its comparison of the selling of term papers to college students with the President's hiring of speech writers overlooks an important difference between these two practices. The awesome responsibilities and complex, time-consuming duties that burden a President of the United States make it impossible for him to write every speech he gives and, therefore, justify the employment of speech writers. The public understands and accepts the practice. A college student is not so burdened. Moreover, the obvious fraudulence of falsifying the authorship of term papers and the prohibition against it are clearly understood and accepted by most college students.

This example illustrates an important weakness in arguing by analogy; an analogy frequently breaks down by ignoring basic differences in the two things being compared. When you use analogy to buttress an argument, therefore, keep its limitations in mind. It can clarify a point made in an argument, but it cannot settle the argument.

EXERCISE 24

A. Factual information and the testimony of experts could be used to support the following generalizations. In the blanks below each statement list the kinds of factual information you could use and an authority you might consult.

EXAMPLE   Americans have become more health conscious.

1. statistics on increase in number of health food stores, joggers, purchases of physical fitness equipment and clothing; on decrease of smokers; popularity of diet books, and so on
2. emphasis on physical fitness of executives in American business and industry today as contrasted with situation in the past
3. opinions of leaders of American Medical Association, physical fitness experts, book publishers

1. During periods of economic stagnation, black teenagers in the cities suffer.

————————————————————————————

————————————————————————————

————————————————————————————

2. Jogging has become an increasingly popular activity in the United States in the past few years.

————————————————————————————

————————————————————————————

————————————————————————————

3. Terrorism remains a serious problem for governments and law enforcement agencies throughout the world.

————————————————————————————

————————————————————————————

————————————————————————————

4. Home ownership for families with modest incomes has become increasingly difficult in the 1980s.

————————————————————————————

————————————————————————————

————————————————————————————

5. College students are becoming more vocationally oriented in their selection of courses and majors.

    _____

    _____

    _____

B. Classify the following arguments as inductive or deductive.

1. Roger Reynolds is calm under pressure, undemonstrative, and selfassured. Such behavior is not surprising; Roger is English. _____

2. Each summer David Barkesdale spends two weeks hiking in the Sierras with his friend Brendon. Each spring and fall he goes fishing off the coast of Baja California at Cabo San Lucas. And once or twice a month he goes up to his cabin in the San Bernardino mountains. David obviously loves the outdoors. _____

3. Oil company stocks have lost value on the New York Stock Exchange lately. The price of gasoline in the United States has held steady or dropped slightly for the past year. The number of service stations has declined dramatically throughout the United States in recent years. And the OPEC nations have had to cut back oil production because of a drop in world demand. It is clear that the oil industry is not flourishing as well as it did a decade ago. _____

4. Madeline Shadbolt is financially independent. She has a house on Balboa Island and spends her summers in Europe. Moreover, she wears designer clothers, dines at the best French restaurants, and drives a new BMW 633. She is, obviously, a financially successful woman. _____

5. The Civil Liberties Union opposes school prayer. They must be atheists.

    _____

C. Scale down the following sweeping generalizations.

    EXAMPLE   Young people today have abandoned morality.

    REVISED   A higher percentage of young people today are living together before, or instead of, getting married than was true a generation ago.

1. Television commercials are stupid and tasteless.

    REVISED _____

    _____

2. Jews are an exceptionally gifted people.

   REVISED _____

   _____

3. Americans worship youth.

   REVISED _____

   _____

4. Government sponsored welfare programs in the United States have failed.

   REVISED _____

   _____   _____

5. American parents are too permissive in rearing their children.

   REVISED _____

   _____

D. Weaknesses in inductive arguments discussed in the preceding pages include the following:

   1. sampling of evidence too selective
   2. lack of sufficient evidence
   3. incompetent or biased authority
   4. generalization based on deceptive statistics
   5. hasty or sweeping generalization
   6. post hoc fallacy
   7. false analogy

Each of the following arguments demonstrates one or more of these weaknesses, though usually one type predominates. Identify these weaknesses by placing one or more of the numbers in this list after the argument.

1. The school board's plan to scale down interscholastic athletic programs to cope with reduced tax income was opposed by all ten speakers at the board meeting last night. The speakers, all members of the Sunday Morning Quarterback Club, vociferously opposed any reduction in financial support. It is clear that interscholastic athletic programs are very popular in River City. _____

2. Wesley Wainright—a successful, highly respected attorney—met Daphne Sodbury in the fall of 1978 at an alumni party. He began to date her thereafter and continued to do so for the next five years. In January

1984, she inherited $630,000 from her favorite aunt. In June 1984, Wesley and Daphne were married. Apparently Wesley could no longer resist Daphne's charms when they were reinforced by $630,000.   ———

3. I don't see why Professor Moriarity won't let us use our books on his history exams. Doctors examine x-rays of their patients before they operate, and lawyers read over their notes before they address the jury.   ———

4. Who says skiing is a healthful, exciting sport? The last two times I've skied I broke my skis each time after hitting a tree. The second time I also banged my head on a rock and was hospitalized for ten days.   ———

5. Carter Ravenal, the owner of Holiday Travel Tours, returned from a two-week trip to the Far East. Accompanied by an interpreter, he spoke with several Japanese businessmen and enjoyed his trip immensely. He was particularly impressed with the Japanese culture. In his monthly newsletter he spoke highly of the Japanese and stated that, in his opinion, Japanese automobile exports represent no real threat to the American automobile industry.   ———

6. According to Samuel Johnson, English lexicographer and writer, "A woman preaching is like a dog walking on its hind legs. It is not done well, but you are surprised to find it done at all."   ———

7. Uncle Schuyler is more generous than my Uncle Dudley. In 1980 Uncle Schuyler increased his contributions to charity by 50 percent, whereas Uncle Dudley didn't increase his at all.   ———

8. Montgomery Fitzgerald, director of a local bank in Arroyo Seco, has been accused of laundering drug money for the Mafia. Mr. Fitzgerald, however, is clearly innocent of such charges. Two of his associates at the bank testified without reservation about his honesty and good character.   ———

9. The news media were definitely biased in their coverage of the 1980 presidential campaign. Slanted television reporting, distorted newspaper reporting, and prejudicial radio news commentary caused President Carter's defeat.   ———

10. In 1938 Leslie Harper was elected mayor of the city of Mesa Grande, Nevada. In his campaign speeches he promised to reduce unemployment, which at that

time was running about 17 percent. He won the election. In 1942 he ran for a second term. In the latter campaign he argued that he should be reelected because he had reduced unemployment to 3 percent since his election in 1938. Obviously, he deserved another term as mayor.

———————

E. Provide at least two hypotheses to explain the set of circumstances narrated below. What additional facts would make one of them more credible?

Monty Sayers, basketball coach of Western State University, had two very successful seasons in his first two years as coach. His star guards, Mike Garcia and Larry Harper, were selected as the two best guards in their league. Because of his coaching success, he urged the student athletic council to approve an emergency request for funds so that he could attend a coaching seminar at Northeastern University. The council approved his request, though the vice-president of the council, Sydney Walton, objected. That spring Sayers attended the seminar at Northeastern, his alma mater, where he was an All-American basketball player. On returning to Western, Sayers informed the athletic director and the president of the college that he would be leaving Western to become head basketball coach at Northeastern University in the fall. In his sports column in the college paper, the sports page editor revealed that Garcia and Harper had applied for admission to Northeastern University four weeks before Sayers had appeared before the student athletic council.

F. Read the following selections carefully and evaluate the logic used in each. In the space provided after each passage identify the main weaknesses in the arguments advanced.

1. Some Congressmen, editorial writers, and defense analysts have been saying that the United States must reinstate the draft to demonstrate American resolve against Soviet expansionism. This argument, however, is a smoke screen put up by American militarists who simply want to reassert their influence in American foreign policy. I've talked to several of my fraternity brothers, and we agree that the draft is not needed. We think the voluntary system is adequate to provide soldiers and sailors for defense if we just increase their pay. With all the modern equipment and weapons in the American arsenal, there is no real need for more men. Reestablishing the draft would increase world tensions. It would be like throwing a lighted match onto a pile of gunpowder. Any time you conscript young men to strengthen an army, generals will use it. Look at Hitler.

——————————————————————————————

——————————————————————————————

——————————————————————————————

2. Reasons for the present decline of morals among our young people are not hard to find. It is not surprising that pornographic movie houses, dirty book stores, lewd television programs, and sex crimes have increased dramatically in recent years. What can you expect when high-school students are allowed to read obscene modern novels in their English classes and enroll in sex education courses? Oh, I know that English teachers and librarians claim that no one was ever morally corrupted or committed a crime because he read a book; but every police officer in the country knows how common it is to find stacks of pornographic books and dirty pictures among the possessions of minors picked up for sex offenses. I read the other day about some young punk who had committed a brutal murder and admitted that he was inspired to commit it after having read the memoirs of the Marquis de Sade. Progressive educators argue that sex education courses make sense, but statistics reveal that one out of four high-school girls has engaged in intercourse within two years after having had such a course, and one out of three within three years. Allowing students to read dirty books and to see films on sex is bound to stimulate prurient thoughts. After all, if you let a group of hungry horses loose in an alfalfa field, they're bound to eat.

G. Write a short paper, one or two paragraphs, on one of the following topics, using an inductive process. That is, investigate the subject firsthand, record your observations in note form, consult relevant experts, and then write up the results of your investigation. Present your data first and your conclusion near or at the end of your paper.

1. student attitudes toward success, their teachers, or marriage

2. part-time work done by students

3. political preference or affiliation of students or faculty

4. educational objectives of students, motivation for attending college

5. student conceptions of the ideal job

6. student preferences regarding entertainment

THE DEDUCTIVE ARGUMENT

In the preceding pages we have studied the relation between inductive reasoning and writing, but, as we mentioned there, writing uses both induction and deduction. In induction you examine a number of particulars and formulate a conclusion to account for them. If the conclusion is a generalization, you can then, by means of a deductive process, apply the generalization to a particular case. For example, if you learn through personal experience that salespeople are extroverts, you can apply this information to the salesperson sitting beside you on a train and anticipate a lively conversation. Your reasoning process could be patterned as follows:

INDUCTIVE PROCESS

1. Salesperson$_1$ is an extrovert.
2. Salesperson$_2$ is an extrovert.
3. Salesperson$_3$ is an extrovert.

CONCLUSION: All salespeople are extroverts.

DEDUCTIVE PROCESS

1. All salespeople are extroverts.
2. The person sitting beside me is a salesperson.

CONCLUSION: The person sitting beside me is an extrovert.

This argument is an example of the *categorical syllogism* described earlier. It has three parts: two premises followed by a conclusion. The *major premise* makes a general statement about something—an object, an idea, a circumstance. In the example above, "All salespeople are extroverts" is the major premise. The *minor premise* contains further information about one of the terms in the major premise. "The person sitting beside me is a salesperson" is the minor premise of the example. And the *conclusion* is a logical inference to be derived from the premises. The last sentence in our syllogism is its conclusion.

The movement of this kind of syllogism is from the general to the specific, from a statement about a larger group to a statement about an individual member of that group. The categorical syllogism simply classifies an individual, object, or idea as a member of a group and assumes that the object so classified will have qualities of that group. Unlike the inductive argument ending in a generalization, which moves from the specific to the general, the categorical syllogism moves from the general to the specific. But the essential difference between a deductive and an inductive argument is not this direction of movement but the fact that the conclusion of a deductive argument can be proven to follow necessarily from the premises, whereas, as explained earlier, the conclusion of an inductive argument is always somewhat uncertain.

Here is a syllogism with its premises and conclusion indicated:

1. MAJOR PREMISE   All human beings are mortal beings.
    MINOR PREMISE   Socrates is a human being.
    CONCLUSION   Socrates is a mortal being.

The major premise commonly precedes the minor premise, but it need not:

2. MINOR PREMISE   Tippy is a cocker spaniel.
    MAJOR PREMISE   Cocker spaniels are dogs.
    CONCLUSION   Tippy is a dog.

The Valid Conclusion

If the conclusion of a syllogism logically follows from the ideas contained in the premises, as in the syllogisms above, the conclusion is said to be *valid*. A conclusion that doesn't follow, an invalid conclusion, is called a *non sequitur*. It is possible to determine the validity of the conclusion of the kind of basic syllogism illustrated in these pages by learning and applying a few simple rules:

1. The syllogism must have three, and only three, terms.
2. The middle term must be "distributed" in one of the premises.
3. The middle term must not shift its meaning.

A *term* is the subject or predicate of a statement. In a syllogism with a valid conclusion, each term will appear twice in the three statements.

3. MAJOR PREMISE   All children are curious.
    MINOR PREMISE   Stephen is a child.
    CONCLUSION   Stephen is curious.

The three terms of this syllogism are *children, curious,* and *Stephen.* The *middle term* is the term that appears in both the major and minor premise (but not in the conclusion), in this case *child. Child* and *children* are considered just one term since they both refer to the same thing.

The second rule, that the middle term be "distributed," simply means that the middle term must appear in a premise that includes or excludes all the members of its class. For example, the term *chemists* is distributed in each of these statements: "All chemists are intelligent." "No chemists are intelligent." In syllogism (3) above, the term *children* is distributed in the major premise. But in this next syllogism

4. MAJOR PREMISE   All Italians are music lovers.
    MINOR PREMISE   Gilbert is a music lover.
    CONCLUSION   Gilbert is an Italian.

the middle term, *music lover,* is not distributed in either premise. Neither premise includes or excludes all music lovers. The term *Italian* is distributed in the major premise, but it is not the middle term; and the conclusion is a non sequitur.

A syllogism in which the meaning of the middle term changes from major to minor premise also produces an invalid conclusion because the term signifies a different thing in each premise, and hence there are four terms. In the following syllogism the meaning of *democratic* differs in the two premises, and the conclusion therefore doesn't follow.

5. MAJOR PREMISE   All political leaders having democratic sympathies are popular.
   MINOR PREMISE   Governor Fagin has Democratic sympathies.
   CONCLUSION   Governor Fagin is popular.

The pattern of valid and invalid deductions is usually clarified by the use of diagrams. For example, in syllogism (3) the major premise states "All children are curious." If we draw a small circle to represent children and a larger one to represent individuals who are curious and then place the small circle within the larger (p. 248), we can diagram the relationship between children and curiosity contained in the major premise.

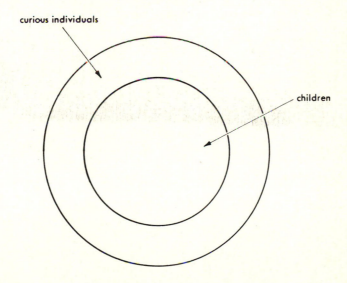

curious individuals

children

By drawing a still smaller circle to represent Stephen and placing it within the circle marked "children" we can diagram the minor premise, "Stephen is a child."

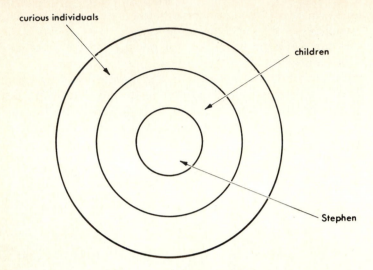

As the diagram now shows, the smallest circle is necessarily included in the largest circle, and the conclusion is thus valid: Stephen *is* curious.

Using the same system of circles to diagram syllogism (4), we can clearly see that its conclusion does not follow. The major premise, "All Italians are music lovers," can be represented thus:

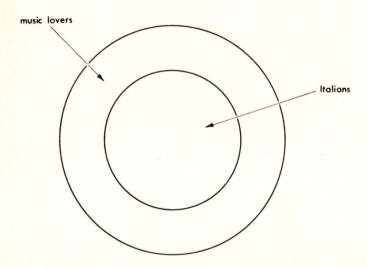

The minor premise, "Gilbert is a music lover," allows us to place the circle representing Gilbert any place within the larger circle: it does not have to be placed within the circle marked "Italians."

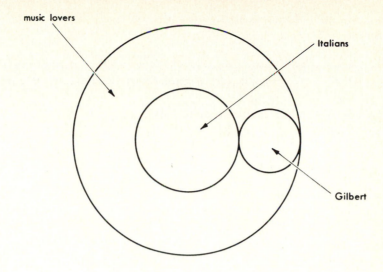

music lovers

Italians

Gilbert

Therefore, the conclusion "Gilbert is an Italian" is a non sequitur—it does not follow.

The True Conclusion
and the Probable Conclusion

We have defined a valid conclusion as a conclusion that follows from the ideas expressed in the premises, but a valid conclusion is not necessarily a *true conclusion*. The premises must be true before the argument can produce a true conclusion. The more firmly rooted in accurate observation the major premise is—the more thorough the process of induction that produced it—the sounder it is. "All human beings are mortal beings" is an accurate premise: it is a generalization born of universal human experience. Any syllogism based on it may yield a true conclusion. Few premises, however, are so demonstrably accurate. Arguments based on such sweeping, faulty premises as "Americans are crass materialists" or "Blondes have more fun" will not produce true conclusions.

Though arguments based on universally accepted generalizations do produce true conclusions when the rules governing syllogisms are followed, most of the generalizations you will use as major premises will not be absolutely accurate, unquestionably accepted. Most of them will be qualified; they might apply to many or most of the members of a class, but not to all of them. A major premise such as "All Democrats favor welfare programs supported and administered by the federal government" is likely to encounter resistance from an informed, intelligent audience. Modified, it becomes the basis of a more acceptable argument:

MAJOR PREMISE   Most Democrats favor welfare programs supported and administered by the federal government.

MINOR PREMISE   Harvey Ritter is a Democrat.

CONCLUSION   Harvey Ritter is likely to favor welfare programs supported and administered by the federal government.

This type of syllogism, a modification of the categorical syllogism since the middle term, Democrat, is not distributed, produces a *probable conclusion*. The greater the percentage of Democrats who favor welfare programs supported and administered by the federal government, the stronger the probability that Harvey Ritter does so too.

The criteria for the valid conclusion and the true conclusion mentioned above do not cover all syllogisms, but they are sufficient for our purposes here. In the section that follows we will consider several fallacies that are a blend of inductive, deductive, and emotional fallacies; but before we leave the syllogism, let us focus briefly on the problem of the *concealed premise*.

The Concealed Premise

A writer or speaker frequently omits one of the premises of a syllogism. Such a syllogism is not necessarily unreliable, but it presents a problem for an inexperienced writer or listener, who may accept an argument without realizing it is an argument and that its implied premises must be tested. The statement "Realtors make good school-board members; therefore, Henry Babbit should be elected to the school board" is a syllogism with its minor premise, "Henry Babbit is a realtor," missing. In such cases the minor premise is easily supplied and tested. Greater care, however, needs to be taken when the major premise is missing. The statement "The current tax bill before Congress should be passed: the United States Chamber of Commerce favors it" contains the concealed premise that the kind of tax legislation promoted by this organization is good for all Americans and should be enacted. The truth of this assumption is open to serious question—many economists would certainly oppose it—and because it is so central to the argument, the writer cannot ignore it without weakening her case.

Examine your own arguments, then, to see that they are not based on hidden, untenable premises. And when reading or discussing an

issue with others, analyze the arguments proposed for the same purpose. If any contain concealed premises, supply the missing premises
and test them for accuracy.

MISCELLANEOUS FALLACIES

Begging the Question

An argument that begs the question assumes that the point the argument ought to be establishing is proven. This fallacy is also known as
the circular argument, for the conclusion of the argument is merely a
restatement in the same words or synonyms of the basic premises,
leaving readers no wiser at the end of the argument than they were at
the beginning. The following arguments illustrate this fallacy:

1. Man will never be able to control the weather because it is impos-
    sible.

2. Genuine tax reform will be a Herculean task because it is so difficult.

3. People who favor gun control are really hopeless because they can't
    be very bright.

Frequently a circular argument extends over several sentences:

> I am adamantly opposed to the appointment of James Virdon
> as head of the committee to investigate charges of rent gouging
> in the city. The chairman of such a committee should not be a
> controversial figure. Since I am opposed to him, he is a contro-
> versial figure; and he should be removed from the chairmanship
> of this committee.

The core of this argument is (1) I object to James Virdon because he
is controversial, and (2) he is controversial because I object to him. The
argument runs in circles with the conclusion simply repeating the original assertion. The writer should either give reasons for his opposition
to Virdon or provide another reason why he is controversial. As it
stands, it is no argument at all since the conclusion of an argument
requires some basis in fact or judgment. As this example illustrates, the
lack of logic and supporting evidence makes the circular argument a
poor risk with careful readers.

Oversimplification

Oversimplification is a common fallacy in argumentation. Persons who are frustrated with the complexity of modern life and who desire simple, direct solutions for its problems commonly indulge in oversimplification. The rabid segregationist who regards civil rights legislation as indicative of the federal government's desire to tyrannize the South, the radical reactionary who believes that abolishing the income tax would solve the unemployment problem, and the military leader who feels that American security can be ensured by simply brandishing nuclear weapons—all these views are oversimplifications of complex problems.

A characteristic tendency of people who oversimplify is to divide people, ideas, and things into two or three sharply contrasting groups. There is a right way and a wrong way to do things, a moral way and an immoral way. Democrats are good, Republicans are bad; the federal government is bad, local government is good; economic systems are socialistic or capitalistic. The weakness of such conclusions is that they omit the possibility of other alternatives: they reject any middle ground between these polar positions. Few economic systems in the world, for example, are either purely capitalistic or purely socialistic. When revising your papers, therefore, reexamine your statements to see that you have not oversimplified issues. An intelligent reader will not be persuaded by simple answers to difficult questions.

Evading the Issue

The evidence used to prove an argument not only must be sufficient and representative, as explained earlier; it must be pertinent as well. When a writer or speaker engaged in a dispute presents evidence that does not relate to the point of his opponent's argument, he commits the error of evading the issue. An arguer who evades the issue often uses one of the following techniques: (1) the "smear" technique, (2) the "transfer" technique, and (3) the "bandwagon" technique. In the first of these, the arguer attacks the person instead of dealing with the issues he or she introduces. The following arguments illustrate the smear technique:

1. I can't imagine why Jeanette Crosley is such a popular actress. Her militant support of left-wing causes is disgraceful.

2. We should ignore the warnings of the president of the Auto Workers' Union on the increase of Japanese automobile imports. He simply wants to get more money for his union and bolster his image as a protector of the working man and woman.

3. I swear, Senator Parker doesn't have both oars in the water. His opposition to the Equal Rights Amendment is medieval. He thinks women should be permanently relegated to the status of second-class citizens. He's a political Neanderthal.

In each of these examples, the writer uses abuse rather than relevant evidence to support her argument. Jeanette Crosley's militant support of left-wing causes, for example, is not a relevant consideration in an evaluation of her acting ability.

The transfer technique involves an appeal to authority—to a famous name or universally sanctioned idea—to validate an argument. Advertisers, newspapers editors, and politicians frequently attempt to gain acceptance for a product or a point of view by using this technique.

1. Olympic skier Claude Savant drives an Alpine Roadster. He says . . . .

2. Rock star Michele Donovan brushes her teeth with Lustrous tooth paste.

3. Benjamin Franklin would never have approved of such a huge federal debt.

4. Henry Kissinger, discussing recent developments in modern art, said . . . .

All these statements illustrate the fallacy of the simple appeal to authority. What Benjamin Franklin said may no longer be relevant in today's world. Nor can one accept Henry Kissinger's opinion on art simply because he is widely known. Of course, if these individuals were quoted on subjects within their competence, this fallacy would not apply. Skier Savant's knowledge might be relevant in a discussion of the winter Olympics and Henry Kissinger's in one about international relations.

Speakers or writers who ignore the issue through an appeal to the passions and prejudices of the crowd use the bandwagon approach. For example, a political campaigner frequently modifies his approach to accommodate his audience. In Harlem he appeals to his listeners as blacks; in Arkansas he appeals to them as farmers. The following passage illustrates this emotional appeal:

I know that the people of this great nation will not reject a man who has throughout his entire public life worked and fought for the good of America. I know that they will not reject a man of the people, a man dedicated to the preservation of American freedoms against the threat of godless communism.

Advertisers also use this device:

> Don't be left behind. Join the crowd and switch to Blitz beer.

The weakness of the bandwagon approach is that in its appeal to the emotions of the audience it submits little or no factual or logical evidence for consideration.

The Loaded Question

The fallacy of the loaded question, like that of begging the question, assumes the truth of something that has not been proved, but it also implies wrongdoing on the part of the person to whom the question is directed. One cannot answer such a question without incriminating himself or committing himself to something he doesn't believe. The question "Why does the government permit big unions to seriously disrupt the economy of this country?" assumes two things, that big unions do seriously disrupt the economy of the country and that the federal government permits it, both of which have not been established. One really cannot reply to such a question. The best one can do is to point out that the question is faulty because it contains unproven assumptions.

EXERCISE 25

A. Place a V after each of the following syllogisms that has a valid conclusion and an I after each one that has an invalid conclusion. (Diagram each syllogism on a piece of scratch paper to help you determine its validity.) Indicate the cause of an invalid argument by writing one of the following numbers next to an I: (1) undistributed middle term, (2) more than three terms used, (3) shift in meaning of middle term.

EXAMPLE   All dogs drool.
Hugo drools.
Hugo is a dog.   <u> I,1 </u>

1. All logicians are concerned about clear thinking.
Professor Chun is a logician.
Professor Chun is concerned about clear thinking.   _____

2. The monsoon is a powerful wind.
This wind is powerful.
This wind is a monsoon.   _____

3. All smoking nuisances should be eliminated in this city.
Erich is a smoking nuisance.
Erich should be eliminated in this city.   _____

4. All vegetarians won't eat beef.
Roger is a fastidious eater.
Roger is a vegetarian.   _____

5. All laws that promote inflation are bad.
This law promotes inflation.
This law is bad.   _____

B. In the following syllogisms some conclusions are true, some are valid, and some are invalid. If the conclusion is true, place a T in the blank after it. If it is valid, place a V in the blank, and if it is invalid, place an I in the blank. (Remember that a true conclusion and a valid conclusion follow logically from the premises, but only a true conclusion follows from sound, accurate premises.)

1. Successful persons are those who have acquired financial independence.
My stockbroker is a successful person.
My stockbroker has acquired financial independence.   _____

2. All persons who deliberately misreport their income on their income tax forms are unethical.
Some Americans deliberately misreport their income on their income tax forms.
Some Americans are unethical.   _____

3. People who obey laws they don't like deserve praise.

Jim Ratlin, a trucker, doesn't like the 55 mph speed limit, but he obeys it.
Jim Ratlin deserves praise.   _____

4.   All extroverts are conceited boobs.
     Peter Per Scott is a conceited boob.
     Peter Per Scott is an extrovert.   _____

5.   All students who can use their native language effectively have a good
     chance to succeed in their university studies.
     John Cassidy is a student who can use his native language effectively.
     John Cassidy has a good chance to succeed in his university studies.

                                                                _____

C.   The following items are deductive arguments with hidden premises. Supply
     the missing premise of each argument.

     EXAMPLE   Of course Clampson Dental Cream is good; it's advertised in
               Peek magazine.
     Missing Premise   Products advertised in *Peek* magazine are good.

1.   Professor Walker is obviously an excellent teacher. Her students rave about
     her sense of humor.

     Missing Premise _____

     _____

2.   Cyril Percy is an Englishman, so he probably believes in strict gun control.

     Missing Premise _____

     _____

3.   *The Bountiful Boudoir* is obviously a good book; it sold more than two million
     copies the first year of its publication.

     Missing Premise _____

     _____

4.   A sports columnist in the *Los Angeles Times* criticized the exorbitant salaries
     paid to basketball players. Very likely he doesn't like basketball.

     Missing Premise _____

     _____

5.   Of course Japanese cars sell well in the United States. They are reasonably
     priced, fuel efficient, and durable.

     Missing Premise _____

     _____

D. Identify the fallacies in the following arguments.

1. People who question the validity of a law reveal that they do not respect our country's legal system, and therefore they are criminals at heart. Either people accept the laws of the land and are law abiding citizens or they don't and are crooks.

_____

2. The X-rated movies are a disgrace to American moral values because they are offensive to the American people's sense of decency and good taste.

_____

3. Senator Lafarge is obviously going to oppose increasing the minimum wage. He owns several textile mills, and he's certainly not going to support legislation that will cost him money.

_____

4. I'm surprised that a newspaper reporter at a White House news conference hasn't asked the President why he wants to bust the big unions.

_____

5. *Modern Times* is an up-to-date, thoughtful, influential journal of opinion. You should subscribe to it today. Seventy-five percent of its readers are college graduates with incomes above $50,000 per year.

_____

6. The furor in Europe over the neutron bomb is confusing to Americans. Do the Europeans want to defend themselves against the Russians, or don't they? If they do, they should want the bomb.

_____

THE SYLLOGISM AS THE BASIS OF ARGUMENTATIVE WRITING

The syllogism can form the basis of an argumentative paragraph or essay. If, for example, you want to argue that working while attending college is beneficial, your first step would be to construct a syllogism with your proposition as the conclusion of your argument. Then devise a minor premise to connect your conclusion to a major premise.

MAJOR PREMISE   Experience that helps students to become more self-reliant, purposeful, and responsible helps them in their studies.

MINOR PREMISE   Working while attending college helps students to become more self-reliant, purposeful, and responsible.

CONCLUSION   Working while attending college helps students in their studies.

In developing your paragraph or essay from this syllogism, you would first support your major premise, then the minor premise, and end with your conclusion. The major premise in this pattern is extremely important. It should be one your reader will accept as probably true, as is the case in the example above. If your major premise is reasonable and your minor premise well supported and logically linked to the major premise, your conclusion should be convincing.

A syllogism forms the organizing principle of the following brief essay on senior citizens. It can be formulated approximately as follows:

MAJOR PREMISE   Any population group whose members on the whole receive a reasonable yearly income, whose expenses have been stabilized, and who are given special reductions in the prices of goods and services should not be homogenously lumped together as poor.

MINOR PREMISE   America's senior citizens on the whole receive a reasonable yearly income, have stabilized incomes, and receive special reductions in the prices of goods and services.

CONCLUSION   America's senior citizens should not be homogenously lumped together as poor.

Old and Needy?

It is not surprising that Americans, particularly younger Americans, believe that older people deserve special attention and consideration. Newspaper and magazine articles and television commentaries have, in recent years, focused on the plight of the aged neglected by their families and ignored by a penurious, indifferent government. Stories and films about old people rotting away in convalescent homes, standing in lines at soup kitchens, and staggering under a heavy burden of medical expense have been in the news and on the minds of millions of Americans. To many of these Americans, old means poor, deprived, neglected. But just how needy are America's senior citizens? Does "old" necessarily mean "poor"?

Minor Premise

Any humane society should be concerned about the welfare of its citizens, about their income and expenses, their ability to maintain themselves in a reasonable standard of living. Any population group that enjoys a reasonable yearly income, stabilized expenses, and special perquisites and benefits is not really poor. And by these standards, senior citizens are not, as a whole, poor. For example, recent census figures indicate that people over sixty-five have a per capita annual income after taxes of $6,299, $335 more than the national average, and a poverty rate of 14%, about that of the general population. Their per capita income is twice that of families headed by a single woman. Moreover, their Social Security payments have been adjusted upward annually to protect them against inflation, an advantage not enjoyed by millions of young factory workers in recent years. And speaking of Social Security benefits, the typical retired person gets back more than four times as much money from Social Security as he or she has contributed to the system. According to *U.S. News and World Report,* a married man who began contributing to Social Security in 1937, retired in 1982, and whose wife did not work would have got back all of his payroll contributions in just fourteen months.[3]

Minor Premise

Senior citizens not only receive reasonable incomes, they also have more stabilized expenses than other groups; and they get special benefits as well. Proponents of increased governmental assistance for the elderly frequently refer to their fixed incomes in arguing their case, but older people's expenses are more stabilized than those of other groups. Their medical expenses, though substantial, are mitigated by Medicare, and supplemental coverage can be obtained through private insurance companies at a nonprohibitive cost. About 70% of them own their own homes; others

[3] Teresa Anderson, "The Best Years of Their Lives," *Newsweek,* January 7, 1985, p. 7.

have sold theirs for a tidy, untaxed profit. They also receive an extra deduction on their income taxes. Public transportation is cheap: in Portland, Oregon, for instance, senior citizens can ride anywhere in the city for a quarter, in Minneapolis for a dime. And they are given reduced prices for a host of services and amusements, from haircuts to hotel rooms to European package tours. To be sure, we must treat senior citizens with kindness and consideration, with respect for their experience and wisdom. We must *Conclusion*   meet their real needs. But if we are to do this effectively, we must not lump them all together as poor, as a "homogenous blob of senile men and women eating cat food in lonely rooms."[4]

EXERCISE 26

A. Construct a syllogism for each of the following propositions. As in the preceding essay, use the proposition as the conclusion of your argument and construct a minor premise to link your conclusion to a major premise that would probably be accepted.

1. Nuclear energy is not a satisfactory source of power today.

2. A restrictive gun control law should (should not) be passed by Congress.

3. Apartment owners should (should not) have the right to refuse to rent to families with children.

B. Use the syllogism you developed for one of the items in A above as the basis of a paragraph or a brief essay.

TRACING CAUSE AND EFFECT RELATIONSHIPS

Another method of structuring an argument is to trace cause and effect relationships, as, for example, when you wish to explain the cause of a problem as a means of convincing your reader to approve of a solution you propose. Causal analysis is similar to sequence or process analysis discussed in Chapter Three (pp. 82–83), for each involves actions that occur in chronological order. They are not the same, however, for a sequence or process analysis simply tells *how* actions or steps are related, not *why*. In a report on the bombing of Pearl Harbor in 1941, for instance, you could simply relate the sequence of events that took

[4] Anderson, p. 7.

place or attempt a more ambitious analysis of the cause and effect of the attack.

Cause and effect writing is a common ingredient in much writing today because it attempts to get at the reasons that underlie events and human behavior, and people want and need to know the causes and effects of forces that influence or govern their lives. Tracing cause and effect is common in systematic, scientific investigation and in the writing of political scientists, historians, and economists; but it is not limited to such formal, argumentative uses. It may be used in expository writing where its purpose is simply to inform, clarify, or perhaps to amuse, rather than to argue a case.

Causal analysis may be used in a number of ways. You may describe an event and emphasize the consequences that followed from it. In a paragraph or paper about a change in graduation requirements—adding a test on writing ability for graduating seniors, let's say—you might briefly mention the substance of the change and the faculty action that produced it and then devote more space to the effects of the change. A second approach would be to describe the event, this time focusing on the causes that produced it. Using this approach, you would proceed as above in describing the new writing requirement and then focus your attention on why the change was enacted. A third strategy would be to deal with both cause and effect after presenting the action. This approach would likely require more than a single paragraph, particularly if your causal analysis formed the basis of an argument.

Whether you write a single paragraph or a longer essay will depend on how thoroughly you wish to explore your subject. In a short paper you would commonly limit yourself to *immediate* causes and effects, those close in time to the event. In a longer paper you could explore *ultimate* causes and effects, those more remote in time from the event. In the case of the graduation requirement referred to above, the immediate cause of the change might simply be the faculty action and the immediate effect the necessity of students to make arrangements to take the test. Dealing with the ultimate causes, you might uncover the following: faculty displeasure with general student writing ability, pressure from the public, and perhaps pressure from state legislators as well. An investigation of ultimate effects would likely turn up these: an increase in student demand for tutorial assistance, changes in students' schedules, the addition of composition classes to the curriculum, delays in graduation, and added student frustration.

A final word. As you're making your investigation and writing your analysis, keep in mind what you've learned about reasoning in this chapter:

1. Avoid oversimplification. Investigate your subject carefully and objectively, and don't claim too much for your analysis.

2. Avoid the *post hoc* fallacy. Don't assume that something that happens before or after something else is a cause or effect of it.

3. Let your reader see the evidence or the reasoning that supports your attribution of cause and effect relationships.

The two paragraphs below are developed by causal analysis, the first focusing on cause, the second on effect.

Faced with these awkward facts, realists in the West began to search for more sophisticated explanations for the superior competitiveness of the Japanese. One reason for it, some people suggested, was that Japanese industry had been fortunate enough to have most of its plants bombed off the face of the earth during World War II and thus, unlike American industry, had been left with no choice but to replace obsolescent factories and mills with more modern and efficient ones. An even more intriguing suggestion was the concept of "Japan, Inc." developed by American business consultant James Abegglen. This was a vision of the Japanese economy as a kind of seamless web in which politicians, bureaucrats and businessmen all worked industriously toward mutually agreed-upon ends. As oversimplified by some of its popularizers, however, it was often reduced to the proposition that unlike the U.S. Government, the Government of Japan invariably seeks, by fair means or foul, to strengthen private industry and advance its interests. [From Robert C. Christopher, *The Japanese Mind,* Linden Press, 1983.]

What has the telephone done to us, or for us, in the hundred years of its existence? A few effects suggest themselves at once. It has saved lives by getting rapid word of illness, injury, or famine from remote places. By joining with the elevator to make possible the multistory residence or office building, it has made possible—for better or worse—the modern city. By bringing about a quantum leap in the speed and ease with which information moves from place to place, it has greatly accelerated the rate of scientific and technological change and growth in industry. Beyond doubt it has crippled if not killed the ancient art of letter writing. It has made living alone possible for persons with normal social impulses; by so doing, it has played a role in one of the greatest social changes of this century, the breakup of the multigenerational household. It has made the waging of war chillingly more efficient than formerly. Perhaps (though not probably) it has prevented wars that might have arisen out of international misunderstanding caused by written communication. Or perhaps—again not probably—by magnifying and extending irrational personal conflicts based on voice contact, it has caused wars. Certainly it has extended the scope of human conflicts, since it impartially disseminates the useful knowledge of scientists and the babble of bores, the affection of the affectionate and the malice of the malicious. [From John Brooks, *Telephone: The First Hundred Years,* Harper & Row, 1975, 1976.]

EXERCISE 27

A. In a paragraph of 100 to 150 words describe the effects of one of the following situations. In the first two or three sentences present your topic sentence and a brief description of the event; then move on to effects.

1. the invention of the automobile, jet airplane, or pocket calculator (Use the paragraph on the telephone, pp. 263–64, as a model.)

2. the availability of contraceptive devices

3. the continuation of a strong dollar internationally

4. the failure of the male head of a household to find a job

5. students dropping out of high school

B. In a paragraph of 100 to 150 words speculate about the causes of one of the following. Follow the same procedure in structuring your paragraph as explained in A above.

1. the increase in the divorce rate

2. the dramatic improvement in performance in the Olympic Games over the past fifty years

3. the popularity of diet books, soap operas, jogging, horror or catastrophe movies

4. the continuing high percentage of American high school students who seek a college education

5. the particular behavior pattern or eccentricity of a friend

C. Select one of the following topics, or one listed in A or B above, and write a 300-word (three-paragraph) essay treating both cause and effect. Either one of the following strategies will help you to organize your paper: (1) In the first paragraph focus on effects, in the second on causes, and in the third on a solution, your recommendation for a course of action; or (2) in the first paragraph describe the problem at some length, in the second deal with causes, and in the third deal with effects. This assignment will require library research to provide you with relevant evidence to substantiate your ideas and arguments.

1. the dramatic increase in the number of working women in the past fifty years

2. the increasing emphasis upon vocational-technical education among college students

3. student cheating

4. the pressure upon college students to get good grades

5. mass transit in the United States—a growing problem

PERSUASION

Persuasive writing is not solely a matter of logic: it is also a matter of language, attitude, and character. We persuade others by an appeal to their emotions as well as to their reason, and by the strength of our personality and character, too. To convince your reader, you must attend to the clarity, honesty, and emotional impact of your arguments as well as to their logical construction. You must present yourself as a person of good sense, integrity, and good will.

Analyzing Your Audience

Persuasive writing, like expository writing, is directed to an audience. In school you will be writing for your instructors and classmates for the most part. Out of school your reader may be a prospective employer, a newspaper editor, a legislator, or a personal friend. In any case you should analyze your audience before you plan your arguments since their interests, educational and social background, knowledge, loyalties, and motives will affect their receptivity to your arguments. What persuades one audience will not necessarily persuade another, as you have undoubtedly learned in arguing the same subject with a number of friends, or with friends and your parents. The *tone* you assume, the *words and sentence patterns* you use, the *length of your paragraphs*, the *arguments* you select—all will vary to accord with your audience. In the essays and reports you write in college, for example, your tone will probably be more serious, your diction more formal, and your sentences and paragraphs longer than would be the case in articles you write for student magazines or in letters you write to friends. The following arguments could be used to support the proposition that living away from home in apartments is beneficial to college students: (1) promotes self-reliance, (2) reduces parental control over choice of friends, (3) helps the student learn to manage a budget, (4) permits a less inhibited life style, (5) reduces household chores, and (6) promotes self-discovery and creativity in human relationships. If you were arguing this proposition with your parents, you would stress arguments 1, 3, and 6. If you were attempting to convince a potential roommate, you would stress 2, 4, and 5.

If you keep your audience in mind, you will keep your arguments more specific, more relevant. By adjusting your tone to the sensitivities of your readers, you will make them more receptive to what you say, less inclined to tune you out. And a knowledge of your audience will often save you needless effort in explaining terms and concepts that are already known and understood.

Defining Important Terms

An awareness of the intellectual level and knowledge of your audience does limit the need of defining familiar terms. But accurate, precise definition of terms is, nonetheless, important, especially when they are subject to varied interpretation. Words like *liberty, freedom, truth, justice, liberal, conservative, radical,* and *propaganda* need to be pinned down. Consider the following passage:

> The American people have been deceived about the nature of their government. They have been taught that the United States is a democracy, when actually it is a republic. Consequently, proposals to modify the system of electing a president to make it more democratic are irrelevant.

This passage is vague because of the writer's failure to tell us what she means by *democracy* and *republic*. Since both terms can be used to describe forms of government in which the power resides in the voters who elect representatives to decide public issues, the writer should specify the sense in which she is using these terms if she is to convince rather than confuse us. The revision below eliminates this confusion, although one may still not agree with the conclusions.

> A republic is commonly defined as a form of government in which the voters elect representatives to meet and decide public issues. A pure democracy is a form of government in which the voters themselves assemble in one place to decide these issues. Accepting this distinction, we can describe the United States as a republic rather than a democracy. Hence, proposals to modify the system of electing a president to make it *more* democractic are irrelevant.

VAGUE	IMPROVED
It is time Americans recognized the danger of extremist groups. The subversives should be controlled before they do real damage to the American way of life.	Political groups and organizations that advocate radical measures to meet the problems of our time threaten the stability of American life. What constitutes a "radical" measure is, of course, open to dispute, but most Americans would probably agree that the term could be applied to such actions as bombing federal buildings to express opposition to governmental policies; advocating elimination of welfare programs, Medicare, and the Social Security system; and establishing local guerrilla "armies." Although radical groups have a right to express their opinions and gain adherents to their cause, they should be watched carefully to see that they do not break any laws.

Appealing to the Emotions

An appeal to the emotions of an audience can be very persuasive, a fact long recognized by writers, propagandists, political leaders. All of us at one time or another are moved to action or to change our opinions through our emotions. Sound, carefully reasoned arguments should be the foundation of your attempts to persuade, but on occasion you will want to couple logic with an appeal to your reader's feelings, loyalties, and aspirations. Martin Luther King, Jr., used an emotional appeal to great effect in persuading Americans of the justice of the civil rights movement:

> We have waited for more than 340 years for our constitutional and God-given rights. The nations of Asia and Africa are moving with jetlike speed toward gaining political independence, but we still creep at horse-and-buggy pace toward gaining a cup of coffee at a lunch counter. Perhaps it is easy for those who

have never felt the stinging darts of segregation to say, "Wait."
But when you have seen vicious mobs lynch your mothers and
fathers at will and drown your sisters and brothers at whim;
when you have seen hate-filled policemen curse, kick and even
kill your black brothers and sisters; when you see the vast majority of your twenty million Negro brothers smothering in an
airtight cage of poverty in the midst of an affluent society; when
you suddenly find your tongue twisted and your speech stam-
mering as you seek to explain to your six-year-old daughter why
she can't go to the public amusement park that has just been
advertised on television, and see tears welling up in her eyes
when she is told that Funtown is closed to colored children, and
see ominous clouds of inferiority beginning to form in her little
mental sky, and see her beginning to distort her personality by
developing an unconscious bitterness toward white people . . .
[From Martin Luther King, Jr., "Letter from Birmingham Jail,"
April 16, 1963, *Why We Can't Wait,* Harper & Row, 1963.]

An emotional appeal is a legitimate weapon in any writer's arsenal,
but it needs to be used honestly and carefully, for it can backfire if it
becomes obvious to readers, particularly well-informed and thoughtful
readers, that the writer is simply pandering to their biases to further
his or her own interests. Advertisers, editorial writers, lawyers, politicians, extremists in favor of one cause or another have on occasion
deviated from the truth with emotional appeals; but those who continually use such appeals for unscrupulous purposes ultimately damage
whatever cause they serve. In your own efforts at persuasion avoid
routine exaggeration and highly charged language or the abuse of those
whose opinions you do not share. In the paragraph below the writer's
anger clearly gets the best of his judgment.

The welfare mess in this country can be laid to the door of
those muddle-headed, fuzzy-minded liberals who for the past
four decades have bemoaned the sad fate of the chiseling, ignorant misfits among us who are too lazy to get off their duffs
and get a job. If Americans ever hope to eliminate this some-
thing-for-nothing boondoggle, they will simply have to put their
feet down and demand that the paper-shuffling bureaucrats in
Washington stop squandering taxpayers' money on socialistic
schemes that perpetuate sloth and irresponsibility. [From William F. Smith and Robert G. Wicks, *Communicating Through Word
and Image,* Winthrop Publishers, 1975.]

Such phrases as "chiseling, ignorant misfits," "paper-shuffling bureaucrats," and "socialist schemes" tell us more about the writer's state of mind than about his subject. Here are examples of exaggerated statements with suggested revisions:

EXAGGERATED	REVISED
The foreign aid program succeeds in doing nothing but pouring money down a rat hole. It is a vast giveaway program that aids no one.	Our foreign aid program needs to be examined carefully to see if we can eliminate some of the waste and mismanagement in its operation.
The lessons of history are unmistakable. Either we reduce our tax rate, or the U.S. faces imminent economic chaos and disaster.	Reducing tax rates in the countries of Western Europe after the Second World War provided a needed stimulus to their economies. In all likelihood, lower taxes in the U.S. would produce a similar expansion.

Emotive Language

As noted earlier, an emotional appeal may involve loaded or slanted words, words that reveal the user's feelings and attitudes, approval or disapproval. Loaded words are rather commonly used in situations in which people's feelings are aroused—political discussions, for example. In the opinion of one person, Senator Jones is intelligent, fair, compassionate in his regard for the underdog. To another he is opinionated, rigid, a maudlin do-gooder. In the course of a conversation between these two persons, people working in Washington, D.C., might be referred to as intellectuals or eggheads, public servants or bureaucrats, faithful employees or time-servers.

The following passage provides further illustration of the use of loaded words. The opinions are those of a Mississippi circuit judge on the subject of Mississippi whiskey.

If when you say whiskey you mean the devil's brew, the poison scourge, the bloody monster, that defiles innocence, dethrones reason, destroys the home, creates misery and poverty, yea, literally takes the bread from the mouths of little children; if you mean the evil drink that topples the Christian man and woman from the pinnacle of righteous, gracious living into the bottomless pit of degradation and despair, and shame, and help-lessness, and hopelessness, then certainly I am against it.

But if when you say whiskey you mean the oil of conversation, the philosophic wine, the ale that puts a song in their hearts and laughter on their lips, and the warm glow of contentment in their eyes; if you mean Christmas cheer; if you mean the stimulating drink that puts the spring into the old gentleman's step on a frosty, crispy morning; if you mean the drink which enables a man to magnify his joy, and his happiness, and to forget, if only for a little while, life's great tragedies, and heart-aches, and sorrows; if you mean that drink, the sale of which pours into our treasuries untold millions of dollars, which are used to provide tender care for our little crippled children, our blind, our deaf, our dumb, our pitiful aged and infirm; to build highways and hospitals and schools, then certainly I am for it.

This is my stand, I will not retreat from it. I will not compro-mise. [From Kenneth Vinson, "Prohibition's Last Stand," *The New Republic*, October 16, 1965, p. 11.]

As these differences of opinion about Senator Jones and about whis-key reveal, special feelings and associations attach to words. The person who approves of Senator Jones describes him in words that arouse favorable feelings—*intelligent, fair, compassionate*. The person who dis-approves of the senator uses words that arouse unfavorable feelings—*opinionated, rigid, do-gooder*. Similarly, one who refers to whiskey as the *oil of conversation,* the *philosophic wine, Christmas cheer* clearly approves of it; one who regards it as the *devil's brew,* the *poison scourge,* the *bloody monster* rather clearly disapproves of it. The suggestions and associations that cluster about a word make up its *connotative* meaning. The conno-tations of *firm,* for instance, are positive: the word suggests determina-tion, courage, solidity—all attractive qualities. The connotations of *rigid,* however, are negative: it suggests stubbornness, inflexibility, a narrow-minded unwillingness to compromise—all unattractive qualities. The tendency to use words with favorable connotations, honorific words, in referring to what we like can be seen in a common practice today, the substitution of a word with more pleasant associations for one that conveys a less pleasant reality. These sugar-coated words and phrases are called *euphemisms*.

Words have *denotative* meanings as well as connotative meanings. The denotative meaning of a word signifies its literal, explicit meaning—the object or idea it stands for. The denotation of "firm" and "rigid" is the same—unyielding, difficult to move. The distinction, then, between the connotative and denotative meaning of a word is that its connotation includes the feelings and attitudes associated with it; its denotation does not. And, as illustrated, the connotation of a word may be positive or negative.

Emotive words, words with strong connotations, vary in their power to arouse feeling. *Political nonconformist, reactionary, fascist*—all evoke feelings of anger in many people's minds. But *fascist* evokes a stronger reaction than does *political nonconformist*. Because emotive words can powerfully influence people's opinions, some writers employ them frequently to condemn persons and ideas they do not like. By using loaded words, such as *traitor, subversive, demagogue,* and the like, they hope to lead their readers into forming unfavorable opinions of their subjects without examining the supporting evidence.

Although emotive language is customarily used by those who distort and exaggerate, it need not be avoided absolutely. Persuasive writing deliberately and legitimately appeals to the emotions of the reader. Many respected writers and speakers employ emotion successfully to persuade others of the truth of their ideas. But it must be used with care. If your readers believe that you are substituting emotion for credible evidence, that you are trying to browbeat them into agreement, they are apt to dismiss your arguments as biased and unreliable. In short, deal honestly with your readers. If you use an emotional appeal, let them see the evidence that justifies it.

Countering the Opposition

To achieve the results you want in a persuasive paper, you will often have to do more than make a strong case for your own point of view, especially when your reader is well informed and thoughtful. You will have to consider and counter important opposition arguments. Countering opposing arguments makes sense for several reasons. First, if you do not, your reader may conclude that you are ignorant of the complexities of your subject and reject your arguments as one-sided and simplistic. Second, even if your reader is unaware of opposing arguments, he or she will be impressed with your fairness; and as we mentioned earlier, a writer's integrity is an important element in persuasion. And, finally, countering opposition arguments is strategically wise: once you have demolished the primary arguments of the opposition, your own arguments will stand more securely.

Note how clearly and judiciously the student writer of the following editorial considers and counters opposition arguments:

Opposition   When the dean of men used his veto power last week to
Argument   squash a Student Commission proposal to pay part of the
                 costs of a radio station on campus, he was well within his
                 rights. As policy now stands, the adviser's veto on the

*Counter
Argument*

Student Commission measures is meant to prevent unwise action on the part of student leaders. Though ostensibly sound, however, this procedure actually renders commissioners impotent before the dean of men.

*Opposition
Argument*

*Counter
Argument*

The dean's suggestion that the Board of Trustees be requested to put up the $10,000 in question seemed to make sense. However, the commission had hoped to allocate funds while the money was available, as it presently is in the Associated Student Body reserve fund, and not allocated for other less worthy projects. Commission members also feel that the board may not come through with the funds. Although Dr. Robert Winslow, chancellor of the college district, is reportedly highly enthusiastic about the radio station, he vacates his post in June. Since the student government does not operate during the summer months, the board may not get around to considering the radio funds requested until September. Then, with a new chancellor, the $10,000 may be hard to get.

*Counter
Argument*

When presented with the facts, student commissioners can be presumed to have as sound a judgment as one administration adviser. The adviser's function is to spell out to commissioners the implications of their proposals, not to block them because of personal preference. The commission, of course, should weigh carefully every suggestion of the adviser, and the adviser should be allowed to veto commissioners' proposals when he disagrees with the conclusions commissioners have drawn. After the veto, however, the commissioners, if they are convinced of the rightness of their decisions, should be allowed to override that veto with, say, a two-thirds vote. Commission members would not be inclined to abuse their veto-overriding power since measures that have hurdled the veto still must be approved by the President's Council. This change in policy would therefore not imperil college stability. Because those proposals having unanimous or near unanimous support of the Student Commission would have direct access to the president, actions strongly desired by the students would be more seriously considered, and student government would become more efficient and meaningful.

This next essay is a longer essay using the same strategy of countering the opposition. In it the writer presents her case against the growing tendency of school boards and other groups to censor books considered obscene or subversive. Because of the length and amplitude of the essay, the writer is justified in devoting a full paragraph to the introduction and to the conclusion. In the first paragraph she introduces her subject broadly and narrows to her thesis at the end of the paragraph. In developing her case, she follows the strategy suggested on page 273 and illustrated on pages 273–74, introducing and countering important opposition arguments. Note that, in the second and fourth paragraphs, the writer begins by presenting an opposition argument and then counters it with her own. In the fifth and sixth paragraphs, having previously disposed of the opposition, she now concentrates on her own strongest arguments.

Surveying the theme as a whole, we can see how she has achieved emphasis through position and proportion. The opening paragraph leads into the subject. The more fully developed middle paragraphs carry the main burden of her case. And the final paragraph, reminding the reader of an important point made in the opening paragraph, the protection of intellectual freedom guaranteed by the First Amendment, forcefully concludes the essay with a quoted passage.

A Deadly Virus

Freedom of speech has long been considered the foundation of American democracy, a principle that antedates and engenders all the other freedoms guaranteed in the Bill of Rights. Because of the First Amendment, Americans have been relatively free of governmental interference in expressing their ideas and opinions in speech and writing. But this restraint has been less characteristic of volunteer censors, of private groups that have wanted to control or curtail free expression to protect people from religious heresy, moral corruption, or unwelcome political ideas. At one time or another, *Huckleberry Finn, The Canterbury Tales, The Merchant of Venice, Grapes of Wrath* and many other classics have felt the hot breath of the censor. In recent years efforts to remove books from public libraries and schoolrooms have increased significantly, due, in part at least, to a resurgent fundamentalist spirit of the Moral Majority, though liberal groups have also on occasion favored suppression of books and films they considered big-

Thesis   oted or reactionary. Whether censorship originates from the right or left, however, from governmental agencies or private groups, it must be opposed.

Opposition   Those who favor book banning, or even burning, fre-
Argument   quently argue that "dirty" books corrupt the morals and

pervert the psychological orientation of the young toward love and sex. They deplore the "degrading" sexual behavior, the coarse language, the disreputable characters in books their children are exposed to; and they want them suppressed. One need only scan the offerings of a typical newsstand or note the aggressive vulgarity of much prime time television to be aware that the reading and viewing tastes of the American public are not burdened by a Victorian prudery. It is also true that parents and teachers need to exercise care and judgment in guiding the reading of elementary school children and adolescents to protect immature minds and sensibilities unable to understand or emotionally cope with the harsh reality of immoral behavior depicted in adult fiction. But when sensible precaution *Counter* is carried to the point of banning books in high schools *Argument* and removing them from public libraries, it is misguided, harmful, and, at times, ludicrous.

The primary purpose of serious literature is to communicate human experience, and since illicit sex and immoral behavior are a part of human experience, it follows that serious writers will deal with sex and human depravity on occasion. The candid representation of such matters may be shocking and offensive to some readers, but the writer's purpose in depicting sinful acts is not to dwell on salacious details for their own sake nor to arouse an interest in evil, but to reveal aspects of his vision of reality. Hiding such situations from students will not help them to understand and deal with such problems as adults. Moreover, the books that have been proscribed for their vivid descriptions of sexuality and alleged obscenity include many written by famous authors: Shakespeare, Chaucer, Hawthorne, Hemingway, Steinbeck, Faulkner, Huxley, Vonnegut, and Salinger, to name but a few. And passages from the Bible have not escaped the wrath of some purists.

Opposition   Censors also want to prohibit the expression of ideas
Argument   they regard as pernicious, subversive, or un-American. The conflicts and violent ideologies of the twentieth century, in particular the growth of communism and its attendant evils, account for much of the drive of reactionary political groups to rid America of "alien" ideas by banning books and other printed matter that seem communist inspired or directed. The works of Karl Marx have often been denounced and their study by college students de-

plored. But there are censors on the left as well, who speak on behalf of minorities. *Mary Poppins* was banned from the San Francisco Public Library because it reflected racist attitudes, *The Merchant of Venice* has been condemned because of its alleged anti-Semitism, and a homosexual organization in New York City attempted to persuade the city to withdraw its cooperation from the production of a film in which homosexuals were depicted unfavorably. But whatever their motives and however sincere their beliefs, censors are misguided and dangerous. They are misguided, for they assume the wisdom and authority to decide which ideas are safe and which not, not only for members of their own groups but for others as well. Ironically, they demand freedom of expression for the ideas they support and suppression of those they oppose. And censors are dangerous because of the constrictive, chilling effect they can have on the free and open discussion of ideas, which is the lifeblood of American political and cultural life.

Counter Argument

Counter Argument

The argument against censorship does not mean that books may not have negative as well as positive effects on readers. It does not mean that pornography doesn't exist, that printed matter is never, under any circumstance, truly subversive. But it does mean that outright censorship and suppression of books, or films, is seldom justified. Admittedly, the reading and viewing of children should be prudently supervised in accordance with their level of maturity. Older youths, however, should not be subject to such close supervision and adults not at all, except in the case of a work "utterly without redeeming social importance" and therefore subject to legal restriction by the courts. As mentioned earlier, many books proscribed by school boards and religious groups in recent years have been regarded as classics. Moreover, banning books because of their alleged obscenity is often self-defeating, for it simply stimulates students to want to read them. Removing books from libraries because they offend the political or social beliefs of some group would just about empty our libraries.

Counter Argument

The urge to censor written words has existed in every society since man learned to write. Modern tyrannies, in particular, seek to control their subjects and keep them contented by rigorously preventing their exposure to troubling ideas in books and periodicals. But this attempt at mind control—and censorship is just that—runs counter to important American values. If successful it would place Americans, young and old, in intellectual and spiritual bondage. Censors and book banners surfacing in school districts across the nation imply that ideas must be made safe for students, whereas, in truth, students must be made safe for ideas. And to be made safe, they must be given the opportunity to develop the capacity to examine books and ideas and to judge their merit for themselves. This process is not always a soothing experience for adults, but then neither is democracy in action. As Professor Bishin of the University of Southern California College of Law reminds us, ". . . the literature and art which the First Amendment protects does not consist of only that which makes us comfortable or happy. The reason why speech and press must be protected from the majority by a constitutional amendment is precisely because humanity is endowed with the stubborn, blind tendency to strike down the new and unconventional, to view it as a threat which must be put down, rather than a possibility to be studied and criticized."[5]

[5] William R. Bishin, "The Supreme Court vs. Obscenity," *Los Angeles Times,* October 30, 1968, Part II, p. 9.

EXERCISE 28

A. Read the following passage carefully. Underline the emotive terms, list them below, and indicate their connotations.

Standard off-the-rack liberals drip tears of compassion for the wife of a convicted murderer facing execution in the gas chamber, but few of these salon socialists put on such a display for the widow of a murdered policemen. The monster who cold-bloodedly slays the owner of a liquor store or brutally molests a child invariably evokes sympathy as his case moves through the courts. The victims of these moral outrages are forgotten. Sentimental sociologists and cocktail-hour psychologists spout the nonsense that capital punishment represents "cruel and unusual" punishment and should therefore be ruled unconstitutional. What about the "cruel and unusual" punishment suffered by those criminally assaulted? Do-gooders and other mental midgets maintain the fiction that life imprisonment is a more effective and moral deterrent than capital punishment. The truth is, however, that few killers spend the rest of their lives in prison, a fact conveniently overlooked by those who agonize over violence. The degenerates who murder decent citizens deserve no such concern. They should be brought to justice and executed.

EMOTIVE WORDS	CONNOTATIONS
———————	———————
———————	———————
———————	———————
———————	———————
———————	———————
———————	———————
———————	———————
———————	———————
———————	———————
———————	———————

B. Opposite each of the words or phrases in the following list, place a word or phrase with roughly the same denotation as the word in the left-hand column but with a different connotation as directed.

EXAMPLE   tax loophole (more favorable)—tax incentive

1. an elderly spinster (less favorable) _____

2. flexible (less favorable) _____

3. taxpayers' money (more favorable) _____

4. law officer (less favorable) _____

5. soldier of fortune (less favorable) _____

6. crammed hard but flunked the test (more favorable) _____

_____

7. courageous (less favorable) _____

8. maid (more favorable) _____

9. made a pile of dough on slick real estate deals (more favorable)

_____

_____

10. used car (more favorable) _____

C. The words in the following lists have about the same denotation, but their connotations vary markedly. Rank them in order of the favorability of their connotations, beginning with the word with the most favorable associations.

1. ignorant, innocent, naive, uninformed

_____

2. obese, fat, portly, stout, pudgy

_____

3. playboy, swinger, *bon vivant*, hedonist, lecher

_____

4. eccentric, odd, nonconformist, weird, individualistic

_____

5. devout, godly, sanctimonious, religious, pious

_____

D. The following list contains ten euphemisms (sugar-coated words or phrases substituted for words and phrases with less favorable connotations). For each euphemism select the word or phrase for which it is a substitute.

1. refuse station ————————————————————————————

2. antisocial act ————————————————————————————

3. revenue enhancements ——————————————————————

4. substandard housing ——————————————————————

5. career apparel ——————————————————————————

6. petrochemical dispenser ————————————————————

7. lady of the evening ——————————————————————

8. language facilitator ——————————————————————

9. affected by an inordinate use of intoxicants ——————————

10. passed on ——————————————————————————————

E. The following newspaper column comments upon the reaction of Lord Killanin, former president of the International Olympic Committee, to the decision by President Carter to boycott the Olympic Games held in Moscow in the summer of 1980. Read the column carefully, and in a brief essay evaluate its persuasiveness. Does the writer support his judgments with sound reasoning, factual detail? Does he use emotive terms? Is he fair with the opposition? Support your judgments with specific illustrations.

HIS LORDSHIP: ENOUGH TO GET YOUR IRISH UP

"For the great Gaels of Ireland," Chesterton wrote, "are the men that God made mad, for all their wars are merry and all their songs are sad."

Lord Killanin, the departing president of the International Olympic Committee, may have fit that description once. Not now. Not recently.

When his lordship ascended to the position of chief playground director, he brought with him a reputation as an urbane, whisky-drinking Irish wit whose scholarship matched his sense of humor. He goes out on a note of petty spite, having a tantrum because the United States chose not to attend his farewell party.

"If they understand other matters as well as they understand sport, God help us all," Killanin said on the eve of the Summer Olympics in Moscow. He was talking about the Americans, who were not present.

They are not there because President Carter and most of his countrymen, repelled by what is euphemistically called the Soviet "intervention" in Afghanistan, decided that playing games with the aggressor is not the most suitable response to armed aggression.

"They did not understand how sport is organized in the world," Killanin said, still throwing rocks at the U.S. "They did not understand how the national Olympic committees work, or the working of the IOC.

"To my mind, they had no knowledge of sport other than American football and baseball. If football and baseball had been in the Olympic Games, perhaps we would not have had a boycott."

Living too long in a playpen does something to full-grown men. It isolates them from the real world, it subordinates facts to fantasy.

Waxing Prosaic

Before he won star billing in the Olympic waxworks, Killanin knew that since the modern Games began in 1896, those people with no knowledge of sport other than football and baseball had won more medals in track and field, rowing, swimming, basketball, boxing and weight lifting than anybody else.

Those people who do not understand how the IOC and national Olympic committees work ran the Winter and Summer Games of 1932 and the Winter Games of 1980 and are preparing to hold the Summer Games of 1984.

Killanin's predecessor as dominant penguin in the Olympic colony was an American, the unmitigated Avery Brundage. Slavery Avery, as the athletes called him, was not the chief custodian of sandbox and blocks forever. It only seemed that way. But he had the job long enough to set the intellectual pattern.

It would not be accurate to say that Killanin's countrymen had no knowledge of sport other than hurling and Gaelic football, but the fact is that when a young Irishman wants to learn footracing, he comes over to Villanova.

Just Super

The arrogance of the IOC and the people who head the organization surpasses understanding. It isn't generally known that there are no U.S. representatives on the committee. The IOC is a supergovernment, and citizenship works in reverse. Two of its members represent it in the U.S.

It goes without saying that nobody can choose the name, anthem or flag of a country except the people of that country. If some international body decided that the U.S. should be known henceforth as New Spain, that the flag should be a tri-color of red, blue and green and the anthem a ditty by Arlo Guthrie, somebody named Reagan or Carter or something else might raise a holler.

Little things like that don't daunt the IOC.

Killanin was in a sweat to bring China into the Olympic family during his administration, but Peking insisted that there could be only one China. The Chinese on Taiwan call their nation the Republic of China. Making the political decision that there was no such country, the IOC told the people on Taiwan to change their name, flag and anthem or get out.

Now the U.S. government tells the Soviet Union and the IOC that it doesn't want its flag raised and anthem played in the closing ceremony of the Moscow Games. It is the custom to do this in salute to the country that will hold the Games four years hence.

Killanin says it doesn't matter what the U.S. wants. "My own view," he says, "is that we should stick to protocol because this has to do with the next Games and not the present Games." [From a column by Red Smith, "His Lordship: Enough to Get Your Irish Up," *International Herald Tribune*, Paris, July 21, 1980. © Copyright 1980 by The New York Times Company. Reprinted by permission.]

F. Using the essay on pp. 275–78 as a model, write a five paragraph essay on one of the topics listed below. In your first paragraph introduce your subject, beginning broadly and narrowing down to a thesis at the end of the paragraph. In the next two paragraphs begin with an opposition argument and then counter that argument. In the fourth and fifth paragraphs focus solely on your own arguments and provide a strong conclusion in your last paragraph. In working up a scratch outline for your paper, jot down the two or three strongest arguments you can think of against your position and provide a counter to each. Then list two or three final arguments of your own. Your sheet might look something like this:

OPPOSITION ARGUMENTS   COUNTER ARGUMENTS

1. _____   1. _____

2. _____   2. _____

FINAL ARGUMENTS SUPPORTING YOUR OWN POSITION

1. _____

2. _____

TOPICS

1. You had planned to study medicine and become a doctor. At the end of your sophomore year, you decide to change your major to business administration. Your father, who is a doctor, and mother strongly oppose your decision. They provide full support for your education and threaten to cut off your support if you make the change.

2. You have been going steady with the same person for three years. You are both twenty-two and juniors in college. You plan to marry when you graduate. You inform your parents that you are going to move in together until you marry. Your parents strongly object.

3. You are a college sophomore whose parents have continually urged you to go to college so that you can find a profession and meet someone who also will be financially successful and share a comfortable life with you. Your parents were very happy when you were dating a medical student but are totally opposed to your present plan to drop out of school and marry a sales clerk whom you began to date when you broke up with the med student.

4. You are finishing your second year in college but getting tired of school. You are uncertain about your future, your course of study, and you want to drop out of college for a year to rethink your goals and renew your energy and enthusiasm. Your parents oppose your plan. Neither went to college. They fear that you won't want to return to college after a year off.

SUMMARY

Effective argumentative writing requires the ability to think logically—to reason correctly from the evidence or premises—and to persuade others to accept your reasoning. In this chapter we have briefly investigated the basic processes of reasoning, induction and deduction, and examined some common fallacies in reasoning. We have said that generalizations resulting from induction must be adequately supported; that is, there must be sufficient, relevant evidence to justify the generalization, and the evidence must be representative, accurate, and verifiable. And if testimony is used, the authority quoted must be qualified and objective. A deductive argument produces a sound conclusion when the premises are accurate and the conclusion follows logically from the premises.

Persuasive writing requires that you analyze your audience and use an appropriate tone, diction, sentence and paragraph pattern, and choice of argument in appealing to their legitimate interests. Persuasive writing, though directed primarily to your readers' reasoning powers, also uses an emotional and ethical appeal. Appealing to the emotions of your readers is a legitimate, honorable tactic, but it needs to be used with care, for if your readers believe that you are substituting emotion for credible evidence, that you are trying to bully them, they will dismiss your arguments as biased and unreliable. You must convince your readers of your integrity, so deal honestly with them by avoiding fallacies and highly charged language, unless the latter is clearly justified by the evidence you present.

PART TWO
READER

ONE

NARRATION

JAMES THURBER

University Days

This essay is based on the author's experiences as a student at Ohio State University during World War I, and was first published over fifty years ago; but its subject and style continue to appeal to college students today. Like most of Thurber's work, it reveals his capacity for converting seemingly commonplace and insignificant conflicts or problems into uncommon and significant humor. Although the situations and characterizations are undoubtedly exaggerated for humorous effect, they are never pushed quite beyond the point of credibility. Much of the success of Thurber's humor lies in his skillful use of this technique.

As you read, note how the author moves from one scene to another to develop a composite picture of his college experience.

(1) I passed all the other courses that I took at my University, but I could never pass botany. This was because all botany students had to spend several hours a week in a laboratory looking through a microscope at plant cells, and I could never see through a microscope. I never once saw a cell through a microscope. This used to enrage my instructor. He would wander around the laboratory pleased with the progress all the students were making in drawing the involved and, so I am told, interesting structure of flower cells, until he came to me. I would just be standing there. "I can't see anything," I would say. He would begin patiently enough, explaining how anybody can see through a microscope, but he would always end up in a fury, claiming that I could *too* see through a microscope but just pretended that I couldn't. "It takes away from the beauty of flowers anyway," I used to tell him. "We are not concerned with beauty in this course," he would say. "We are concerned solely with what I may call the *mechanics* of flars." "Well," I'd say, "I can't see anything." "Try it just once again," he'd say, and I would put my eye to the microscope and see nothing at all, except now and again, a nebulous milky substance—a phenomenon of maladjustment.

You were supposed to see a vivid, restless clockwork of sharply defined plant cells. "I see what looks like a lot of milk," I would tell him. This, he claimed, was the result of my not having adjusted the microscope properly; so he would readjust it for me, or rather, for himself. And I would look again and see milk.

(2) I finally took a deferred pass, as they called it, and waited a year and tried again. (You had to pass one of the biological sciences or you couldn't graduate.) The professor had come back from vacation brown as a berry, bright-eyed, and eager to explain cell-structure again to his classes. "Well," he said to me, cheerily, when we met in the first laboratory hour of the semester, "we're going to see cells this time, aren't we?" "Yes, sir," I said. Students to right of me and to left of me and in front of me were seeing cells; what's more, they were quietly drawing pictures of them in their notebooks. Of course, I didn't see anything.

(3) "We'll try it," the professor said to me, grimly, "with every adjustment of the microscope known to man. As God is my witness, I'll arrange this glass so that you see cells through it or I'll give up teaching. In twenty-two years of botany, I—" He cut off abruptly for he was beginning to quiver all over, like Lionel Barrymore, and he genuinely wished to hold onto his temper: his scenes with me had taken a great deal out of him.

(4) So we tried it with every adjustment of the microscope known to man. With only one of them did I see anything but blackness or the familiar lacteal opacity, and that time I saw, to my pleasure and amazement, a variegated constellation of flecks, specks, and dots. These I hastily drew. The instructor, noting my activity, came back from an adjoining desk, a smile on his lips and his eyebrows high in hope. He looked at my cell drawing. "What's that?" he demanded, with a hint of a squeal in his voice. "That's what I saw," I said. "You didn't, you didn't, you *didn't!*" he screamed, losing control of his temper instantly, and he bent over and squinted into the microscope. His head snapped up. "That's your eye!" he shouted. "You've fixed the lens so that it reflects! You've drawn your eye!"

(5) Another course that I didn't like, but somehow managed to pass, was economics. I went to that class straight from the botany class, which didn't help me any in understanding either subject. I used to get them mixed up. But not as mixed up as another student in my economics class who came there direct from a physics laboratory. He was a tackle on the football team, named Bolenciecwcz. At that time Ohio State University had one of the best football teams in the country, and Bolenciecwcz was one of its outstanding stars. In order to be eligible to play it was necessary for him to keep up in his studies, a very difficult matter, for while he was not dumber than an ox he was not any smarter. Most of his professors were lenient and helped him along. None gave him

more hints, in answering questions, or asked him simpler ones than the economics professor, a thin, timid man named Bassum. One day when we were on the subject of transportation and distribution, it came Bolenciecwcz's turn to answer a question. "Name one means of transportation," the professor said to him. No light came into the big tackle's eyes. "Just any means of transportation," said the professor. Bolenciecwcz sat staring at him. "That is," pursued the professor, "any medium, agency, or method of going from one place to another." Bolenciecwcz had the look of a man who is being led into a trap. "You may choose among steam, horse-drawn, or electrically propelled vehicles," said the instructor. "I might suggest the one which we commonly take in making long journeys across land." There was a profound silence in which everybody stirred uneasily, including Bolenciecwcz and Mr. Bassum. Mr. Bassum abruptly broke this silence in an amazing manner. "Choo-choo-choo," he said, in a low voice, and turned scarlet. He glanced appealingly around the room. All of us, of course, shared Mr. Bassum's desire that Bolenciecwcz should stay abreast of the class in economics, for the Illinois game, one of the hardest and most important of the season, was only a week off. "Toot, toot, too-tooooooot!" some student with a deep voice moaned; and we all looked encouragingly at Bolenciecwcz. Somebody else gave a fine imitation of a locomotive letting off steam. Mr. Bassum himself rounded off the little show. "Ding, dong, ding, dong," he said, hopefully. Bolenciecwcz was staring at the floor now, trying to think, his great brow furrowed, his huge hands rubbing together, his face red.

(6) "How did you come to college this year, Mr. Bolenciecwcz?" asked the professor. "*Chuffa* chuffa, *chuffa* chuffa."

(7) "M'father sent me," said the football player.

(8) "What on?" asked Bassum.

(9) "I git an 'lowance," said the tackle, in a low, husky voice, obviously embarrassed.

(10) "No, no," said Bassum. "Name a means of transportation. What did you *ride* here on?"

(11) "Train," said Bolenciecwcz.

(12) "Quite right," said the professor. "Now, Mr. Nugent, will you tell us—"

(13) If I went through anguish in botany and economics—for different reasons—gymnasium work was even worse. I don't even like to think about it. They wouldn't let you play games or join in the exercises with your glasses on and I couldn't see with mine off. I bumped into professors, horizontal bars, agricultural students, and swinging iron rings. Not being able to see, I could take it but I couldn't dish it out. Also, in order to pass gymnasium (and you had to pass it to graduate) you had to learn to swim if you didn't know how. I didn't like the swimming

pool, I didn't like swimming, and I didn't like the swimming instructor, and after all these years I still don't. I never swam but I passed my gym work anyway, by having another student give my gymnasium number (978) and swim across the pool in my place. He was a quiet, amiable blonde youth, number 473, and he would have seen through a microscope for me if we could have got away with it, but we couldn't get away with it. Another thing I didn't like about gymnasium work was that they made you strip the day you registered. It is impossible for me to be happy when I am stripped and being asked a lot of questions. Still, I did better than a lanky agricultural student who was cross-examined just before I was. They asked each student what college he was in—that is, whether Arts, Engineering, Commerce, or Agriculture. "What college are you in?" the instructor snapped at the youth in front of me. "Ohio State University," he said promptly.

(14) It wasn't that agricultural student but it was another a whole lot like him who decided to take up journalism, possibly on the ground that when farming went to hell he could fall back on newspaper work. He didn't realize, of course, that that would be very much like falling back full-length on a kit of carpenter's tools. Haskins didn't seem cut out for journalism, being too embarrassed to talk to anybody and unable to use a typewriter, but the editor of the college paper assigned him to the cow barns, the sheep house, the horse pavilion, and the animal husbandry department generally. This was a genuinely big "beat," for it took up five times as much ground and got ten times as great a legislative appropriation as the College of Liberal Arts. The agricultural student knew animals, but nevertheless his stories were dull and colorlessly written. He took all afternoon on each of them, because he had to hunt for each letter on the typewriter. Once in a while he had to ask somebody to help him hunt. "C" and "L," in particular, were hard letters for him to find. His editor finally got pretty much annoyed at the farmer-journalist because his pieces were so uninteresting. "See here, Haskins," he snapped at him one day, "why is it we never have anything hot from you on the horse pavilion? Here we have two hundred head of horses on this campus—more than any other university in the Western Conference except Purdue—and yet you never get any real lowdown on them. Now shoot over to the horse barns and dig up something lively." Haskins shambled out and came back in about an hour; he said he had something. "Well, start it off snappily," said the editor. "Something people will read." Haskins set to work and in a couple of hours brought a sheet of typewritten paper to the desk; it was a two-hundred word story about some disease that had broken out among the horses. Its opening sentence was simple but arresting. It read: "Who has noticed the sores on the tops of the horses in the animal husbandry building?"

(15) Ohio State was a land grant university and therefore two years

of military drill was compulsory. We drilled with old Springfield rifles and studied the tactics of the Civil War even though the World War was going on at the time. At 11 o'clock each morning thousands of freshmen and sophomores used to deploy over the campus, moodily creeping up on the old chemistry building. It was good training for the kind of warfare that was waged at Shiloh but it had no connection with what was going on in Europe. Some people used to think there was German money behind it, but they didn't dare say so or they would have been thrown in jail as German spies. It was a period of muddy thought and marked, I believe, the decline of higher education in the Middle West.

(16) As a soldier I was never any good at all. Most of the cadets were glumly indifferent soldiers, but I was no good at all. Once General Littlefield, who was commandant of the cadet corps, popped up in front of me during regimental drill and snapped, "You are the main trouble with this university!" I think he meant that my type was the main trouble with the university but he may have meant me individually. I was mediocre at drill, certainly—that is, until my senior year. By that time I had drilled longer than anybody else in the Western Conference, having failed at military at the end of each preceding year so that I had to do it all over again. I was the only senior still in uniform. The uniform which, when new, had made me look like an interurban railway conductor, now that it had become faded and too tight made me look like Bert Williams in his bell-boy act. This had a definitely bad effect on my morale. Even so, I had become by sheer practice little short of wonderful at squad manoeuvres.

(17) One day General Littlefield picked our company out of the whole regiment and tried to get it mixed up by putting it through one movement after another as fast as we could execute them: squads right, squads left, squads on right into line, squads right about, squads left front into line, etc. In about three minutes one hundred and nine men were marching in one direction and I was marching away from them at an angle of forty degrees, all alone. "Company, halt!" shouted General Littlefield, "That man is the only man who has it right!" I was made a corporal for my achievement.

(18) The next day General Littlefield summoned me to his office. He was swatting flies when I went in. I was silent and he was silent too, for a long time. I don't think he remembered me or why he had sent for me, but he didn't want to admit it. He swatted some more flies, keeping his eyes on them narrowly before he let go with the swatter. "Button up your coat!" he snapped. Looking back on it now I can see that he meant me although he was looking at a fly, but I just stood there. Another fly came to rest on a paper in front of the general and began rubbing its hind legs together. The general lifted the swatter cautiously. I moved restlessly and the fly flew away. "You startled him!" barked

General Littlefield, looking at me severely. I said I was sorry. "That won't help the situation!" snapped the General, with cold military logic. I didn't see what I could do except offer to chase some more flies toward his desk, but I didn't say anything. He stared out the window at the faraway figures of co-eds crossing the campus toward the library. Finally, he told me I could go. So I went. He either didn't know which cadet I was or else he forgot what he wanted to see me about. It may have been that he wished to apologize for having called me the main trouble with the university; or maybe he had decided to compliment me on my brilliant drilling of the day before and then at the last minute decided not to. I don't know. I don't think about it much any more.

QUESTIONS AND EXERCISES

VOCABULARY

1. nebulous (*paragraph* 1)
2. lacteal (4)
3. opacity (4)
4. variegated (4)
5. anguish (13)
6. amiable (13)
7. husbandry (14)
8. arresting (14)
9. mediocre (16)
10. interurban (16)

LANGUAGE AND RHETORIC

1. Why does the author begin new paragraphs at 2, 5, 13, 14, and 15?
2. A single topic sentence in paragraph 1 serves not only for that paragraph but for paragraphs 2, 3, and 4. Identify that sentence.
3. Locate the topic sentence that serves for paragraphs 5 through 11. Is there any controlling idea in this section?
4. Why are paragraphs 7 through 12 treated as separate paragraphs?
5. Why does paragraph 18 have no explicit controlling idea? What is the purpose of the paragraph?
6. If you were in a position to revise this essay and were required to drop one incident from the narrative, which would you choose, and why?

DISCUSSION AND WRITING

1. What implicit comment about college athletics does the section portraying the economics class make? Do you agree or disagree with the author? Why?
2. What implicit comment about required courses do the sections dealing with the botany, gym, and ROTC classes make? Have you ever had similar attitudes toward a college regulation or requirement? If so, write a paper explaining your attitude and the reasons for it.
3. Describe an interesting or unusual instructor you have had, focusing on a single trait that makes him or her interesting or unusual.

4. Recount a particularly interesting or humorous incident from your own college experience, presenting the incident as concretely as you can.
5. Develop a list of your own instructors and personal educational experiences that you might draw from to write additional essays.

GORDON PARKS

My Mother's Dream for Me

This essay by Gordon Parks recalls several important experiences in his early life and their continuing impact on his later years. His recollections of family relationships, of violence and death, and of the constant undercurrent of prejudice around them go well beyond the personal narrative to make a subtle but powerful social statement.

Note how Parks ties the different dimensions of his subject together to present a unified, coherent whole.

(1) The full meaning of my mother's death had settled over me before they lowered her into the grave. They buried her at two-thirty in the afternoon; now, at nightfall, our big family was starting to break up. Once there had been fifteen of us and, at sixteen, I was the youngest. There was never much money, so now my older brothers and sisters were scraping up enough for my coach ticket north. I would live in St. Paul, Minnesota, with my sister Maggie Lee, as my mother had requested a few minutes before she died.

(2) Poppa, a good quiet man, spent the last hours before our parting moving aimlessly about the yard, keeping to himself and avoiding me. A sigh now and then belied his outer calm. Several times I wanted to say that I was sorry to be going, and that I would miss him very much. But the silence that had always lain between us prevented this. Now I realized that probably he hadn't spoken more than a few thousand words to me during my entire childhood. It was always: "Mornin', boy"; "Git your chores done, boy"; "Goodnight, boy." If I asked for a dime or nickel, he would look beyond me for a moment, grunt, then dig through the nuts and bolts in his blue jeans and hand me the money. I loved him in spite of his silence.

(3) For his own reasons Poppa didn't go to the depot, but as my sister and I were leaving he came up, a cob pipe jutting from his mouth, and stood sideways, looking over the misty Kansas countryside. I stood awkwardly waiting for him to say something. He just grunted—three short grunts. "Well," Maggie Lee said nervously, "won't you be kissin'

your poppa goodbye?" I picked up my cardboard suitcase, turned and kissed his stubbly cheek and started climbing into the taxicab. I was halfway in when his hand touched my shoulder. "Boy, remember your momma's teachin'. You'll be all right. Just you remember her teachin'." I promised, then sat back in the Model T taxi. As we rounded the corner, Poppa was already headed for the hog pens. It was feeding time.

(4) Our parents had filled us with love and a staunch Methodist religion. We were poor, though I did not know it at the time; the rich soil surrounding our clapboard house had yielded the food for the family. And the love of this family had eased the burden of being black. But there were segregated schools and warnings to avoid white neighborhoods after dark. I always had to sit in the peanut gallery (the Negro section) at the movies. We weren't allowed to drink a soda in the drugstore in town. I was stoned and beaten and called "nigger," "black boy," "darky," "shine." These indignities came so often I began to accept them as normal. Yet I always fought back. Now I considered myself lucky to be alive; three of my close friends had already died of senseless brutality, and I was lucky that I hadn't killed someone myself. Until the very day that I left Fort Scott on that train for the North, there had been a fair chance of being shot or perhaps beaten to death. I could easily have been the victim of mistaken identity, of a sudden act of terror by hate-filled white men, or, for that matter, I could have been murdered by some violent member of my own race. There had been a lot of killing in the border states of Kansas, Oklahoma and Missouri, more than I cared to remember.

(5) I was nine years old when the Tulsa riots took place in 1921. Whites had invaded the Negro neighborhood, which turned out to be an armed camp. Many white Tulsans were killed, and rumors had it that the fight would spread into Kansas and beyond. About this time, a grown cousin of mine decided to go south to work in a mill. My mother, knowing his hot temper, pleaded with him not to go, but he caught a freight going south. Months passed and we had no word of him. Then one day his name flashed across the nation as one of the most-wanted men in the country. He had killed a white millhand who spat in his face and called him "nigger." He killed another man while fleeing the scene and shot another on the viaduct between Kansas City, Missouri, and Kansas City, Kansas.

(6) I asked Momma questions she couldn't possibly answer. Would they catch him? Would he be lynched? Where did she think he was hiding? How long did she think he could hold out? She knew what all the rest of us knew, that he would come back to our house if it was possible.

(7) He came one night. It was storming, and I lay in the dark of my room, listening to the rain pound the roof. Suddenly, the window next to my bed slid up, and my cousin, wet and cautious, scrambled through the opening. I started to yell as he landed on my bed, but he quickly covered my mouth with his hand, whispered his name, and cautioned me into silence. I got out of bed and followed him. He went straight to Momma's room, kneeled down and shook her awake. "Momma Parks," he whispered, "it's me, it's me. Wake up." And she awoke easily and put her hand on his head. "My Lord, son," she said, "you're in such bad trouble." Then she sat up on the side of the bed and began to pray over him. After she had finished, she tried to persuade him to give himself up. "They'll kill you, son. You can't run forever." But he refused. Then, going to our old icebox, he filled a sack with food and went back out my window into the cornfield.

(8) None of us ever saw or heard of him again. And I would lie awake nights wondering if the whites had killed my cousin, praying that they hadn't. I remember the huge sacks of peanut brittle he used to bring me and the rides he gave me on the back of his battered motorcycle. And my days were full of fantasies in which I helped him escape imaginary white mobs.

(9) When I was eleven, I became possessed of an exaggerated fear of death. It started one quiet summer afternoon with an explosion in the alley behind our house. I jumped up from under a shade tree and tailed Poppa toward the scene. Black smoke billowed skyward, a large hole gaped in the wall of our barn and several maimed chickens and a headless turkey flopped about on the ground. Then Poppa stopped and muttered, "Good Lord." I clutched his overalls and looked. A man, or what was left of him, was strewn about in three parts. A gas main he had been repairing had somehow ignited and blown everything around it to bits.

(10) Then once, with two friends, I had swum along the bottom of the muddy Marmaton River, trying to locate the body of a Negro man. We had been promised fifty cents apiece by the same white policeman who had shot him while he was in the water trying to escape arrest. The dead man had been in a crap game with several others who had managed to get away. My buddy, Johnny Young, was swimming beside me; we swam with ice hooks which we were to use for grappling. The two of us touched the corpse at the same instant. Fear streaked through me and the memory of his bloated body haunted my dreams for nights.

(11) One night at the Empress Theater, I sat alone in the peanut gallery watching a motion picture, *The Phantom of the Opera*. When the curious heroine, against Lon Chaney's warning, snatched away his mask, and the skull of death filled the screen, I screamed out loud and ran

out of the theater. I didn't stop until I reached home, crying to Momma, "I'm going to die! I'm going to die."

(12) Momma, after several months of cajoling, had all but destroyed this fear when another cruel thing happened. A Negro gambler called Captain Tuck was mysteriously killed on the Frisco tracks. Elmer Kinard, a buddy, and I had gone to the Cheney Mortuary out of youthful, and perhaps morbid, curiosity. Two white men, standing at the back door where bodies were received, smiled mischievously and beckoned to us. Elmer was wise and ran, but they caught me. "Come on in, boy. You want to see Captain Tuck, don't you?"

(13) "No, no," I pleaded. "No, no, let me go."

(14) The two men lifted me through the door and shoved me into a dark room. "Cap'n Tuck's in here, boy. You can say hello to him." The stench of embalming fluid mixed with fright. I started vomiting, screaming and pounding the door. Then a smeared light bulb flicked on and, there before me, his broken body covering the slab, was Captain Tuck. My body froze and I collapsed beside the door.

(15) After they revived me and put me on the street, I ran home with the old fear again running the distance beside me. My brother Clem evened the score with his fists the next day, but from then on Poppa proclaimed that no Parks would ever be caught dead in Cheney's. "The Koonantz boys will do all our burying from now on," he told Orlando Cheney.

(16) Another time, I saw a woman cut another woman to death. There were men around, but they didn't stop it. They all stood there as if they were watching a horror movie. Months later, I would shudder at the sight of Johnny Young, one of my closest buddies, lying, shot to death, at the feet of his father and the girl he loved. His murderer had been in love with the same girl. And not long after, Emphry Hawkins, who had helped us bear Johnny's coffin, was also shot to death.

(17) As the train whistled through the evening, I realized that only hours before, during what seemed like a bottomless night, I had left my bed to sleep on the floor beside my mother's coffin. It was, I knew now, a final attempt to destroy this fear of death.

(18) But in spite of the memories I would miss this Kansas land that I was leaving. The great prairies filled with green and cornstalks; the flowering apple trees, the tall elms and oaks bordering the streams that gurgled and the rivers that rolled quiet. The summers of long, sleepy days for fishing, swimming and snatching crawdads from beneath the rocks. The endless tufts of high clouds billowing across the heavens. The butterflies to chase through grass high as the chin. The swallowtails, bobolinks and robins. Nights filled with soft laughter, with fireflies and restless stars, and the winding sound of the cricket rubbing dampness

from its wing. The silver of September rain, the orange-red-brown Octobers and Novembers, and the white Decembers with the hungry smells of hams and pork butts curing in the smokehouses. Yet, as the train sped along, the telegraph poles whizzing toward and past us, I had a feeling that I was escaping a doom which had already trapped the relatives and friends I was leaving behind. For, although I was departing from this beautiful land, it would be impossible ever to forget the fear, hatred and violence that Negroes had suffered upon it.

(19) It was all behind me now. By the next day, there would be what my mother had called "another kind of world, one with more hope and promising things." She had said, "Make a man of yourself up there. Put something into it, and you'll get something out of it." It was her dream for me. When I stepped onto the chilly streets of St. Paul, Minnesota, two days later, I was determined to fulfill that dream.

QUESTIONS AND EXERCISES

VOCABULARY

1. belied (*paragraph* 2)
2. staunch (4)
3. viaduct (5)
4. cajoling (12)
5. morbid (12)

LANGUAGE AND RHETORIC

1. How does Parks use his opening lines to establish the tone and purpose of what is to follow? What is the relationship between his opening and concluding paragraphs?
2. This essay deals with several important aspects of the author's early life. What are they, and how does he tie them together?
3. The author uses a personal narrative to make some points about prejudice. What are some of the advantages and disadvantages of Parks' approach?

DISCUSSION AND WRITING

1. Parks records several incidents in the increasing awareness of his own mortality. If you have had such an experience yourself, write a personal narrative recounting that experience and its effect on you.
2. Fear of death is, of course, common. If you have experienced this emotion, write an essay dealing with the fear and how it was—or might be—overcome.
3. There are several examples of prejudice in this essay, both obvious and subtle. Have you ever been involved in a situation where you were either the victim or the source of prejudice? If so, write an essay recalling that situation and your role in it.

EDWARD ABBEY

Disorder and Early Sorrow

Readers familiar with the works of Edward Abbey will find in this essay a departure—literally as well as figuratively—from what many have come to expect in his books and articles. Rejecting the labels of "naturalist" and "nature writer," Abbey characterizes his nonfiction writing as a kind of "personal history." This essay is a backward glance down a little traveled road in that history. One can only marvel at the single-mindedness and good humor with which he pursues his objective.

Consider the author's tone and intention as you read.

(1) The first time I investigated Big Bend National Park was a long time ago, way back in '52 during my student days at the University of New Mexico. My fiancée and I drove there from Albuquerque in her brand-new Ford convertible, a gift from her Father. We were planning a sort of premature, premarital honeymoon, a week in the wilderness to cement, as it were, our permanent relationship. Things began well. With all the other tourists (few enough in those days), we followed the paved road down from Marathon and into the park at Persimmon Gap, paused at the entrance station for instruction and guidance, as per regulations, and drove up into the Chisos Mountains that form the heart of this rough, rude, arid national park. We camped for a few days in the Chisos Basin, hiking the trails to Lost Mine, to the Window, to Emory Peak and Casa Grande. Some of the things I saw from those high points, looking south, attracted me. Down in those blue, magenta, and purplish desert wastes are odd configurations of rock with names like Mule Ear Peaks and Cow Heaven Anticline. I was interested; my fiancée was satisfied with long-distance photographs.

(2) When I inquired of a ranger how to get down there, he told me we'd have to backpack it; there was, he said, "no road." I showed him my 1948 Texaco map; according to the map there was a road—unpaved, ungraded, primitive to be sure, but a road all the same—leading from the hamlet of Castolon near the southwest corner of the park to Rio Grande Village at the east-central edge of the park. Fifty miles of desert road.

(3) "That road is closed," the ranger told me.

(4) "Closed?"

(5) "Not fit for travel," he explained. "Permanently washed out. Not patrolled. Not safe. Absolutely not recommended."

(6) My sweetheart listened carefully.

(7) I thanked him and departed, knowing at once where I wanted to go. Had to go. Since we were not equipped for backpacking, it would

have to be on wheels. My fiancée expressed doubts: I reassured her. We drove down the old road along Alamo Creek—the only road at that time—to the mouth of Santa Elena Canyon. We contemplated the mouth of Santa Elena Canyon for a day, then headed east to Castolon, where we stocked up on water and food. I made no further inquiries about the desert road; I did not wish to expose myself to any arguments.

(8) A short distance beyond Castolon we came to a fork in the road. The left-hand fork was marked by a crude, hand-painted wooden sign that said:

Staked in the middle of the right-hand fork was a somewhat more official-looking board that said:

(9) The left-hand fork led northeasterly, up a rocky ravine into a jumble of desert hills. The other fork led southeasterly, following the course of the Rio Grande into the wastelands of southern Big Bend. One would have liked to meet Mr. Hartung but his road was not our road.

(10) I pulled up the No Road sign, drove through, stopped, replaced the sign. Our tire tracks in the dust showed clearly on each side of the warning sign, as if some bodiless, incorporeal ghost of a car had passed through. That should confuse the park rangers, I thought, if they ever came this way. My fiancée meanwhile was objecting to the whole procedure; she felt it was time to turn back. Gently but firmly I overruled her. We advanced, cautiously but steadily, over the rocks and through

the sand, bound for Rio Grande Village—an easy fifty-mile drive somewhere beyond those mountains and buttes, mesas and ridges and anticlines on the east.

(11) All went well for half a mile. Then we came to the first of a hundred gulches that lie transverse to the road, formed by the rare flash floods that drain from the hills to the river. The gulch was deep, narrow and dry but filled with sand and cobbles. The drop-off from the bank to streambed was two feet high. Time to build road. I got out the shovel, beveled off the edge of the cut bank on either side, removed a few of the larger rocks, logs, and other obstacles. Revving the Ford's hearty V-8 engine, I put her in low and charged down, across the rocks, and up the other side. A good little car, and it made a game effort, hanging to the lip of the far embankment while the rear wheels spun furiously in the sand and gravel. Not quite sufficient traction; we failed to make it. I backed down into the bottom of the gulch, opened the trunk, took out the luggage and filled the trunk with rocks. That helped. Gunning the engine, we made a second lunge for the top and this time succeeded, though not without cost. I could smell already the odor of burning clutch plate.

(12) Onward, though my fiancée continued to demur. We plunged into and up out of another dozen ravines, some of them deeper and rougher than the first, sometimes requiring repeated charges before we could climb out. Although the car had less than 5,000 miles to its career, some parts began to give under the strain. The right-hand door, for example, would no longer latch. Evidently the frame or body had been forced a trifle askew, springing the door. I wired it shut with a coat hanger. My sweetheart, in a grim mood by this time, suggested again that we turn around. I pointed out that the road ahead could hardly be as bad as what we had come through already and that the only sensible course lay in a resolute advance. She was doubtful; I was wrong, but forceful. I added water to the boiling radiator, diluting the manufacturer's coolant, and drove on.

(13) There seemed no choice. After all, I reasoned, we had already disregarded a park ranger's instructions and a clear warning sign. Our path was littered not only with bolts, nuts, cotter pins, and shreds of rubber, but broken law as well. Furthermore, I had to see what lay beyond the next ridge.

(14) In the afternoon we bogged down halfway through a stretch of sand. I spent two hours shoveling sand, cutting brush and laying it on the roadway, and repeatedly jacking up the rear of the car as it advanced, sank, stopped. I could have partially deflated the tires and got through more easily but we had no tire pump, and ahead lay many miles of stony trail.

(15) By sundown of the first day we had accomplished twenty miles. The car still ran but lacked some of its youthful élan. The bright enamel finish was scarred and scoriated, dulled by a film of dust. We made camp and ate our meal in silence. Coyotes howled like banshees from the foothills of Backbone Ridge, gaunt Mexican cattle bellowed down in the river bottom, and across the western sky hung the lurid, smoldering fires of sunset, a spectacle grim and ghastly as the announcement of the end of the world. A scorpion scuttled out of the shadows past our mesquite fire, hunting its evening meal. I made our bed in a dusty clearing in the cactus, but my beloved refused to sleep with me, preferring, she said, to curl up in the back seat of her car. The omens multiplied and all were dark. I slept alone under the shooting stars of Texas, dreaming of rocks and shovels.

(16) Dawn, and a dusty desert wind, and one hoot owl hooting back in the bush. I crawled out of my sack and shook my boots out (in case of arachnids), made breakfast and prepared for another struggle through the heat, the cactus, the rock, and, hardest of all, the unspeaking enmity of my betrothed.

(17) The second day was different from the first. Worse. The washouts rougher than before, the ravines deeper, the sandy washes broader, the stones sharper, the brush thornier. In the morning we had our first flat. No repair kit, of course; no pump, no tire irons. I bolted on the spare tire, which meant that for the next thirty miles we would have no spare. Onward. We thrashed in and out of more gullies and gulches, burning up the pressure plate, overheating the engine, bending things. Now the other door, the one on the driver's side, had to be secured with coathanger wire. Sprung doors were always a problem with those old Ford convertibles.

(18) We clattered on. Detouring an unnecessarily bad place on the road, I veered through the cactus and slammed into a concealed rock. Bent the tie-rod. Taking out the lug wrench, I hammered the tie-rod as straight as I could. We drove on with the front wheels toed in at a cockeyed angle. Hard to steer and not good for the tires, which were compelled, now one, now the other, or both at once, to slide as well as roll, forward. They might or might not endure for the twenty miles or so that, according to my Texaco road map and the record of the odometer, we still had to cover.

(19) As in any medical disorder, one malady aggravates another. Because of the friction in the front end I found it harder to negotiate the car across the washes and up out of the ravines. It was no longer sufficient merely to gear down into low, pop and clutch, and *charge!* up the far side. I had to charge *down* as well as *up*. The clutch still functioned, but it was going. I prayed for the clutch, but it was the oil pan

I worried about. My fiancée, clutching at the dashboard with both hands, jaw set and eyes shut, said nothing. I thought of iron seizures, bleeding crankcases, a cracked block.

(20) Nevertheless: forward. Determination is what counts.

(21) Cactus, sand pits, shock-busting chuckholes, axle-breaking wash-outs, rocks. And more rocks. Embedded like teeth in the roadway, points upward, they presented a constant nagging threat to my peace of mind. No matter how slowly I drove forward, lurching over the ruts at one mile an hour, there was no way I could avoid them all. I missed a few, but one of them got us, five miles short of the goal, late in the afternoon of the second day. A sharp report rang out, like a gunshot, followed by the squeal of hot air, the sigh of an expiring tire, and I knew we were in difficulty.

(22) I stopped to inspect the damage, for form's sake, but there was really nothing I could do. Nothing practical, that is, except maybe pull the wheel and roll it on to Rio Grande Village by hand where, possibly, I could have it fitted with a new tire, and roll it back here to the stricken Ford. I suggested this procedure to my one and only. She objected to being left alone in this scorching wilderness full of animals and Mexicans while I disappeared to the east. Did she wish to walk with me? No, she didn't want to do that either.

(23) That helped make up my mind. I got back in the car, started the engine and drove on, flat tire thumping on the roadway, radiator steam-ing, clutch smoking, oil burning, front wheels squealing, the frame and all moving parts a shuddering mass of mechanical indignation. The car clanked forward on an oblique axis, crabwise, humping up and down on the eccentric camber of the flat. Scraps of hot, smoking rubber from the shredded tire marked our progress. Late in the evening, on scal-loped wheel rim and broken heart, we rumbled painfully into Rio Grande Village, pop. 22 counting dogs.

(24) My fiancée took the first bus out of town. She had most of our money. I was left behind to hitchhike through west Texas with two dollars and forty-seven cents in my pocket. The car, as I later heard, was salvaged by my sweetheart and her friends, but never recovered to its original *esprit de Ford*. Nor did I ever see my fian-cée again. Our permanent relationship had been wrecked, perma-nently. Not that I could blame her one bit. She was fully justified. Who could question that statement? All the same it hurt; the pain lingered for weeks. Small consolation to me was the homely wis-dom of the philosopher, to wit:

> A woman is only a woman
> But a good Ford is a car.

QUESTIONS AND EXERCISES

VOCABULARY

1. configurations (*paragraph* 1)
2. incorporeal (10)
3. anticlines (10)
4. transverse (11)
5. demur (12)
6. élan (15)
7. scoriated (15)
8. banshees (15)
9. lurid (15)
10. mesquite (15)
11. arachnids (16)
12. malady (19)
13. oblique (23)
14. camber (23)
15. esprit (24)

LANGUAGE AND RHETORIC

1. Describe the author's tone. Is he solemn, bitter, playful, mock serious? At the outset of his narrative, he refers to his companion as his "sweetheart" and "fiancée." Later he refers to her as his "betrothed" and "my one and only." What do these expressions reveal about the author's attitude toward his fiancée? Does it change? If so, why? Identify the allusion in the final two lines.
2. In paragraphs 1, 7, and 12, the writer uses the compound sentence with a semicolon to connect two clauses. Would a coordinating conjunction with a comma work as well to join the clauses? Explain.
3. Point out examples of parallel structure in paragraphs 10,17,19, and 23.
4. Point out examples of vigorous, lively diction that helps to convey meaning and describe scenes vividly.
5. The author makes effective use of the verbal phrase to add variety and vigor to his style. Find examples in paragraphs 11, 17, and 18. He also makes frequent use of the sentence fragment in paragraphs 7, 11, 17, 18, 20, 21, and 22. Can these fragments be justified? Reread pages 205–7 to refresh your memory about appropriate use of the fragment.
6. This story reveals something about the effect of youthful male determination and stubbornness (perhaps chauvinism) on an engagement of marriage and on the intelligent use of automobiles. Which of these two effects does the writer consider more important? Consider your response to question 1 before you formulate your answer, since tone qualifies theme in this story. In particular, consider the last two lines.

DISCUSSION AND WRITING

1. To what extent is this experience merely an adventure in youthful folly? Is there anything to be learned from it? If so, what?
2. Compare and contrast the attitudes toward male-female relationships expressed in the essay by Erich Fromm (pp. 397–400) and those expressed in this essay by Edward Abbey. Do you think that Fromm would approve of young Abbey in this regard? Support your answer with specifics.
3. Examine the author's attitude toward his female companion throughout this essay. Does he demonstrate any feeling for her? Any concern? How would you characterize their relationship?

4. What is your impression of the author as a person, in light of the experience related here? What is your basis for that impression? Be specific.
5. Try to recapture on paper an experience from your life having to do with a male-female relationship under extremely demanding conditions. If the situation has the potential for a humorous treatment, you might see if you can render it in the same spirit that Abbey has in this essay.

T. H. WATKINS

Little Deaths

It has been more than ten years since the day my cousin let me walk his traplines with him. We never see each other now. Our worlds, never very close, have grown even farther apart. He left California several years ago to become a trapping supervisor somewhere in Nevada, while I have joined the ranks of those who would cheerfully eliminate his way of life. He would, rightly enough, consider me one of his natural enemies, and it is not likely that we would have much to say if we did meet. Still, I am grateful to him for giving me a glimpse into the reality of a world normally hidden from us, a dark little world where death is the only commonplace.

At the time, my cousin was a lowly field trapper at the beck and call of any rancher or farmer who made an official complaint to the trapping service about varmint troubles—coyotes or wildcats getting after newborn lambs, foxes sneaking into chicken coops, that sort of thing. His current assignment was to trap out the varmint population of some ranchland high in the Diablo Hills southeast of Oakland, a country of rolling grassland, scrub oak, and chaparral dominated by the 3,000-foot upthrust of Mount Diablo. His base was a house trailer planted on the edge of one of the ranches he was servicing near Livermore, although he got into Oakland quite a lot for weekend visits to a lady of his acquaintance. I lived in Oakland at the time, and he usually made a point of stopping by to see my children, of whom he was particularly fond.

I was then a practicing student of western history and thoroughly intrigued by the glittering adventure that pervaded my reading—especially in the stories of the mountain men, those grizzled, anarchic beings with a lust for far places and far things, stubborn individualists who had lived freer than any Indian and had followed their quest for beaver pelts into nearly all the mysterious blanks of the American West, from Taos, New Mexico, to Puget Sound, from the Marys River of the northern Rockies to the Colorado River of the Southwest; hopelessly romantic creatures with a predilection for Indian women, a talent for profanity, and a thirst for liquor profound enough to melt rivets. And here was my cousin, the literary—if not lineal—descendant of the mountain man. True, he was neither grizzled nor given much to profanity, nor had he, so far as I knew, ever offered his blanket to an Indian woman. Still, he was a *trapper,* by God, and when on one of his visits he invited me to accompany him on his rounds, I was entranced with the notion.

Late one spring afternoon I bundled wife and children into the car and drove down to Livermore and out to the ranch where he was staying. After a dinner cooked in the trailer's tiny kitchen, my wife and the children bedded down in the trailer's two little bunks. "When we get back tomorrow afternoon," my cousin told the children. "I'll take you out and show you some spring lambs. You'd like that, right?" he added, giving them a pinch and tickle that set them to giggling in delight. He and I bundled up in sleeping bags on the ground outside.

It was pitch black when he woke me that next morning at five o'clock. After shocking ourselves out of sleep by bathing our faces in water from the outside faucet, we got into his pickup and drove off for breakfast at an all-night diner on the road. Dawn was insinuating itself over the dark hills by the time we finished breakfast, and had laid a neon streak across the sky when we finally turned off the highway and began climbing a rutted dirt road that led to the first trapline (we would be walking two traplines, my cousin explained, one on the western side of the hills, one on the eastern; these were two of the six he had scattered over the whole range, each of them containing between 15 and 20 traps and each checked out and reset or moved to a new location every ten days or so). As we bumped and rattled up the road, daylight slowly illuminated the hills. For two or three months in the spring, before the summer sun turns them warm and brown, these hills look as if they had been transplanted whole from Ireland or Wales. They are a celebration of green, all shades of green, from the black-green of manzanita leaves to the bright, pooltable green of the grasses. Isolated bunches of cows and sheep stood almost motionless, like ornaments added for the effect of contrast, and morning mist crept around the base of trees and shrouded dark hollows with the ghost of its presence. Through all this, the exposed earth of the road cut like a red scar, and the sounds of the pickup's engine and the country-western music yammering out of its radio intruded themselves on the earth's silence gracelessly.

We talked of my cousin's father, whom he worshipped and emulated. My cousin was, in fact, almost literally following in his father's footsteps, for "the old man" had been a state trapper himself and was now trapping supervisor. Before that, back in the deep of the Depression, he had been a lion hunter for the state, when a mountain lion's ears were good as money, and before that he had "cowboyed some," as he put it; at one time, according to family tradition, his grandfather's ranch had encompassed much of what became the town of San Bernardino in Southern California. At one point in his life, he had led jaguar-hunting trips to the jungles of northwestern Mexico, and he was still a noteworthy hunter, though now he confined himself principally to an occasional deer, antelope, or bear. My cousin had grown up in a house where skins of various types served as rugs and couch-throws, where stuffed heads glared unblinkingly from the walls, where sleek hounds were always in-and-out, where hunting magazines dominated the tables, hunting talk dominated the conversations, and everywhere was the peculiarly masculine smell of newly oiled guns, all kinds of guns—pistols (including an old Colt once used by my cousin's great-grandfather, legend had it, to kill a man), rifles, shotguns. It was a family that had been killing things for a long time, sometimes for meat, sometimes for a living, sometimes for what was called the sport of it, and one of my cousin's consuming ambitions was to bag a bighorn sheep, something his father had never managed to do.

I had never killed anything in my life except fish, and since fish neither scream, grunt, squeal, nor moan when done in, it had never seemed like killing at all. In any case, I was by no means prepared for the first sight of what my cousin did to earn his bread. I don't know what I had expected with my romantic notions of the trapper's life, but surely it was something other than what I learned when we crawled up the road through increasingly heavy underbrush and stopped to check out the first of my cousin's traps.

We got out of the truck and beat our way through the brush to a spot perhaps 30 feet from the road. I did not see the animal until we were nearly on top of it. It was a raccoon, the first raccoon I had ever seen in person, and at that moment I wished that I never had seen one. It was dead, had been dead for several days, my cousin informed me. "Hunger, thirst, and shock is what kills them, mostly," he said in response to my question. "That, and exhaustion, I reckon." The animal seemed ridiculously tiny in death. It lay on its side, its small mouth, crawling with ants, open in a bared-tooth grin, and its right rear leg in the clutch of the steel trap. It was easy to see how the animal had exhausted itself; it had been at its leg. A strip of flesh perhaps three inches in width had been gnawed away, leaving the white of bone and a length of tendon exposed. Tiny flies sang about the ragged wound and over the pool of dried blood beneath the leg. There was a stink in the air, and it suddenly seemed very, very warm to me there in the morning shadows of the brush.

"Once in a while," my cousin said, prying open the curved jaws of the trap, "one of them will chew his way loose, and if he doesn't lose too much blood he can live. I caught a three-legged coyote once. Too stupid to learn, I guess."

"Do you ever find one of them still alive?" I asked.

"Sometimes."

"What do you do with them?"

He looked up at me. "Do with them? I shoot them," he said, patting the holstered pistol at his waist. He lifted the freed raccoon by the hind legs and swing it off into the brush. "Buzzard meat," he said. He then grabbed the steel stake to which the trap was attached by a chain and worked it out of the ground. "I've had this line going for over a month, now. The area's just about trapped out." He carried the trap back to the road, threw it in the back of the pickup, and we drove up the increasingly rough road to the next trap. It was empty, as was the one after it. I was beginning to hope they would all be empty, but the fourth one contained a small skunk, a black-and-white pussycat of a creature that had managed to get three of its feet in the trap at once and lay huddled in death like a child's stuffed toy. It, too, was disengaged and tossed into the brush. A little further up the ridge, and we found a fox, to my cousin's visible relief. "Great," he said. "That has to be the mate to the one I got a couple of weeks ago. Pregnant, too. There won't be any little foxes running around this year." Into the brush the animal went.

By the time we reached the top of the long ridge on which my cousin had set his traps, the morning had slipped toward noon and our count had risen to seven animals: three raccoons, three skunks, and the pregnant fox. There was only one trap left now, but it was occupied by the prize of the morning, a bobcat. "I'll be damned," my cousin said, "I've been after that bugger all month. Just about give up hope." The bobcat had not died well, but in anger. The marks of its rage and anguish were laid out in a torn circle of earth described by the length of the chain that had linked the animal to its death. Even the brush had been ripped and clawed at, leaves and twigs stripped from branches, leaving sweeping scars. Yellow tufts of the animal's fur lay scattered on the ground, as if the bobcat had torn at its own body for betraying it, and its death-mask was a silent howl of outrage. My cousin took it out of the trap and heaved it down the side of the hill. Buzzard meat.

We had to go back down the hills and around the range in order to come up the eastern slopes and check out the second trapline, and on the way we stopped at a small roadhouse in Clayton for a hamburger and a beer. I found I could eat, which surprised me a little, and I certainly had a thirst for the beer. We sat side-by-side at the bar, not saying much. Something Wallace Stegner had once written kept flashing through my mind. "Like most of my contemporaries," he had said, "I grew up careless. I grew up killing things." I wondered if my cousin would know what Stegner had been talking about, and decided it would be best not to bring it up. I could have cancelled out right there, I suppose, asking him to take me back to his camp, explaining that I had seen enough, too much, of the trapper's life. I could always plead exhaustion. After all, the day's hiking had been more real exercise than I had had in months, and I was, in fact, tired. A stubborn kernel of pride would not let me do it. I would see the day through to the end.

So the ritual continued. We climbed back up into the hills on the east side of the range in the oven-heat of a strong spring sun. The day's count rose even more as the pickup bounced its way up the ragged weedgrown road: two more skunks, another fox, two more raccoons. The work went more slowly than the mornings's run, for this was a new line, and each trap had to be reset. My cousin performed this task with an efficient swiftness and the kind of quiet pride any craftsman takes in his skill, snapping and locking the jaws of the traps, covering them with a thin scattering of earth and twigs, sprinkling the ground about with dog urine from a plastic squeeze bottle to cover up the man-smell. By the time we were ready to approach the last three traps of the line, it was well after three o'clock. We were very high by then, well up on the slopes of Mount Diablo itself, and we had to abandon the pickup to hike the rest of the way on foot. We broke out of the brush and walked along a spur of the hills. About 1,500 feet below us and some miles to the east, we could see the towns of Pittsburg and Martinez sending an urban haze into the air. Ahead of me, my cousin suddenly stopped.

"Wait a minute. Listen," he said.

A distant thrashing and rattling sound came from the slope below us. "That's where the trap is," he said. "Might be a bobcat, but I didn't expect to get him so soon. Come on."

The slope was very steep, and we slid much of the way down to the trap on our bottoms, slapped at and tangled by brush. The animal was not a bobcat. It was a dog, a large, dirty-white mongrel whose foreleg was gripped in the trap. The dog snarled at us as we approached it. Saliva had gathered at its lips and there was a wildness in its eyes.

"Dammit," my cousin said. He had owned dogs all his life. "A wild dog. Probably abandoned by somebody. They do it all the time. Dogs turn wild and start running in packs. Some people ought to be shot."

I didn't know what he wanted to do. He hadn't pulled out his gun. "Can we turn him loose? Maybe he isn't wild. Maybe he just wandered up here on his own."

My cousin looked at me. "Maybe. There's a noose-pole in the back of the truck—a kind of long stick with a loop of rope at the end. Why don't you get it?'

I scrambled back up the slope and made my way back to the pickup, where I found the noose-pole. As thick as a broomhandle and about five feet in length, it looked like a primitive fishing-pole. When I got back down to the trap, the dog was still snarling viciously. My cousin took the pole from me, opened the loop at the end, and extended it toward the dog. "If I can hook him," he said, "I'll hold his head down while you open the trap. You've seen how I do it."

It was useless. The dog fought at the loop frantically in a madness of pain and fear. After perhaps 15 minutes, my cousin laid the pole down. "He just isn't going to take it."

"What'll we do?" I asked, though I'm sure I knew.

He shrugged. "Can't just leave him here to die." He unsnapped his holster and pulled out the gun. He duck-walked to within a couple of feet of the animal, which watched him suspiciously. "I'll try to do it with one shot," he said. The gun's discharge slammed into the silence of the mountain. The dog howled once, a long, penetrating song of despair that ran in echoes down the hill. My cousin nudged the animal with his boot. It was dead. He opened the trap, freed the leg, and heaved the body down the slope. The crashing of its fall seemed to go on for a long time. My cousin reset the trap. "Come on," he said. "It's getting late."

The last trap of the day held a dead raccoon.

My cousin was pleased with the day's work. "If it keeps up like this," he said as we rattled down the highway toward his trailer, "I could be out of here in a month."

"What's the hurry?"

He indicated a small housing development by the side of the road. "Too much civilization around here for me. Too many people. I need to get back up into the mountains."

There was plenty of light left when we got back, and true to his promise, my cousin took the children out into the fields to see a newborn lamb. While its mother bleated in protest, he ran one down and brought it to my children so they could pet it. I watched his face as he held the little creature. There was no hint in it of all the death we had harvested that day, no hint of the half-eaten legs we had seen, no hint of the fearful thrashing agony the animals had endured before dying. No hint, even, of the death-howl of the dirty white dog that may or may not have been wild. There was neither irony nor cynicism in him. He held the lamb with open, honest delight at the wonder my children found in touching this small, warm, live thing.

My cousin is not an evil man. We are none of us evil men.

TWO
DESCRIPTION

DEEMS TAYLOR
The Monster

Much has been written about the effect of conformity on the creative mind. In this essay, Deems Taylor describes a genius who refused to be devoured by or to compromise with society. The title suggests the personality and behavior of Taylor's subject, paragraph 2 sharpens the focus, and the body of the article develops in detail the central impression of the man. In the concluding paragraphs, Taylor evaluates "the monster's" artistic achievements and asks the essential question: Is society willing to pay the price of genius?

This is one of the best selections in the book for the study of topic sentences; be especially conscious of where and how they are used.

(1) He was an undersized little man, with a head too big for his body—a sickly little man. His nerves were bad. He had skin trouble. It was agony for him to wear anything next to his skin coarser than silk. And he had delusions of grandeur.

(2) He was a monster of conceit. Never for one minute did he look at the world or at people, except in relation to himself. He was not only the most important person in the world, to himself; in his own eyes he was the only person who existed. He believed himself to be one of the greatest dramatists in the world, one of the greatest thinkers, and one of the greatest composers. To hear him talk, he was Shakespeare, and Beethoven, and Plato, rolled into one. And you would have had no difficulty in hearing him talk. He was one of the most exhausting conversationalists that ever lived. An evening with him was an evening spent in listening to a monologue. Sometimes he was brilliant; sometimes he was maddeningly tiresome. But whether he was being brilliant or dull, he had one sole topic of conversation: himself. What *he* thought and what *he* did.

(3) He had a mania for being in the right. The slightest hint of disagreement, from anyone, on the most trivial point, was enough to

set him off on a harangue that might last for hours, in which he proved himself right in so many ways, and with such exhausting volubility, that in the end his hearer, stunned and deafened, would agree with him, for the sake of peace.

(4) It never occurred to him that he and his doing were not of the most intense and fascinating interest to anyone with whom he came in contact. He had theories about almost any subject under the sun, including vegetarianism, the drama, politics, and music; and in support of these theories he wrote pamphlets, letters, books . . . thousands upon thousands of words, hundreds and hundreds of pages. He not only wrote these things, and published them—usually at somebody else's expense—but he would sit and read them aloud, for hours, to his friends and his family.

(5) He wrote operas; and no sooner did he have the synopsis of a story, but he would invite—or rather summon—a crowd of his friends to his house and read it aloud to them. Not for criticism. For applause. When the complete poem was written, the friends had to come again, and hear *that* read aloud. Then he would publish the poem, sometimes years before the music that went with it was written. He played the piano like a composer, in the worst sense of what that implies, and he would sit down at the piano before parties that included some of the finest pianists of his time, and play for them, by the hour, his own music, needless to say. He had a composer's voice. And he would invite eminent vocalists to his house, and sing them his operas, taking all the parts.

(6) He had the emotional stability of a six-year-old child. When he felt out of sorts, he would rave and stamp, or sink into suicidal gloom and talk darkly of going to the East to end his days as a Buddhist monk. Ten minutes later, when something pleased him, he would rush out of doors and run around the garden, or jump up and down on the sofa, or stand on his head. He could be grief-stricken over the death of a pet dog, and he could be callous and heartless to a degree that would have made a Roman emperor shudder.

(7) He was almost innocent of any sense of responsibility. Not only did he seem incapable of supporting himself, but it never occurred to him that he was under any obligation to do so. He was convinced that the world owed him a living. In support of this belief, he borrowed money from everybody who was good for a loan—men, women, friends, or strangers. He wrote begging letters by the score, sometimes groveling without shame, at others loftily offering his intended benefactor the privilege of contributing to his support, and being mortally offended if the recipient declined the honor. I have found no record of his ever paying or repaying money to anyone who did not have a legal claim upon it.

(8) What money he could lay his hands on he spent like an Indian rajah. The mere prospect of a performance of one of his operas was

enough to set him running up bills amounting to ten times the amount of his prospective royalties. On an income that would reduce a more scrupulous man to doing his own laundry, he would keep two servants. Without enough money in his pocket to pay his rent, he would have the walls and ceiling of his study lined with pink silk. No one will ever know—certainly he never knew—how much money he owed. We do know that his greatest benefactor gave him $6,000 to pay the most pressing of his debts in one city, and a year later had to give him $16,000 to enable him to live in another city without being thrown into jail for debt.

(9) He was equally unscrupulous in other ways. An endless procession of women marches through his life. His first wife spent twenty years enduring and forgiving his infidelities. His second wife had been the wife of his most devoted friend and admirer, from whom he stole her. And even while he was trying to persuade her to leave her first husband he was writing to a friend to inquire whether he could suggest some wealthy woman—*any* wealthy woman—whom he could marry for her money.

(10) He was completely selfish in his other personal relationships. His liking for his friends was measured solely by the completeness of their devotion to him, or by their usefulness to him, whether financial or artistic. The minute they failed him—even by so much as refusing a dinner invitation—or began to lessen in usefulness, he cast them off without a second thought. At the end of his life he had exactly one friend left whom he had known even in middle age.

(11) He had a genius for making enemies. He would insult a man who disagreed with him about the weather. He would pull endless wires in order to meet some man who admired his work, and was able and anxious to be of use to him—and would proceed to make a mortal enemy of him with some idiotic and wholly uncalled-for exhibition of arrogance and bad manners. A character in one of his operas was a caricature of one of the most powerful music critics of his day. Not content with burlesquing him, he invited the critic to his house and read him the libretto aloud in front of his friends.

(12) The name of this monster was Richard Wagner. Everything that I have said about him you can find on record—in newspapers, in police reports, in the testimony of people who knew him, in his own letters, between the lines of his autobiography. And the curious thing about this record is that it doesn't matter in the least.

(13) Because this undersized, sickly, disagreeable, fascinating little man was right all the time. The joke was on us. He *was* one of the world's great dramatists; he *was* a great thinker; he *was* one of the most stupendous musical geniuses that, up to now, the world has ever seen. The world did owe him a living. People couldn't know those things at the time, I suppose; and yet to us, who know his music, it does seem as

though they should have known. What if he did talk about himself all the time? If he talked about himself for twenty-four hours every day for the span of his life he would not have uttered half the number of words that other men have spoken and written about him since his death.

(14) When you consider what he wrote—thirteen operas and music dramas, eleven of them still holding the stage, eight of them unquestionably worth ranking among the world's greatest musico-dramatic masterpieces—when you listen to what he wrote, the debts and heartaches that people had to endure from him don't seem much of a price. Edward Hanslick, the critic whom he caricatured in *Die Meistersinger* and who hated him ever after, now lives only because he was caricatured in *Die Meistersinger*. The women whose hearts he broke are long since dead; and the man who could never love anyone but himself has made them deathless atonement, I think, with *Tristan und Isolde*. Think of the luxury with which for a time, at least, fate rewarded Napoleon, the man who ruined France and looted Europe; and then perhaps you will agree that a few thousand dollars' worth of debts were not too heavy a price to pay for the *Ring* trilogy.

(15) What if he was faithless to his friends and to his wives? He had one mistress to whom he was faithful to the day of his death: Music. Not for a single moment did he ever compromise with what he believed, with what he dreamed. There is not a line of his music that could have been conceived by a little mind. Even when he is dull, or downright bad, he is dull in the grand manner. There is a greatness about his worst mistakes. Listening to his music, one does not forgive him for what he may or may not have been. It is not a matter of forgiveness. It is a matter of being dumb with wonder that his poor brain and body didn't burst under the torment of the demon of creative energy that lived inside him, struggling, clawing, scratching to be released; tearing, shrieking at him to write the music that was in him. The miracle is that what he did in the little space of seventy years could have been done at all, even by a great genius. Is it any wonder that he had no time to be a man?

QUESTIONS AND EXERCISES

VOCABULARY

1. grandeur (*paragraph* 1)
2. mania (3)
3. harangue (3)
4. vegetarianism (4)
5. callous (6)
6. groveling (7)
7. scrupulous (8)
8. infidelities (9)
9. caricature (11)
10. libretto (11)

LANGUAGE AND RHETORIC

1. Underline the topic sentence for each paragraph. When you have done this, you will have a virtual summary of the entire selection.
2. Examine the division of this article by paragraphs. Explain why in paragraphs 3 through 11 the author begins each new paragraph at that particular point.
3. The name of the subject, Richard Wagner, is withheld until paragraph 12. Why? What difference would it make if the name had been introduced immediately?
4. Write a thesis statement expressing the main idea of this selection in your own words.

DISCUSSION AND WRITING

1. The author says in effect that Wagner's contributions as an artist make his shortcomings as a man relatively unimportant. Do you agree or disagree? Why?
2. If Wagner had been a failure as an artist, would his personal weaknesses be unimportant? Should we be willing to tolerate the disagreeable qualities of the artistic failure as well as those of the artistic success, or should some distinction be made? If the latter, where and how would you draw the line?
3. It has been said that, rather than geniuses adjusting to society, society must adjust to its geniuses. What is the basis for this view? Do you agree or disagree? Why?
4. If you have known a particularly gifted person in some field of the arts, write a paper describing that person as a human being and as an artist. If you are not personally familiar with someone in the arts, select a public figure as your subject.

GEORGE ORWELL

Marrakech

World travelers have made the Moroccan city of Marrakech a fashionable place to visit and a major tourist attraction in Northwest Africa. The city described here, however, presents a very different picture—one not likely to reinforce the popular image. George Orwell focuses on the ten percent of the townspeople who own "literally nothing except the rags they stand up in," and it would appear that the appeal of the city to travelers has developed despite this other view.

Note how Orwell uses a number of different scenes to convey a dominant impression of life in Marrakech.

(1) As the corpse went past the flies left the restaurant table in a cloud and rushed after it, but they came back a few minutes later.

(2) The little crowd of mourners—all men and boys, no women—

threaded their way across the market-place between the piles of pomegranates and the taxies and the camels, wailing a short chant over and over again. What really appeals to the flies is that the corpses here are never put into coffins, they are merely wrapped in a piece of rag and carried on a rough wooden bier on the shoulders of four friends. When the friends get to the burying-ground they hack an oblong hole a foot or two deep, dump the body in it and fling over it a little of the dried-up, lumpy earth, which is like broken brick. No gravestone, no name, no identifying mark of any kind. The burying-ground is merely a huge waste of hummocky earth, like a derelict building-lot. After a month or two no one can even be certain where his own relatives are buried.

(3) When you walk through a town like this—two hundred thousand inhabitants, of whom at least twenty thousand own literally nothing except the rags they stand up in—when you see how the people live, and still more how easily they die, it is always difficult to believe that you are walking among human beings. All colonial empires are in reality founded upon that fact. The people have brown faces—besides, there are so many of them! Are they really the same flesh as yourself? Do they even have names? Or are they merely a kind of undifferentiated brown stuff, about as individual as bees or coral insects? They rise out of the earth, they sweat and starve for a few years, and then they sink back into the nameless mounds of the graveyard and nobody notices that they are gone. And even the graves themselves soon fade back into the soil. Sometimes, out for a walk, as you break your way through the prickly pear, you notice that it is rather bumpy underfoot, and only a certain regularity in the bumps tells you that you are walking over skeletons.

(4) I was feeding one of the gazelles in the public gardens.

(5) Gazelles are almost the only animals that look good to eat when they are still alive, in fact, one can hardly look at their hindquarters without thinking of mint sauce. The gazelle I was feeding seemed to know that this thought was in my mind, for though it took the piece of bread I was holding out it obviously did not like me. It nibbled rapidly at the bread, then lowered its head and tried to butt me, then took another nibble and then butted again. Probably its idea was that if it could drive me away the bread would somehow remain hanging in mid-air.

(6) An Arab navvy working on the path nearby lowered his heavy hoe and sidled slowly towards us. He looked from the gazelle to the bread and from the bread to the gazelle, with a sort of quiet amazement, as though he had never seen anything quite like this before. Finally he said shyly in French:

(7) "*I* could eat some of that bread."

(8) I tore off a piece and he stowed it gratefully in some secret place under his rags. This man is an employee of the Municipality.

(9) When you go through the Jewish quarters you gather some ideas of what the medieval ghettoes were probably like. Under their Moorish rulers the Jews were only allowed to own land in certain restricted areas, and after centuries of this kind of treatment they have ceased to bother about overcrowding. Many of the streets are a good deal less than six feet wide, the houses are completely windowless, and sore-eyed children cluster everywhere in unbelievable numbers, like clouds of flies. Down the center of the street there is generally running a little river of urine.

(10) In the bazaar huge families of Jews, all dressed in the long black robe and little black skull-cap, are working in dark fly-infested booths that look like caves. A carpenter sits crosslegged at a prehistoric lathe, turning chair-legs at lightning speed. He works the lathe with a bow in his right hand and guides the chisel with his left foot, and thanks to a lifetime of sitting in this position his left leg is warped out of shape. At his side his grandson, aged six, is already starting on the simpler parts of the job.

(11) I was just passing the coppersmith's booths when somebody noticed that I was lighting a cigarette. Instantly, from the dark holes all round, there was a frenzied rush of Jews, many of them old grandfathers with flowing grey beards, all clamoring for a cigarette. Even a blind man somewhere at the back of one of the booths heard a rumor of cigarettes and came crawling out, groping in the air with his hand. In about a minute I had used up the whole packet. None of these people, I suppose, works less than twelve hours a day, and every one of them looks on a cigarette as a more or less impossible luxury.

(12) As the Jews live in self-contained communities they follow the same trades as the Arabs, except for agriculture. Fruit-sellers, potters, silversmiths, blacksmiths, butchers, leatherworkers, tailors, water carriers, beggars, porters—whichever way you look you see nothing but Jews. As a matter of fact there are thirteen thousand of them, all living in the space of a few acres. A good job Hitler wasn't here. Perhaps he was on his way, however. You hear the usual dark rumors about the Jews, not only from the Arabs but from the poorer Europeans.

(13) "Yes, mon vieux, they took my job away from me and gave it to a Jew. The Jews! They're the real rulers of this country, you know. They're got all the money. They control the banks, finance—everything."

(14) "But," I said, "isn't it a fact that the average Jew is a laborer working for about a penny an hour?"

(15) "Ah, that's only for show! They're all moneylenders really. They're cunning, the Jews."

(16) In just the same way, a couple of hundred years ago, poor old

women used to be burned for witchcraft when they could not even work enough magic to get themselves a square meal.

(17) All people who work with their hands are partly invisible, and the more important the work they do, the less visible they are. Still, a white skin is always fairly conspicuous. In northern Europe, when you see a laborer ploughing a field, you probably give him a second glance. In a hot country, anywhere south of Gibraltar or east of the Suez, the chances are that you don't even see him. I have noticed this again and again. In a tropical landscape one's eye takes in everything except the human beings. It takes in the dried-up soil, the prickly pear, the palm tree and the distant mountain, but it always misses the peasant hoeing at his patch. He is the same color as the earth, and a great deal less interesting to look at.

(18) It is only because of this that the starved countries of Asia and Africa are accepted as tourist resorts. No one would think of running cheap trips to the Distressed Areas. But where the human beings have brown skins their poverty is simply not noticed. What does Morocco mean to a Frenchman? An orange-grove or a job in Government service. Or to an Englishman? Camels, castles, palm trees, Foreign Legionnaires, brass trays, and bandits. One could probably live there for years without noticing that for nine-tenths of the people the reality of life is an endless, back-breaking struggle to wring a little food out of an eroded soil.

(19) Most of Morocco is so desolate that no wild animal bigger than a hare can live on it. Huge areas which were once covered with forest have turned into a treeless waste where the soil is exactly like broken-up brick. Nevertheless a good deal of it is cultivated, with frightful labor. Everything is done by hand. Long lines of women, bent double like inverted capital L's, work their way slowly across the fields, tearing up the prickly weeds with their hands, and the peasant gathering lucerne for fodder pulls it up stalk by stalk instead of reaping it, thus saving an inch or two on each stalk. The plough is a wretched wooden thing, so frail that one can easily carry it on one's shoulder, and fitted underneath with a rough iron spike which stirs the soil to a depth of about four inches. This is as much as the strength of the animals is equal to. It is usual to plough with a cow and a donkey yoked together. Two donkeys would not be quite strong enough, but on the other hand two cows would cost a little more to feed. The peasants possess no harrows, they merely plough the soil several times over in different directions, finally leaving it in rough furrows, after which the whole field has to be shaped with hoes into small oblong patches to conserve water. Except for a day or two after the rare rainstorms there is never enough water. Along the edges of the fields channels are hacked out to a depth of thirty or forty feet to get at the tiny trickles which run through the subsoil.

(20) Every afternoon a file of very old women passes down the road outside my house, each carrying a load of firewood. All of them are mummified with age and the sun, and all of them are tiny. It seems to be generally the case in primitive communities that the women, when they get beyond a certain age, shrink to the size of children. One day a poor old creature who could not have been more than four feet tall crept past me under a vast load of wood. I stopped her and put a five-sou piece (a little more than a farthing) into her hand. She answered with a shrill wail, almost a scream, which was partly gratitude but mainly surprise. I suppose that from her point of view, by taking any notice of her, I seemed almost to be violating a law of nature. She accepted her status as an old woman, that is to say as a beast of burden. When a family is traveling it is quite usual to see a father and a grownup son riding ahead on donkeys, and an old woman following on foot, carrying the baggage.

(21) But what is strange about these people is their invisibility. For several weeks, always at about the same time of day, the file of old women had hobbled past the house with their firewood, and though they had registered themselves on my eyeballs I cannot truly say that I had seen them. Firewood was passing—that was how I saw it. It was only that one day I happened to be walking behind them, and the curious up-and-down motion of a load of wood drew my attention to the human being beneath it. Then for the first time I noticed the poor old earth-colored bodies, bodies reduced to bones and leathery skin, bent double under the crushing weight. Yet I suppose I had not been five minutes on Moroccan soil before I noticed the overloading of the donkeys and was infuriated by it. There is no question that the donkeys are damnably treated. The Moroccan donkey is hardly bigger than a St. Bernard dog, it carries a load which in the British Army would be considered too much for a fifteen-hands mule, and very often its pack-saddle is not taken off its back for weeks together. But what is peculiarly pitiful is that it is the most willing creature on earth, it follows its master like a dog and does not need either bridle or halter. After a dozen years of devoted work it suddenly drops dead, whereupon its master tips it into the ditch and the village dogs have torn its guts out before it is cold.

(22) This kind of thing makes one's blood boil, whereas—on the whole—the plight of the human beings does not. I am not commenting, merely pointing to a fact. People with brown skins are next door to invisible. Anyone can be sorry for the donkey with its galled back, but it is generally owing to some kind of accident if one even notices the old woman under her load of sticks.

(23) As the storks flew northward the Negroes were marching south-ward—a long, dusty column, infantry, screwgun batteries, and then

more infantry, four or five thousand men in all, winding up the road with a clumping of boots and a clatter of iron wheels.

(24) They were Senegalese, the blackest Negroes in Africa, so black that sometimes it is difficult to see whereabouts on their necks the hair begins. Their splendid bodies were hidden in reach-me-down khaki uniforms, their feet squashed into boots that looked like blocks of wood, and every tin hat seemed to be a couple of sizes too small. It was very hot and the men had marched a long way. They slumped under the weight of their packs and the curiously sensitive black faces were glistening with sweat.

(25) As they went past a tall, very young Nergo turned and caught my eye. But the look he gave me was not in the least the kind of look you might expect. Not hostile, not contemptuous, not sullen, not even inquisitive. It was the shy, wide-eyed Negro look, which actually is a look of profound respect. I saw how it was. This wretched boy, who is a French citizen and has therefore been dragged from the forest to scrub floors and catch syphilis in garrison towns, actually has feelings of reverence before a white skin. He has been taught that the white race are his masters, and he still believes it.

(26) But there is one thought which every white man (and in this connection it doesn't matter twopence if he calls himself a socialist) thinks when he sees a black army marching past. "How much longer can we go on kidding these people? How long before they turn their guns in the other direction?"

(27) It was curious, really. Every white man there had this thought stowed somewhere or other in his mind. I had it, so had the other onlookers, so had the officers on their sweating chargers and the white N.C.O.'s marching in the ranks. It was a kind of secret which we all knew and were too clever to tell; only the Negroes didn't know it. And really it was like watching a flock of cattle to see the long column, a mile or two miles of armed men, flowing peacefully up the road, while the great white birds drifted over them in the opposite direction, glittering like scraps of paper.

QUESTIONS AND EXERCISES

VOCABULARY

1. bier (*paragraph* 2)
2. hummocky (2)
3. derelict (2)
4. gazelles (4)
5. navvy (6)
6. sidled (6)
7. frenzied (11)
8. clamoring (11)
9. khaki (24)

LANGUAGE AND RHETORIC

1. Paragraphs 9, 10, 11, and 12 form a unit. What sentence serves as a topic sentence for these paragraphs? Why does the author place the detail in these paragraphs before that of paragraphs 13, 14, and 15?

2. What device is used in the first sentence of paragraph 18 to connect it with paragraph 17? What is the antecedent of the word *this*? How is the thought of paragraph 18 related to that of 17?

3. The controlling idea of paragraph 19 is actually contained in two sentences. What are they? What method of paragraph development is used to support the controlling idea in this paragraph?

4. How do paragraphs 16, 22, and 27 relate to the several paragraphs immediately preceding each of them?

5. Point out examples of parallelism in paragraphs 2 and 3. What other means does the author use to provide coherence in paragraph 3?

6. In this selection, the author presents a number of scenes that convey his impression of life in Marrakech. What dominant impression does he convey of the quality of this life, of its effect upon the people? Though a general tone pervades the piece it varies slightly. How, for example, does the writer's attitude vary in paragraphs 3, 16, 18, 21, and 27?

7. What method of paragraph development is used in paragraphs 17 and 21?

DISCUSSION AND WRITING

1. Orwell observes that white visitors to Marrakech, himself included, are by and large more attentive to, and concerned about, abuse to animals than to brown-skinned humans. Comment on this observation and the basis for it. Is there any relationships between the way people treat animals and the way they treat other humans? Support your answer.

2. Consider Orwell's point about how it is possible to ignore poverty and its victims in order to maintain one's personal comfort, as, for example, with tourists. Does it have merit? Can you offer specific examples to either support or refute it?

3. Describe in some detail the experience of poverty as you have known it yourself or observed it in others. Pay particular attention to the specific details and to the central impression you want to convey.

4. If you have ever found yourself in the midst of people who were "different" from you or among whom you felt ill at east, describe your reaction to that situation. Again, try to focus on a single overall impression.

5. Write a descriptive essay about a place you have visited where the people made a particular impression on you. Follow Orwell's general pattern in focusing on the people in their familiar setting. Try to select your subjects and details in such a way as to convey a single dominant impression.

BARRY LOPEZ
Weekend

The casual and routine quality of the title of this piece offers little indication of what is to come, and therein lies a great deal of its irony. During the weekend, and in this writing that provides a permanent record of it, Barry Lopez explores central and eastern Oregon on a Memorial Day journey to "get away from it all." What he finds—and fails to find—marks another milestone of not only how far this nation has come but where we have already gone.

The author depends heavily on specific details to make his description as effective as possible. Take note of the way in which he does this.

(1) You can camp in the Oregon desert for a week and see no one at all, no more than the glow of headlights hovering over a dirt road miles distant, disappearing soundlessly over the curve of the Earth. You can see, as you wander over those dry flats, that man has been there, that vast stretches of sagebrush have replaced the bunchgrass grazed off by his cattle and sheep. Against a hill you can find the dry-rotting foundation of a scuttled homestead. But the desert is not scarred by man's presence. It is still possible to be alone out there, to stare at your hands for an hour and have no one ask why. It is possible to feel the cracks in the earth, to sense the enormity of space, to roll, between the tips of your fingers, the dust of boulders gone to pieces.

(2) I thought I would go there on Memorial Day weekend to look for fossils. I would watch the full moon rise, and golden eagles disappear in the eye of the sun.

(3) I left on Saturday morning, feeling smug about avoiding Friday night's traffic. I crested the Santiam Pass in the Cascades and came down into Sisters, Oregon, on the east slope of that range of volcanoes. As I drove southeast toward Christmas Lake Valley I could feel the mountains behind me, blanketed with snow and blinding white.

(4) Six miles east of Christmas Lake Valley lies an alkali flat called Fossil Lake. The flat is flanked by massive sand dunes, and there isn't a town once you're past Christmas Lake Valley. There had been an illfated land boom in Christmas Lake Valley in the early 1960s, and I expected to see the unfinished town looming over the flats like a dehydrated circus. It came up slowly, like an automobile wreck.

(5) On the dirt road west of town there was a Christmas tree—a two-dimensional latticework of weather-beaten wood, flaking green paint, edged with shredded wisps of silver tinsel. The town, shimmering in the heat a half mile ahead, seemed larger than it was because of the vacant concrete buildings, the faded street signs at barren intersections,

the unconnected bits of fence strung out in the sage. There was a general store with a bar and a few gas pumps, some scattered, dilapidated mobile homes, and another gas station on the edge of town. The dirt road widened to three car widths in front of the store, and a pall of white, alkali dust hung over a tangle of pickups, trail bikes, and people. In the still, desert air all you could hear was the *brrrrup-brrrrup* of winding-up motorbikes and the yelling conversation of dust-encrusted men and their sons. Women sat in the baking heat of truck cabs, staring through opaque glasses.

(6) I stopped for gas and water at the second gas station. The girl at the pumps said I couldn't miss Fossil Lake. "It's probably crawling with dune buggies." She ducked back out of the sun and away from conversation.

(7) You could not tell from a distance that anything at all was going on out there. Perhaps the girl was joking. I drove along at 45 miles per hour steering a path between sections of hard washboard. Even with the windows up it was impossible to keep the dust out. Pickups, their beds loaded with motorcycles and spare tires, surged by at 60 mph and disappeared in the boiling dust. Perhaps she wasn't joking.

(8) The turnoff to Fossil Lake was marked with strands of blue and red ribbon fluttering in the thin breeze. Still there was no sign of concentrated activity—only the full-bore traffic of mechanized recreation equipment going, I presumed, to the same place, like a mobile home rendezvous of 500 silver trailers beneath Mount Rushmore. Hope for a lonely weekend spent poking in the desert balanced on a vibrating piano wire. *This is the middle of the goddam desert,* I thought.

(9) If there were too many people at Fossil Lake, I decided, I would drive across the alkali flat to the far side, drive away from wherever all these people were and camp. I very much wanted to hold onto the stone bones of some long forgotten fish, to prove that what I sensed lay over the horizon would somehow pass.

(10) The one-lane road to Fossil Lake ended in a knot of motor homes, dune buggies, tent trailers, house trailers, motorbikes, pickups, four-wheel drives, tents, barbecues, and yellow-and-green lawn furniture. It dawned on me for the first time that they were there to stay. I rolled down the window to the smell of gasoline and the hammering rap of two-cycle engines and stared at the boiling mass. The route across the flat was blocked, and I desperately considered flooring my van and surging over the sagebrush around the roadblock. But with a spinning of wheels in the dust and a fumbling of gears I managed to get turned around and left.

(11) On my detailed map I saw a place five miles to the north, on the other side of the dunes, a little basin that looked just fine. I'd camp there and leave in the morning if I couldn't get into the flats alone.

(12) I wondered about the people at Fossil Lake. I had thought no one would be there, but they were there, and they were there first. Hunting fossils, or the simple desire to be alone, wasn't going to mix well with a lot of desert traffic, so that was that. It was understandable, however. Coming over the mountains I had seen a half-and-half mixture of in- and out-of-state plates. Here in the desert there were only Oregon plates. Oregonians have long maintained that out-of-staters take over their mountain and coastal regions during the summer. So they go to places the collective "Californians" have never heard of. The fact that I witnessed the brutal weekend take-over of this delicate environment, saw fossil bones of fish with unpronounceable names pounded to dust under the wheels of a wide-tired dune buggy, saw the demythologization of all I felt the desert to be—well, that was my problem.

(13) Fossil Lake, however, was simply an outpost. The north side of the dunes was the center of activity. I stopped a mile short of the concentration of recreational equipment and tried to pull off the road into a grassy arroyo. The one-lane road had been ground almost eight inches into the desert, and I got stuck, half in and half out. I reached into the van for my shovel. It was gone. I had lent it to a neighbor the day before. I could only wait until someone came along, and I appreciated the irony of my predicament. Half an hour later two men came by in a new Oldsmobile. The vehicle, its stereo blaring, seemed no more incongruous in the desert than did the name of Christmas Lake Valley, or adjacent Chicago Valley.

(14) They had a shovel. They said they were treasure hunters. The back seat was loaded with sophisticated metal detectors, shovels, crowbars, and picks. Their families, they said, were camped at the dunes, and they'd gone to scout an abandoned dwelling. No luck. "You can't find much anymore," said the older man. "Too many people been through these old places already."

(15) We dug my van out and got it settled on solid ground. I told them I'd come out here to get away from people and that I wasn't having much luck. The younger man said, "Well, you ought to get yourself a hobby for your vacation. Not much sense being out in a place like this with nothing to do."

(16) They left.

(17) I put a pot of tea water on the portable stove and started fixing dinner. In the distance I could hear the whining and grunting of engines. The sun set, and the noise continued. The miracle of the headlight. Coyotes called, were drowned out, and fell silent. I sat on a hill and watched the moon rise.

(18) Later in the evening a jeepful of men came by. The vehicle seemed, in the moonlight, like a commercial version of the Lunar Rover, with its chrome wheels, wide tires, open cockpit, winch, tow chain looped

over the front bumper, fire extinguisher lashed to the roll bars, the throaty, modified V-8 engine, and its bank of high-intensity driving lamps.

(19) I waved them to a halt to ask about the condition of the road farther on. They were a little drunk and began arguing over who knew what about which road. I thanked them and they blasted off. I spent the evening trying to stay interested in a book on bird physiology, trying to shut out the voices, the noise coming over the desert, the rage of unmitigated recreation down the road. I believed I bore them no ill will. It was more a matter of suddenly realizing that the last ball game had started and you were not on the team, that *this* would be the game, and henceforth there would be no room for other games.

(20) I was gone before sunrise. The desert was quiet and the air thick and cool, the sky black and blue. I guessed that if I went north, up on the John Day River, things would be better. Thirty-eight miles of dirt road and I hit the highway. A few miles farther I passed an alkali flat, where a dark, irregular mass was shimmering in the heat waves. I squinted but couldn't make it out. When I got home I read about the twenty-two thousand drums sitting out there, more than a million gallons of herbicide and pesticide manufacturing wastes that no one knows what to do with. The barrels are leaking. In the middle of the desert.

(21) I drove most of the day, stopping to buy groceries in the town of John Day, stopping at the John Day fossil beds, where a woman in yellow cotton shorts and red sneakers was shoveling specimens into a plastic garbage bucket. Traffic was thin. Apparently most people had reached their destination. The drivers I passed looked dazed, hunched over the wheels of small foreign cars whizzing by at 80 mph, dull, NoDoz stares anchored on the horizon. One car with a ski-laden roof was pulling a trailer with two black-and-red snowmobiles. An enormous motor home, with two motorbikes stacked on the extended rear bumper and an aluminum boat on the roof, was hauling a jeep. Prepared for anything.

(22) Late in the afternoon I stopped at the town of Spray to ask about two U.S. Forest Service campgrounds nearby. The man in the air-conditioned general store said there would be room in both of them. "We don't get many tourists over here like you do in western Oregon."

(23) The first one, an "unimproved campground," was three-quarters full. The other, called Bull Prairie, was "improved" and packed to capacity. Bull Prairie campground was on Bull Prairie Lake, land donated by a lumber company. The water was buzzing with motorboats and ringed with fishermen. I sat in the parking lot and watched a man get into a Pontiac Safari station wagon, wedged between a Chevrolet Blazer and a hatchet-scarred ponderosa pine, and drive 250 feet to the boat ramp. He got out of the car, locked it, walked to the ramp, and

yelled for Raymond. Raymond had caught a turtle. His father told him he couldn't take it home. The boy winged the turtle as far as he could toward the middle of the lake and jumped into the car.

(24) The campground trees were wired together with clotheslines draped with bathing suits, underwear, and wet clothing. A woman sat at a picnic table reading a magazine and painting her nails a bright blue. Her head was encased in a pink, plastic bag plugged into a hot-air blower, the blower plugged into a portable generator. An obese man in khaki safari shorts was lying on the same table with his hat over his face. The table was chained to a bolt in the ground. A long-haired collielike dog, lying on his side with his tongue in the dust, was chained to the tent camper. The trash cans were overflowing. A wad of used disposable diapers was piled next to one can.

(25) Until that day I had never seen, except in an advertisement, a portable, gasoline-powered generator, or a pair of red, Styrofoam water shoes for walking over lakes, or a television set tuned to a golf match in the middle of a national forest.

(26) Bull Prairie Lake was an absurd counterpoint. It looked like the sort of small mountain tarn you'd find by accident deep in a wilderness area, marked on the Forest Service map but still unnamed. The edge of the lake was thick with cattails dotted with birds' nests.

(27) At the entrance to the campground there was a suggestion box. It was full. Through the plastic I could read one of the cards. It said, "Cut down the cattails. This would improve the view and get rid of insects." It was signed by a man and his wife from Tacoma, Washington.

(28) I drove out of the national forest, down to the John Day River, and began looking for a place to camp. At a bend in the road I saw a trail through the brush. I followed it to the edge of the river and parked the van on a grassy flat. There was a small beach of black sand, criss-crossed with the tracks of deer, coyote, killdeer, geese, raccoon, and porcupine. The only sound was the river crashing over the rocks. The sun flashed off canyon walls decorated with red, green, and yellow patches of lichen, and a streak of white droppings below a chukar nest. With my binoculars I found a red-tailed hawk's nest and watched its inhabitants circling near the rim, riding the thermals.

(29) With the respite from the road—on which during the past hour I had counted twenty-two dead animals—and with the horror of the desert dunes and Bull Prairie fading, I took off my clothes and went down to the river's edge. The water was a deep olive drab and opaque with the residue of cattle manure and raw sewage from the little towns upriver. It did not seem to matter. As I lay on the beach I realized what I had known all along—that it would be like this, that there would be no getting away, even in the remote corners of frontier Oregon.

(30) It was not at all odd that the tracks in the sand led to offaled

waters. This is the way it is, short of packing into a wilderness area, and even their days seem numbered. What was odd, lying there by the polluted river, fifty miles from a town of more than five hundred people, watching the hawks circle, was that I was alone and it was quiet. I felt blessed. What about those, I wondered, back in New York and down in Los Angeles who were hanging on for a few more bucks before they broke away, strung out on visions of the pristine, unspoiled expanse of Oregon? Who would tell them it was already too late?

(31) At dusk a cattle truck came down the trail. The man owned the little beachhead and said he didn't mind people camping there as long as they cleaned up. He had come to tell me the place was infested with rattlesnakes. We talked about the number of people on the road. He said he didn't understand people anymore, that he'd caught three boys who'd shotgunned twenty-nine Canada geese for the hell of it, that the deer and chukar were scarce because people "from Portland" were coming down and blasting away at anything that moved.

(32) "I don't know what the hell to think anymore. Why, I saw a man sitting inside his car shooting out the window at a rattlesnake with a 30/30. He must have taken twenty shots at the thing before he was through. I turn in the license plates, but that's all you can do. They won't let you take their guns away."

(33) We talked about snakebite remedies and predators and folk cures and hawks and the pitfalls of farming. He reminded me about the rattlers and told me not to drink out of the river.

(34) I sat by the John Day River that night and sipped my tea and felt like a man in prison.

(35) I stayed by the river until almost noon the next day, half afraid of going out on the road, not wanting to abandon the little bit of peace I'd found. Thoughts of the evening crush going back over the mountains and the possibility of beating it with an early departure moved me to leave.

(36) On the way back I passed through the town of Madras. There is a sign outside of town that boasts: MADRAS, HOME OF ROUND BUTTE DAM, THE MOST SPECTACULAR VIEW IN AMERICA. I saw on the map that I could take a shortcut home and see Round Butte Dam, which promised, if not spectacle, at least the answer to a sign I'd read twenty times.

(37) It was, looking down from above, something short of a spectacular sight. One was almost embarrassed for the Madras Chamber of Commerce for their grasping at such straws, at such commercial desperation among the tourist-hungry city fathers of this town of 1,700.

(38) The visitors' building overlooking the dam was outfitted with dioramas and drawings explaining how the land was being changed to provide electricity and a reservoir for recreation. A set of black-and-

white photographs, the only thing in the room not locked up or behind glass, introduced you to the region's wildlife. One photograph had been pulled out of the frame and left hanging in mid-theft. Two of the frames were empty.

(39) I sat at a picnic table in the little park and ate lunch. A sign indicated that the building and park, surrounded by a cyclone fence topped with barbed wire, were there courtesy of Portland General Electric, the people who built the dam.

(40) A convoy of campers came in through the barbed-wire gate and the people went off to the edge of the canyon to see the dam. Noting the flag was at half-mast, a man yelled over to the attendant, "Somebody else get it?"

(41) "No, it's Memorial Day."

(42) "Oh."

(43) A young girl shouted to her father, "What should I do with the dog?"

(44) "Where is he?"

(45) "In the truck."

(46) "Leave him."

(47) "But it's hot."

(48) "Everybody's hot. Your idea to bring him anyway."

(49) My shortcut led down into the canyon to Lake Billy Chinook, named for the Indian who, along with Kit Carson, guided Captain John Frémont through Oregon. At the end of the road, on the lip of the canyon, was a sign indicating the "overflow campground." It was full.

(50) Halfway down the canyon road I pulled into a turnout to look down on the expanse of water. I looked back up to the rim and was surprised to see a waterfall. As I traced the water's course down the canyon wall to a pit and through a culvert to the reservoir, I realized I'd made a mistake. It was a sewage outfall from the campground above. The fecal smear swelled out into the lake, forming a stain perhaps sixty feet across. In the middle of this mess a man was fishing. The lake was crisscrossed with the wakes of powerboats, fishing boats, racing boats, and water-skiers, and dotted here and there with buoys that meant scuba-divers were below.

(51) I drove down to the edge of the lake. There wasn't a place to park. A sign saying No Parking Beyond This Point had been bulldozed aside by a motor home. Beyond that point there were fourteen campers, two motor homes, twelve cars, nineteen boat trailers, and eleven boats. The chrome V-8 Chevrolet engine of a sleek, low, fiberglass racing boat flashed in the sunlight like the blade of a hunting knife. It could drive the boat over Lake Billy Chinook at a speed approaching 150 mph.

(52) I drove past the graffiti on the canyon wall, news that George

loved Maureen and that Bill Green had visited the area on 6/22/71, past shopping bags of garbage piled by the side of the road, past teenagers waiting around for something to happen, gunning the engines of their trail bikes.

(53) On the opposite rim there was an aquamarine mobile home decked out with flapping plastic banners advertising Round Butte Valley Estates.

(54) The freshly paved road—its tar boiling into an oily slick in the hot desert sun—turned to dirt, the two lanes turned to one and a half, and then to one. After a few more miles I came to a junction and an abandoned school sitting in a clump of junipers. The desks were gone, the walls covered with obscene graffiti and riddled with bullet holes. The back doors had been crowbarred off and thrown out into the yard. There was a cast-iron stove in the vestibule, its porcelain face shattered by a shotgun blast. The door to an anteroom had been blown off its hinges, and a series of shotgun blasts had opened a hole in one wall. The window frames were gone, the floor littered with A&W root beer cups, an empty Colonel Sanders chicken bucket, Olympia and Blitz beer cans, crumpled cigarette packs, human offal, broken glass and rocks, rocks apparently used to break the windows before someone took the frames.

(55) There was nothing after that but the drive home, in lockstep with the others who had decided to go home early and beat the traffic. I was the thirty-first in a line of fifty-nine cars going over the pass.

(56) There were twenty state residents killed in recreational accidents over the weekend in Oregon: eleven by drowning, four in auto wrecks, one in a motorcycle wreck, three in a light plane crash, and the last was a woman killed on the coast when a log came in on the surf and crushed her. In Eugene, Oregon, the city had been unsuccessful in keeping a throng of holiday swimmers out of a polluted lake in the city's showcase Alton Baker Park.

(57) There was no news of what had happened to the desert.

QUESTIONS AND EXERCISES

VOCABULARY

1. alkali (*paragraph* 4)
2. latticework (5)
3. demythologization (12)
4. arroyo (13)
5. incongruous (13)
6. unmitigated (17)
7. physiology (19)
8. respite (29)
9. offaled (30)
10. pristine (30)
11. dioramas (38)
12. culvert (50)
13. fecal (50)
14. graffiti (52)
15. vestibule (54)

LANGUAGE AND RHETORIC

1. How effective is the title of this selection? Why didn't Lopez use a more dramatic title to underscore his point? What *is* his point?
2. What is the significance of the events described here taking place on Memorial Day weekend? What use does the author make of this fact? How does it fit into his overall intention?
3. This selection includes extensive use of both narrative and descriptive techniques. Why, in classifying it according to basic rhetorical type, do the authors/editors list it as description rather than narration? Can you make a case for classifying it as narration?
4. Paragraphs 20 and 21 both end in sentence fragments. Why doesn't Lopez use complete sentences at those points?
5. Lopez depends heavily on specific details to make his description as effective as possible. Point out several examples of this and comment on their effectiveness.
6. Reread the first two paragraphs and then the last two. What is the author doing with his introduction and conclusion? How do they relate to one another? To the thesis of the essay?

DISCUSSION AND WRITING

1. Compare and contrast the attitude expressed by Lopez in this selection with that expressed by Sagan (pp. 361–67). Would Lopez be likely to "praise" science and technology as Sagan does? Why or why not? On what points might they agree? Support your answer.
2. Compare the author's attitude toward the desert with that of the author of "Disorder and Early Sorrow" (pp. 300–304). What does each author feel about the subject, and what evidence reveals their feelings?
3. Do you think the author is overly sensitive to the problem he describes here? Has he taken an extreme position? Defend your answer.
4. Describe one of your own attempts to "get away from it all," but do not necessarily restrict yourself to an attempt that failed. Rather, let your reader know what you were seeking and what you found, using specific details to enable the reader to share that experience.

RICHARD SELZER

In the Shadow of the Winch

It is not the great vessels I am after. The aortic arch with its branches, the carotids, the subclavian. There is a man, you see, waiting at the hospital. His own aorta has blown. It is a thin-walled blister that crowds his chest, pressing upon his heart and lungs, eroding the high pile of his vertebrae. On one side, it is grooved by his ribs. Here and there, it is barnacled with plaques of calcium. At any moment, it will burst: when he sneezes, perhaps, or bends to tie his shoe. So I am here, harvesting the organs of beasts for transplantation.

A little money has been paid.

In my bag, a packet of sterile instruments, sterile jars, rubber gloves. Everything is ready.

This slaughterhouse is kosher. The Gentiles make the cut too low on the neck. We need as much length on the arteries as we can get. The slaughterer wears hip boots and a skullcap. He mutters prayers. Blessings, I imagine. He and I are joined here for different purposes. To the cattle it is all the same.

One is chosen. Compared to a cheetah or a python, she would be almost vegetable—slow, planted, something whose destiny it is to be bitten off and chewed, as she has mowed many meadows. Nor would I compare her to the performing hawk, whose grace is exteriorized to the interface that flames between wing and wind. No. A cow has none of the bestial graces. And in the shadow of the Winch, she falls clumsier still.

Commotion! Behind a gate too high for leaping, a wild eye backs away from the prod. There is a scudding, a side-wise bumping into walls.

There is the sound of chains, and another sound like bagpipes skirling. A great wheel turns. What a scrabbling of hoofs! The head of the cow dips, is no longer to be seen above the gate. Over a pulley set in the roof, the chain pulls taut. In a minute she is lifted, upside down, one hind leg grappled by the chain. First seen rising is that braceleted hoof. The hind leg follows, pulled rigid by the weight of the hoisted cow. The other hind leg is held out from the side. It is thick, like the thigh of a fat woman. After, come the rump and tail, the torso; then there is the head, eyes bursting, sweet blunt horns remonstrating.

Her passion begins. Only now, as she is assumed, does she begin to low. She extends her head to look about. Her moo stretches breath to the limit. Behind the gate, the others listen. They thump and shove, then fall still. I think they know.

The height is convenient for the man in the hip boots and skullcap. His knife flashes. He steps forward.

"Cut high," I say. "Last time, the carotids were too short."

The slaughterer is good. One stroke across the neck beneath the mandible. She is caught in mid-groan, her lips and tongue working on. The fall of her whole blood to the stone floor is like the plash of her endless urinations. For as long as it can, her heart pumps the steaming blood to the floor, to the drain at the center, where the flies wait. The rushing out of her blood causes her to turn and gyrate on the chain. Soon enough, the fall slows to a woven strand. It lazes. At last, a trickle, a wavy thread. Then, drop follows drop. And still, she revolves, graceful at last, floating, airborne, she who stumbled and twitched below.

Perhaps, had she not gone lovely, I would not reach up my hand to still her motion. But I do. My palm comes to rest upon her belly. I press, and the swinging stops. She hangs. Now it is that I feel transmitted to my touch, a stirring. It is muffled, fur covered. Yet it quickens, insists. Again! It kicks, soft, to knock at my mind. Who's there! What lingers here to complete itself!

A calf almost, almost lives, unmindful, seeing still a world enough and time, as only the fetal might. I step to face the belly of the cow, press my ear against the warm pink skin where the fine hairs whorl at midline. Above, the velvety udders hang, touching my hair. There! I feel it again. It lives!

My knife! Hurry! I tear open the sterile pack and rummage for the knife. I have it! Now! One long slit, and I shall lift it free. My own blood hurtles. My lungs flood with it. I seem to be remembering my own birth, the battering choking abrading blinding of it, the loss of all that was moist and warm, the bright that was more than bright.

Now! I raise my knife.

But I do not cut into the belly of the cow. I pause; I think: there is pro; there is con. Human ruminations have ever been the ruination of cattle. My knife clatters to the floor.

But I am so close to the heat of the beast's underparts. Her smell! Once more I press my ear to her abdomen. As I do, yes, as I do, her forelegs take me gently about the hips, her hoofs dangling. It is a reflex, I know. I stand in the embrace, the delicate embrace of the creature that, beyond death, offers herself in place of her calf.

The winched cow has stopped her plink, plink dripping upon the stones.

The carcass roars with silence.

The winch unwinds. The meat is lowered.

THREE

ILLUSTRATION

STEVEN M. WEISS

I Remember Max

College teachers have been urged in recent years to let their students know they care about them. In this essay, Steven M. Weiss, a college teacher himself, takes a different view as he recalls his own freshman English teacher. "Max was the best professor I ever had," says Weiss, and "I hated his guts." Although this essay was originally intended for an audience of college teachers, it presents a point of view that students, whether or not they agree, would do well to consider.

Notice how the author uses the single extended example of "Max" to illustrate his point.

(1) I remember Max very well. He had a Ph.D. from Princeton. He was a Chaucerian. He was brilliant, eloquent, and professorial. He possessed everything respectable in a human being—a good mind, a sound professional ethic, a sense of learning's place in the universe. Max was truly an educator.

(2) But there is one thing I haven't told you about Max: I hated his guts.

(3) Max was my freshman-English teacher. And while he was, in a sense, everything I desired to be (that is, a gentleman and a scholar), he was also a man who force-fed me for 15 weeks on literature and grammar (and what a foul stew it was!).

(4) Today, I am a college teacher myself, and have discovered that very few students are encountering their own version of Max.

(5) This is not to say that younger, up-and-coming professors are less erudite or well trained than Max was. On the contrary, the scarcity of academic-job opportunities has virtually assured that colleges can choose from among the best-trained young scholars in the world.

(6) Neither am I suggesting that it is impossible for a student to find a genuinely loathsome professor. (I have enough personal evidence that the potential for real animosity between teacher and student does exist.

We all have encountered the student who fantasized the most heinous retribution for that despicable faculty member who dared give him a C.)

(7) What made Max unique was neither his mental prowess nor his propensity to be disliked. Rather, it was his aloofness.

(8) Max didn't "care" about his students. He wasn't worried about whether they were passing his course. He didn't really seem concerned that most of them never expressed a passion for the subjects of his lectures. And, most of all, Max didn't give a damn how his students felt about him.

(9) Chances are, most students are thankful that "Maxish" professors are an endangered species. Further, I'll wager that many professors are proud and pleased they are not Maxes (or Maxines). The reason is that, today, college teachers, individually and collectively, "care" about their students.

(10) The explanation for the decline in Maxism is not really relevant to my point, but one might nonetheless speculate that a general decline in college enrollment, and consequently in available teaching positions, has led some young professors to believe that they have to be popular.

(11) The college classroom has become, for some of these "hungry" young men and women, a battleground in their war against job insecurity. Their weapons are a strong response demonstrated by their students (in terms of attendance) coupled with ostensibly strong acceptance (in terms of student evaluations—which actually measure little more than the congeniality of the professor).

(12) The knowledge that academics are more sympathetic to their students than Max was would be heartening, indeed, except for one very curious fact: Max was the best teacher I ever had. That's right. The very best teacher I ever had was the one who didn't give a damn about me or anyone else, the one who never tried to make me feel "comfortable," who didn't even know my name.

(13) How could so cavalier an attitude, so profound an indifference, have led to such resounding pedagogical success?

(14) The answer involves an analysis of Max's philosophy in educating adults who were not unlike himself, save in their lack of enlightenment. Max did not care about his students because he cared about something more important to a scholar. Max cared about knowledge—or truth, if you will. Max was an intellectual, a man about the business of discovering and imparting knowledge, and not necessarily about the business of caring.

(15) Max may have cared about his family and friends, but he didn't care about his students if caring about them meant making them comfortable in his classroom. He knew caring about them could never rival

educating them. And the fact remains that he did educate them—better than I've seen anyone educate anyone else before or since.

(16) I'm not urging professors to stop caring about students. It's probably too late now to go back to just lecture and recitation. I make only a modest proposal, one that entails little more than a change in the *ethos* of the college professor.

(17) What concerns me is the attitude (exemplified perfectly in the "evaluative instruments" so often used by administrators to ascertain "teaching effectiveness") that lead students to ask such questions as these about their education:

> Are my instructors nice?
> Do I like my instructor?
> Do my instructors like me?
> Am I comfortable in class?
> Will the instructor be sure not to embarrass me?

(18) To these questions, I recommend only that the professor say, once and for all, "Who cares?"

(19) A more meaningful set of questions for students to ask might sound something like this:

> Does my instructor know something I don't?
> Will he or she frankly point out my ignorance?
> Can I bear criticism as a price of being educated?
> Can I remember that knowledge is not necessarily a "comfortable" thing to acquire?
> Can I learn something from someone who doesn't care about me?

(20) Until significant numbers of students start asking something resembling the second set of questions, the world is running a great risk of producing a generation suffering from "Maxlessness"—copious caring and minuscule thinking.

(21) Recently, a student told me that my lectures were boring, pseudointellectual, and pedantic. (Believe me, she didn't use the same vocabulary.) She seemed dissatisfied with the notion of knowledge *per se* as the purpose and rationale of a course. She wanted to know if things would get more interesting, more entertaining.

(22) Rather than respond as Max would have, I chose to speak as a teacher who *cared*. I carefully and patiently explained why and how the esoteric balderdash in my lectures might eventually have relevance to her "nuts and bolts" experience. I never once considered, as Max would have, that the knowledge I have might be inherently worthwhile; that it probably overshadowed all her knowledge by a long shot; and that,

as far as she and I were concerned, it was exceeded only by her ignorance.

(23) I suggest that it is not entirely a student's determination that guarantees his or her educability. There is a greater burden that falls on me and my colleagues—to conceive of education as courageously as Max did, to realize that learning should be a handshake instead of a kiss.

(24) Succinctly, my proposal is this: The next time a student tells you, "Gee, I really enjoyed your class," try a new response. Say: "You weren't supposed to enjoy it; you were supposed to study and learn from it and think about it."

(25) Your students may hate you for talking that way. But I would rather they hate me, as I hated Max, so long as they also learn what a lovely thing knowledge can be.

QUESTIONS AND EXERCISES

VOCABULARY

1. Chaucerian (*paragraph* 1)
2. erudite (5)
3. animosity (6)
4. heinous (6)
5. propensity (7)
6. cavalier (13)
7. pedagogical (13)
8. ethos (16)
9. copious (20)
10. minuscule (20)
11. pseudointellectual (21)
12. pedantic (21)
13. *per se* (21)
14. esoteric (22)
15. balderdash (22)

LANGUAGE AND RHETORIC

1. What is the author's thesis, and what is his basic method of developing it?
2. Why is the essay written from a first-person point of view? Couldn't the same effect have been achieved if Weiss had described Max objectively?
3. Weiss uses the word "care" in its various forms seven times in this essay, starting in paragraphs 8 and 9, where he sets the word off in quotation marks. What tone does this establish, and how does it support his thesis?
4. This essay originally appeared in a tabloid newspaper format, which is one reason the paragraphs tend to be so brief. Regroup the paragraphs to develop them more fully and be prepared to defend your groupings.

DISCUSSION AND WRITING

1. What is your reaction to the author's comments about caring? He equates caring about students with making them comfortable in the classroom. Is it as important for an instructor to care about students as it is for an instructor to care about subject matter? Is it necessary to choose between the two?

2. Weiss dismisses most student evaluations of instructors as of little or no significance. What do you think of his "meaningful set of questions for students to ask" (paragraph 19)?

3. Many students have had instructors they disliked, only to find later that they had benefited greatly from their teaching. If you have had such an experience, write an essay describing the instructor and how you benefited from his/her teaching.

4. Write an essay in which you describe the instructor who had the greatest impact on your education to date. In addition to describing the instructor, be sure to show how he/she influenced you.

BARBARA LAWRENCE

Dirty Words Can Harm You

In this essay, Barbara Lawrence deals directly and explicitly with "four-letter words," leaning heavily on scholarly background to temper as well as to support her remarks. She focuses attention on the use of sexual language that, according to her, is intended to reduce women to mere sex objects.

As you read, pay particular attention to the author's use of multiple examples to develop her thesis.

(1) Why should any words be called obscene? Don't they all describe natural human functions? Am I trying to tell them, my students demand, that the "strong, earthy, gut-honest"—or, if they are fans of Norman Mailer, the "rich, liberating, existential"—language they use to describe sexual activity isn't preferable to "phony-sounding, middleclass words like 'intercourse' and 'copulate'?" "Cop You Late!" they say with fancy inflections and gagging grimaces. "Now, what is *that* supposed to mean?"

(2) Well, what is it supposed to mean? And why indeed should one group of words describing human functions and human organs be acceptable in ordinary conversation and another, describing presumably the same organs and functions, be tabooed—so much so, in fact, that some of these words still cannot appear in print in many parts of the English-speaking world?

(3) The argument that these taboos exist only because of "sexual

hangups" (middle-class, middle-age, feminist), or even that they are a result of class oppression (the contempt of the Norman conquerors for the languge of their Anglo-Saxon serfs), ignores a much more likely explanation, it seems to me, and that is the sources and functions of the words themselves.

(4) The best known of the tabooed sexual verbs, for example, comes from the German *ficken,* meaning "to strike"; combined, according to Partridge's etymological dictionary *Origins,* with the Latin sexual verb *futuere;* associated in turn with the Latin *fustis,* "a staff or cudgel"; the Celtic *buc,* "a point, hence to pierce"; the Irish *bot,* "the male member"; the Latin *battuere,* "to beat"; the Gaelic *batair,* "a cudgeller"; the Early Irish *bualaim,* "I strike"; and so forth. It is one of what etymologists sometimes call "the sadistic group of words for the man's part in copulation."

(5) The brutality of this word, then, and its equivalents ("screw," "bang," etc.), is not an illusion of the middle class or a crotchet of Women's Liberation. In their origins and imagery these words carry undeniably painful, if not sadistic, implications, the object of which is almost always female. Consider, for example, what a "screw" actually does to the wood it penetrates; what a painful, even mutilating, activity this kind of analogy suggests. "Screw" is particularly interesting in this context, since the noun, according to Partridge, comes from words meaning "groove," "nut," "ditch," "breeding sow," "scrofula" and "swelling," while the verb, besides its explicit imagery, has antecedent associations to "write on," "scratch," "scarify," and so forth—a revealing fusion of a mechanical or painful action with an obviously denigrated object.

(6) Not all obscene words, of course, are as implicitly sadistic or denigrating to women as these, but all that I know seem to serve a similar purpose: to reduce the human organism (especially the female organism) and human functions (especially sexual and procreative) to their least organic, most mechanical dimension; to substitute a trivializing or deforming resemblance for the complex human reality of what is being described.

(7) Tabooed male descriptives, when they are not openly denigrating to women, often serve to divorce a male organ or function from any significant interaction with the female. Take the word "testes," for example, suggesting "witnesses" (from the Latin *testis*) to the sexual and procreative strengths of the male organ; and the obscene counterpart of this word, which suggests little more than a mechanical shape. Or compare almost any of the "rich," "liberating" sexual verbs, so fashionable today among male writers, with that much-derided Latin word "copulate" ("to bind or join together") or even that Anglo-Saxon phrase (which seems to have had no trouble surviving the Norman Conquest) "make love."

(8) How arrogantly self-involved the tabooed words seem in comparison to either of the other terms, and how contemptuous of the female partner. Understandably so, of course, if she is only a "skirt," a "broad," a "chick," a "pussycat" or a "piece." If she is, in other words, no more than her skirt, or what her skirt conceals; no more than a breeder, or the broadest part of her; no more than a piece of human being or a "piece of tail."

(9) The most severely tabooed of all the female descriptives, incidentally, are those like a "piece of tail," which suggest (either explicitly or through antecedents) that there is no significant difference between the female channel through which we are all conceived and born and the anal outlet common to both sexes—a distinction that pornographers have always enjoyed obscuring.

(10) This effort to deny women their biological identity, their individuality, their humanness, is such an important aspect of obscene language that one can only marvel at how seldom, in an era preoccupied with definitions of obscenity, this fact is brought to our attention. One problem, of course, is that many of the people in the best position to do this (critics, teachers, writers) are so reluctant today to admit that they are angered or shocked by obscenity. Bored, maybe, unimpressed, aesthetically displeased, but—no matter how brutal or denigrating the material—never angered, never shocked.

(11) And yet how eloquently angered, how piously shocked many of these same people become if denigrating language is used about any minority group other than women; if the obscenities are racial or ethnic, that is, rather than sexual. Words like "coon," "kike," "spic," "wop," after all, deform identity, deny individuality and humanness in almost exactly the same way that sexual vulgarisms and obscenities do.

(12) No one that I know, least of all my students, would fail to question the values of a society whose literature and entertainment rested heavily on racial or ethnic pejoratives. Are the values of a society whose literature and entertainment rest as heavily as ours on sexual pejoratives any less questionable?

QUESTIONS AND EXERCISES

VOCABULARY

1. copulate (*paragraph* 1)
2. inflections (1)
3. etymological (4)
4. crotchet (5)
5. sadistic (4)
6. analogy (5)
7. denigrated (5)
8. procreative (6)
9. pornographers (9)
10. aesthetically (10)
11. pejoratives (12)

LANGUAGE AND RHETORIC

1. In addition to her use of multiple examples, Lawrence uses several other methods of development. What are they?
2. What is the thesis and where is it presented?
3. This essay has a clearly defined beginning, middle, and end. Where do the divisions occur? How does the author attempt to arouse interest in her subject at the beginning?
4. Why are the words "rich" and "liberating" quoted in paragraph 7? The general tone of this essay can be described as earnest and serious. This tone changes a bit in paragraph 7. Explain.

DISCUSSION AND WRITING

2. Despite the apparent freedom with which Lawrence discusses "four-letter" or "dirty" words, she nevertheless manages to avoid explicitly using one common word central to her discussion (see paragraph 4). Does this omission—if it is one—weaken her essay in any way? Support your answer.
3. Do you find the author's argument that sexual obscenity demeans women a valid one? Why or why not?
4. In her final two paragraphs, Lawrence relates the use of sexual pejoratives to the use of racial and ethnic pejoratives, suggesting that the one is as questionable as the other as a reflection of the values of our society. What is her basis for that connection? Do you consider her comparison of the two in this context to be a valid one? Why or why not?
5. Some English instructors are reluctant to use selections such as this one because they believe that the actual use of the language under examination is likely to offend some of their students. Discuss the arguments for and against that point of view, and arrive at a position of your own on the issue if you have not already done so. Write an essay stating your position and explaining the basis for it, using specific examples to illustrate your point.

N. SCOTT MOMADAY

A Vision Beyond Time and Space

The life of N. Scott Momaday bridges two cultures. As a Kiowa Indian, he recalls—and responds to—the heritage of his people, a heritage that he perpetuates as a writer of both fiction and nonfiction. As a Professor of English at Stanford University, he is part of a contemporary culture of quite another kind. This selection deals with the contrast between these two cultures by focusing on the world view of the Kiowa, "a vision beyond time and place" that, according to the author, makes the Indian "perhaps the most culturally secure of all Americans."

This selection is an excellent example of how a writer effectively combines methods of development. Framing his subject with the example of "old man Cheney" at both beginning and end, Momaday focuses on the contrast between cultures and shows its significance for our time.

When my father was a boy, an old man used to come to [my grand-father] Mammedaty's house and pay his respects. He was a lean old man in braids and was impressive in his age and bearing. His name was Cheney, and he was an arrowmaker. Every morning, my father tells me, Cheney would paint his wrinkled face, go out, and pray aloud to the rising sun. In my mind I can see that man as if he were there now. I like to watch him as he makes his prayer. I know where he stands and where his voice goes on the rolling grasses and where the sun comes up on the land. There, at dawn, you can feel the silence. It is cold and clear and deep like water. It takes hold of you and will not let you go. (From *The Way to Rainy Mountain*. The University of New Mexico Press.)

(1) I often think of old man Cheney, and of his daily devotion to the sun. He died before I was born, and I never knew where he came from or what of good and bad entered into his life. But I think I know who he was, essentially, and what his view of the world meant to him and to me. He was a man who saw very deeply into the distance, I believe, one whose vision extended far beyond the physical boundaries of his time and place. He perceived the wonder and meaning of Creation itself. In his mind's eye he could integrate all the realities and illusions of the earth and sky; they became for him profoundly intelligible and whole.

(2) Once, in the first light, I stood where Cheney has stood, next to the house which my grandfather Mammedaty had built on a rise of land near Rainy Mountain Creek, and watched the sun come out of the black horizon of the world. It was an irresistible and awesome emergence, as waters gather to the flood, of weather and of light. I could not have been more sensitive to the cold, nor than to the heat which came upon it. And I could not have *foreseen* the break of day. The shadows on the rolling plains became large and luminous in a moment, impalpable, then faceted, dark and distinct again as they were run through with splinters of light. And the sun itself, when it appeared, was pale and immense, original in the deepest sense of the word. It is no wonder, I thought, that an old man should pray to it. It is no wonder . . . and yet, of course, wonder is the principal part of such a vision. Cheney's prayer was an affirmation of his wonder and regard, a testament to the realization of a quest for vision.

(3) This native vision, this gift of seeing truly, with wonder and delight, into the natural world, is informed by a certain attitude of reverence

and self-respect. It is a matter of extrasensory as well as sensory perception, I believe. In addition to the eye, it involves the intelligence, the instinct, and the imagination. It is the perception not only of objects and forms but also of essences and ideals, as in this Chippewa song:

> *as my eyes*
> *search*
> *the prairie*
> *I feel the summer*
> *in the spring*

Even as the singer sees into the immediate landscape, he perceives a now and future dimension that is altogether remote, yet nonetheless real and inherent within it, a quality of evanescence and evolution, a state at once of being and of becoming. He beholds what is there; nothing of the scene is lost upon him. In the integrity of his vision he is wholly in possession of himself and of the world around him; he is quintessentially alive.

(4) Most Indian people are able to see in these terms. Their view of the world is peculiarly native and distinct, and it determines who and what they are to a great extent. It is indeed the basis upon which they identify themselves as individuals and as a race. There is something of genetic significance in such a thing, perhaps, an element of being which resides in the blood and which is, after all, the very nucleus of the self. When old man Cheney looked into the sunrise, he saw as far into himself, I suspect, as he saw into the distance. He knew certainly of his existence and of his place in the scheme of things.

(5) In contrast, most of us in this society are afflicted with a kind of cultural nearsightedness. Our eyes, it may be, have been trained too long upon the superficial, and *artificial,* aspects of our environment; we do not see beyond the buildings and billboards that seem at times to be the monuments of our civilization, and consequently we fail to see into the nature and meaning of our own humanity. Now, more than ever, we might do well to enter upon a vision quest of our own, that is, a quest after vision itself. And in this the Indian stands to lead by his example. For with respect to such things as a sense of heritage, of a vital continuity in terms of origin and of destiny, a profound investment of the mind and spirit in the oral traditions of literature, philosophy, and religion—those things, in short, which constitute his vision of the world—the Indian is perhaps the most culturally secure of all Americans.

(6) As I see him, that old man, he walks very slowly to the place where he will make his prayer, and it is always the same place, a small mound where the grass is sparse and the hard red earth shows through. He limps a little, with age, but when he plants his feet he is tall and straight

and hard. The bones are fine and prominent in his face and hands. And his face is painted. There are red and yellow bars under his eyes, neither bright nor sharply defined on the dark, furrowed skin, but soft and organic, the colors of sandstone and of pollen. His long braids are wrapped with blood-red cloth. His eyes are deep and open to the wide world. At sunrise, precisely, they catch fire and close, having seen. The low light descends upon him. And when he lifts his voice, it enters upon the silence and carries there, like the call of a bird.

QUESTIONS AND EXERCISES

VOCABULARY

1. perceived (*paragraph 1*)
2. intelligible (1)
3. impalpable (2)
4. faceted (2)
5. extrasensory (3)
6. evanescence (3)
7. quintessentially (3)

LANGUAGE AND RHETORIC

1. What kind of audience does the author seem to have in mind for this selection? How can you tell?
2. What is his point of view in relation to that audience; that is, where does he stand in this matter? What clues helped you to determine your answer?
3. The author uses the example of "old man Cheney" to open and close his essay. Could he have achieved the same results if he had placed that example in the middle? Why or why not?

DISCUSSION AND WRITING

1. Sift through your memory to identify some of the friends, family, and associates who have particularly influenced you regarding the kinds of things dealt with in this essay: time, nature, the outdoors; a sense of place, heritage, or culture. Select a likely person and write an essay showing how he or she influenced you.
2. If you have ever had the experience of feeling intensely alive in a natural setting, write a paper describing or recounting that experience and its effect on you.
3. How do you respond to Momaday's comments on the "cultural nearsightedness" that afflicts most of us in the non-Indian culture? Is there a basis in fact for his generalization about not seeing beyond the superficial and artificial aspects of our environment? Support your conclusions in an essay.
4. Momaday says that the Indian is "perhaps the most culturally secure of all Americans." Others have argued to the contrary: that the Indian is caught

between two cultures, that of the Native American heritage and that of the contemporary "Anglo." Advocates of this position maintain that the American Indian totally lacks a sense of personal identity. Investigate this subject in your campus library and explore some possible topics for writing.

MARK TWAIN (SAMUEL CLEMENS)

Corn-Pone Opinions

Fifty years ago, when I was a boy of fifteen and helping to inhabit a Missourian village on the banks of the Mississippi, I had a friend whose society was very dear to me because I was forbidden by my mother to partake of it. He was a gay and impudent and satirical and delightful young black man—a slave—who daily preached sermons from the top of his master's woodpile, with me for sole audience. He imitated the pulpit style of the several clergymen of the village, and did it well, and with fine passion and energy. To me he was a wonder. I believed he was the greatest orator in the United States and would some day be heard from. But it did not happen; in the distribution of rewards he was overlooked. It is the way, in this world.

He interrupted his preaching, now and then, to saw a stick of wood; but the sawing was a pretense—he did it with his mouth; exactly imitating the sound the bucksaw makes in shrieking its way through the wood. But it served its purpose; it kept his master from coming out to see how the work was getting along. I listened to the sermons from the open window of a lumber room at the back of the house. One of his texts was this:

"You tell me whar a man gits his corn pone, en I'll tell you what his 'pinions is."

I can never forget it. It was deeply impressed upon me. By my mother. Not upon my memory, but elsewhere. She had slipped in upon me while I was absorbed and not watching. The black philosopher's idea was that a man is not independent, and cannot afford views which might interfere with his bread and butter. If he would prosper, he must train with the majority; in matters of large moment, like politics and religion, he must think and feel with the bulk of his neighbors, or suffer damage in his social standing and in his business prosperities. He must restrict himself to cornpone opinions—at least on the surface. He must get his opinions from other people; he must reason out none for himself; he must have no first-hand views.

I think Jerry was right, in the main, but I think he did not go far enough.

1. It was his idea that a man conforms to the majority view of his locality by calculation and intention.

This happens, but I think it is not the rule.

2. It was his idea that there is such a thing as a first-hand opinion; an original opinion; an opinion which is coldly reasoned out in a man's head, by a searching analysis of the facts involved, with the heart unconsulted, and the jury room closed against outside influences. It may be that such an opinion has been born somewhere, at some time or other, but I suppose it got away before they could catch it and stuff it and put it in the museum.

I am persuaded that a coldly-thought-out and independent verdict upon a fashion in clothes, or manners, or literature, or politics, or religion, or any other matter that is projected into the field of our notice and interest, is a most rare thing—if it has indeed ever existed.

A new thing in costume appears—the flaring hoop skirt, for example—and the passers-by are shocked, and the irreverent laugh. Six months later everybody is reconciled; the fashion has established itself; it is admired, now, and no one laughs. Public opinion resented it before, public opinion accepts it now, and is happy in it. Why? Was the resentment reasoned out? Was the acceptance reasoned out? No. The instinct that moves to conformity did the work. It is our nature to conform; it is a force which not many can successfully resist. What is its seat? The inborn requirement of self-approval. We all have to bow to that; there are no exceptions. Even the woman who refuses from first to last to wear the hoop skirt comes under the law and is its slave; she could not wear the skirt and have her own approval; and that she *must* have, she cannot help herself. But as a rule our self-approval has its source in but one place and not elsewhere—the approval of other people. A person of vast consequences can introduce any kind of novelty in dress and the general world will presently adopt it—moved to do it, in the first place, by the natural instinct to passively yield to that vague something recognized as authority, and in the second place by the human instinct to train with the multitude and have its approval. An empress introduced the hoop skirt, and we know the result. A nobody introduced the bloomer, and we know the result. If Eve should come again, in her ripe renown, and reintroduce her quaint styles—well, we know what would happen. And we should be cruelly embarrassed, along at first.

The hoop skirt runs its course and disappears. Nobody reasons about it. One woman abandons the fashion; her neighbor notices this and follows her lead; this influences the next woman; and so on and so on, and presently the skirt has vanished out of the world, no one knows how nor why; or cares for that matter. It will come again, by and by, and in due course will go again.

Twenty-five years ago, in England, six or eight wine glasses stood grouped by each person's plate at a dinner party, and they were used, not left idle and empty; today there are but three or four in the group, and the average guest sparingly uses about two of them. We have not adopted this new fashion yet, but we shall do it presently. We shall not think it out; we shall merely conform, and let it go at that. We get our notions and habits and opinions from outside influences; we do not have to study them out.

Our table manners, and company manners, and street manners change from time to time, but the changes are not reasoned out; we merely notice and conform. We are creatures of outside influences, as a rule we do not think, we only imitate. We can not invent standards that will stick; what we mistake for standards are only fashions, and perishable. We may continue to admire them, but we drop the use of them. We notice this in literature. Shakespeare is a standard, and fifty years ago we used to write tragedies which we couldn't tell from—from somebody else's; but we don't do it any more, now. Our prose standard, three-quarters of a century ago, was ornate and diffuse; some authority or other changed it in the direction of compactness and simplicity, and conformity followed, without argument. The historical novel starts up suddenly, and sweeps the land. Everybody writes one, and the nation is glad. We had historical novels before; but nobody read them, and the rest of us conformed—without reasoning it out. We are conforming in the other way, now, because it is another case of everybody.

The outside influences are always pouring in upon us, and we are always obeying their orders and accepting their verdicts. The Smiths like the new play; the Joneses go to see it, and they copy the Smith verdict. Morals, religions, politics, get their following from surrounding influences and atmospheres, almost entirely; not from study, not from thinking. A man must and will have his own approval first of all, in each and every moment and circumstance of his life—even if he must repent of a self-approved act the moment after its commission, in order to get his self-approval *again:* but, speaking in general terms, a man's self-approval in the large concerns of life has its source in the approval of the peoples about him, and not in a searching personal examination of the matter. Mohammedans are Mohammedans because they are born and reared among that sect, not because they have thought it out and can furnish sound reasons for being Mohammedans; we know why Catholics are Catholics; why Presbyterians are Presbyterians; why Baptist are Baptists; why Mormons are Mormons; why thieves are thieves; why monarchists are monarchists; why Republicans are Republicans and Democrats, Democrats. We know it is a matter of association and sympathy, not reasoning and examination, that hardly a man in the world has an opinion upon morals, politics, or religion which he got otherwise than through his associations and sympathies. Broadly speaking, there are none but corn-pone opinions. And broadly speaking, corn-pone stands for self-approval. Self-approval is acquired mainly from the approval of other people. The result is conformity. Sometimes conformity has a sordid business interest—the bread-and-butter interest—but not in most cases, I think. I think that in the majority of cases it is unconscious and not calculated; that it is born of the human being's natural yearning to stand well with his fellows and have their inspiring approval and praise—a yearning which is commonly so strong and so insistent that it cannot be effectually resisted, and must have its way.

A political emergency brings out the corn-pone opinion in fine force in its two chief varieties—the pocketbook variety, which has its origin in self-interest, and the bigger variety, the sentimental variety—the one which can't bear to be outside the pale; can't bear to be in disfavor; can't endure the averted face and the cold shoulder; wants to stand well with his friends, wants to be smiled upon, wants to be welcome, wants to hear the precious words, *"He's* on the right track!" Uttered, perhaps by an ass, but still an ass of high degree, an ass whose approval is gold and diamonds to a smaller ass, and confers glory and honor and happiness, and membership in the herd. For these gauds many a man will dump his life-long principles into the street, and his conscience along with them. We have seen it happen. In some millions of instances.

Men think they think upon great political questions, and they do; but they think with their party, not independently; they read its literature, but not that of the other side; they arrive at convictions, but they are drawn from a partial view of the matter in hand and are of no particular value. They swarm with their party, they feel with their party, they are happy in their party's approval; and where the party leads they will follow, whether for right and honor, or through blood and dirt and a mush of mutilated morals.

In our late canvass half of the nation passionately believed that in silver lay salvation, the other half as passionately believed that that way lay destruction. Do you believe that a tenth part of the people, on either side, had any rational excuse for having an opinion about the matter at all? I studied that mighty question to the bottom—came out empty. Half of our people passionately believe in high tariff, the other half believe otherwise. Does this mean study and examination, or only feeling? The latter, I think. I have deeply studied that question, too—and didn't arrive. We all do no end of feeling, and we mistake it for thinking. And out of it we get an aggregation which we consider a boon. Its name is public opinion. It is held in reverence. It settles everything. Some think it the voice of God.

FOUR

FACTS AND JUDGMENTS

JEFFREY CRESSY

Air Bags Are a Proven "Vaccine"

As one of 5,000 annual victims of spinal cord damage due to automobile accidents, Jeffrey Cressy knows his subject from personal experience. But Cressy has gone beyond his own experience to investigate this matter on a broader basis. In the process he has uncovered some surprising facts and figures that suggest we may indeed be facing a national problem. The irony is that we know its cause and already have a potential solution—the air bag. Nevertheless, neither the auto manufacturers nor the federal government is inclined to adopt such a safety measure regardless of the consequences of failing to do so.

Cressy has done a commendable job of using factual details to support his judgments. Pay attention to the interaction between these two aspects of his argument as you read.

(1) The spinal cord is only about as big around as your little finger. Because it carries impulses between the brain and the rest of the body, bringing messages of movement and sensation, it's one of the most important structures in the body. If these impulses are interrupted, paralysis results.

(2) I am no casual observer of spinal-cord injury. Eight years ago, my neck was broken and my spinal cord was damaged at the C-6 cervical level, leaving me with only limited use of my arms and hands. I have been a quadriplegic living in a wheelchair ever since. Were my neck broken about an inch higher, I would have been on a respirator for the rest of my life.

(3) I was 18 years old and I had just finished my first year of college when a split-second, 25-mile-per-hour crash permanently changed my life. I remember sitting there waiting for the rescue crew, unable to remove my hands from the steering wheel. I hadn't had the luxury of an air bag, nor the common sense to buckle up. I wish I had had both.

(4) In the past eight years not a day has passed that I haven't thought

of my life before wheels. My "new wheels" constantly remind me of how inadequate the safety devices in our larger vehicles are.

(5) Last year, more than 42,000 people died in auto accidents; 5,000 who survived were left with serious spinal-cord injuries. A spinal-cord injury—a permanent disabling condition—takes only a fraction of a second to happen. But in that same split second, an air bag would inflate. Since the first patent was applied for more than 30 years ago, the air bag has become a proven, relatively cheap device which works automatically.

(6) Auto crashes are the leading killer and crippler of people like me, those who are under 35 years in age. The air bag is a proven "vaccine" for this most deadly and disabling "disease." But tragically, it has been withheld from the American public. After limited experiments, the automakers—with one exception—decided not to allow you and me to have this lifesaving device in our cars. And even last week, the federal government seemed reluctant to force the industry to provide it.

(7) I recently testified before a Department of Transportation hearing in Los Angeles on auto safety, and while waiting my turn, I heard incredible things. People standing on two legs criticized the air bag because it *only* works in frontal crashes. More than half of the fatal car crashes are frontal crashes. Others maintained that the air bag is just another example of government regulation. Yet the issue here is not one of airline fares or gasoline prices but unnecessary injuries and deaths. I had the freedom not to wear my seat belt so now I'm confined to a wheelchair. What about my freedom to choose to use an air bag?

(8) During the Los Angeles hearing, I also heard American auto manufacturers complain that the cost of installing an air bag is too high—that the extra cost would discourage potential buyers of new cars at a time of growing sales and renewed prosperity in their industry. A poll conducted for the Insurance Institute for Highway Safety has found that 9 out of 10 car buyers favor passive restraints as standard or optional equipment in new cars. And in a recent Gallup poll, Americans were increasingly concerned about auto safety. By a margin of 2 to 1, 60 percent to 31 percent, those surveyed said they favored a law that would require air bags in all new cars.

(9) A few hundred dollars extra to install an air bag hardly compares to the catastrophic cost of caring for a person with a severe spinal-cord injury. Lifetime costs for one victim average $350,000. And there are about 10,000 new victims in the United States every year, 40 percent of them injured in auto accidents. That's $1.4 billion in health-care costs incurred each year because of car crashes, a tab for spinal-cord patients that is paid for in part by taxpayers through the Medicaid system. The hidden costs to society include higher health-, auto- and life-insurance premiums and an increased tax burden. The price tag on the psycho-

logical effects of a disabling injury are impossible to calculate. Air bags are a cost-effective measure for everyone.

(10) At Rancho Los Amigos Hospital where I work, we get about 170 new spinal-cord-injury patients every year. Half of them are under the age of 25, and 70 percent are on Medi-Cal, California's Medicaid system. The hospital is full of patients who were injured in car crashes: most were not wearing seat belts at the time of their accidents. And as you might expect, many are now air-bag supporters. Unfortunately, some cannot speak.

(11) My crash was a very simple one. I was driving around a sharp turn on a country road when my back wheels went off the pavement. I ended up careening front-end first into a small ditch. A simple accident paralyzed me.

(12) Last November a man in Texas was driving 50 miles per hour when his car left the road and flew 40 feet through the air, landing in a deep ravine. Bob LaRoche walked away from that accident—similar to mine yet a more powerful crash—because he was driving an air-bag equipped Mercedes. His wife suffered a broken back and severe bruises and lacerations; the passenger side of the car was not air-bag equipped.

(13) How many Americans can afford a $45,000 Mercedes-Benz? Should auto safety be reserved only for the wealthy? Seat belts work, I know, and I wish I had been wearing mine that summer night eight years ago. But now when I think of auto safety, I also think of a fire extinguisher. Hanging on the wall, it is useless in putting out a fire unless someone has the presence of mind to point it toward the flame. But a sprinkler system, mandatory in many places, is automatic.

(14) That's the beauty of the air bag. It is truly the proverbial ounce of prevention that is worth a pound of cure. "Procrastination," someone once said, "is the thief of time." In the continuing case of air bags, procrastination is the thief of young lives. As a victim and as a provider of health care, I know that air bags would significantly reduce the incidence of spinal-cord injuries—and the waste of human lives.

QUESTIONS AND EXERCISES

VOCABULARY

1. cervical (*paragraph 2*)
2. quadriplegic (2)
3. catastrophic (9)
4. careening (11)
5. procrastination (14)

LANGUAGE AND RHETORIC

1. What is your reaction to the comparison of spinal cord injury to a disease and the air bag to a vaccine. Is it effective? Explain your response. Can you suggest other comparisons that might work well here?
2. This selection is a good example of the use of facts and judgments to develop a thesis. Can you find any judgments that do not appear to be well supported by facts? If so, point them out.
3. Cressy combines personal experience with a number of factual details. Would you change the balance between the two in any way? If so, why and how?
4. What rhetorical function does the first paragraph serve? Is it placed at the most appropriate point, or would the essay be stronger if the author opened with paragraph two, citing his personal experience?

DISCUSSION AND WRITING

1. How convincing do you find Cressy's argument? Write an essay based on this one in which you either support or refute his thesis. Try to incorporate factual details from other sources, but in any event be sure to support your judgments.
2. Some people claim that *mandatory* use of seat belts, air bags, or other safety devices constitutes an infringement on the rights of the individual. What do you think of this view? What is your basis for it? Write an essay defending your position.
3. If you have been involved in an automobile accident, write a paper recounting your experience. Like Cressy, you may wish to consider causes and effects, but regardless, be sure that you support any judgments you offer.

LOIS TIMNICK

Electronic Bullies

The marvels of the electronic age may add to our lives a number of unanticipated—and in some cases unwelcome—dimensions. Even some of the smartest among us may be inclined to place greater confidence in what a computer or calculator says than in what we believe to be true. When things reach this point, says author Lois Timnick, we had better beware of deluding ourselves into believing that a machine can function perfectly and find out who—or what—is really in charge.

Central to the author's subject is a university research study. Notice how she organizes her article around that report.

(1) Laura McKinley certainly wasn't feeling like a member of an endangered species when she dialed the downtown branch of Los Angeles's largest bank. What she *was* feeling was angry, having just opened

her statement to find herself erroneously charged with an $800 over-draft and assessed finance charges to boot.

(2) A robotlike voice at the other end of the line insisted that the computerized statement was correct. "Just go over your figures again and check your daily balances," the woman told her. "I'm sure you'll find your mistake." Persisting, McKinley eventually found that human error or a glitch in the computer's labyrinthine circuitry had deducted her home-mortgage payments from her account twice in the same month, depleting her otherwise sufficient funds.

(3) Laura McKinleys seem to be increasingly scarce these days. Faced with computerized figures that don't jibe with their own, a surprising number of people never bother to reconcile the discrepancy. Many simply scratch their heads, assume that the bank is right, and make the appropriate adjustments in their checkbooks. Even large mistakes often go undetected, unchallenged, and uncorrected as we become increasingly dependent on machines, trusting in their infallibility and reluctant to challenge their authority.

(4) Now a disturbing study—the first of its kind—from the University of Missouri at Columbia has confirmed just how blind our faith in that authority is. A team of researchers found that even the brightest students and adults, it seems, tend to take the word of a machine—in this case a hand-held calculator—over their own good sense, even when their rough calculations are correct and the machine is off by as much as 50 percent.

(5) As if it weren't bad enough that even the smartest among us doubt our own abilities when pitted against a calculator, what of our duller counterparts who lack even the basic skills that would enable them to detect or suspect mechanical mistakes and miscalculations? In effect, their calculators use them, not the other way around.

(6) Sometimes the cost of such dependence may be slight—a confused bank statement, an overcharge in the supermarket checkout line—although, assuming that we notice them at all, even small snafus can take their toll in frustration and in anger.

(7) But overreliance on machines can also be potentially dangerous—and not just in science fiction, such as the film "2001: A Space Odyssey," in which astronaut Bowman belatedly realizes that the humanoid computer, Hal, has turned murderer.

(8) Three times within the last two and a half years, computer malfunctions in our military warning system gave off false alarms indicating that the Soviets had fired missiles at the United States, triggering a complex set of preparatory measures. In the most recent incidents, bomber engines were actually being warmed up and missile technicians had been alerted when the mistakes—failures in 46-cent-circuits—were discovered.

(9) As our technology grows increasingly complex, perhaps only a healthy skepticism about what machines can and cannot do, along with routine double checks of their results, can save us from catastrophe. We need to realize that even simple machines—those calculators and computers supposedly created to simplify our lives by providing quick solutions to time-consuming problems—are no substitute for certain basic thinking and reasoning skills.

(10) Robert E. Reys, a mathematics educator at the University of Missouri in Columbia and the principal investigator involved in the calculator study, says that his findings should not be misinterpreted as an argument against allowing students to use hand-held calculators. Instead, he says, that results underline the importance of students developing an awareness of calculator errors and an unwillingness to be intimidated by a result that doesn't square with their ballpark estimate of the answer. The same attitudes will eventually have to develop in people who use the verbal counterparts of calculators—the newfangled machines and programs that supposedly correct bad punctuation and misspelled words. Psychologist Susan Chipman, assistant director of learning and development at the National Institute of Education (NIE) in Washington, warns that despite the claims of the ads in microcomputer magazines, "in truth, there are still serious limitations on what can be done with language processors and artificial intelligence."

(11) Reys and his associates, who included three math teachers, conducted a yearlong, $63,000 study for the NIE on what they call "the most neglected skill in the mathematics curriculum—computational estimation." They wanted to find out what processes teenagers and adults use when neither pencil nor calculator is available, to decide, say, what size package is the better buy at the supermarket, how large a tip to leave at a restaurant, or whether that $10 bill in their pocket will cover the items in the shopping cart.

(12) Researchers tested nearly 1,200 students (grades seven through 12) and adults in St. Louis, Columbia, and Cape Girardeau, Missouri, and in Escondido, California, on their ability to make mathematical estimates: the ones who scored in the top 10 percent were culled for follow-up interviews. Predictably, the researchers found that the best "estimators"—not necessarily those able to do quick and exact mental arithmetic but those who could roughly estimate the answers to math problems—arrived at their conclusions by using shortcuts that included rounding off numbers or working with only the first digits. The good estimators tended to have a command of basic arithmetic processes and concepts, to be self-confident, and to have a tolerance for error. It's important, said one seventh-grader in explaining the ease with which he gave estimates, to "tell yourself not to end up getting bothered by being off some."

(13) Reys believes that such skills are more critical than ever in an era when more than 80 percent of secondary-school students have access to calculators. Hence, a portion of the interview involved asking subjects to estimate the answers to seven problems and then to compare the accuracy of their estimates with results obtained by using a calculator. Some of the problems: $436 + 972 + 79$; $42,962 \div 73$; 252×1.2.

(14) There was one catch, however: The researchers had programmed the calculators to make systematically increasing errors in computing, giving answers that were from 10 percent to 50 percent above the real answer and above the range that they had determined as acceptable. Thirty-three students and 12 adults participated in this phase of the study. Thirty-one were male, 14 female. The results are surprising and disturbing. Only 20 percent of the participants—all of them male—recognized the unreasonableness of the result and voiced suspicion of the calculator after the first exercise. Most looked puzzled, hesitated, repunched the sequence, or asked to work the problem out with pencil and paper, but did not directly voice any doubt before proceeding to the next problem.

(15) By the time they reached the final problem, 36 percent of the females and 77 percent of the males had caught on. But almost a quarter of the males and nearly two-thirds of the females proceeded through all seven problems without verbally expressing *any* concern about the accuracy of the calculator.

(16) "I must have entered it wrong on the calculator; either that or I'm thinking wrong," one student said. Another remarked: "It doesn't look right, but if that's what the calculator says, then it's probably right. It still doesn't look right."

(17) One ninth-grader was typical of those who stayed confused to the very end. In Exercise 1, he was asked to add $436 + 972 + 79$. The acceptable interval was 1,450–1,600, and the student estimated 1,480; the calculator said 1,627. The student mused, "So I was about 140 off," and went on to the next problem. After five highly accurate estimates on other problems, for which the calculator was "off" by 50 to 1,700, the student was totally puzzled. On Exercise 7, multiplying 252×1.2, he estimated 312.4, explaining that he had "multiplied 252 by 1, then 252 by .2, then added them together."

(18) "So should that be pretty close?" the investigator asked.

(19) "The way I'm going, I wouldn't say anything right now."

(20) The student then used the calculator, which came up with 452.4, far above the acceptable interval of 252–350.

(21) "Do you think that's pretty close?"

(22) "My answer is about three-fourths of it."

(23) "So you're satisfied."

(24) "Yes, pretty much. More than the last one."

(25) "As we look back, it looks like all of the exact answers are higher than your estimates."

(26) "Yes, I usually underestimate except with money. . . ."

(27) "What do you think about your estimates?"

(28) "They're pretty . . . okay, I guess, except for 22 × 39."

(29) "Why?"

(30) "I don't understand why my numbers are so far off. Can I round down the numbers?"

(31) "Yes."

(32) "I don't know what to think."

(33) "What could be wrong?"

(34) "I don't know."

(35) Reys concedes that his numbers are small, that the calculator used may have been unfamiliar to the subjects, and that the interviewer may have been viewed as an authority figure. Ed Esty, the NIE's math research specialist, cautions: "Remember, this was an unrealistic situation." The machine, an HP-65, which is a complex, programmable model, may have been "assumed to be special and accurate"; the project involved "good estimators who were sophisticated in numerical-estimation skills but not in the tricks of wily investigators."

(36) Still, the researchers feel justified in making several general observations:

(37) ● Males were more likely than females to challenge the calculator's results. Reys speculates that this may be because "the boys were less intimidated, more aggressive, more willing to risk and tolerate something other than the exact answer."

(38) ● No single factor, other than sex, appeared to separate the challengers from the accepters. Adults were no more skeptical than the younger students (although they tended to do better on the estimation exercises, presumably because they had had more experience). And neither mathematical prowess, self-confidence, nor other personality characteristics appeared to differentiate the two groups.

(39) ● Even subjects making good estimates were reluctant to challenge the calculator's answers.

(40) These findings, the researchers say, show that "an aura of infallibility surrounds the calculator." In a subsequent interview, Reys added that the true incidence of overdependence on calculators may be even worse than his study indicates: The team used only good students in accelerated classrooms and adults who held professional jobs. Since the bright and confident, who can arrive at reasonable estimates, reject them in favor of a calculator's unreasonable answers, he says, it is hard to expect more from those who are poor at math and lacking in the ability to recognize a wrong answer when they see one.

(41) Reys says that the unwillingness of many good estimators to trust themselves suggests that a challenging task lies ahead for math teachers. But he is optimistic, recalling one seventh-grader who commented at the end of the very first problem. "This doesn't seem right." He plugged the calculator in again and concluded. "This *can't* be right. The calculator's messed up." "Can that be?" the interviewer asked. "Of course," the youngster replied. "Mine at home messes up all the time."

(42) Having developed an awareness of calculator errors and the ease with which wrong keys can be pressed, this unintimidated youngster was well on his way to using the calculator properly, Reys said—as a helpful but not infallible tool. Other students were nearly as good, sometimes detecting something "fishy" several problems before they became sure enough to question openly the calculator's answers. One 12th-grader said at Problem 3 that something about the calculator had "smelled slightly" in Problem 2, and went on to say, "I have a sneaking suspicion that your calculator is multiplying it [the answer] by a certain small constant."

(43) In business circles a disenchantment of sorts with computers may be setting in already, after an initial burst of overenthusiasm. A recent report in *The New York Times* found that more and more small-business owners are finding that computers do not always perform as promised and that a business can become so dependent on them for billing and accounting that a faulty computer could bankrupt a firm before its human officers realized that anything was wrong.

(44) An Illinois insurance agent, for example, bought a computer three years ago to automate his mailings and records. Despite a college course on computers and days and nights spent working with his new toy (which culminated in his being hospitalized for exhaustion and bronchial pneumonia), he could never get it to work properly. Finally, he gave up. "I took the computer out of here," he told a reporter. "I couldn't stand the sight of it." It now sits gathering dust in his basement, and he is suing the manufacturer for fraudulently misrepresenting its product's capabilities.

(45) That kind of frustration may well turn out to be one of the most insidious prices of overreliance on computers and other technological marvels and gadgetry—be they assembly-line robots, microwave ovens, fancy automobiles, or defense systems—whose complexities often mean only more things to go wrong and break down. "The general rule is that the more dependent you are on anything, the more apt you are to become infuriated—spontaneously, impulsively enraged—when it does not work to perfection," says Mel Mandel, a psychiatrist in Los Angeles who is president-elect of the Southern California Psychiatric Society. Because machinery normally performs as expected, he says, "we lose

our sense of the fallible and expect infallible behavior. We have deluded ourselves into believing that a machine can function perfectly, and when that delusion is exposed by failure, we become utterly enraged at the machinery.

(46) "Of course, we are really angry at ourselves."

QUESTIONS AND EXERCISES

VOCABULARY

1. glitch (*paragraph 2*)
2. labyrinthine (2)
3. skepticism (9)
4. wily (35)
5. aura (40)
6. infallibility (40)

LANGUAGE AND RHETORIC

1. How does the title reflect both the subject and the thesis of this selection?
2. The bulk of this selection is devoted to reporting the results of the University of Missouri study by Professor Reys. Show how the author organizes her article around that report.
3. The other essays in this section utilize a broad range of sources, while this selection limits itself to one report. What are some of the advantages and disadvantages of each approach?
4. The concluding quotation could have been included in the previous paragraph. What is the result of setting it apart as the author does?

DISCUSSION AND WRITING

1. If you have ever had an experience similar to Laura McKinley's, in which a computer or other machine error created a serious problem for you, write an essay recounting that experience and how you handled it.
2. Timnick suggests in paragraph 9 that we need to develop "a healthy skepticism" about what machines can and cannot do for us. How would you go about developing it? Explore this question in some preliminary form, such as a journal, to see if you can come up with any ideas.
3. Some teachers refuse to let students use calculators in classes. What might Timnick say about this attitude? What is your view on the subject and what are your reasons for it? Write a paper defending your position.
4. How do you respond to Professor Reys' speculation that males were more likely than females to challenge calculator results because males were "less intimidated, more aggressive," and "more willing to risk"?
5. Is there any significant difference between the willingness to accept machine calculations and conclusions and the willingness to accept whatever one sees in print? If so, what is it?

CARL SAGAN

In Praise of Science and Technology

Technology has been cited by some writers as the main cause of many of our environmental problems. In the following essay, Carl Sagan writes in praise of both science and technology, while recognizing that they "have not been pursued with sufficient attention to their ultimate humane objectives." In analyzing the reasons behind this situation, Sagan points to the public's limited understanding of science and technology and the inadequacies of our school systems in fulfilling this part of their mission.

Observe the author's use of a combination of factual detail and judgment to develop his argument.

(1) In the middle of the 19th century, the largely self-educated British physicist, Michael Faraday, was visited by his monarch, Queen Victoria. Among Faraday's many celebrated discoveries, some of obvious and immediately practical benefit, were more arcane findings involving electricity and magnetism, then little more than laboratory curiosities. In the traditional dialogue between heads of state and heads of laboratories, the queen asked Faraday of what use such studies were, to which he is said to have replied: "Madame, of what use is a baby?" Faraday had an idea that there might someday be something practical in electricity and magnetism.

(2) At about the same time the Scottish physicist James Clerk Maxwell set down four mathematical equations, based on the work of Faraday and his experimental predecessors, relating electrical charges and currents with electric and magnetic fields. The equations exhibited a curious lack of symmetry, and this bothered Maxwell. To improve the symmetry Maxwell proposed that one of the equations should have an additional term which he called the displacement current. His argument was fundamentally intuitive; there was no experimental evidence of such a current. Maxwell's proposal had astonishing consequences. The corrected Maxwell equations implied the existence of electromagnetic radiation, encompassing gamma rays, x-rays, ultraviolet light, visible light, infrared and radio. Faraday's laboratory work and Maxwell's theoretical work together have led, one century later, to a technical revolution on the planet Earth. Electric lights, telephones, phonographs, radio, television, refrigerator trains making fresh produce available far from the farm, cardiac pacemakers, hydroelectric power plants, automatic fire alarms and sprinkler systems, electric trolleys and subways and the electronic computer are a few devices in the direct evolutionary line from the arcane intellectual endeavors of Faraday and Maxwell. Few would argue that the net effect of these inventions has not been

positive. Many who are profoundly disenchanted with Western technological civilization still retain a passionate fondness for certain aspects of high technology—for example high fidelity electronic music systems.

(3) Some of these inventions have changed profoundly the character of our society. Ease of communication has deprovincialized many parts of the globe; but cultural diversity has been likewise diminished. The practical advantages of these inventions are recognized in virtually all human societies; it is remarkable how infrequently emerging nations are concerned with the negative effects of high technology (environmental pollution, for example); they clearly have decided that the benefits outweigh the risks. One of Lenin's aphorisms was that socialism plus electrification equals communism. But there has been no more vigorous or inventive pursuit of high technology than in the West. The resulting rate of change has been so rapid that many of us find it difficult to keep up. There are still people alive today, born before the first airplane, who have lived to see Viking land on Mars, and Pioneer 10 (the first interstellar spacecraft) be ejected from the solar system; or who were raised under a sexual code of Victorian severity, and now find themselves living under a regimen of sexual freedom brought about by widespread availability of effective contraceptives.

(4) The rate of change has been disorienting for many, and it is easy to understand the nostalgic appeal of a return to an earlier and simpler existence. But the standard of living and conditions of work for most people in, say, Victorian England, were degrading and demoralizing compared to industrial societies today, and the life expectancy and infant mortality statistics were appalling. If science and technology are partly responsible for many of the problems which face us today, it is because public understanding of science and technology is desperately inadequate and because insufficient effort has been made to accommodate our society to these new technologies. Technology is a tool, not a panacea. Considering these facts, I find it remarkable that we have done as well as we have. Luddite alternatives can solve nothing. More than one billion people alive today owe the margin between starvation and barely adequate nutrition to high agricultural technology. Probably an equal number have survived or avoided disfiguring, crippling or fatal diseases because of high medical technology. Were high technology to be abandoned, these people also would be abandoned. Science and technology may be the cause of some of our problems; but they are certainly essential to any solution for those same problems—both in this country and planet-wide.

(5) Science and, particularly, technology have not been pursued with sufficient attention to their ultimate humane objectives. For example, it has gradually dawned on us that human activities can have an adverse effect not only on the local but also on the global environment. By

accident a few research groups in atmospheric photochemistry discovered that halocarbon propellants from aerosal spray cans will reside for very long periods in the atmosphere, circulate to the stratosphere, partially destroy the ozone there, and let ultraviolet light from the sun leak down to the Earth's surface. Increased skin cancer for light-skinned people is the most widely advertised consequence (blacks are much more immune). Very little public attention has been given to the considerably more serious possibility that microorganisms, occupying the base of an elaborate food pyramid with man at the top, might also be destroyed by the increased ultraviolet light. Steps finally have been taken, although reluctantly, to ban halocarbons from spray cans (although nobody seems to be worrying about the same molecules used in refrigerators); as a result the immediate dangers probably are slight. What is most worrisome about this incident is how accidental was the discovery that the problem existed at all. One group approached this problem because it had written the appropriate computer programs, but in a quite different context: these scientists were concerned with the chemistry of the atmosphere of the planet Venus, which contains hydrochloric and hydrofluoric acids. A broad and diverse set of problems in pure science clearly is required for our survival. But what other problems, even more severe, exist that we do not know about, because no research group happens as yet to have stumbled on them? For each problem we have uncovered, such as the effect of halocarbons on the ozonosphere, might there not be another dozen lurking around the corner? It is astonishing that nowhere in the federal government, major universities or private research institutes is there a single highly competent, broadly empowered and adequately funded research group whose function it is to seek out and defuse future catastrophes resulting from the development of new techniques.

(6) The establishment of such organizations will require political courage. Technological societies have a tightly knit industrial ecology, an interwoven network of economic assumptions. It is too difficult to tug on one string in the network without causing the whole system to tremble. Any decision to halt a technological development because it will have adverse human consequences will cost somebody money. For example, the du Pont Company, the principal manufacturers of halocarbon propellants, took the curious position in public debates that all conclusions about halocarbons destroying the ozonosphere were "theoretical." Du Pont seemed to be saying that it would stop making halocarbons only after the conclusions were tested experimentally—that is, when the ozonosphere was destroyed. There are some problems where inferential evidence is all that we will have; where once the catastrophe arrives it is too late to deal with. A new Energy Research and Development Administration, or a new Department of Energy, can be effec-

tive only if it can maintain a distance from vested commercial interests. It must be free to pursue new options even if such options imply loss of profits for some industries. The same is true of pharmaceutical research, in the pursuit of alternatives to the internal combustion engine and on many other technological frontiers. Development of new technologies should not be left to those who control old technologies; the temptation to suppress the competition is too great. If organizations devoted to technological innovation are not challenging (and perhaps even offending) at least some powerful groups, they are not accomplishing their purpose.

(7) Many practical technological developments are not being pursued for lack of government support. The government spends millions on cancer research. But as dreadful a disease as cancer is, I do not think it can be said that our civilization is threatened by it. If cancer were cured completely, the average life expectancy would be extended by only a few years, until some other disease, which does not now have its chance at cancer victims, takes over. On the other hand our civilization *is* fundamentally threatened by the lack of adequate fertility control. Exponential increases of population will dominate any arithmetic increases in the availability of food and resources (even those brought about by heroic technological initiatives), as Malthus long ago realized. Some industrial nations have approached zero population growth, but this is not the case for the world as a whole. Minor climatic fluctuations can destroy entire populations with marginal economies. In many societies where the technology is meager and reaching adulthood an uncertain prospect, having many children is the only possible hedge against a desperate and uncertain future. Such a society, in the grip of a consuming famine, for example, has little to lose. At a time when nuclear weapons are proliferating unconscionably, when an atomic device is almost a home handicraft industry, widespread famine and stark disparities in affluence pose serious dangers to both the developed and the underdeveloped parts of the world. The solution to such problems certainly requires better education and at least a degree of technological self-sufficiency. But it cries out for entirely adequate contraception— long-term, safe birth control pills, available for men as well as for women, perhaps to be taken once a month or over even longer intervals. Such a development also would be useful here at home, because of concern about the side effects of the conventional estrogen oral contraceptives. Why is there no major effort for such a development?

(8) Many other technological initiatives deserve to be treated seriously. These proposals range from very cheap to extremely expensive. At one end is soft technology—for example, the development of closed ecological systems involving algae, shrimp and fish which could be maintained in rural ponds and provide nutritious and low-cost dietary supplements.

At the other end of the economic scale is the proposal of Gerard O'Neill of Princeton University to construct large orbital cities which would be self-propagating. One city would be able to construct another using lunar and asteroidal materials. Such cities in Earth orbit might be able to convert sunlight into microwave energy and beam power down to Earth. The idea of independent cities in space—each perhaps built on differing social, economic or political assumptions, or having different ethnic antecedents—is appealing, an opportunity for those deeply disenchanted with terrestrial civilizations to strike out on their own somewhere else. In its earlier history America provided such an opportunity for the restless, ambitious and adventurous. Space cities would be a kind of America in the skies. They also would greatly enhance the potential for survival of the human species. The project would be expensive, costing at minimum about the same as one Vietnam war (in resources, not in lives).

(9) Clearly, there are more technological projects now possible than we can possibly afford. Some of them may be extremely cost-effective, but may have such large start-up costs that they are impractical. In other cases a daring initial investment of resources may work a benevolent revolution in our society. We must consider our options carefully. The most prudent strategy calls for combining low risk/moderate yield and moderate risk/high yield endeavors.

(10) In order for such technological initiatives to muster the support they need, improvements in public understanding of science and technology are essential. We are thinking beings. Our minds are our distinguishing characteristic as a species. We are not stronger or swifter than many other animals that share this planet with us. We are only smarter. In addition to the immense practical benefit of having a scientifically literate public, the contemplation of science and technology permits us to exercise our intellectual faculties to the limits of our capabilities. Science is an exploration of the intricate, subtle and awesome universe we inhabit. Those who practice it know, at least on occasion, a rare kind of exhilaration that Socrates said was the greatest of human pleasures. It is a communicable pleasure. To allow informed public participation in technological decision-making, to decrease the alienation which too many citizens feel from our technological society, and for the sheer joy which comes from knowing a deep thing well, we need better science education, a superior communication of its powers and delights. One way to start is by reversing the self-destructive decline in federal scholarships and fellowships for science researchers and science teachers at the college, graduate and post-doctoral levels.

(11) The most effective agents communicating science to the public are television, motion pictures and newspapers. But the science offerings in these media often are dreary, inaccurate, ponderous, grossly

caricatured, or (as with much Saturday morning commercial television programming for children) openly hostile to science. There have been astonishing recent findings concerning the exploration of the planets, the role of small brain proteins in affecting our emotional lives, the collisions of continents, the evolution of the human species (and the extent to which our past prefigures our future), the ultimate structure of matter (and the question of whether there are elementary particles or an infinite regress of them), the attempt to communicate with civilizations on planets of other stars, the nature of the genetic code (which determines our heredity and makes us cousins to all the other plants and animals on our planet), and the ultimate questions of the origin, nature and fate of life, worlds and the universe as a whole. These are deep questions. Many of them have been asked for the entire history of our species. These developments can be understood by any intelligent person. Why are they so rarely discussed in the media, in schools, in everyday conversation?

(12) Civilizations can be characterized by how they approach such questions of ultimate concern, how they nourish the mind as well as the body. The modern scientific pursuit of these questions represents an attempt to acquire a generally accepted view of our place in the cosmos; it requires open-minded creativity, tough-minded skepticism and a fresh sense of wonder. These questions are different from the practical issues which I discussed earlier; but they are connected with such issues and—as in the example of Faraday and Maxwell—the encouragement of pure research may be the most reliable guarantee available that we will have the intellectual and technical wherewithal to deal with the practical problems which face us.

(13) Only a small fraction of the most able young people enter scientific careers. I am often amazed at how much more capability and enthusiasm for science there is among elementary school youngsters than among college students. Something happens in the school years to discourage interest in science and mathematics; it is important to understand and circumvent this discouragement. No one can predict where the future leaders of science will come from. Albert Einstein as a teenager would today without a doubt be described as a hippie. It is clear that he became a scientist despite, not because of, his schooling. In his *Autobiography* Malcolm X describes a numbers runner who never wrote down a bet, but carried a lifetime of transactions perfectly in his head. What contributions would such a person have made to society, Malcolm asked, if society had given him adequate education and encouragement? The most brilliant youngsters are a national resource. They require special care and feeding. Many of the problems which are facing us may be soluble, but only if we are willing to embrace brilliant, daring and complex solutions. Such solutions require brilliant, daring

and complex people. I believe that there are many more of them around—in every nation, ethnic group and degree of affluence—than we realize. The training of such young people must not, of course, be restricted to science and technology; indeed the compassionate application of new technology to human problems requires a deep understanding of human nature and human culture, a general education in the broadest sense.

(14) We are at a crossroads in human history. We are the first species to have taken our evolution into our own hands. For the first time we possess the means for intentional or inadvertent self-destruction. We also have, I believe, the means for passing through this stage of technological adolescence into a long-lived, rich and fulfilling maturity for all the members of our species. There is not much time to determine down which fork of the road we are committing our children and our future.

QUESTIONS AND EXERCISES

VOCABULARY

1. arcane (*paragraph* 1)
2. intuitive (2)
3. deprovincialized (3)
4. aphorisms (3)
5. panacea (4)
6. Luddite (4)
7. vested (6)
8. exponential (7)
9. disparities (7)
10. affluence (7)
11. ecological (8)
12. terrestrial (8)
13. caricatured (11)
14. regress (11)
15. cosmos (12)
16. circumvent (13)

LANGUAGE AND RHETORIC

1. Identify the three major divisions of the structure of this essay and explain the function of each part.
2. What is the thesis of this essay? Where is it first introduced?
3. The author relies heavily on factual detail and judgment. Which method is dominant in the first three paragraphs? In paragraphs 10, 11, and 12? The paragraphs in this essay are uniformly longer than those of most of the other essays in this book. Why?
4. Paragraph 3 could be divided into two paragraphs. At what point?
5. What is the topic sentence of paragraph 4?
6. Analyze paragraph 8 in terms of its topic sentence and primary and secondary supporting sentences.
7. What devices does the author employ in paragraph 10 to achieve coherence?
8. Point out examples of parallel structure in the final paragraph. What purposes does it serve in this paragraph?

DISCUSSION AND WRITING

1. According to Sagan, "development of new technologies should not be left to those who control old technologies; the temptation to suppress the competition is too great." What are the implications of this statement for the development of nuclear and solar energy by the power companies? For the development of alternatives to gasoline by the oil industry? Do you agree with the author? Why or why not? What other options are available? Investigate some aspect of this subject through related reading and prepare a paper based on your findings.

2. The author suggests that "the idea of independent cities in space—each perhaps built on differing social, economic or political assumptions, or having different ethnic antecedents—is appealing, an opportunity for those deeply disenchanted with terrestrial civilizations to strike out on their own somewhere else." Does the idea appeal to you? Why or why not?

3. A scientist and university professor himself, Sagan says that public understanding of science and technology is "desperately inadequate" and that this is one of the reasons for the problems we have with it; he later states that the solution to such problems requires better education. Still later he charges that "something happens in the school years to discourage interest in science and mathematics." Consider your own education in science and/or technology. To what extent has it prepared you to deal with the things discussed in this essay? How would you improve the process? Get some of your reflections down on paper, and use them to develop an essay in response to these questions.

4. The author is also critical of television, motion pictures, and newspapers for science offerings that "often are dreary, inaccurate, ponderous, grossly caricatured, or . . . openly hostile to science." Evaluate an appropriate offering by one of these media in light of this statement and report your findings in an essay that makes use of facts to support your judgments.

FRANCES MOORE LAPPÉ

A Vegetarian Manifesto

Perhaps, in these times, we ought to expect a certain amount of fuzzy thinking about meat prices, and certainly the spokesmen for agribusiness have good reason to confuse what dollars can command with what bodies need to function. The truth, however, is another matter. America faces no "protein shortage." On the contrary, we are a nation consuming well beyond our protein needs with a diet geared to a protein source that is the most protein-costly of all to produce—namely beef.

Currently most Americans eat two times their recommended daily protein allowance. In fact, we could *reduce* our livestock population by one-quarter and still provide every single American with one-half pound of meat and poultry every day of the year. This is enough to supply every person's recommended protein allowance in meat and poultry alone—with no help at all from milk products, eggs, cereal products, nuts and beans, which presently provide more than half of our daily protein. But perhaps most surprisingly, *we could completely eliminate meat, fish, and poultry from our national diet and still ingest our recommended daily protein in all the other high protein foods we eat regularly.*

Heavy meat consumption is presently common to all but the poorest fifth of the American population. On the average, Americans in the lower 50 percent of family levels eat more than a half pound of meat and poultry each day. This is enough protein to supply an adult's daily allowance entirely by itself. Individuals in families with incomes in the upper 50 percent eat on the average a *whole pound* of meat and poultry daily.

Since protein cannot be stored in the body and since we can only use a limited amount to replace the small amount that is broken down and excreted every day, what happens to all this extra protein? It is, quite simply, wasted. Our bodies cannot use the excess as protein but instead convert it into energy-giving fuel as if it were carbohydrate. For many Americans the last vestige of our Puritan heritage is the belief that throwing away food is a sin; yet few realize that our very consumption pattern means we are "throwing away" that most precious of all human nutrients—protein.

For most of us meat is no longer a luxury but a staple we demand and expect. Steak on a week-day night is part of the American dream. Yet throughout man's history a carbohydrate has been the "staff of life" (be it bread or rice) and animal protein (be it fish or meat) has played a purely supplementary role. This is the pattern that correctly reflects the body's nutritional needs as well as the earth's capacity to support Man as an ecological dominant.

Well over a hundred years ago, the earth's population increased beyond the point at which it could conceivably be supported by a meat-centered diet. Such a diet requires three and one-half acres of arable land per person. But according to most estimates, the earth now offers only *one* acre of agricultural land per person. One acre per person is not enough for meat in the volume to which we are accustomed, but it is adequate to provide a fully nutritious plant-centered diet—*if the land is shared equally.*

As it happens, however, we Americans do not have to face up to this reality. To us, plant-centered diets are what "yet to be developed" peasants or young "food freaks" deserve to eat. We are permitted this myopia partly because our soils and climate produce an unparalleled agricultural wealth. More important, American economic, military and political power prevents other peoples with real food needs from making effective demands on our protein wealth and at the same time allows us to make demands on *their* resources to inflate our own bloated diet.

This we do, for example, by importing almost 40 percent of all beef in world trade. Although the amount of meat we import seems small (8 pounds per capita annually), this portion would represent a 50 percent increase in present meat consumption in the poor nations of the world. It would, moreover, provide an appreciable portion of the minimum daily protein allowance for many of the world's hungry.

Ironically, much of the meat we import comes from the poorest countries in Central America, which do, in fact, face a "protein shortage." The U.S. government, for its part, controls the influx of meat as a safety valve against rising prices. Beyond these tragic absurdities, the trade has a devasting effect on the land economy of food production in the poor nations. Tom Bodenheimer has reported, for example, that Costa Rica once had a "relatively well-developed milk industry with a per capita consumption of 0.85 pounds per day . . . but because of the recent U.S. policy to import beef from Central America, Costa Rican milk farmers are leaving the dairy industry in order to raise more profitable beef cattle. Thus Costa Rica's milk production is dropping, and the future of the industry is in doubt."[1]

The U.S. is also a leading importer of seafood—fully as valuable a source of protein as meat. More than one-quarter of all fresh and frozen fish and about one-third of all shell fish in world trade is directed into the American market-place. (Recall that we represent only six percent of the world's population.) Many of these protein riches come from poor countries like India, Panama and Mexico. When it is available, we import enough fishmeal (containing about twice the protein as the same amount of meat) from Chile and Peru to meet the protein requirements of the Peruvian population for an entire year.

While America thus absorbs protein from the underdeveloped countries, it does not return it as protein-rich food. In fact, most of our food exports go to the wealthy areas—Europe, Japan and Canada. We currently ship three times more agricultural products to Europe than to Latin America and Africa *combined.* Of the ten leading U.S. agricultural exports, four—hides, tallow, cotton and tobacco—are not edible at all, and of the remaining six, only two are high in protein—nonfat dry milk and soybeans. Most of the soybeans go to Japan, Western Europe and Canada, where they are fed to livestock. As for the one million tons of protein imported annually by the rich nations from the poor nations, much if not most of it comes from the soil of the underdeveloped world and goes into the mouths of European livestock in the form of high-protein seed meals like that made from African peanuts.

[1] Tom Bodenheimer, "Food for Profit, *"NACLA Newsletter,* Vol. 5, No. 3, p. 8.

In this regard, Americans benefit from the historical relationships of colonialism, according to which the poor countries become "hooked" economically on growing luxury crops for export to the rich. In many poor countries most of the best land is used to supply us and the rest of the rich world with such items as cocoa, coffee, tea, sugar and bananas, and with industrial goods like rubber and jute.

For the poor countries this pattern means more than economic dependency and usurpation of needed agricultural land. As a West African agronomist put it, "With every ton of cocoa exported, there goes out also a big chunk of African land fertility which must be replaced by chemical or other fertilizer." Conversely, with every such ton America imports, there comes a big chunk of land fertility which relieves the pressure on U.S. resources. If it were not for access to the agricultural products from the poor, we would be forced to use our *own* land to produce substitutes and thus have less to devote to our own overconsumption.

Under these circumstances we can afford to make the American Way of Eating the most resource-squandering diet of all, and it is not by coincidence that our diet is centered around beef, the most resource-expensive way to meet man's need for protein. In fact, over the past ten years we have increased our dependence on beef, so that now we each eat 32 pounds more beef per year than we did a decade ago (on the average, of course). It so happens that for every pound of beef we eat, some steer has been fed over *21 pounds* of protein. (Other livestock, e.g., poultry, are more efficient in converting plant protein into meat protein.)

Given that meat, and particularly beef, is not a luxury but a staple we demand in excess of all need, it should come as no surprise that we are willing to devote most of our agricultural production to its supply. Not only do we use *one-third* to *one-half* of our continental land surface for grazing but we feed 86 percent of all of our corn, barley, oats, and grain sorghum, and over 90 percent of our nonexported soybean crop, to livestock. We feed about 42 percent as much wheat to animals in this country as we eat ourselves. And we give livestock the benefit of large quantities of highly nutritious wheat germ and bran which are considered impurities in the milling process.

American generosity, they say, provides hungry children around the world with milk. But the ads neglect to point out that we use twice as much milk to feed animals as we export abroad for *all* purposes including "charity." Ironically, the protein that is produced in livestock as a result of this feeding is of lower quality than the original milk protein the animals are fed. (That is, one gets about 12 percent *more* if he eats milk protein than if he eats the same amount of beef protein.)

Totalling this up, we can say that of all the crops produced on our agricultural land, *half* is fed to livestock. That amounts to an incredible waste: about 20 million tons of humanly edible and nutritious protein are fed to livestock yearly in America and only about 2 million tons get back to the American people as meat on their plates. The rest, about 90 percent, is irrevocably lost and constitutes almost the entire protein deficit of the world each year!

This really makes no sense at all, and it would not be too outlandish to suppose that our willingness to so concentrate on meat production and pay any price for it suggests something more than a liking for the taste. We seem to have deified meat, and created a theology to go with it. We have become disciples of the Great American Steak Religion, in the words of a European friend of mine. And, as true believers, we hold tenaciously to certain tenets of this religion on faith alone—for example, that there is no substitute for meat, or that meat is essential to good health and strength. Recently a hearty-looking young man said to me, "A vegetable diet might be OK for you because all you do is sit around the house all day" (not true, I thought, but best take one issue at a time!). "But," he protested, "I couldn't make out on that stuff. I'm an athlete. I need lots of *meat* protein." Now, in fact, it is much more useful and accurate to think of *all* food proteins—meat and vegetable— as part of a continuum related to their quantity and usability. Then meaningful comparisons can be made.

• *Quantity:* how much protein by weight the food contains. Most people think that meat is *pure* protein and thus richer in protein than any other food. Actually meat is only about 25 percent protein. Certain non-meat foods have more protein than meat—soy flour and Parmesan cheese, for example. Other non-meat foods such as peanuts and dry beans have about the same amount of protein as meat, while others— grains and milk, for example—have less protein than meat.

• *Usability:* how closely the amino acid pattern of the protein matches the one pattern that the human body can fully use. Generally animal protein is more usable by the body than vegetable protein. But here also there is some overlapping, and the most usable protein of all is neither meat nor vegetable but egg protein. Next best is milk. It is important to realize that there is no such thing as a perfect protein, or, as some people say, a "complete" protein—one that the body can use *completely.* Egg is closest, but it's probably no more than 95 percent usable; and milk, second best, is only 82 percent usable. Meat, most often thought of as a "complete" protein, is between 70 and 75 percent usable. Most vegetable proteins rank between 40 and 70 percent usable. More important, it is possible to combine certain non-meat proteins in the same meal and thereby create a more usable protein—one equal or better than that of meat. The trick is simply to match foods with certain complementary amino acids. Since the relationships hold for whole food categories—like beans plus grains, for example—it is not hard to learn what foods "go together."

Thus meat is not unique and irreplaceable as a protein source. But many believe that meat is the sole repository of essential vitamins and minerals—another myth. Although meat supplies 42 percent of our protein, it carries with it an equivalent contribution of vitamins and minerals in only three out of eleven cases. And in none of the three is meat the sole source. Obviously we get most of these essential vitamins and minerals from non-meat sources.

But there are other components of our "Steak Religion" even less related to nutritional fact. I often encounter such ego-involved ratio-nalizations as: "Well, I am a 'steak-and-potatoes' man myself!" Or, I have heard women refer to their husbands with pride: "He sure likes his steak and potatoes!" The association of meat eating and masculinity seems to be very much a part of our culture.

However the mainstay of the "Religion" most effective in discouraging heretics is undoubtedly the firm belief that, to quote a noted nutritionist and agriculturist, "All vegetarian diets are rated as monotonous. There is a paucity of form and flavors."

But wait now. Think about it for a minute. There are basically five different kinds of meat. But there are 40 to 50 different kinds of commonly eaten vegetables, 24 different kinds of peas, beans and lentils, 20 different fruits, 12 different nuts and 9 different grains. Now where is the paucity?

The national consensus about meat-centered diets has made us ig-norant of the qualities of non-meat or low-meat diets. Sometimes our ignorance is truly amazing. A recent *New York Times* article reported that the department of foods science of the University of Illinois had just discovered that soybeans could be used for human food. The sci-entists reported that all you have to do is cook them! The Chinese would, no doubt, be relieved to learn of this great *American* discovery— inasmuch as the soybean has been a staple in their diet for almost five thousand years. China presently consumes about five million tons of soybean products, and Japan about half that, and those soybeans are treated with a real cultural genius. Commonly eaten in 12 different forms, they play quite a variety of roles in the diet.

Some people do, of course, benefit from this meat myopia, and it is certainly no mere accident that the meat industry uses advertising to link meat consumption with status and success. I ran across an ad recently for a mail order steak at $6.95 a pound. "These are the steaks," the ad said, "you would serve if you were out to out-do your brother-in-law. . . ." Similar psychology is used to convince the public to pay more to get a meat product as opposed to a plant product, on the grounds that plant food is undesirable. Cereal has become so despicable that it is not even good enough for our pets. We are told to buy ALPO because it has "not a speck of cereal. . . ."

If the meat industry is the prime beneficiary of this national obsession, then the people of the poor nations are the big losers. They are said to go hungry because the world's resources simply cannot support the world's population. Birth control, we are told, is the only answer.

In effect, this reasoning places responsibility for hunger and starvation on fate and the poor themselves. It is faulty reasoning. The nutrients are available to provide an adequate food supply for all mankind, but the realities of the world economic system insure that the fat will get fatter and the undernourished will go hungry. It is this system which must be changed if the world's food problems are to be solved, and with it must change the American fixation on meat.

FIVE

COMPARISON AND CONTRAST

ROGER EBERT
Not Being There

The pleasure we derive from watching movies may seem identical to most of us whether we do so in a commercial theater or in a home setting. Not so, says movie reviewer and critic Roger Ebert. Regardless of the similarities between the two situations, there are fundamental differences in the quality and character of the media, and for Ebert, at least, "to experience a movie fully, you have to go to the movies." Here he tells you why.

Ebert develops his thesis largely by means of comparison and contrast, with the emphasis on the latter. As you assess his argument, see to what extent his response to the two experiences matches your own.

(1) Like most other people whose tastes began to form before television became the dominant entertainment medium, I have a simple idea of what it means to go to the movies. You buy your ticket and take a seat in a large dark room with hundreds of strangers. You slide down in your seat and make yourself comfortable. On the screen in front of you, the movie image appears—enormous and overwhelming. If the movie is a good one, you allow yourself to be absorbed in its fantasy, and its dreams become part of your memories.

(2) Television is not a substitute for that experience, and I have never had a TV-watching experience of emotional intensity comparable to my great movie-going experiences. Television is just not first class. The screen is too small. The image is technically inferior. The sound is disgracefully bad. As the viewer I can contain telvision—but the movies are so large they can contain me. I can't lose myself in a television image, and neither, I suspect, can most other people. That is why people are forever recreating movie memories in great detail, but hardly ever reminisce about old TV programs.

(3) I believe, then, that to experience a movie fully you have to go to the movies. I enjoy television for other purposes, and my favorite TV

programs are the live ones (sports, news, elections, talk shows), where immediacy helps compensate for the loss in intensity. Unlike a lot of movie buffs, I am not a fan of *The Late Show.* If a movie is good enough to stay up late for, it's too good to be watched through the dilution of television. I'll catch it later at a revival theater or a film society, or, if I never catch it again at least I'll think of it as a *movie* and not as late-night programming.

(4) Maybe it's no wonder, then, that, with these personal biases, I was disturbed by some of the things I heard last March during a conference I went to in Colorado. The American Film Institute had taken over the Aspen Institute for three days, and invited forty-five people to gather for a discussion of the future of the feature film. By "feature film," they meant both theatrical and made-for-TV features, the latter including docudramas and TV miniseries.

(5) The conference was weighted toward the TV people, among them executives of various pay-cable companies, and although several of us professed an interest in a discussion of content (that is, what movies are *about* these days), most of the talk was about "delivery" (how to sell television programming at a profit). What actually went out on the airwaves or cable systems would presumably take care of itself.

(6) Many panelists' remarks were couched in a technological Newspeak that I had trouble understanding at first. *Software,* for example, was the word for TV programming—software to feed the hardware of our new home video entertainment centers. ("Software?" they said. "You know. That's a word for product." "Product?" I asked. "Yeah. Like a movie.") *Television consuming units* was another expression that gave me trouble until I realized it was a reference to human beings. *Windows* was a very interesting word. It referred to the various markets that a new movie could be sold to (or "shown through") once it was made. First there would be the theatrical window, a traditional booking in a movie theater. Then came the network window—sale to commercial television. After that the windows came thick and fast: the paycable window, video cassette window, video disc window, airline in-flight window, and so on. In the hierarchy of these windows, the traditional practice of showing the movie in a theater seemed furthest from everybody's mind; the theatrical run was sort of a preliminary before the other markets could be carved up.

(7) One of the enticing things about all the windows, I learned, was that a new movie could now be in the position of turning a profit before it was made. The pre-sales of subsidiary viewing rights would take the risk out of the initial investment.

(8) The chilling thought occurred to me that, if a movie was already

in profit, actually showing it in theaters could be risky because promotion, advertising, and overhead would be seen as liabilities instead of (in the traditional view) as an investment risk with a hope of profitable return. But no, I was assured, that was wrong. Movies would still have to play in theaters because the theatrical run "legitimatized" them: they thus became "real" movies in the eyes of people buying them on cassettes or over pay cable.

(9) Wonderful, I thought. The theatrical feature film, the most all-encompassing art form of the twentieth century, has been reduced to a necessary marketing preliminary for software.

(10) If this was a pessimistic view, it was mild compared to some of the visions of the future held by the conference participants. An important TV writer-producer, one of the most likable people at the conference, calmly predicted that in ten years people would be sitting at home in front of their wall-size TV screens while (and I am indeed quoting) "marauding bands roam the streets." I thought he was joking, until he repeated the same phrase the next day.

(11) What about going out to the movies? Another television executive said he used to go, but he had stopped. "You have to stand in line and be crowded in with all those people. And it's too expensive."

(12) Well, apart from the fact that he could no doubt afford to buy a ticket for everyone in line, and that higher ticket prices only reflect general inflation, his view overlooked the fact that video cassettes and pay cable are at least as expensive as going out to the movies, especially when you consider the initial "hardware" investment. And for your money, you get to watch a TV image made up of dots arranged in 625 lines—an image that, even assuming your set has perfect adjustment and color control, does not and cannot approach the quality of an image projected by light through celluloid.

(13) But those technical considerations aside, why did this man and some of his colleagues have such a distaste for going out to the movies? I do it all the time. I feel it adds something to a movie-going experience to share it with other people. It's communal. A lot of the fun of seeing a movie such as *Jaws* or *Star Wars* comes, for me, from the massed emotion of the theater audience. When the shark attacks, we all levitate three inches above our seats, and come down screaming and laughing.

(14) Watching *Jaws* on network TV isn't a remotely comparable experience. And watching a *comedy* in isolation can actually be a depressing experience. Our laughter during a movie comedy is an act of communication; an audience roaring with laughter is expressing its shared opinion about what's funny. I've watched comedies while I was alone in a room, and I've noticed that I don't laugh at all. Why should I? Who's to hear? And, perhaps because I don't laugh, those comedies don't seem

as funny. Maybe it's essential to comedy that we're conscious of sharing it with other people; maybe, in human development, the first communication was a scream and the second was a laugh, and then they got around to words.

(15) I made a modest proposal at Aspen. I suggested that some time and attention be given to perfecting cheaper and better home 16-mm movie projection systems, and that 16-mm rental and lending libraries be set up, like the Fotomat video cassette centers. I've gotten a lot of enjoyment out of 16-mm movie prints. The picture is larger, sharper, and brighter than television, so you can get a good idea of what the director had in mind. My suggestion was received with polite indifference, although, later, there was a lot of enthusiasm about reports that they're improving those giant-size TV screens you see in bars.

(16) As anyone who has seen one knows, giant TV screens aren't the answer because they further dilute the already washed-out TV image. The TV signal has only 625 lines to contain its information no matter *how* large the screen is, and so a larger screen means a faded picture. TV retail outlets report that consumers seem to understand this, and that 17- and 19-inch sets are preferred to 21- and 24-inch screens because of the sharper image.

(17) One evening over dinner, I finally got an interesting response to my suggestion about home 16-mm movie projectors. The problem with those, I was told, is that they can't be programmed by the pay-TV systems. You sit in your own house operating your own projector, and the cable operators don't have access to it. They can't pipe their software into it and charge you for it. Why, you decide for yourself what and when to watch!

(18) What is clearly happening is very alarming.

(19) A superior system of technology—motion pictures—is being sold out in favor of an inferior but more profitable system—pay video hardware/software combinations. The theatrical motion picture, which remains such a desirable item that it's used to sell home cassette systems, is in danger of being held hostage. Truly daring and offbeat film subjects will become increasingly risky because they can't be easily presold for showing through other "windows."

(20) The two edges that movies have enjoyed over television are greater quality and impact of image, and greater freedom of subject matter. Now television is poised to absorb and emasculate the movies, all in the name of home entertainment. It will serve us right, as we sit in front of our fuzzy giant-screen home video systems ten or twenty years from now, if there's nothing new or interesting to watch on them. Count me in with the marauding bands.

QUESTIONS AND EXERCISES

VOCABULARY

1. reminisce (*paragraph* 2)
2. dilution (3)
3. docudramas (4)
4. hierarchy (6)
5. subsidiary (7)
6. marauding (10)
7. levitate (13)
8. emasculate (20)

LANGUAGE AND RHETORIC

1. The title of this essay alludes to the Jerzy Koszinski novel of the same name, later made into a motion picture starring Peter Sellers. Does this information enhance your response to the title, or would it be just as effective without your knowing it? Can you suggest other titles that would not depend on such references?
2. The selection is clearly organized into an introduction, body, and conclusion. Which paragraphs comprise each section and how does the author use each to advance his argument?
3. The author, Roger Ebert, is a well-known movie reviewer for both a Chicago daily newspaper and a national television network. The conference he refers to was attended largely by other professionals in the field. What seems to be his intended audience and how can you tell?
4. In paragraph 10, the author quotes a TV writer-producer who refers to "marauding bands" roaming the streets. What is meant by this remark? In the conclusion, Ebert includes himself among those bands. What is the significance of his doing so, and how effective a conclusion does it make? Support your answer.

DISCUSSION AND WRITING

1. Make a point of viewing the same motion picture both in a movie theater and on television. Using Ebert's essay as a basis, carefully compare the two experiences and either validate or refute Ebert's thesis.
2. Discuss Ebert's thesis with your classmates and others to get their ideas on the subject. Then conduct an informal survey of a limited number of students on your campus to determine their opinions. Prepare a written report of your findings.
3. Write a paper in which you make a case for television viewing as superior to movies. Use points of comparison and contrast as one means of supporting your argument.
4. Ebert says that movies have enjoyed an edge over television in terms of "quality and impact of image" and "greater freedom of subject matter." Apply his criteria to the two media yourself and write an essay in which you come to your own conclusions.

ROBIN LAKOFF

You Are What You Say

> *The language of sexism, like the language of racism, is by now well documented. Yet it is one thing to be an unconscious victim of a society's use of language and quite another to contribute to that condition yourself—whether unwitting or not. Linguist Robin Lakoff shows here how women's language differs from men's. She goes on to reveal that women have not only accepted that difference; they have helped to promote it, and by so doing, have reinforced their second-class status.*
>
> *This selection originally appeared in* Ms *Magazine. Consider the implication of that fact for how the author addresses her subject and her audience.*

(1) "Women's language" is that pleasant (dainty?), euphemistic, never-aggressive way of talking we learned as little girls. Cultural bias was built into the language we were allowed to speak, the subjects we were allowed to speak about, and the ways we were spoken of. Having learned our linguistic lesson well, we go out in the world, only to discover that we are communicative cripples—damned if we do, and damned if we don't.

(2) If we refuse to talk "like a lady," we are ridiculed and criticized for being unfeminine. ("She thinks like a man" is, at best, a left-handed compliment.) If we do learn all the fuzzy-headed, unassertive language of our sex, we are ridiculed for being unable to think clearly, unable to take part in a serious discussion, and therefore unfit to hold a position of power.

(3) It doesn't take much of this for a woman to begin feeling she deserves such treatment because of inadequacies in her own intelligence and education.

(4) "Women's language" shows up in all levels of English. For example, women are encouraged and allowed to make far more precise discriminations in naming colors than men do. Words like *mauve, beige, ecru, aquamarine, lavender,* and so on, are unremarkable in a women's active vocabulary, but largely absent from that of most men. I know of no evidence suggesting that women actually *see* a wider range of colors than men do. It is simply that fine discriminations of this sort are relevant to women's vocabularies, but not to men's; to men, who control most of the interesting affairs of the world, such distinctions are trivial—irrelevant.

(5) In the area of syntax, we find similar gender-related peculiarities of speech. There is one construction, in particular, that women use conversationally far more than men: the tag question. A tag is midway

between an outright statement and a yes-no question; it is less assertive than the former, but more confident than the latter.

(6) A *flat statement* indicates confidence in the speaker's knowledge and is fairly certain to be believed; a *question* indicates a lack of knowledge on some point and implies that the gap in the speaker's knowledge can and will be remedied by an answer. For example, if, at a Little League game, I have had my glasses off, I can legitimately ask someone else: "Was the player out at third?" A *tag question*, being intermediate between statement and question, is used when the speaker is stating a claim, but lacks full confidence in the truth of that claim. So if I say, "Is Joan here?" I will probably not be surprised if my respondent answers "no"; but if I say, "Joan is here, isn't she?" instead, chances are I am already biased in favor of a positive answer, wanting only confirmation. I still want a response, but I have enough knowledge (or think I have) to predict that response. A tag question, then, might be thought of as a statement that doesn't demand to be believed by anyone but the speaker, a way of giving leeway, of not forcing the addressee to go along with the views of the speaker.

(7) Another common use of the tag-question is in small talk when the speaker is trying to elicit conversation: "Sure is hot here, isn't it?"

(8) But in discussing personal feelings or opinions, only the speaker normally has any way of knowing the correct answer. Sentences such as "I have a headache, don't I?" are clearly ridiculous. But there are other examples where it is the speaker's opinions, rather than perceptions, for which corroboration is sought, as in "The situation in Southeast Asia is terrible, isn't it?"

(9) While there are, of course, other possible interpretations of a sentence like this, one possibility is that the speaker has a particular answer in mind—"yes" or "no"—but is reluctant to state it baldly. This sort of tag question is much more apt to be used by women than by men in conversation. Why is this the case?

(10) The tag question allows a speaker to avoid commitment, and thereby avoid conflict with the addressee. The problem is that, by so doing, speakers may also give the impression of not really being sure of themselves, or looking to the addressee for confirmation of their views. This uncertainty is reinforced in more subliminal ways, too. There is a peculiar sentence intonation-pattern, used almost exclusively by women, as far as I know, which changes a declarative answer into a question. The effect of using the rising inflection typical of a yes-no question is to imply that the speaker is seeking confirmation, even though the speaker is clearly the only one who has the requisite information, which is why the question was put to her in the first place:

(Q) When will dinner be ready?
(A) Oh . . . around six o'clock . . . ?

It is as though the second speaker were saying, "Six o'clock—if that's okay with you, if you agree." The person being addressed is put in the position of having to provide confirmation. One likely consequence of this sort of speech-pattern in a woman is that, often unbeknownst to herself, the speaker builds a reputation of tentativeness, and others will refrain from taking her seriously or trusting her with any responsibilities, since she "can't make up her mind," and "isn't sure of herself."

(11) Such idiosyncrasies may explain why women's language sounds much more "polite" than men's. It is polite to leave a decision open, not impose your mind, or views, or claims, on anyone else. So a tag question is a kind of polite statement, in that it does not force agreement or belief on the addressee. In the same way a request is a polite command, in that it does not force obedience on the addressee, but rather suggests something be done as a favor to the speaker. A clearly stated order implies a threat of certain consequences if it is not followed, and—even more impolite—implies that the speaker is in a superior position and able to enforce the order. By couching wishes in the form of a request, on the other hand, a speaker implies that if the request is not carried out, only the speaker will suffer; noncompliance cannot harm the addressee. So the decision is really left up to addressee. The distinction becomes clear in these examples:

Close the door.
Please close the door.
Will you close the door?
Will you please close the door?
Won't you close the door?

(12) In the same ways as words and speech patterns used *by* women undermine her image, those used to *describe* women make matters even worse. Often a word may be used of both men and women (and perhaps of things as well); but when it is applied to women, it assumes a special meaning that, by implication rather than outright assertion, is derogatory to women as a group.

(13) The use of euphemisms has this effect. A euphemism is a substitute for a word that has acquired a bad connotation by association with something unpleasant or embarrassing. But almost as soon as the new word comes into common usage, it takes on the same old bad connotations, since feelings about the things or people referred to are not altered by a change of name; thus new euphemisms must be constantly found.

(14) There is one euphemism for *women* still very much alive. The

word of course, is *lady*. *Lady* has a masculine counterpart, namely *gentleman*, occasionally shortened to *gent*. But for some reason *lady* is very much commoner than *gent(leman)*.

(15) The decision to use *lady* rather than *woman*, or vice versa, may considerably alter the sense of a sentence, as the following examples show:

> (a) A woman (lady) I know is a dean at Berkeley.
> (b) A woman (lady) I know makes amazing things out of shoelaces and old boxes.

(16) The use of *lady* in (a) imparts a frivolous, or nonserious, tone to the sentence: the matter under discussion is not one of great moment. Similarly, in (b), using *lady* here would suggest that the speaker considered the "amazing things" not to be serious art, but merely a hobby or an aberration. If *woman* is used, she might be a serious sculptor. To say *lady doctor* is very condescending, since no one ever says *gentleman* doctor or even *man doctor*. For example, mention in the *San Francisco Chronicle* of January 31, 1972, of Madalyn Murray O'Hair as the *lady atheist* reduces her position to that of scatterbrained eccentric. Even *woman atheist* is scarcely defensible: sex is irrelevant to her philosophical position.

(17) Many women argue that, on the other hand, *lady* carries with it overtones recalling the age of chivalry: conferring exalted stature on the person so referred to. This makes the term seem polite at first, but we must also remember that these implications are perilous: they suggest that a "lady" is helpless, and cannot do things by herself.

(18) *Lady* can also be used to infer frivolousness, as in titles of organizations. Those that have a serious purpose (not merely that of enabling "the ladies" to spend time with one another) cannot use the word *lady* in their titles, but less serious ones may. Compare the *Ladies' Auxiliary* of a men's group, or the *Thursday Evening Ladies' Browning and Garden Society* with *Ladies' Liberation* or *Ladies' Strike for Peace*.

(19) What is curious about this split is that *lady* is in origin a euphemism—a substitute that puts a better face on something people find uncomfortable—for *women*. What kind of euphemism is it that subtly denigrates the people to whom it refers? Perhaps *lady* functions as a euphemism for *women* because it does not contain the sexual implications present in *woman*: it is not "embarrassing" in that way. If this is so, we may expect that, in the future, *lady* will replace woman as the primary word for the human female, since *woman* will have become too blatantly sexual. That this distinction is already made in some contexts at least is shown in the following examples, where you can try replacing *woman* with *lady*:

(a) She's only twelve, but she's already a woman.
(b) After ten years in jail, Harry wanted to find a woman.
(c) She's my woman, see, so don't mess around with her.

(20) Another common substitute for *woman* is *girl*. One seldom hears a man past the age of adolescence referred to as a boy, save in expressions like "going out with the boys," which are meant to suggest an air of adolescent frivolity and irresponsibility. But women of all ages are "girls": one can have a man—not a boy—Friday, but only a girl—never a woman or even a lady—Friday; women have girlfriends, but men do not—in a nonsexual sense—have boyfriends. It may be that this use of *girl* is euphemistic in the same way the use of *lady* is: in stressing the idea of immaturity, it removes the sexual connotations lurking in *woman*. *Girl* brings to mind irresponsibility: you don't send a girl to do a woman's errand (or even, for that matter, a boy's errand). She is a person who is both too immature and too far from real life to be entrusted with responsibilities or with decisions of any serious or important nature.

(21) Now let's take a pair of words which, in terms of the possible relationships in an earlier society, were simple male-female equivalents, analogous to *bull : cow*. Suppose we find that, for independent reasons, society has changed in such a way that the original meanings now are irrelevant. Yet the words have not been discarded, but have acquired new meanings, metaphorically related to their original senses. But suppose these new metaphorical uses are no longer parallel to each other. By seeing where the parallelism breaks down, we discover something about the different roles played by men and women in this culture. One good example of such a divergence through time is found in the pair, *master : mistress*. Once used with reference to one's power over servants, these words have become unusable today in their original master-servant sense as the relationship has become less prevalent in our society. But the words are still common.

(22) Unless used with reference to animals, *master* now generally refers to a man who has acquired consummate ability in some field, normally nonsexual. But its feminine counterpart cannot be used this way. It is practically restricted to its sexual sense of "paramour." We start out with two terms, both roughly paraphrasable as "one who has power over another." But the masculine form, once one person is no longer able to have absolute power over another, becomes usable metaphorically in the sense of "having power over *something*." *Master* requires as its object only the name of some activity, something inanimate and abstract. But *mistress* requires a masculine noun in the possessive to precede it. One cannot say: "Rhonda is a mistress." One must be *someone's* mistress. A man is defined by what he does, a woman by her sexuality, that is, in terms of one particular aspect of her relationship to men. It

is one thing to be an *old master* like Hans Holbein, and another to be an *old mistress*.

(23) The same is true of the words *spinster* and *bachelor*—gender words for "one who is not married." The resemblance ends with the definition. While *bachelor* is a neuter term, often used as a compliment, *spinster* normally is used pejoratively, with connotations of prissiness, fussiness, and so on. To be a bachelor implies that one has the choice of marrying or not, and this is what makes the idea of a bachelor existence attractive, in the popular literature. He has been pursued and has successfully eluded his pursuers. But a spinster is one who has not been pursued, or at least not seriously. She is old, unwanted goods. The metaphorical connotations of *bachelor* generally suggest sexual freedom; of *spinster,* puritanism or celibacy.

(24) These examples could be multiplied. It is generally considered a *faux pas,* in society, to congratulate a woman on her engagement, while it is correct to congratulate her fiancé. Why is this? The reason seems to be that it is impolite to remind people of things that may be uncomfortable to them. To congratulate a woman on her engagement is really to say, "Thank goodness! You had a close call!" For the man, on the other hand, there was no such danger. His choosing to marry is viewed as a good thing, but not something essential.

(25) The linguistic double standard holds throughout the life of the relationship. After marriage, bachelor and spinster become man and wife, not man and woman. The woman whose husband dies remains "John's widow"; John, however, is never "Mary's widower."

(26) Finally, why is it that salesclerks and others are so quick to call women customers "dear," "honey," and other terms of endearment they really have no business using? A male customer would never put up with it. But women, like children, are supposed to enjoy these endearments, rather than being offended by them.

(27) In more ways than one, it's time to speak up.

QUESTIONS AND EXERCISES

VOCABULARY

1. euphemistic (*paragraph* 1)
2. syntax (5)
3. elicit (7)
4. corroboration (8)
5. subliminal (10)
6. intonation (10)
7. inflection (10)
8. idiosyncrasies (11)

  9. noncompliance (11)
 10. frivolous (16)
 11. aberration (16)
 12. condescending (16)
 13. denigrates (19)
 14. pejoratively (23)
 15. prissiness (23)
 16. celibacy (23)
 17. *faux pas* (24)

LANGUAGE AND RHETORIC

1. What indications are there that this essay was initially intended primarily for a female audience? Point out specific evidence in the writing itself.
2. Lakoff divides her essay into two basic sections. What are they, and how do they relate to one another?
3. The author brings to bear on this subject both her expertise as a linguist and her experience as a woman. How does she manage to avoid letting that expertise lead to an excessively technical essay for the general reader?
4. Evaluate the title of this selection. In your own words, what does it mean? How does it relate to the subject? Is it an appropriate and effective title, or could you improve it?

DISCUSSION AND WRITING

1. Using this essay as a basis, write a paper defining and illustrating "men's language." Emphasize the contrast between it and "women's language." Use original examples to make your point rather than repeating those provided here.
2. Can you make a case for a "pleasant, euphemistic, never-aggressive" way of talking? Must such a use of language be taken as totally negative? Support your answer in an essay of your own.
3. Examine a dictionary for its use of words associated with male and female. See if in fact the word associations for the former tend to be positive and the latter negative. Write a paper reporting your findings.
4. The language of sexism has received considerable attention in recent years. Investigate the subject in your campus library and develop a list of potential topics for future writing projects.

ELLEN GOODMAN

The Right to Live vs. the Right to Die: No Single Yardstick

> *The issue reflected in the headline of this newspaper column has stirred controversy throughout the country for some time now. If author Ellen Goodman is right, much of that controversy results from people seeking simple answers to complex questions. Goodman compares the cases of an 85-year-old man in New York and a 26-year-*

old woman in California and concludes that there is no "single moral yardstick" for making such decisions, that, despite superficial similarities, each must be decided in light of its own unique circumstances.

Observe how the author has selected comparable cases but concentrates on the differences rather than the similarities between them to illustrate her thesis.

(1) An 85-year-old man died in Syracuse, N.Y., last weekend. By all accounts, G. Ross Henninger had lived a full life: college president, author, technical counselor to the military, husband, father.

(2) Yet it could also be said that his life was cut short, that he committed suicide in the Syracuse nursing home where he lived since his stroke last May. He simply stopped eating 45 days before his death.

(3) The private nursing-home administrators, caught between a mandate to take care of their patients and a law that gives patients the right to refuse care, had taken his case to court. There, Justice Miller of the State Supreme Court ruled that the nursing home had neither the obligation nor the right to force-feed their elderly patient.

(4) The justice wrote, "This court is heavily burdened by these questions. . . .(but) I will not, against his wishes, order this man to be operated upon and/or to be force-fed." A day later, the man was dead of starvation.

(5) But while the family of the elderly Mr. Henninger was planning his funeral, on the other side of the country, in Riverside, Calif., a 26-year-old woman, severely handicapped by cerebral palsy, was still alive because she is being force-fed. Elizabeth Bouvia had gone to a different judge in a different state. She sued for the right to have medical help, pain-killers and hygienic care, while she starved to death. The judge denied her request in December, and recently the doctors won the right to force-feed her as long as she's in the hospital.

(6) Here we have two people with the same wish—to die. Two cases that consistently pit the right-to life advocates against the right-to-die advocates. Surely we can decide: either we should or shouldn't intervene to prevent suicide. Either a person does or doesn't have the right to end his or her own life.

(7) But in fact, these cases are so provocative that I, like many others, agree with both these opposite decisions. Having just written disapproval of Ms. Bouvia's legal plea, I nevertheless approve of the ruling in Mr. Henninger's case.

(8) We are so often told that our attitudes should remain consistent about issues, that we may easily forget the details of the human life at its center. It occurs to me now that our apparent inconsistencies may say the most about these questions of life and death. They remind us that we're dealing with individual lives.

(9) Almost six decades separated Elizabeth Bouvia and G. Ross Hen-

ninger. Suicide, they say, is a permanent solution to a temporary problem. But the problems of an 85-year-old stroke victim are not temporary.
His choice, like that of a terminal cancer patient, was to be respected.

(10) Ms. Bouvia's physical condition isn't a temporary problem either.
But her depression may be. Any young woman who had just ended a
marriage, lost the hope of child-bearing and belief in a career within
the same year, could be despairing. Wasn't there some ambiguity in her
decision to seek suicidal help in a psychiatric ward?

(11) There was a subtle legal difference as well between these two
cases. The Bouvia case tested the right of a patient to prescribe her own
medical treatment. The Henninger case tested the right of a patient to
resist medical treatment. In both decisions, the courts chose the less
intrusive path.

(12) But when all is said and done, the courts were required to judge
individually the seriousness of the illness, the permanence of the problem. They were asked to determine whether each person's desire to die
was "rational."

(13) It is disturbing, bewildering, to try and decipher someone's right
to live or die on the basis of their age, their illness, their pain, their life
expectancy, their psyche. Where do you draw the line between the 26-
year-old and the 85-year-old, between rescuing one back into life and
comforting another into death? At 50, 60, 70? For cancer, paralysis,
stroke?

(14) How long does it take before we believe that Ms. Bouvia has
permanently, not temporarily, lost the will to live. One year, five years?
How long can we force-feed a patient and how many measures can we
take to prevent suicide?

(15) These stories raise questions that set our minds to spinning. It
would be easier if we could apply a single moral yardstick. But in the
end, these cases must be judged as human tales, one by one, whether
in a family setting or a hospital room or a courtroom. At times, you see,
there is simply no way to be both consistent and humane.

QUESTIONS AND EXERCISES

VOCABULARY

1. mandate (*paragraph* 3)
2. provocative (7)

LANGUAGE AND RHETORIC

1. Evaluate the title of this piece in terms of subject matter, thesis, length, and
   overall effectiveness.
2. As with a number of the other selections in this book, this one first appeared

as a newspaper column. Accordingly, the paragraphing reflects that format. Review the paragraphs to see if you can combine any of them without disrupting the author's argument or the reader's response.

3. The author employs two extended examples and comparison/contrast to develop her argument. Show how she uses one method to reinforce the other.

DISCUSSION AND WRITING

1. There are those who would argue that Ellen Goodman's thesis reflects a kind of moral cowardice, that the situation calls for absolute judgments: people either have a right to die or they don't. Consider these two conflicting views through discussion and reading; then prepare a paper defending your own position.
2. Put yourself in the position of a judge in one of these two cases. Based solely on the information presented here, write an original essay reflecting your own decision and the basis for it. If additional information is available to you, pursue it. In the event that you wish to change your decision, write another paper expressing the reasons why.
3. Emerson has said that "A foolish consistency is the hobgoblin of little minds." What is meant by that statement? Would Ellen Goodman agree? Would you? Why or why not? Support your answer in a paper using appropriate supporting techniques.

ERICA JONG

Creativity vs. Generativity: The Unexamined Lie

> . . . *sitting at the table, thinking of the book I have written, the child which I have carried for years and years in the womb of the imagination as you carried in your womb the children you love, and of how I had fed it day after day out of my brain and memory . . .*
>
> —James Joyce to Nora

Only a man (or a woman who had never been pregnant) would compare creativity to maternity, pregnancy to the creation of a poem or novel. The comparison of human gestation to human creativity is by now a conventional metaphor—as largely unexamined as the dead metaphors in our everyday speech (i.e. arm of a chair, leg of a table)—but it is also thoroughly inexact.

Although the *idea* for a poem or novel often comes as if unbidden, a gift from the Muse (or the communal unconscious), and although at rare, blessed moments, one may write *as if* automatically, as if in the grip of an angel who seems to push one's pen across the page, still, most often, literary creativity is sheer hard labor, quite different from the growing of a baby in the womb, which goes on despite one's conscious will and is, properly speaking, God's miracle, or nature's, and does not belong to the individual woman who provides it with a place to happen. On the contrary, the growing of the fetus in the womb is DNA's triumph, the triumph of the genes, the triumph of the species. The woman whose body is the site of this miracle is, in a sense, only being used by the species temporarily in its communal passion to survive. The writing of a book can, of course, be seen as the Muse working through the voice, hand and will of an individual creator, but that individual creator must labor hard indeed to be worthy of being a vessel for the Muse since she is a stern taskmistress and will withdraw her favors from the lazy, slovenly or self-pitying artist. Nature, on the other hand, is all-forgiving. Any womb, any woman, may be the vessel for her continuance. Willing assent is hardly even necessary: only a healthy womb, and the will not to deliberately destroy the fetus.

How much more passive pregnancy is than creativity! Creativity demands conscious, active will; pregnancy only demands the absence of ill-will. Perhaps the desire to equate them arises from the artists' ancient wish that creativity be as effortless, easy and unconscious as the creation of a fetus. Or perhaps the male artist's desire to equate the two arises out of his envy of the female ability to generate life. Like most forms of envy, it is absurd. One might as well envy the hummingbird for being able to stand still in mid-air, or the flounder for having two eyes on one side of its head. Whatever joys there are in pregnancy (and there are many) they are not the joys of consciousness, nor the joys of intellect, nor the joys of art, nor the joys of civilization. Pregnancy is perhaps most enjoyable to the over-civilized, over-intellectualized woman precisely for that reason.

Certainly this was true for me. All my life I had mistrusted my body and overvalued my mind. I had sought a very high degree of control over my environment and my body—a degree of control perhaps best represented by the fact that I never became pregnant, not even "accidentally," until well after my 35th birthday, and well after having spent a year or more consciously wishing for pregnancy and trying to become pregnant. I had dreaded pregnancy as a loss of control over my destiny, my body and my life. I had fantasies of death in childbirth, the death of my creativity during pregnancy, the alteration of my body into something monstrous, the loss of my intelligence through mysterious hormonal sabotage, the loss of my looks, my energy, my robustness.

But I ought to have known that the ruler of the cosmos is nothing if not a Joker—and all the opposite things happened. For the first time in my life, I controlled my weight effortlessly; my face grew thinner, my skin clearer, my eyes brighter. I never felt sick or lacked energy. I worked as hard at my writing as I ever had in my life—and, in fact, worked with greater consistency. I wrote a number of poems, continued to toil productively at the novel I had begun a year before becoming pregnant, and even undertook a grueling book tour for my second novel when I was in my fifth and sixth months of pregnancy. Certainly I worked as hard as I did partly to undercut the myth that pregnant woman are somehow incapacitated (or else "too fulfilled" by burgeoning life to need creative work as well), but mostly, it was a case of genuinely feeling good, feeling very much myself (only now freed from the gnawing anxiety that I would never have a child) and having genuine gusto for creative work. Whatever pregnancy "fulfilled" in me (and I do not underestimate that fulfillment at all), it was a wholly different order of fulfillment from the one I seek through my creative work. Might as well compare the delights of swimming or skiing with the delights of writing or researching. They simply aren't comparable; and every life needs both physical and mental challenges.

Pregnancy felt particularly good to me, I think, because it was an affirmation of life for one who had once been prone to a romantic infatuation with death. At twenty-five I may have wished with Keats "to cease upon the midnight with no pain," but at thirty-five I had turned away from the romantic infatuation with death, the worship of poetic suicides, the idealization of poets who died of TB, or poets who died as martyrs to woman's lot—and I now wished to show myself (and perhaps also the world) that both poets and women could be survivors. It was a turn from romantic to classic, from martyr to survivor, from self-destroyer to self-affirmer, from worshipper of sickness to worshipper of health. And having a successful, easy pregnancy was a way of telling myself that the core of my being was healthy and could not only confer life upon myself, but on others as well.

I think that to a large extent the artists and intellectuals in our society worship illness, as if it were illness that conferred art rather than art that conferred a temporary reprieve from illness. In part, this is one legacy of 19th-century Romanticism, but in part it also stems from the misconception that the mind can only be nourished at the expense of the body—as if health were a finite commodity (like oil or electricity) and one could only fill one area by depleting others. This is one of the many falsehoods inherent in materialism, and often it corrupts our view of artistic creativity. Critics sometimes fault artists for being too prolific—as if creativity were a material substance, a sort of natural resource which could be depleted by too wanton use. In fact, the contrary is true. Both creativity and health are self-replenishing; the more they are used, the more they flourish and regenerate.

Bodily health and artistic creativity were seen as complementary, not opposing, characteristics by the Greeks and Romans, and it was only when the scourging of the flesh came to be considered of spiritual benefit by the medieval Christian church that we began to move toward the modern attitude that mortification of the flesh somehow propitiates the creative powers of the mind. The worship of suicidal artists, consumptive poets, alcoholic or insane artists, is an outgrowth of this essentially Christian view that the mind can only flourish at the expense of the body.

Women inherit a double legacy of mistrust in regard to the body. First they share the western Christian heritage that dictates chastity and mortification of the flesh as prerequisites to the spiritual life. But they also inherit the medieval church's primitive attitude toward womankind, childbearing and the female body. For a woman artist, the choice of physical robustness coupled with fertile creativity has been particularly hard—both for psychological and practical reasons. Until the advent of dependable birth control (which is less than a century old) childbearing was not really optional for women except for the deliberately abstinent or accidentally sterile. Pregnancy was too compulsory to be experienced as a choice. But even after the advent of birth control, complex social and psychological forces conspired to make all but the most adamantly individualistic women marry and bear children for most of their adult lives. Pregnancy could hardly be seen as an affirmation of life and health when it was so compulsory, so fraught with dangers for mother and child, and so *constant*. It often did, in fact, herald the end of other forms of creativity, and the fact that many women artists avoided it like the plague and then referred to their books or paintings as "their children" is not surprising.

I belong to one of the first generations of women artists for whom pregnancy is not compulsory (despite the psychological pressures for motherhood that still do exist, not to mention the increasing legal threats to reproductive freedom) and therefore one of the first generations of women artists to be able to examine the paradox of artistic creativity vs. biological generativity. Neither George Eliot nor Jane Austen had that option. Even Edith Wharton and Virginia Woolf were not really able to regard childbearing as a choice; the legacy of Victorian womanhood was too close and too frightening. In their time the only way for a woman artist to combat the Victorian stereotype of "the angel in the house" was to turn around and become the devil (or else to assert that they were mothers of books, and thus *had* fulfilled the ideal of womanhood, albeit in another way).

For years I was determined not to have a child precisely because many of the women writers I admired most had not had children. If childlessness was good enough for Virginia Woolf and Jane Austen, it ought to be good enough for me. One could also mention Emily Dickinson, Edith Wharton, George Eliot, and, closer to our own time, Simone de Beauvoir and Edna St. Vincent Millay. Yet the worm of desire for a child gnawed at me constantly and gnawed at my poems as well. Precisely because I was so afraid of childbearing, I was drawn to it, for I had found that all the greatest steps in my development as an individual were made possible by my doing the very things I feared the most. Having a child seemed to me a rite of passage (without which one could still certainly be a perfectly fulfilled woman, prolific artist and spiritually developed person), but also without which one would have failed to have one of the crucial experiences of the human race. What point would there be in having passed a whole incarnation in a female body without experiencing, at least once, all the potentialities of that body? It would be like being incarnated as a bird and never flying. But still, I hesitated. Childbearing had always taken too much of a toll of women. It had meant jeopardizing the things writers needed most—peace, quiet, a lack of interruptions. It had meant diluting passions which one wanted undiluted for one's work. It was not only the drudgery of childbearing which seemed threatening to art, but the pleasures. Babies are most distracting when they are most pleasurable. Besides, it had taken me years to free myself of the guilt I felt toward my parents and the men in my life when I shut myself away to write. How would I ever deal with the guilt created by a creature who *really* needed me for its physical survival?

There was no way to solve all these problems in advance. I would have to take the plunge and find the solutions later. I would have to give up my constant need to control and manipulate my life, to control and manipulate the future. Control of the future is a delusion anyway, for the future always defeats our most carefully made plans, and the belief that we can control it is merely an instance of human hubris. I came to the conclusion that whatever was lost by introducing this great element of uncertainty into my life would be more than repaid by the new experiences and insights it would bring. For I had belatedly discovered that art cannot exist without life, and that those writers who are overcareful to limit their lives (in the hope of screening out all interruptions) often wind up with nothing to write about, or else are so spiritually impoverished by denying themselves human relationships that all their psychic wounds fester and they destroy themselves and their creativity in various other ways—alcoholism, destructive marriages, other addictions.

I tried to hedge my bets as best I could—controlling as much as possible without trying to control everything. I did not become pregnant until I found a man who really wanted to share all aspects of childrearing with me and I waited for a time in my life when there was enough money for plenty of help. Had those two conditions never arisen, I would probably never have risked becoming pregnant. Whether this makes me cowardly or prudent, I cannot say. I will never be able to claim that I sacrificed all to have a child, but then I am not quite sure that rearing a child in such a spirit of sacrifice is a favor either to the child or to the mother. All I know is that I did the only thing I *could* do at the time. For the first thirty-five years of my life, writing was so much more important to me than anything else, that I could not risk *any* turn of fate that might jeopardize my own still shaky self-confidence as a writer or my need to establish a sense of vocation, regular work habits, and a pattern of self-discipline. For one cannot become a novelist or poet overnight. Even if the talent is there, it takes years to form the *habit* of writing, the sitting down at the desk in the morning, the knowledge of one's own evasions, one's fears of writing, fears of failure, fears of success. Women who bear children *before* they establish these habits of work may never establish them at all, however easy their economic circumstances may be. Having been defined first as mothers (rather than as writers) they may never be able to see themselves in another light and the demands of their children may always drown out the demands of their books.

I only know that I am grateful to have been born into a time when it was possible for a women to delay childbearing until other life patterns were firmly established. Does it bespeak optimism or pessimism for the human race to recognize that (with the possible exception of the prehistoric matriarchies) this is the best time for women the western world has ever known? The discrimination against us is still rampant and virulent. Given how many practical obstacles stand in the way of most of us doing creative work at all, the malignity with which that work is often treated is nothing less than criminal. But still, the fact that we choose when and whether to bear children has changed our lives to a degree unthinkable for the thousands upon thousands of mute, laboring generations of women. The very fact that no generation before ours has really been in a position to challenge the lie that creativity and generativity are one and the same makes us privileged beyond any earlier generations. And that privilege rests almost entirely upon motherhood remaining optional for us. It is the key to all our freedoms—even the freedom to dwell seriously on the meaning of pregnancy and childbirth. For one only has the luxury of philosophical contemplation when a degree of detachment is present. As long as motherhood was constant and compulsory, women *could* not examine motherhood compassionately (and without rage), nor probably could men resist idealizing it.

I think we have never quite considered the implications of the fact that most of the literature about pregnancy and birth has been written either by men or by women who forswore childbearing in order to do their creative work. Even after women writers began to have children more frequently (in the last two generations) they often resisted writing

directly about their experiences for fear of criticism according to patriarchal standards ("don't wear your ovaries on your sleeve") or for
fear of seeming sentimental or trivial. Pregnancy and birth were considered minor, foolish, "female" subjects, and women writers who aspired to the heights of Parnassus often disdained them as their male
mentors had taught them to do. So the lie that creativity and generativity
were somehow interchangeable continued unchallenged for generations. Even in our own day, it has been insufficiently examined.

Neither the women who denied the childbearing urge in order to
create books, nor the men who had wives to bear children for them,
were in a position to chart the terra incognita of pregnancy and childbirth. Both were prejudiced parties, outsiders, partisans of the party
of childlessness. Similarly, women who bore children under various
compulsions (no abortions, no birth control, fear of parental disapproval, a husband's wrath, abandonment by those one loved, the
dreaded loss of the imprimatur of "good woman") were in no position
to dispassionately examine the meaning of childbirth and pregnancy.
Mute, enraged, trapped first by their own bodies, then by society, they
could feel only fury at their helplessness and loss of control—however
much they may have loved the infants they produced. (The record of
recent feminist literature is full of such testaments to rage at men and
simultaneous love of children—the classic female ambivalence).

So, now we stand at a literary crossroads made entirely possible by
childbirth having become a choice. All efforts to withdraw that choice
must be seen as efforts to put women back into the mute rage from
which they have so recently begun to emerge. What untold wonders
would world literature contain if it told the story of pregnancy, childbirth, and childbearing as well as the story of childlessness? What untold
stories might we hear if mothers as well as fathers were able to relate
their tales? The history of world literature is the history of the literature
of the male, the white man, the aristocrat, the affluent bourgeois, and
the childless woman. How different it might look if mothers were writers
too! It might be like discovering the lost continent of Atlantis—right in
our kitchens and bedrooms. It might be like irrigating the desert and
suddenly seeing it bloom. It would certainly put an end, once and for
all, to the notion that books are like babies, and babies even remotely
are like books. For a book's creative demands upon its author end at
the moment of publication; while a baby only begins to call forth *conscious* creativity, after it emerges from the unconscious Eden of the
womb.

SIX

ANALYSIS (DIVISION AND CLASSIFICATION)

ERICH FROMM

Is Love an Art?

According to Erich Fromm, love is the only satisfactory answer to the problem of human existence, and yet most people have very little understanding of the nature of love. The following section, the first chapter from Dr. Fromm's book The Art of Loving, *considers the premises underlying most popular attitudes about love and urges that love be approached in the same searching spirit and with the same effort of will that characterizes the pursuit of any art.*

In terms of rhetorical techniques, the essay is noteworthy for its coherence, which is achieved in part by a careful enumeration of points and in part by effectively tying one paragraph to another.

(1) Is love an art? Then it requires knowledge and effort. Or is love a pleasant sensation, which to experience is a matter of chance, something one "falls into" if one is lucky? This little book is based on the former premise, while undoubtedly the majority of people today believe in the latter.

(2) Not that people think that love is not important. They are starved for it; they watch endless numbers of films about happy and unhappy love stories, they listen to hundreds of trashy songs about love—yet hardly anyone thinks that there is anything that needs to be learned about love.

(3) This peculiar attitude is based on several premises which either singly or combined tend to uphold it. Most people see the problem of love primarily as that of *being loved,* rather than that of *loving,* of one's capacity to love. Hence the problem to them is how to be loved, how to be lovable. In pursuit of this aim they follow several paths. One, which is especially used by men, is to be successful, to be as powerful and rich as the social margin of one's position permits. Another, used especially by women, is to make oneself attractive, by cultivating one's body, dress, etc. Other ways of making oneself attractive, used both by men and

women, are to develop pleasant manners, interesting conversation, to be helpful, modest, inoffensive. Many of the ways to make oneself lovable are the same as those used to make oneself successful, "to win friends and influence people." As a matter of fact, what most people in our culture mean by being lovable is essentially a mixture between being popular and having sex appeal.

(4) A second premise behind the attitude that there is nothing to be learned about love is the assumption that the problem of love is the problem of an *object,* not the problem of a faculty. People think that to *love* is simple, but that to find the right object to love—or to be loved— is difficult. This attitude has several reasons rooted in the development of modern society. One reason is the great change which occurred in the twentieth century with respect to the choice of a "love object." In the Victorian age, as in many traditional cultures, love was mostly not a spontaneous personal experience which then might lead to marriage. On the contrary, marriage was contracted by convention—either by the respective families, or by a marriage broker, or without the help of such intermediaries; it was concluded on the basis of social considerations, and love was supposed to develop once the marriage had been con- cluded. In the last few generations the concept of romantic love has become almost universal in the Western world. In the United States, while considerations of a conventional nature are not entirely absent, to a vast extent people are in search of "romantic love," of the personal experience of love which then should lead to marriage. This new con- cept of freedom in love must have greatly enhanced the importance of the *object* as against the importance of the *function.*

(5) Closely related to this factor is another feature characteristic of contemporary culture. Our whole culture is based on the appetite for buying, on the idea of a mutually favorably exchange. Modern man's happiness consists in the thrill of looking at the shop windows, and in buying all that he can afford to buy, either for cash or on installments. He (or she) looks at people in a similar way. For the man an attractive girl—and for the woman an attractive man—are the prizes they are after. "Attractive" usually means a nice package of qualities which are popular and sought after on the personality market. What specifically makes a person attractive depends on the fashion of the time, physically as well as mentally. During the twenties, a drinking and smoking girl, tough and sexy, was attractive; today the fashion demands more do- mesticity and coyness. At the end of the nineteenth and the beginning of this century, a man had to be aggressive and ambitious—today he has to be social and tolerant—in order to be an attractive "package." At any rate, the sense of falling in love develops usually only with regard to such human commodities as are within reach of one's own possibilities for exchange. I am out for a bargain; the object should be desirable

from the standpoint of its social value, and at the same time should want me, considering my overt and hidden assets and potentialities. Two persons thus fall in love when they feel they have found the best object available on the market, considering the limitations of their own exchange values. Often, as in buying real estate, the hidden potentialities which can be developed play a considerable role in this bargain. In a culture in which the marketing orientation prevails, and in which material success is the outstanding value, there is little reason to be surprised that human love relations follow the same pattern of exchange which governs the commodity and the labor market.

(6) The third error leading to the assumption that there is nothing to be learned about love lies in the confusion between the initial experience of *"falling"* in love, and the permanent state of *being* in love, or as we might better say, of "standing" in love. If two people who have been strangers, as all of us are, suddenly let the wall between them break down, and feel close, feel one, this moment of oneness is one of the most exhilarating, most exciting experiences in life. It is all the more wonderful and miraculous for persons who have been shut off, isolated, without love. This miracle of sudden intimacy is often facilitated if it is combined with, or initiated by, sexual attraction and consummation. However, this type of love is by its very nature not lasting. The two persons become well acquainted, their intimacy loses more and more its miraculous character, until their antagonism, their disappointments, their mutual boredom kill whatever is left of the initial excitement. Yet, in the beginning they do not know all this: in fact, they take the intensity of the infatuation, this being "crazy" about each other, for proof of the intensity of their love, while it may only prove the degree of their preceding loneliness.

(7) This attitude—that nothing is easier than to love—has continued to be the prevalent idea about love in spite of the overwhelming evidence to the contrary. There is hardly any activity, any enterprise, which is started with such tremendous hopes and expectations, and yet, which fails so regularly, as love.If this were the case with any other activity, people would be eager to know the reasons for the failure, and to learn how one could do better—or they would give up the activity. Since the latter is impossible in the case of love, there seems to be only one adequate way to overcome the failure of love—to examine the reasons for this failure, and to proceed to study the meaning of love.

(8) The first step to take is to become aware that *love is an art,* just as living is an art; if we want to learn how to love we must proceed in the same way we have to proceed if we want to learn any other art, say music, painting, carpentry, or the art of medicine or engineering.

(9) What are the necessary steps in learning any art?

(10) The process of learning an art can be divided conveniently into

two parts: one, the mastery of the theory; the other, the mastery of the practice. If I want to learn the art of medicine, I must first know the facts about the human body, and about various diseases. When I have all this theoretical knowledge, I am by no means competent in the art of medicine. I shall become a master in this art only after a great deal of practice, until eventually the results of my theoretical knowledge and the results of my practice are blended into one—my intuition, the essence of the mastery of any art. But, aside from learning the theory and practice, there is a third factor necessary to becoming a master in any art—the mastery of the art must be a matter of ultimate concern; there must be nothing else in the world more important than the art. This holds true for music, for medicine, for carpentry—and for love. And, maybe, here lies the answer to the question of why people in our culture try so rarely to learn this art, in spite of their obvious failures: in spite of the deep-seated craving for love, almost everything else is considered to be more important than love: success, prestige, money, power—almost all our energy is used for the learning of how to achieve these aims, and almost none to learn the art of loving.

(11) Could it be that only those things are considered worthy of being learned with which one can earn money or prestige, and that love, which "only" profits the soul, but is profitless in the modern sense, is a luxury we have no right to spend much energy on?

QUESTIONS AND EXERCISES

VOCABULARY

1. premise (*paragraph* 1)
2. intermediaries (4)
3. mutually (5)
4. domesticity (5)
5. coyness (5)
6. facilitated (6)
7. consummation (6)
8. antagonism (6)
9. prevalent (7)
10. theoretical (10)

LANGUAGE AND RHETORIC

1. The coherence in this essay is derived in part from the author's constant attempts to clarify relationships by means of analysis. Point out specific examples of this practice.
2. Coherence is also established by the manner in which one paragraph is tied to another. Examine the first sentence of each paragraph, and show how many of these sentences employ transitional devices.
3. Could paragraphs 1 and 2 be combined? Why are they presented as separate paragraphs?
4. Analyze paragraphs 3, 4, and 5 in terms of the topic sentence and the controlling idea for each.

DISCUSSION AND WRITING

1. According to the author, how do most people define love? How does he define it? Write an essay in which you define love as you understand it. You might try using types, steps, or stages to help organize your paper.

2. The author enumerates some of the ways in which people seek to make themselves lovable. What are some of the ways that he does not mention? Develop a list of such ways as a possible source for a paper on the subject.

3. Discuss the advantages and disadvantages of each of the two approaches to marital love mentioned in paragraph 4—the traditional idea of the marriage contract that would hopefully give rise to love and the modern idea of romantic love as a motive for marriage. Write a paper in which you enumerate the reasons why you believe one method is superior to the other.

4. If you are prepared to accept what the author suggests about "the art of loving," what specific things can you do to act in accord with his ideas? How, apart from reading Dr. Fromm's book, might you go about mastering the "art"? Make a list of the things that might be done and use it as the basis for an essay of your own.

JUDY SYFERS

Why I Want a Wife

If a woman's "proper place" is in the home as a "housewife," Judy Syfers says she would like to take advantage of those services too—but from a male perspective. Why would a woman want a wife? Syfers offers a host of reasons as she raises some fundamental questions about sex roles and responsibilities in the American family.

As you read, notice how the author adapts the title as a recurring line to organize her essay, and enumerates the "duties" of a housewife accordingly.

(1) I belong to that classification of people known as wives. I am A Wife. And, not altogether incidentally, I am a mother.

(2) Not too long ago a male friend of mine appeared on the scene from the Midwest fresh from a recent divorce. He had one child, who is, of course, with his ex-wife. He is obviously looking for another wife. As I thought about him while I was ironing one evening, it suddenly occurred to me that I, too, would like to have a wife. Why do I want a wife?

(3) I would like to go back to school so that I can become economically independent, support myself, and, if need be, support those dependent upon me. I want a wife who will work and send me to school. And while I am going to school I want a wife to take care of my children. I want a wife to keep track of the children's doctor and dentist appointments. And to keep track of mine, too. I want a wife to make sure my

children eat properly and are kept clean. I want a wife who will wash the children's clothes and keep them mended. I want a wife who is a good nurturant attendant to my children, arranges for their schooling, makes sure that they have an adequate social life with their peers, takes them to the park, the zoo, etc. I want a wife who takes care of the children when they are sick, a wife who arranges to be around when the children need special care, because, of course, I cannot miss classes at school. My wife must arrange to lose time at work and not lose the job. It may mean a small cut in my wife's income from time to time, but I guess I can tolerate that. Needless to say, my wife will arrange and pay for the care of the children while my wife is working.

(4) I want a wife who will take care of *my* physical needs. I want a wife who will keep my house clean. A wife who will pick up after my children, a wife who will pick up after me. I want a wife who will keep my clothes clean, ironed, mended, replaced when need be, and who will see to it that my personal things are kept in their proper place so that I can find what I need the minute I need it. I want a wife who cooks the meals, a wife who is a *good* cook. I want a wife who will plan the menus, do the necessary grocery shopping, prepare the meals, serve them pleasantly, and then do the cleaning up while I do my studying. I want a wife who will care for me when I am sick and sympathize with my pain and loss of time from school. I want a wife to go along when our family takes a vacation so that someone can continue to care for me and my children when I need a rest and a change of scene.

(5) I want a wife who will not bother me with rambling complaints about a wife's duties. But I want a wife who will listen to me when I feel the need to explain a rather difficult point I have come across in my course of studies. And I want a wife who will type my papers for me when I have written them.

(6) I want a wife who will take care of the details of my social life. When my wife and I are invited out by my friends, I want a wife who will take care of the babysitting arrangements. When I meet people at school that I like and want to entertain, I want a wife who will have the house clean, will prepare a special meal, serve it to me and my friends, and not interrupt when I talk about the things that interest me and my friends. I want a wife who will have arranged that the children are fed and ready for bed before my guests arrive so that the children do not bother us. I want a wife who takes care of the needs of my guests so that they feel comfortable, who makes sure that they have an ashtray, that they are passed the hors d'oeuvres, that they are offered a second helping of the food, that their wine glasses are replenished when necessary, that their coffee is served to them as they like it. And I want a wife who knows that sometimes I need a night out by myself.

(7) I want a wife who is sensitive to my sexual needs, a wife who

makes love passionately and eagerly when I feel like it, a wife who makes sure that I am satisfied. And, of course, I want a wife who will not demand sexual attention when I am not in the mood for it. I want a wife who assumes the complete responsibility for birth control, because I do not want more children. I want a wife who will remain sexually faithful to me so that I do not have to clutter up my intellectual life with jealousies. And I want a wife who understands that *my* sexual needs may entail more than strict adherence to monogamy. I must, after all, be able to relate to people as fully as possible.

(8) If, by chance, I find another person more suitable as a wife than the wife I already have, I want the liberty to replace my present wife with another one. Naturally, I will expect a fresh, new life; my wife will take the children and be solely responsible for them so that I am left free.

(9) When I am through with school and have acquired a job, I want my wife to quit working and remain at home so that my wife can more fully and completely take care of a wife's duties.

(10) My God, who *wouldn't* want a wife?

QUESTIONS AND EXERCISES

VOCABULARY

1. nurturant (*paragraph* 3)
2. hors d'oeuvres (6)
3. monogamy (7)

LANGUAGE AND RHETORIC

1. What is the tone of this essay? What elements in the essay reflect that tone?
2. The organizational pattern of this piece is based on repetition of the line "I want a wife," followed by a series of clauses. What effect does this technique have on the reader?
3. Review the author's paragraphing. Can you justify the introduction of each new paragraph? Can you suggest any alternatives to the author's pattern?
4. Syfers uses sentence fragments in paragraphs 3 and 4. Point them out and comment on their appropriateness. Could she have achieved the same effect in some other way?
5. What is the author's purpose in writing this essay, and to what extent has she succeeded in fulfilling it? Support your answer.

DISCUSSION AND WRITING

1. Consider your family life as you were growing up. To what extent does this essay reflect the role of wife and husband in your household. Write a paper reflecting those roles and relationships in light of Syfers' thesis.
2. If you are—or have been—a wife, write a response to this essay in terms of

your own experience. If you are—or have been—a husband, write *your* response to it.

3. Write an essay based on this model in which you pursue the reasons why you want a wife or a husband.

JAMES BALDWIN

On Being "White" . . . and Other Lies

The superiority assumed by some white people over other Americans rests in large part on pigmentation. Stated another way, racism in America—whether individual or institutional—is based on skin color. But what in fact is this "white race," where did it come from, who created it, and why? Novelist and essayist James Baldwin raises these questions in the following selection and offers some obvious but easily ignored answers.

Baldwin employs definition as well as analysis to develop his argument, but the latter is the key to his thesis. Examine carefully his specific use of classification for this purpose.

(1) The crisis of leadership in the white community is remarkable—and terrifying—because there is, in fact, no white community.

(2) This may seem an enormous statement—and it is. I'm willing to be challenged. I'm also willing to attempt to spell it out.

(3) My frame of reference is, of course, America, or that portion of the North American continent that calls itself America. And this means I am speaking, essentially, of the European vision of the world—or more precisely, perhaps, the European vision of the universe. It is a vision as remarkable for what it pretends to include as for what it remorselessly diminishes, demolishes or leaves totally out of account.

(4) There is, for example—at least, in principle—an Irish community: here, there, anywhere, or, more precisely, Belfast, Dublin and Boston. There is a German community: both sides of Berlin, Bavaria and York-ville. There is an Italian community: Rome, Naples, the Bank of the Holy Ghost, and Mulberry Street. And there is a Jewish community, stretching from Jerusalem to California to New York. There are English communities. There are French communities. There are Swiss consortiums. There are Poles: in Warsaw (where they would like us to be friends) and in Chicago (where because they are white we are enemies). There are, for that matter, Indian restaurants, and Turkish baths. There is the underworld—the poor (to say nothing of those who intend to become rich) are always with us—but this does not describe a community. It bears terrifying witness to what happened to everyone who

got here, and paid the price of the ticket. The price was to become "white." No one was white before he/she came to America. It took generations, and a vast amount of coercion, before this became a white country.

(5) It is probable that it is the Jewish community—or more accurately, perhaps, its remnants—that in America has paid the highest and most extraordinary price for becoming white. For the Jews came here from countries where they were not white, and they came here, in part, *because* they were not white; and incontestably—in the eyes of the Black American (and not only in those eyes) American Jews have opted to become white, and this is how they operate. It was ironical to hear, for example, former Israeli prime minister Menachem Begin declare some time ago that "the Jewish people bow only to God" while knowing that the state of Israel is sustained by a blank check from Washington. Without further pursuing the implication of this mutual act of faith, one is nevertheless aware that the Jewish translation into a white American can sustain the state of Israel in a way that the Black presence, here, can scarcely hope—at least, not yet—to halt the slaughter in South Africa.

(6) And there is a reason for that.

(7) America became white—the people who, as they claim, "settled" the country became white—because of the necessity of denying the Black presence, and justifying the Black subjugation. No community can be based on such a principle—or, in other words, no community can be established on so genocidal a lie. White men—from Norway, for example, where they were *Norwegians*—became white: by slaughtering the cattle, poisoning the wells, torching the houses, massacring Native Americans, raping Black women.

(8) This moral erosion has made it quite impossible for those who think of themselves as white in this country to have any moral authority at all—privately, or publicly. The multitudinous bulk of them sit, stunned, before their TV sets, swallowing garbage that they know to be garbage, and—in a profound and unconscious effort to justify this torpor that disguises a profound and bitter panic—pay a vast amount of attention to athletics: even though they know that the football player (the Son of the Republic, *their* sons!) is merely another aspect of the money-making scheme. They are either relieved or embittered by the presence of the Black boy on the team. I do not know if they remember how long and hard they fought to keep him off it. I know that they do not dare have any notion of the price Black people (mothers and fathers) paid and pay. They do not want to know the meaning, or face the shame, of what they compelled—out of what they took as the necessity of being white—Joe Louis or Jackie Robinson or Cassius Clay (aka Muhammad Ali) to pay. I know that they, themselves, would not have liked to pay it.

(9) There has never been a labor movement in this country, the proof being the absence of a Black presence in the so-called father-to-son unions. There are, perhaps, some niggers in the window; but Blacks have no power in the labor unions.

(10) Just so does the white community, as a means of keeping itself white, elect, as they imagine, their political (!) representatives. No nation in the world, including England, is represented by so stunning a pantheon of the relentlessly mediocre. I will not name names—I will leave that to you.

(11) But this cowardice, this necessity of justifying a totally false identity and of justifying what must be called a genocidal history, has placed everyone now living into the hands of the most ignorant and powerful people the world has ever seen: And how did they get that way?

(12) By deciding that they were white. By opting for safety instead of life. By persuading themselves that a Black child's life meant nothing compared with a white child's life. By abandoning their children to the things white men could buy. By informing their children that Black women, Black men and Black children had no human integrity that those who call themselves white were bound to respect. And in this debasement and definition of Black people, they debased and defined themselves.

(13) And have brought humanity to the edge of oblivion; because they think they are white. Because they think they are white, they do not dare confront the ravage and the lie of their history. Because they think they are white, they cannot allow themselves to be tormented by the suspicion that all men are brothers. Because they think they are white, they are looking for, or bombing into existence, stable populations, cheerful natives and cheap labor. Because they think they are white, they believe, as even no child believes, in the dream of safety. Because they think they are white, however vociferous they may be and however multitudinous, they are as speechless as Lot's wife—looking backward, changed into a pillar of salt.

(14) However—! White being, absolutely, a moral choice (for there *are* no white people), the crisis of leadership for those of us whose identity has been forged, or branded, as Black is nothing new. We—who were not Black before we got here either, who were defined as Black by the slave trade—have paid for the crisis of leadership in the white community for a very long time, and have resoundingly, even when we face the worst about ourselves, survived and triumphed over it. If we had not survived, and triumphed, there would not be a Black American alive.

(15) And the fact that we are still here—even in suffering, darkness, danger, endlessly defined by those who do not dare define, or even

confront, themselves—is the key to the crisis in white leadership. The past informs us of various kinds of people—criminals, adventurers and saints, to say nothing, of course, of popes—but it is the Black condition, and only that, which informs us concerning white people. It is a terrible paradox, but those who believed that they could control and define Black people divested themselves of the power to control and define themselves.

QUESTIONS AND EXERCISES

VOCABULARY

1. remorselessly (*paragraph* 3)
2. consortiums (4)
3. incontestably (4)
4. subjugation (7)
5. multitudinous (8)
6. pantheon (10)
7. vociferous (13)

LANGUAGE AND RHETORIC

1. What kind of audience do you think Baldwin had in mind for this essay, and how can you tell?
2. Describe the author's tone. Point out specific words, lines, and passages that reveal it to you.
3. Comment on the title of this piece. How do you respond to it, and why? Would another title have been as effective? Suggest at least one of your own.
4. Show how the author employs analysis as a primary method to develop his thesis.

DISCUSSION AND WRITING

1. James Baldwin has been called "an enduring menace to white supremacy." What is meant by that statement? Does this essay reinforce that description? Why or why not?
2. Baldwin argues that there is a "crisis of leadership in the white community" and attributes the source of that problem to the conditions described here. In your opinion, is there any logical basis for him to come to that conclusion? Do you agree with it or not? If yes, write a paper in which you use examples of contemporary white leaders to illustrate your point. If no, write one focusing on a single white leader you believe to be an exception to Baldwin's thesis.
3. Read some of Baldwin's other essays, which should be readily available in your campus library. You might begin with his book *The Fire Next Time*. See if Baldwin is consistent in his thinking on this subject and write a paper in which you classify several of the ideas that are central to his thinking.

MANUEL J. MARTINEZ

The Art of the Chicano Movement,
and the Movement of Chicano Art

To understand the present cultural values of our people, it is necessary to understand the history of Mexico, to which we are still closely related. Mexican history and artistic expressions that bring life and cultural nationalism within emotional grasp.

Unlike many of the styles of contemporary art, many concepts and forms of Chicano art come from its own traditions. This is not to say that Chicano art is an imitation of Indian, Spanish, or Modern Mexican art, in technique or otherwise. The most *ancient* art of our history is purely Indian and is still considered the natural and most vital source of inspiration. Then following the conquest of Mexico came Colonial art which is based fundamentally on Spanish-European principles of the sixteenth and seventeenth centuries. And then came the Modern Mexican art movement dominated by artists who were Mestizo (the offspring of Indian and Spanish blood) and whose work has both Indian and European influences.

Chicano art is a newborn baby with Ancient Indian art as a mother, Spanish Colonial art as a father and Modern Mexican art as a midwife. Or we can see it as a branch extending out into the southwest United States from the great Bronze Tree of Mexican art. Taking the roots of that tree for granted as being Indian and Spanish, we can move up to the trunk of the tree which is known as Modern Mexican art.

It would be wrong if we first looked up definitions of art in textbooks and then used them to determine the past principles from the modern artistic movement of Mexico. We should start from historical facts, not from abstract definitions.

What are some of the historical and artistic facts of the modern art movement in Mexico? Or, from the Mexican point of view what are some of the significant features in the development of this movement? Despite all the conflict, confusion, and bloodshed of the Mexican Revolution, it created a new spirit. A revolutionary spirit that inspired new leadership and began to be felt and expressed by the writers, the musicians, the poets and the painters. Each felt that it was his duty and privilege to share his talents in the social cause of bringing about a new Mexico. Art for art's sake began to die. The new art would no longer serve as a privilege of the rich or a mere decoration. Since Mexico was largely illiterate, painting had to become the medium of visual education, monumental in size, and become public property.

Some of the more advanced artists and pioneers of this new aesthetic concept formed a group in 1922 known as the "Syndicate of painters, sculptors, and intellectual workers." Among those who allied themselves into this group and who brought forth the first original expression of Modern art on this continent were: Ramon Alva de la Canal, Jean Charlot, Fernando Leal, Xavier Guerrero, Carlos Medina, Roberto Montenegro, Jose Clemente Orozco, Fermin Revueltas, Diego Rivera, David Alfaro Sigueiros, and Maximo Pacheco.

The open-mindedness and foresight of Jose Vasconcelos, minister of education, must be given credit for opening the doors to the usefulness of monumental painting on the walls of public buildings. Under his program, Vasconcelos patronized the artists and they were given but one instruction: to paint Mexican subjects. It was the first collective attempt at mural painting in Modern art.

Then followed the fruits of the "Mexican Renaissance": the rebirth of creative enthusiasm and a time for the people to again recognize human values and their expressions in a creative form.

The Mexican painters have shown in their work the long and exciting history of the Mexican people. Great murals were done by men who sought truth and justice for their people and all of humanity. Mexican Modern art was essentially an art of the Revolution. Nowhere else in the world can the people of a country see so much of their own story told pictorially on the big walls of their public buildings.

Like the modern art of Mexico, the new Chicano art is essentially an art of social protest. Generally speaking, however, there are two types of Chicano art. The first is an art that makes up the cultural front of the Chicano movement that is sweeping the Southwest, an art that reflects the greatness and sacrifices of our past, an art that clarifies and intensifies the present desires of a people who will no longer be taken for granted as second class citizens and whose time has come to stand up and fight for what is rightfully theirs as human beings.

The art of the Chicano movement serves as a shield to preserve and protect our cultural values from the mechanical shark of this society, that has been chewing and spitting out our beautiful language, music, literature, and art for over a hundred years. The artists use their own media in their own way to strengthen the unity of our people and they help to educate us about ourselves since the educational system has failed to do so.

The other type of Chicano art is created by artists who find it difficult to allow themselves to be used by any cause, by any institution, or by any government. They realize that the artist has spent centuries to free himself from the domination of a social hierarchy, the church, or government control. They love the past but refuse to be trapped by it.

Their primary interest is to convey a point of view or an idea, whereas the Chicano artist of the movement generally uses any method to achieve his goal.

The Chicano artist who refuses to plunge into the movement, yet wishes to deal with social concerns in this society, cannot escape the realities in his life, in the lives of people around him, and in the times in which he lives. These things will inevitably begin to show in his work. Art works that are characterized as works of social protest are really just the product of the artist having to deal with the realities he sees. How does he respond to these realities? He writes a poem, a play, a song; he paints a picture, a mural; or models clay or wax.

The Chicano artist will work with his own "raw materials" of his social concerns in his own way. Most importantly, the artist is devoted to his art, and he loves color, form, composition, structure, and rhythm.

There are times when the Chicano artist, like other people, attempts to escape his humanness but cannot. His commitment is to himself and to humanity. He loves art and he loves his people. It is this love for humanity that he can reveal to others and in doing so help fulfill their humanness. This does not mean that he is not going to reveal the countless evils of our life but rather to show you that we must get back our humanness if we are to live in this world peacefully.

SEVEN

ANALYSIS (PROCESS)

ANDY ROONEY

A Rich Writer

While not all college students aspire to be writers, let alone "rich" writers, anyone who is serious about higher education must, as we have indicated earlier, come to grips with writing—the process as well as the product. The four essays in this section thus serve a dual function, as examples of process-oriented analyses and as advice to other writers. This first one, by Andy Rooney, treats the subject in the author's characteristically humorous style, focusing on the preliminaries of the process and offering a series of "tips on how to be a writer without the drudgery of actually putting words on paper."

Rooney's essay is an excellent example of a humorous treatment of a serious subject. Consider the implications for his tone and purpose.

(1) "What does your husband do?" I asked a young woman I met at a wedding last weekend.

(2) "He's a writer," she told me.

(3) "What does he write?" I asked and I noticed that as I did, the tone of my voice turned ever so slightly away from conversational to reportorial.

(4) "All sorts of things," she said. "Novels, short stories and . . . you know."

(5) One of the surprising things about being a writer is that a person need not actually write anything to be one.

(6) On further gentle prodding, it turned out that in addition to being a writer, the young woman's husband had also inherited a lot of money. That's the kind of writer I've always wanted to be.

(7) If there is one thing I know a lot about, it's how to keep from writing. For those of you who want to call yourselves writers, here are some tips on how to be a writer without the drudgery of actually putting words on paper.

1—Only write when your mind is free and clear of any other responsibility. Don't try to write if there's something else you could be doing. Finish all your chores first. Sweep out the garage, clean out your bottom drawer and file those papers and old checks.

2—Work in comfortable surroundings. There should be a couch in your office. If you're sleepy or want more time to think through your idea, relax on the couch for a while. Have yourself a little nap if you think it will help.

3—If, after you awake from your little nap, you find that it's almost lunch or dinner time, close up shop. There's no sense trying to write on an empty stomach. And don't try to write on a full stomach, either.

4—Don't try to write with equipment that is anything less than perfect. Nothing physically wrong with your typewriter, paper supply, pencils, pens or paper clips should come between you and the clear flow of an idea. If, just for example, the holes in the *o*'s, *e*'s or *a*'s on your typewriter are clogged with dried ink from your ribbon and are producing a shaded area on the paper instead of a clean blank spot, bend out the end of a paperclip and pick out the clot of ink embedded in the keys.

5—If there's a telephone call you ought to make, make it before you write anything. If you think of an old friend you might call, call him. Make all your calls before you write.

6—There is nothing more distracting for a writer than for him to have the feeling that he's missing out on something good. If you hear the television set on in some other part of the house, go see what it is.

7—A writer ought to have a work area that is free of other materials. If there are letters you haven't read on your desk or copies of old Sunday newspaper sections, *Harper's* magazine, *Playboy* or last week's issue of *TV Guide*, read them and throw them away before you start to write.

8—Smoking can be a big help in not writing. Cigarettes are good but the pipe is far and away the favorite smoke for the writer who isn't going to actually write anything. A pipe can keep a writer busy all morning just cleaning, packing, lighting and relighting it.

9—Don't write unless the temperature is right. You can fuss with the thermostat and if that doesn't work, change your clothes for more or less warmth.

10—All of us need plenty of time to worry. There simply are not enough hours in the day for each of us to do all the worrying there is to be done. If you have a lot of worrying to do, put off writing until you've done some of it.

(8) By following these simples rules, and inheriting a million dollars, you too can be a rich writer.

QUESTIONS AND EXERCISES

VOCABULARY

1. reportorial (*paragraph* 3)
2. drudgery (7)

LANGUAGE AND RHETORIC

1. What is the author's purpose? How does he employ humor to achieve it?
2. See if you can rewrite this piece to make the same points without using humor. What is the result?
3. What does Rooney mean when he says, "The tone of my voice turned ever so slightly away from conversational to reportorial"?
4. What is the significance of the young woman's husband having inherited "a lot of money"? How does that fact relate to the title and the conclusion of this piece? How does it relate to Rooney's thesis?

DISCUSSION AND WRITING

1. If you are not already familiar with Andy Rooney's television commentaries, watch for one at the close of the weekly program *60 Minutes*. See to what extent Rooney's language and style in speaking match his writing and report your findings in a paper.
2. Rooney does an excellent job in this essay of covering a large number of the things people will do to avoid the act of writing. Obviously there are more, and you may have a few of your own. Write an essay in which you enumerate some of the things you have done—or not done—in this regard.
3. Not everyone enjoys Rooney's humor. (He would probably be annoyed if they did.) If you are one of those who do not, write a paper in which you explain why you feel as you do.

PETER ELBOW

Freewriting

Despite the irony of the title and the author's particular desire to help students not enrolled in writing classes, Peter Elbow's book Writing Without Teachers *has had an important influence on writing instructors throughout the nation over the past decade. The first chapter of that brief volume is devoted to freewriting, a process for helping the would-be writer generate words and ideas. In this selection from that chapter, Elbow explains the process and how it helps the writer.*

Perhaps the best measure of the effectiveness of Elbow's essay might be for you to use his explanation as the basis for practicing some freewriting exercises yourself.

(1) The most effective way I know to improve your writing is to do freewriting exercises regularly. At least three times a week. They are sometimes called "automatic writing," "babbling," or "jabbering" exercises. The idea is simply to write for ten minutes (later on, perhaps fifteen or twenty). Don't stop for anything. Go quickly without rushing. Never stop to look back, to cross something out, to wonder how to spell something, to wonder what word or thought to use, or to think about what you are doing. If you can't think of a word or a spelling, just use a squiggle or else write, "I can't think of it." Just put down something. The easiest thing is just to put down whatever is in your mind. If you get stuck it's fine to write "I can't think what to say, I can't think what to say" as many times as you want; or repeat the last word you wrote over and over again; or anything else. The only requirement is that you *never* stop.

(2) What happens to a freewriting exercise is important. It must be a piece of writing which, even if someone reads it, doesn't send any ripples back to you. It is like writing something and putting it in a bottle in the sea. The teacherless class helps your writing by providing maximum feedback. Freewritings help you by providing no feedback at all. When I assign one, I invite the writer to let me read it. But also tell him to keep it if he prefers. I read it quickly and make no comments at all and I do not speak with him about it. The main thing is that a freewriting must never be evaluated in any way; in fact there must be no discussion or comment at all.

(3) Here is an example of a fairly coherent exercise (sometimes they are very incoherent, which is fine):

I think I'll write what's on my mind, but the only thing on my mind right now is what to write for ten minutes. I've never done this before and I'm not prepared in any way—the sky is cloudy today, how's that? now I'm afraid I won't be able to think of what to write when I get to the end of the sentence—well, here I am at the end of the sentence— here I am again, again, again, again, at least I'm still writing—Now I ask is there some reason to be happy that I'm still writing—ah yes! Here comes the question again—What am I getting out of this? What point is there in it? It's almost obscene to always ask it but I seem to question everything that way and I was gonna say something else pertaining to that but I got so busy writing down the first part that I forgot what I was leading into. This is kind of fun oh don't stop writing—cars and trucks speeding by somewhere out the window, pens clittering across peoples' papers. The sky is still cloudy—is it symbolic that I should be mentioning it? Huh? I dunno. Maybe I should try colors, blue, red, dirty words—wait a minute—no can't do that, orange, yellow, arm tired, green pink violet magenta lavender red brown black green—now that I can't think of any more colors—just about done—relief? Maybe.

(4) Freewriting may seem crazy but actually it makes simple sense. Think of the difference between speaking and writing. Writing has the advantage of permitting more editing. But that's its downfall too. Almost everybody interposes a massive and complicated series of editings between the time words start to be born into consciousness and when they finally come off the end of the pencil or typewriter onto the page. This is partly because schooling makes us obsessed with the "mistakes" we make in writing. Many people are constantly thinking about spelling and grammar as they try to write. I am always thinking about the awkwardness, wordiness, and general mushiness of my natural verbal product as I try to write down words.

(5) But it's not just "mistakes" or "bad writing" we edit as we write. We also edit unacceptable thoughts and feelings, as we do in speaking. In writing there is more time to do it so the editing is heavier: when speaking, there's someone right there waiting for a reply and he'll get bored or think we're crazy if we don't come out with *something.* Most of the time in speaking, we settle for the catch-as-catch-can way in which the words tumble out. In writing, however, there's a chance to try to get them right. But the opportunity to get them right is a terrible burden: you can work for two hours trying to get a paragraph "right" and discover it's not right at all. And then give up.

(6) Editing, *in itself,* is not the problem. Editing is usually necessary if we want to end up with something satisfactory. The problem is that editing goes on *at the same time* as producing. The editor is, as it were, constantly looking over the shoulder of the producer and constantly fiddling with what he's doing while he's in the middle of trying to do it. No wonder the producer gets nervous, jumpy, inhibited, and finally can't be coherent. It's an unnecessary burden to try to think of words and also worry at the same time whether they're the right words.

(7) The main thing about freewriting is that it is *nonediting.* It is an exercise in bringing together the process of producing words and putting them down on the page. Practiced regularly, it undoes the ingrained habit of editing at the same time you are trying to produce. It will make writing less blocked because words will come more easily. You will use up more paper, but chew up fewer pencils.

(8) Next time you write, notice how often you stop yourself from writing down something you were going to write down. Or else cross it out after it's written. "Naturally," you say, "it wasn't any good." But think for a moment about the occasions when you spoke well. Seldom was it because you first got the beginning just right. Usually it was a matter of a halting or even garbled beginning, but you kept going and your speech finally became coherent and even powerful. There is a lesson here for writing: trying to get the beginning just right is a formula for failure—and probably a secret tactic to make yourself give up writing. Make some words, whatever they are, and then grab hold of that line

and reel in as hard as you can. Afterwards you can throw away lousy beginnings and make new ones. This is the quickest way to get into good writing.

(9) The habit of compulsive, premature editing doesn't just make writing hard. It also makes writing dead. Your voice is damped out by all the interruptions, changes, and hesitations between the consciousness and the page. In your natural way of producing words there is a sound, a texture, a rhythm—a voice—which is the main source of power in your writing. I don't know how it works, but this voice is the force that will make a reader listen to you, the energy that drives the meanings through his thick skull. Maybe you don't *like* your voice; maybe people have made fun of it. But it's the only voice you've got. It's your only source of power. You better get back into it, no matter what you think of it. If you keep writing in it, it may change into something you like better. But if you abandon it, you'll likely never have a voice and never be heard.

(10) Freewritings are vacuums. Gradually you will begin to carry over into your regular writing some of the voice, force, and connectedness that creep into those vacuums.

(11) I find freewriting offends some people. They accuse it of being an invitation to write garbage.

(12) Yes and No.

(13) Yes, it produces garbage, but that's all right. What is feared seems to be some kind of infection: "I've struggled so hard to make my writing cleaner, more organized, less chaotic, struggled so hard to be less help-less and confused in the face of a blank piece of paper. And I've made some progress. If I allow myself to write garbage or randomness *even for short periods*, the chaos will regain a foothold and sneak back to overwhelm me again."

(14) Bad writing doesn't infect in this way. It might if you did nothing but freewriting—if you gave up all efforts at care, discrimination, and precision. But no one asks you to give up careful writing. It turns out, in fact, that these brief exercises in not caring help you care better afterward.

(15) A word about being "careless." In freewriting exercises you should not stop, go back, correct, or reflect. In a sense this means "be careless." But there is a different kind of carelessness: not giving full attention, focus, or energy. Freewriting helps you pour *more* attention, focus, and energy into what you write. That is why freewriting exercises must be short.

(16) If there is any validity to the infectious model of bad writing, it works the other way around: there is garbage in your head; if you don't let it out onto paper, it really will infect everything else up there.

Garbage in your head poisons you. Garbage on paper can safely be put in the wastepaper basket.

(17) In a sense I'm saying, "Yes, freewriting invites you to write garbage, but it's good for you." But this isn't the whole story. Freewriting isn't just therapeutic garbage. It's also a way to produce bits of writing that are genuinely *better* than usual: less random, more coherent, more highly organized. This may happen soon in your freewriting exercises, or only after you have done them for quite a number of weeks; it may happen frequently or only occasionally; these good bits may be long or short. Everyone's experience is different. But it happens to everyone.

(18) It happens because in those portions of your freewriting that are coherent—in those portions where your mind has somehow gotten into high gear and produced a set of words that grows organically out of a thought or feeling or perception—the integration of meanings is at a finer level than you can achieve by conscious planning or arranging. Sometimes when someone speaks or writes about something that is very important to him, the words he produces have this striking integration or coherence: he isn't having to plan and work them out one by one. They are all permeated by his meaning. The meanings have been blended at a finer level, integrated more thoroughly. Not merely manipulated by his mind, but, rather, sifted through his entire self. In such writing you don't feel mechanical cranking, you don't hear the gears change. When there are transitions they are smooth, natural, organic. It is as though every word is permeated by the meaning of the whole (like a hologram in which each part contains faintly the whole).

(19) It boils down to something very simple. If you do freewriting regularly, much or most of it will be far inferior to what you can produce through care and rewriting. But the *good* bits will be much better than anything else you can produce by any other method.

QUESTIONS AND EXERCISES

VOCABULARY

1. interposes (*paragraph* 4)
2. obsessed (4)
3. inhibited (6)
4. compulsive (9)

LANGUAGE AND RHETORIC

1. Define freewriting in your own words.
2. What does Elbow mean when he says that the most important thing about freewriting is "nonediting"?
3. Why does the author depend upon process rather than definition as the method for developing his ideas? How does it relate to his purpose?
4. Who do you believe is the intended audience for this selection? What clues suggest this to you?

5. What is the author's attitude toward his subject? Point out some specific evidence to support your conclusions.

DISCUSSION AND WRITING

1. Do *not*—repeat *not*—write an essay based on this selection. Instead, practice freewriting exercises as explained here, and share the results of your efforts with your classmates.

WILLIAM STAFFORD

A Way of Writing

All too often we make an unnecessary, and in some senses false, distinction between "creative" writing and other kinds. Happily, poet William Stafford has avoided such premises in this essay and by so doing has produced an explanation of the writing process that should be equally valuable to all writers, whatever form or function their work assumes. His key statement is his opening one, in which he tells us that "A writer is not so much someone who has something to say as he is someone who has found a process that will bring about new things he would not have thought of if he had not started to say them." That sentence sets the stage for all that follows.

As you read, try to determine whether the process explained here is in fact applicable to the kinds of writing you do for your composition class.

(1) A writer is not so much someone who has something to say as he is someone who has found a process that will bring about new things he would not have thought of if he had not started to say them. That is, he does not draw on a reservoir; instead, he engages in an activity that brings to him a whole succession of unforeseen stories, poems, essays, plays, laws, philosophies, religions, or—but wait!

(2) Back in school, from the first when I began to try to write things, I felt this richness. One thing would lead to another; the world would give and give. Now, after twenty years or so of trying, I live by that certain richness, an idea hard to pin, difficult to say, and perhaps offensive to some. For there are strange implications in it.

(3) One implication is the importance of just plain receptivity. When I write, I like to have an interval before me when I am not likely to be interrupted. For me, this means usually the early morning, before others are awake. I get pen and paper, take a glance out the window (often it is dark out there), and wait. It is like fishing. But I do not wait very long, for there is always a nibble—and this is where receptivity comes in. To get started I will accept anything that occurs to me. Something

always occurs, of course, to any of us. We can't keep from thinking. Maybe I have to settle for an immediate impression: it's cold, or hot, or dark, or bright, or in between! Or—well, the possibilities are endless. If I put down something, that thing will help the next thing come, and I'm off. If I let the process go on, things will occur to me that were not at all in my mind when I started. These things, odd or trivial as they may be, are somehow connected. And if I let them string out, surprising things will happen.

(4) If I let them string out. . . . Along with initial receptivity, then, there is another readiness: I must be willing to fail. If I am to keep on writing, I cannot bother to insist on high standards. I must get into action and not let anything stop me, or even slow me much. By "standards" I do not mean "correctness"—spelling, punctuation, and so on. These details become mechanical for anyone who writes for a while. I am thinking about what many people would consider "important" standards, such matters as social significance, positive values, consistency, etc. I resolutely disregard these. Something better, greater, is happening! I am following a process that leads so wildly and originally into new territory that no judgment can at the moment be made about values, significance, and so on. I am making something new, something that has not been judged before. Later others—and maybe I myself—will make judgments. Now, I am headlong to discover. Any distraction may harm the creating.

(5) So, receptive, careless of failure, I spin out things on the page. And a wonderful freedom comes. If something occurs to me, it is all right to accept it. It has one justification: it occurs to me. No one else can guide me. I must follow my own weak, wandering, diffident impulses.

(6) A strange bonus happens. At times, without my insisting on it, my writings become coherent; the successive elements that occur to me are clearly related. They lead by themselves to new connections. Sometimes the language, even the syllables that happen along, may start a trend. Sometimes the materials alert me to something waiting in my mind, ready for sustained attention. At such times, I allow myself to be eloquent, or intentional, or for great swoops (treacherous! not to be trusted!) reasonable. But I do not insist on any of that; for I know that back of my activity there will be the coherence of my self, and that indulgence of my impulses will bring recurrent patterns and meanings again.

(7) This attitude toward the process of writing creatively suggests a problem for me, in terms of what others say. They talk about "skills" in writing. Without denying that I do have experience, wide reading, automatic orthodoxies and maneuvers of various kinds, I still must insist that I am often baffled about what "skill" has to do with the precious

little area of confusion when I do not know what I am going to say and then I find out what I am going to say. That precious interval I am unable to bridge by skill. What can I witness about it? It remains mysterious, just as all of us must feel puzzled about how we are so inventive as to be able to talk along through complexities with our friends, not needing to plan what we are going to say, but never stalled for long in our confident forward progress. Skill? If so, it is the skill we all have, something we must have learned before the age of three or four.

(8) A writer is one who has become accustomed to trusting that grace, or luck, or—skill.

(9) Yet another attitude I find necessary: most of what I write, like most of what I say in casual conversation, will not amount to much. Even I will realize, and even at the time, that it is not negotiable. It will be like practice. In conversation I allow myself random remarks—in fact, as I recall, that is the way I learned to talk—, so in writing I launch many expendable efforts. A result of this free way of writing is that I am not writing for others, mostly; they will not see the product at all unless the activity eventuates in something that later appears to be worthy. My guide is the self, and its adventuring in the language brings about communication.

(10) This process-rather-than-substance view of writing invites a final, dual reflection:

(11) 1. Writers may not be special—sensitive or talented in any usual sense. They are simply engaged in sustained use of a language skill we all have. Their "creations" come about through confident reliance on stray impulses that will, with thrust, find occasional patterns that are satisfying.

(12) 2. But writing itself is one of the great, free human activities. There is scope for individuality, and elation, and discovery, in writing. For the person who follows with trust and forgiveness what occurs to him, the world remains always ready and deep, an inexhaustible environment, with the combined vividness of an actuality and flexibility of a dream. Working back and forth between experience and thought, writers have more than space and time can offer. They have the whole unexplored realm of human vision.

QUESTIONS AND EXERCISES

VOCABULARY

1. receptivity (*paragraph* 3)
2. orthodoxies (7)
3. eventuates (9)
4. elation (12)
5. inexhaustible (12)

1. Why does Stafford place such a premium on receptivity? Why is that quality so important to the writer?
2. How applicable is Stafford's advice to you as a student of composition? Is this essay really that general or is it more appropriately aimed at an audience of creative writers?
3. The author depends upon his own experience to outline the writing process. Could he have reinforced his purpose by also referring to other writers who share similar views and work habits? Why or why not?
4. Where does the author first make his thesis clear? Show how he uses process analysis to develop that thesis. What other methods might he have used?

DISCUSSION AND WRITING

1. Here, as in response to the previous essay, you may wish to try some free-writing. While Stafford may not use that term, the initial step in his process is virtually identical with that proposed by Peter Elbow.
2. Stafford is one of the best known and most respected contemporary American poets. Look for some of his work in your campus library. You might be especially interested in locating a copy of his poem "Traveling Through the Dark" and the essay in which he recalls the source of the poem and the process by which he put it together.

DONALD M. MURRAY

The Maker's Eye: Revising Your Own Manuscripts

When students complete a first draft, they consider the job of writing done—and their teachers too often agree. When professional writers complete a first draft, they usually feel that they are at the start of the writing process. When a draft is completed, the job of writing can begin.

That difference in attitude is the difference between amateur and professional, inexperience and experience, journeyman and craftsman. Peter F. Drucker, the prolific business writer, calls his first draft "the zero draft"—after that he can start counting. Most writers share the feeling that the first draft, and all of those which follow, are opportunities to discover what they have to say and how best they can say it.

To produce a progression of drafts, each of which says more and says it more clearly, the writer has to develop a special kind of reading skill. In school we are taught to decode what appears on the page as finished writing. Writers, however, face a different category of possibility and responsibility when they read their own drafts. To them the words on the page are never finished. Each can be changed and rearranged, can set off a chain reaction of confusion or clarified meaning. This is a different kind of reading, which is possibly more difficult and certainly more exciting.

Writers must learn to be their own best enemy. They must accept the criticism of others and be suspicious of it; they must accept the praise of others and be even more suspicious of it. Writers cannot depend on others. They must detach themselves from their own pages so that they can apply both their caring and their craft to their own work.

Such detachment is not easy. Science fiction writer Ray Bradbury supposedly puts each manuscript away for a year to the day and then rereads it as a stranger. Not many writers have the discipline or the time to do this. We must read when our judgment may be at its worst, when we are close to the euphoric moment of creation.

Then the writer, counsels novelist Nancy Hale, "should be critical of everything that seems to him most delightful in his style. He should excise what he most admires, because he wouldn't thus admire it if he weren't . . . in a sense protecting it from criticism." John Ciardi, the poet, adds, "The last act of the writing must be to become one's own reader. It is, I suppose, a schizophrenic process, to begin passionately and to end critically, to begin hot and to end cold; and, more important, to be passion-hot and critic-cold at the same time."

Most people think that the principal problem is that writers are too proud of what they have written. Actually, a greater problem for most professional writers is one shared by the majority of students. They are overly critical, think everything is dreadful, tear up page after page, never complete a draft, see the task as hopeless.

The writer must learn to read critically but constructively, to cut what is bad, to reveal what is good. Eleanor Estes, the children's book author, explains: "The writer must survey his work critically, coolly, as though he were a stranger to it. He must be willing to prune, expertly and hard-heartedly. At the end of each revision, a manuscript may look . . . worked over, torn apart, pinned together, added to, deleted from, words changed and words changed back. Yet the book must maintain its original freshness and spontaneity."

Most readers underestimate the amount of rewriting it usually takes to produce spontaneous reading. This is a great disadvantage to the student writer, who sees only a finished product and never watches the craftsman who takes the necessary step back, studies the work carefully, returns to the task, steps back, returns, steps back, again and again. Anthony Burgess, one of the most prolific writers in the English-speaking world, admits, "I might revise a page twenty times." Roald Dahl, the popular children's writer, states, "By the time I'm nearing the end of a story, the first part will have been reread and altered and corrected at least 150 times. . . . Good writing is essentially rewriting. I am positive of this."

Rewriting isn't virtuous. It isn't something that ought to be done. It is simply something that most writers find they have to do to discover what they have to say and how to say it. It is a condition of the writer's life.

There are, however, a few writers who do little formal rewriting, primarily because they have the capacity and experience to create and review a large number of invisible drafts in their minds before they approach the page. And some writers slowly produce finished pages, performing all the tasks of revision simultaneously, page by page, rather than draft by draft. But it is still possible to see the sequence followed by most writers most of the time in rereading their own work.

Most writers scan their drafts first, reading as quickly as possible to catch the larger problems of subject and form, then move in closer and closer as they read and write, reread and rewrite.

The first thing writers look for in their drafts is *information*. They know that a good piece of writing is built from specific, accurate, and interesting information. The writer must have an abundance of information from which to construct a readable piece of writing.

Next writers look for *meaning* in the information. The specifics must build to a pattern of significance. Each piece of specific information must carry the reader toward meaning.

Writers reading their own drafts are aware of *audience*. They put themselves in the reader's situation and make sure that they deliver information which a reader wants to know or needs to know in a manner which is easily digested. Writers try to be sure that they anticipate and answer the questions a critical reader will ask when reading the piece of writing.

Writers make sure that the *form* is appropriate to the subject and the audience. Form, or genre, is the vehicle which carries meaning to the reader, but form cannot be selected until the writer has adequate information to discover its significance and an audience which needs or wants that meaning.

Once writers are sure the form is appropriate, they must then look at the *structure,* the order of what they have written. Good writing is built on a solid framework of logic, argument, narrative, or motivation which runs through the entire piece of writing and holds it together. This is the time when many writers find it most effective to outline as a way of visualizing the hidden spine by which the piece of writing is supported.

The element on which writers may spend a majority of their time is *development*. Each section of a piece of writing must be adequately developed. It must give readers enough information so that they are satisfied. How much information is enough? That's as difficult as asking how much garlic belongs in a salad. It must be done to taste, but most beginning writers underdevelop, underestimating the reader's hunger for information.

As writers solve development problems, they often have to consider questions of *dimension*. There must be a pleasing and effective proportion among all the parts of the piece of writing. There is a continual process of subtracting and adding to keep the piece of writing in balance.

Finally, writers have to listen to their own voices. *Voice* is the force which drives a piece of writing forward. It is an expression of the writer's authority and concern. It is what is between the words on the page, what glues the piece of writing together. A good piece of writing is always marked by a consistent, individual voice.

As writers read and reread, write and rewrite, they move closer and closer to the page until they are doing line-by-line editing. Writers read their own pages with infinite care. Each sentence, each line, each clause, each phrase, each word, each mark of punctuation, each section of white space between the type has to contribute to the clarification of meaning.

Slowly the writer moves from word to word, looking through language to see the subject. As a word is changed, cut, or added, as a construction is rearranged, all the words used before that moment and all those that follow that moment must be considered and reconsidered.

Writers often read aloud at this stage of the editing process, muttering or whispering to themselves, calling on the ear's experience with language. Does this sound right—or that? Writers edit, shifting back and forth from eye to page to ear to page. I find I must do this careful editing in short runs, no more than fifteen or twenty minutes at a stretch, or I become too kind with myself. I begin to see what I hope is on the page, not what actually is on the page.

This sounds tedious if you haven't done it, but actually it is fun. Making something right is immensely satisfying, for writers begin to learn what they are writing about by writing. Language leads them to meaning, and there is the joy of discovery, of understanding, of making meaning clear as the writer employs the technical skills of language.

Words have double meanings, even triple and quadruple meanings. Each word has its own potential for connotation and denotation. And when writers rub one word against the other, they are often rewarded with sudden insight, an unexpected clarification.

The maker's eye moves back and forth from word to phrase to sentence to paragraph to sentence to phrase to word. The maker's eye sees the need for variety and balance, for a firmer structure, for a more appropriate form. It peers into the interior of the paragraph, looking for coherence, unity, and emphasis, which make meaning clear.

I learned something about this process when my first bifocals were prescribed. I had ordered a larger section of the reading portion of the glass because of my work, but even so, I could not contain my eyes within this new limit of vision. And I still find myself taking off my glasses and bending my nose towards the page, for my eyes unconsciously flick back and forth across the page, back to another page, forward to still another, as I try to see each evolving line in relation to every other line.

When does this process end? Most writers agree with the great Russian writer Tolstoy, who said, "I scarcely ever reread my published writings, if by chance I come across a page, it always strikes me: all this must be rewritten; this is how I should have written it."

The maker's eye is never satisfied, for each word has the potential to ignite new meaning. This article has been twice written all the way through the writing process, and it was published four years ago. Now it is to be republished in a book. The editors make a few small suggestions, and then I read it with my maker's eye. Now it has been re-edited, re-revised, re-read, re-re-edited, for each piece of writing to the writer is full of potential and alternatives.

A piece of writing is never finished. It is delivered to a deadline, torn out of the typewriter on demand, sent off with a sense of accomplishment and shame and pride and frustration. If only there were a couple more days, time for just another run at it, perhaps then . . .

EIGHT

DEFINITION

SUZANNE BRITT JORDAN

Fun. Oh, Boy. Fun. You Could Die from It.

Some things just don't sit still for easy definition. Fun, self-respect, happiness— all are equally elusive, and all are subject to scrutiny in the next three reading selections. Abstract aspects of the human condition, they call for a personal perception to be shared before arriving at agreement on their definition. In this first instance, Suzanne Britt Jordan, writing for an audience of New York Times readers, appears to be having fun with fun itself. But don't let her title fool you. She treats her topic seriously by working her way through a succession of common examples to arrive at her own definition—yet another example, but this one of her own choosing. The extent to which you can comprehend and accept her definition is up to you.

While reading this essay, consider what alternative methods might have been employed in search of her definition.

(1) Fun is hard to have.

(2) Fun is a rare jewel.

(3) Somewhere along the line people got the modern idea that fun was there for the asking, that people deserved fun, that if we didn't have a little fun every day we would turn into (sakes alive!) Puritans.

(4) "Was it fun?" became the question that overshadowed all other questions: good questions like: Was it moral? Was it kind? Was it honest? Was it beneficial? Was it generous? Was it necessary? And (my favorite) was it selfless?

(5) When pleasure got to be the main thing, the fun fetish was sure to follow. Everything was supposed to be fun. If it wasn't fun, then by Jove, we were going to make it fun, or else.

(6) Think of all the things that got the reputation of being fun. Family outings were supposed to be fun. Sex was supposed to be fun. Education was supposed to be fun. Work was supposed to be fun. Walt Disney was supposed to be fun. Church was supposed to be fun. Staying fit was supposed to be fun.

(7) Just to make sure that everybody knew how much fun we were

having, we put happy faces on flunking test papers, dirty bumpers, sticky refrigerator doors, bathroom mirrors.

(8) If a kid, looking at his very happy parents traipsing through that very happy Disney World, said, "This ain't no fun, ma," his ma's heart sank. She wondered where she had gone wrong. Everybody told her what fun family outings to Disney World would be. Golly gee, what was the matter?

(9) Fun got to be such a big thing that everybody started to look for more and more thrilling ways to supply it. One way was to step up the level of danger or licentiousness or alcohol or drug consumption so that you could be sure that, no matter what, you would manage to have a little fun.

(10) Television commercials brought a lot of fun and fun-loving folks into the picture. Everything that people in those commercials did looked like fun: taking Polaroid snapshots, swilling beer, buying insurance, mopping the floor, bowling, taking aspirin. We all wished, I'm sure, that we could have half as much fun as those rough-and-ready guys around the locker room, flicking each other with towels and pouring champagne. The more commercials people watched, the more they wondered when the fun would start in their own lives. It was pretty depressing.

(11) Big occasions were supposed to be fun. Christmas, Thanksgiving and Easter were obviously supposed to be fun. Your wedding day was supposed to be fun. Your wedding night was supposed to be a whole lot of fun. Your honeymoon was supposed to be the epitome of fundom. And so we ended up going through every Big Event we ever celebrated, waiting for the fun to start.

(12) It occurred to me, while I was sitting around waiting for the fun to start, that not much is, and that I should tell you just in case you're worried about your fun capacity.

(13) I don't mean to put a damper on things. I just mean we ought to treat fun reverently. It is a mystery. It cannot be caught like a virus. It cannot be trapped like an animal. The god of mirth is paying us back for all those years of thinking fun was everywhere by refusing to come to our party. I don't want to blaspheme fun anymore. When fun comes in on little dancing feet, you probably won't be expecting it. In fact, I bet it comes when you're doing your duty, your job, or your work. It may even come on a Tuesday.

(14) I remember one day, long ago, on which I had an especially good time. Pam Davis and I walked to the College Village drug store one Saturday morning to buy some candy. We were about 12 years old (fun ages). She got her Bit-O-Honey. I got my malted milk balls, chocolate stars, Chunkys, and a small bag of M&M's. We started back to her house. I was going to spend the night. We had the whole day to look forward to. We had plenty of candy. It was a long way to Pam's house but every time we got weary Pam would put her hand over her eyes,

scan the horizon like a sailor and say, "Oughta reach home by nightfall," at which point the two of us would laugh until we thought we couldn't stand it another minute. Then after we got calm, she'd say it again. You should have been there. It was the kind of day and friendship and occasion that made me deeply regret that I had to grow up.

(15) It was fun.

QUESTIONS AND EXERCISES

VOCABULARY

1. fetish (*paragraph* 5)
2. licentiousness (9)
3. epitome (11)
4. blaspheme (13)

LANGUAGE AND RHETORIC

1. What kind of definition of fun does Jordan offer here? How effective is it? Support your answer.
2. Try your own definition of fun, using several different kinds of definition. Which of the alternatives works best for you and why?
3. How do you respond to the title of this selection? Is it appropriate? Effective? Can you suggest any alternatives?
4. The author concludes with a simple three-word sentence. Do you think it works well as a conclusion? Why or why not?

DISCUSSION AND WRITING

1. Why does the author object to the notion of fun as exemplified in paragraphs 3 through 11? What is your reaction to these items? What is the basis for your reaction?
2. What is your idea of fun? Write an essay in which you define fun by means of a key example the way Jordan did in her last two paragraphs. Try to capture the specific details of your experience as precisely as possible.

JOHN CIARDI

Is Everybody Happy?

The "pursuit of happiness" is, according to our Constitution, an inalienable right of every American. But how do we go about that pursuit, and how do we know when we are happy, if we do not really know what happiness is? In this essay John Ciardi examines three different concepts of happiness, charging that the ideas of happiness either as a matter of possession or as a matter of spiritual being are equally misleading.

He then proposes an idea of happiness that avoids the two extremes without ignoring them, that defines happiness as neither a thing nor a state but a process.
    Notice how the author employs definition as his primary method of development and comparison as a secondary method.

(1) The right to pursue happiness is issued to Americans with their birth certificates, but no one seems quite sure which way it ran. It may be we are issued a hunting license but offered no game. Jonathan Swift seemed to think so when he attacked the idea of happiness as "the possession of being well-deceived," the felicity of being "a fool among knaves." For Swift saw society as Vanity Fair, the land of false goals.

(2) It is, of course, un-American to think in terms of fools and knaves. We do, however, seem to be dedicated to the idea of buying our way to happiness. We shall all have made it to Heaven when we possess enough.

(3) And at the same time the forces of American commercialism are hugely dedicated to making us deliberately unhappy. Advertising is one of our major industries, and advertising exists not to satisfy desires but to create them—and to create them faster than any man's budget can satisfy them. For that matter, our whole economy is based on a dedicated insatiability. We are taught that to possess is to be happy, and then we are made to want. We are even told it is our duty to want. It was only a few years ago, to cite a single example, that car dealers across the country were flying banners that read "You Auto Buy Now." They were calling upon Americans, as an act approaching patriotism, to buy at once, with money they did not have, automobiles they did not really need, and which they would be required to grow tired of by the time next year's models were released.

(4) Or look at any of the women's magazines. There, as Bernard DeVoto once pointed out, advertising begins as poetry in the front pages and ends as pharmacopoeia and therapy in the back pages. The poetry of the front matter is the dream of perfect beauty. This is the baby skin that must be hers. These, the flawless teeth. This, the perfumed breath she must exhale. This, the sixteen-year-old figure she must display at forty, at fifty, at sixty, and forever.

(5) Once past the vaguely uplifting fiction and feature articles, the reader finds the other face of the dream in the back matter. This is the harness into which Mother must strap herself in order to display that perfect figure. These, the chin straps she must sleep in. This is the salve that restores all, this is her laxative, these are the tablets that melt away fat, these are the hormones of perpetual youth, these are the stockings that hide varicose veins.

(6) Obviously no half-sane person can be completely persuaded either by such poetry or by such pharmacopoeia and orthopedics. Yet someone is obviously trying to buy the dream as offered and spending billions

every year in the attempt. Clearly the happiness-market is not running out of customers, but what is it trying to buy?

(7) The idea "happiness," to be sure, will not sit still for easy definition: the best one can do is to try to set some extremes to the idea and then work in toward the middle. To think of happiness as acquisitive and competitive will do to set the materialistic extreme. To think of it as the idea one senses in, say, a holy man of India will do to set the spiritual extreme. That holy man's idea of happiness is in needing nothing from outside himself. In wanting nothing, he lacks nothing. He sits immobile, rapt in contemplation, free even of his own body. Or nearly free of it. If devout admirers bring him food he eats it; if not, he starves indifferently. Why be concerned? What is physical is an illusion to him. Contemplation is his joy and he achieves it through a fantastically demanding discipline, the accomplishment of which is itself a joy within him.

(8) Is he a happy man? Perhaps his happiness is only another sort of illusion. But who can take it from him? And who will dare say it is more illusory than happiness on the installment plan?

(9) But, perhaps because I am Western, I doubt such catatonic happiness, as I doubt the dreams of the happiness-market. What is certain is that his way of happiness would be torture to almost any Western man. Yet these extremes will still serve to frame the area within which all of us must find sort of balance. Thoreau—a creature of both Eastern and Western thought—had his own firm sense of that balance. His aim was to save on the low levels in order to spend on the high.

(10) Possession for its own sake or in competition with the rest of the neighborhood would have been Thoreau's idea of the low levels. The active discipline of heightening one's perception of what is enduring in nature would have been his idea of the high. What he saved from the low was time and effort he could spend on the high. Thoreau certainly disapproved of starvation, but he would put into feeding himself only as much effort as would keep him functioning for more important efforts.

(11) Effort is the gist of it. There is no happiness except as we take on life-engaging difficulties. Short of the impossible, as Yeats puts it, the satisfactions we get from a lifetime depend on how high we choose our difficulties. Robert Frost was thinking in something like the same terms when he spoke of "The pleasure of taking pains." The mortal flaw in the advertised version of happiness is in the fact that it purports to be effortless.

(12) We demand difficulty even in our games. We demand it because without difficulty there can be no game. A game is a way of making something hard for the fun of it. The rules of the game are an arbitrary imposition of difficulty. When the spoilsport ruins the fun, he always

does so by refusing to play by the rules. It is easier to win at chess if you are free, at your pleasure, to change the wholly arbitrary rules, but the fun is in winning within the rules. No difficulty, no fun.

(13) The buyers and sellers at the happiness-market seem too often to have lost their sense of the pleasure of difficulty. Heaven knows what they are playing, but it seems a dull game. And the Indian holy man seems dull to us, I suppose, because he seems to be refusing to play anything at all. The Western weakness may be in the illusion that happiness can be bought. Perhaps the Eastern weakness is in the idea that there is such a thing as perfect (and therefore static) happiness.

(14) Happiness is never more than partial. There are no pure states of mankind. Whatever else happiness may be, it is neither in having nor in being, but in becoming. What the Founding Fathers declared for us as an inherent right, we should do well to remember, was not happiness but the *pursuit* of happiness. What they might have underlined, could they have foreseen the happiness-market, is the cardinal fact that happiness is in the pursuit itself, in the meaningful pursuit of what is life-engaging and life-revealing, which is to say, in the idea of *becoming*. A nation is not measured by what it possesses or wants to possess, but by what it wants to become.

(15) By all means let the happiness-market sell us minor satisfactions and even minor follies so long as we keep them in scale and buy them out of spiritual change. I am no customer for either puritanism or asceticism. But drop any real spiritual capital at those bazaars, and what you come home to will be your own poorhouse.

QUESTIONS AND EXERCISES

VOCABULARY

1. felicity (*paragraph* 1)	6. varicose (5)	11. gist (11)
2. knaves (1)	7. orthopedics (6)	12. purports (11)
3. insatiability (3)	8. illusory (8)	13. static (13)
4. pharmacopoeia (4)	9. catatonic (9)	14. inherent (14)
5. salve (5)	10. perception (10)	15. cardinal (14)

LANGUAGE AND RHETORIC

1. Explain the reference to "Vanity Fair" in the first paragraph.
2. What is the meaning of the first sentence in paragraph 15? How does the author connect the concluding paragraph with the opening paragraph?
3. In paragraph 7 the author defines happiness from the points of view of a materialist and an Indian holy man. In paragraph 10 he presents Thoreau's idea of happiness. Reread the section of Chapter Three dealing with definition (pp. 85–90), and then fashion each of these three definitions of happiness into a minimum, formal definition.

4. What is the relationship of paragraph 11 to 10 and of paragraph 12 to 11?
5. Paragraph 9 provides an excellent example of a skillfully constructed, coherent paragraph. Explain how each sentence points backward and forward to the sentences preceding and succeeding it.
6. What is the thesis of this essay? Locate the paragraphs that explicitly reveal the author's views on happiness.
7. The author's tone is serious but not solemn, instructive but not dogmatic. Indicate how the thesis and the diction of this essay reveal this tone. Examine in particular paragraphs 2, 7, 9, and 13.
8. Find examples of the effective use of parallel structure.

DISCUSSION AND WRITING

1. What *is* happiness? How do *you* define it? Write an essay in which you attempt to define happiness, using specific examples rather than abstract language.
2. The author states that we Americans "seem to be dedicated to the idea of buying our way to happiness." What basis does he have for this conclusion? Do you agree with him? Explain why or why not in an essay of your own.
3. Does advertising exist "not to satisfy desires but to create them"? Select some popular and effective advertisements and examine them in the light of this statement. Write an essay about your conclusions.
4. Do you feel that the happiness of the contemplative man as described in paragraphs 7 and 8 is as illusory as "happiness on the installment plan"? What are the reasons for your answer? Write a paper in support of your response.
5. Do you agree with the author that happiness depends on effort, that "there is no happiness except as we take on life-engaging difficulties"? Explain why or why not in an essay, using specific examples from your own experience.
6. How does the author distinguish among "having," "being," and "becoming"? What does he mean by these terms? He argues that happiness is exclusively tied to becoming. Can you make a case for happiness as having or happiness as being? If so, write a paper defending your position.

JOAN DIDION

On Self-respect

If the definitions of fun and happiness proposed in the previous selections were difficult to arrive at, consider the subject of self-respect addressed in this one. As Joan Didion makes clear promptly and emphatically, "self-respect has nothing to do with the approval of others"; thus she places responsibility squarely where it belongs: in the hands of the reader. From that point, she goes on to remind us of a literary and cultural heritage that helped us to define self-respect in the past. In the final paragraphs she closes in on the heart of the matter—self-respect as the core of personal integrity.

Given the nature of this subject and Didion's treatment of it, what follows is likely to be one of the more difficult reading selections in this book. Rather than compound any potential problems by trying to identify all the literary and historic references cited, you may wish to accept them at face value and concentrate on the heart of the definition as it applies to you.

(1) Once, in a dry season, I wrote in large letters across two pages of a notebook that innocence ends when one is stripped of the delusion that one likes oneself. Although now, some years later, I marvel that a mind on the outs with itself should have nonetheless made painstaking record of its every tremor, I recall with embarrassing clarity the flavor of those particular ashes. It was a matter of misplaced self-respect.

(2) I had not been elected to Phi Beta Kappa. This failure could scarcely have been more predictable or less ambiguous (I simply did not have the grades), but I was unnerved by it; I had somehow thought myself a kind of academic Raskolnikov, curiously exempt from the cause-effect relationships which hampered others. Although even the humorless nineteen-year-old that I was must have recognized that the situation lacked real tragic stature, the day that I did not make Phi Beta Kappa nonetheless marked the end of something, and innocence may well be the word for it. I lost the conviction that lights would always turn green for me, the pleasant certainty that those rather passive virtues which had won me approval as a child automatically guaranteed me not only Phi Beta Kappa keys but happiness, honor, and the love of a good man; lost a certain touching faith in the totem power of good manners, clean hair, and proven competence on the Stanford-Binet scale. To such doubtful amulets had my self-respect been pinned, and I faced myself that day with the nonplused apprehension of someone who has come across a vampire and has no crucifix at hand.

(3) Although to be driven back upon oneself is an uneasy affair at best, rather like trying to cross a border with borrowed credentials, it seems to me now the one condition necessary to the beginnings of real self-respect. Most of our platitudes notwithstanding, self-deception remains the most difficult deception. The tricks that work on others count for nothing in that very well-lit back alley where one keeps assignations with oneself: no winning smiles will do here, no prettily drawn lists of good intentions. One shuffles flashily but in vain through one's marked cards—the kindness done for the wrong reason, the apparent triumph which involved no real effort, the seemingly heroic act into which one had been shamed. The dismal fact is that self-respect has nothing to do with the approval of others—who are, after all, deceived easily enough; has nothing to do with reputation, which, as Rhett Butler told Scarlett O'Hara, is something people with courage can do without.

(4) To do without self-respect, on the other hand, is to be an unwilling

audience of one to an interminable documentary that details one's failings, both real and imagined, with fresh footage spliced in for every screening. *There's the glass you broke in anger, there's the hurt on X's face; watch now, this next scene, the night Y came back from Houston, see how you muff this one.* To live without self-respect is to lie awake some night, beyond the reach of warm milk, phenobarbital, and the sleeping hand on the coverlet, counting up the sins of commission and omission, the trusts betrayed, the promises subtly broken, the gifts irrevocably wasted through sloth or cowardice or carelessness. However long we postpone it, we eventually lie down alone in that notoriously uncomfortable bed, the one we make ourselves. Whether or not we sleep in it depends, of course, on whether or not we respect ourselves.

(5) To protest that some fairly improbable people, some people who *could not possibly respect themselves,* seem to sleep easily enough is to miss the point entirely, as surely as those people miss it who think that self-respect has necessarily to do with not having safety pins in one's underwear. There is a common superstition that "self-respect" is a kind of charm against snakes, something that keeps those who have it locked in some unblighted Eden, out of strange beds, ambivalent conversations, and trouble in general. It does not at all. It has nothing to do with the face of things, but concerns instead a separate peace, a private reconciliation. Although the careless, suicidal Julian English in *Appointment in Samarra* and the careless, incurably dishonest Jordan Baker in *The Great Gatsby* seem equally improbable candidates for self-respect, Jordan Baker had it, Julian English did not. With that genius for accommodation more often seen in women than in men, Jordan took her own measure, made her own peace, avoided threats to that peace: "I hate careless people," she told Nick Carraway. "It takes two to make an accident."

(6) Like Jordan Baker, people with self-respect have the courage of their mistakes. They know the price of things. If they choose to commit adultery, they do not then go running, in an access of bad conscience, to receive absolution from the wronged parties; nor do they complain unduly of the unfairness, the undeserved embarrassment, of being named co-respondent. In brief, people with self-respect exhibit a certain toughness, a kind of moral nerve; they display what was once called *character,* a quality which, although approved in the abstract, sometimes loses ground to other, more instantly negotiable virtues. The measure of its slipping prestige is that one tends to think of it only in connection with homely children and United States senators who have been defeated, preferably in the primary, for reelection. Nonetheless, character—the willingness to accept responsibility for one's own life—is the source from which self-respect springs.

(7) Self-respect is something that our grandparents, whether or not

they had it, knew all about. They had instilled in them, young, a certain discipline, the sense that one lives by doing things one does not particularly want to do, by putting fears and doubts to one side, by weighing immediate comforts against the possibility of larger, even intangible, comforts. It seemed to the nineteenth century admirable, but not remarkable, that Chinese Gordon put on a clean white suit and held Khartoum against the Mahdi; it did not seem unjust that the way to free land in California involved death and difficulty and dirt. In a diary kept during the winter of 1846, an emigrating twelve-year-old named Narcissa Cornwall noted coolly: "Father was busy reading and did not notice that the house was being filled with strange Indians until Mother spoke about it." Even lacking any clue as to what Mother said, one can scarcely fail to be impressed by the entire incident: the father reading, the Indians filing in, the mother choosing the words that would not alarm, the child duly recording the event and noting further that those particular Indians were not, "fortunately for us," hostile. Indians were simply part of the *donnée*.

(8) In one guise or another, Indians always are. Again, it is a question of recognizing that anything worth having has its price. People who respect themselves are willing to accept the risk that the Indians will be hostile, that the venture will go bankrupt, that the liaison may not turn out to be one in which *every day is a holiday because you're married to me*. They are willing to invest something of themselves; they may not play at all, but when they do play, they know the odds.

(9) That kind of self-respect is a discipline, a habit of mind that can never be faked but can be developed, trained, coaxed forth. It was once suggested to me that, as an antidote to crying, I put my head in a paper bag. As it happens, there is a sound physiological reason, something to do with oxygen, for doing exactly that, but the psychological effect alone is incalculable: it is difficult in the extreme to continue fancying oneself Cathy in *Wuthering Heights* with one's head in a Food Fair bag. There is a similar case for all the small disciplines, unimportant in themselves; imagine maintaining any kind of swoon, commiserative or carnal, in a cold shower.

(10) But those small disciplines are valuable only insofar as they represent larger ones. To say that Waterloo was won on the playing fields of Eton is not to say that Napoleon might have been saved by a crash program in cricket; to give formal dinners in the rain forest would be pointless did not the candlelight flickering on the liana call forth deeper, stronger disciplines, values instilled long before. It is a kind of ritual, helping us to remember who and what we are. In order to remember it, one must have known it.

(11) To have that sense of one's intrinsic worth which constitutes self-respect is potentially to have everything: the ability to discriminate, to

love and to remain indifferent. To lack it is to be locked within oneself, paradoxically incapable of either love or indifference. If we do not respect ourselves, we are on the one hand forced to despise those who have so few resources as to consort with us, so little perception as to remain blind to our fatal weaknesses. On the other, we are peculiarly in thrall to everyone we see, curiously determined to live out—since our self-image is untenable—their false notions of us. We flatter ourselves by thinking this compulsion to please others an attractive trait: a gist for imaginative empathy, evidence of our willingness to give. *Of course I will play Francesca to your Paolo, Helen Keller to anyone's Annie Sullivan: no expectation is too misplaced, no role too ludicrous.* At the mercy of those we cannot but hold in contempt, we play roles doomed to failure before they are begun, each defeat generating fresh despair at the urgency of divining and meeting the next demand made upon us.

(12) It is the phenomenon sometimes called "alienation from self." In its advanced stages, we no longer answer the telephone, because someone might want something; that we could say *no* without drowning in self-reproach is an idea alien to this game. Every encounter demands too much, tears the nerves, drains the will, and the specter of something as small as an unanswered letter arouses such disproportionate guilt that answering it becomes out of the question. To assign unanswered letters their proper weight, to free us from the expectations of others, to give us back to ourselves—there lies the great, the singular power of self-respect. Without it, one eventually discovers the final turn of the screw; one runs away to find oneself, and finds no one at home.

QUESTIONS AND EXERCISES

VOCABULARY

1. amulets (*paragraph* 2)
2. nonplused (2)
3. assignations (3)
4. interminable (4)
5. irrevocably (11)
6. ambivalent (5)
7. absolution (6)
8. liaison (8)
9. liana (10)
10. consort (11)
11. thrall (11)
12. untenable (11)
13. ludicrous (11)

LANGUAGE AND RHETORIC

1. How essential to your understanding and enjoyment of this essay is your ability to understand the author's literary and cultural references?
2. In paragraph 3, Didion says, "The dismal fact is that self-respect has nothing to do with the approval of others . . ." How central is this statement to her thesis? Why does she make it at this point in the essay?
3. The author examines several different kinds of definition. Point out at least three of these and show how they contribute to her thesis.
4. In her final paragraph, Didion moves on to a different dimension of her subject. Why does she introduce it at this point and how does it relate to her overall purpose?

DISCUSSION AND WRITING

1. Make a list of some personal experiences that you feel helped you develop your self-respect. Then make a list of some that detracted from your self-respect. Use these lists to prepare an essay in which you develop personal definition of self-respect.
2. Does Didion make too much of self-respect? Is it really as important as she thinks? If you agree, what is the basis for your position aside from what you find in this essay. If you disagree, explain your reasons.
3. In paragraph 3 of his essay earlier in the book, N. Scott Momaday (p. 343) speaks of the vision that is the subject of his essay as being "informed by a certain attitude of self-respect." What does Momaday mean by self-respect in this context? Would he agree with Joan Didion's definition? Why or why not?

JOEL M. VANCE

Acrophobia Is Its Name

In George Orwell's "1984," a character's will is broken by using against him his secret fear. He has a phobia about rats and has a cageful of them stuck in his face. If he hadn't been afraid of rats before, that would do it.

Well, if they want to control *my* mind, let them drag me, kicking and screaming, to a high place and leave me there, gibbering and slobbering. Threatened with that, I'll confess to any of my crimes. I'll tell about the time I snowballed the cop car and the time I took all the putty out of the windows at the new house down the block and sculpted clay doggies with it.

Yes, I have a secret fear. Acrophobia is its name, and I am its game. I am afraid of heights. I am not the pluperfect acrophobiac who goes into engine lock on seeing a photo of a mountain, but I'm bad enough. When I funk out at a high place, I do so with a walleyed fright that has caused more than one person to reevaluate the image of me as the incarnation of Prince Valiant.

Had my oldest daughter not already begun to doubt her daddy after I tripped over one of her dolls, then proceeded to punt poor Barbie halfway through a wall, she would have done so when I could not climb a fire tower. We had stopped to admire the view, and she craned her neck to look up at the spidery tower. "I want to climb it," she announced. Little mouse-foot fear skittered through me. I knew daddies were supposed to set an example.

I set one, all right—one that earned me an instant berth in the Pusillanimity Hall of Fame. Carrie was spooked by the multiple stairways, the open grillwork, the height of the thing—but she went all the way to the top. I made three stages, about twenty feet off the ground, before my on-board navigation computer flashed me a fatal-error message and refused to return me to my operating system.

I was phobic.

Now a phobia is different from a run-of-the-mill fear where you get a little shaky and dry-mouthed—but you go ahead and do it. A phobia locks you up tighter than your brother-in-law's pocketbook when you need a loan.

Psychologists claim that a phobia is an irrational fear, but I find the fear of heights an eminently sensible one. If God had meant for us to climb cliffs, He would have equipped us with carabiners for belly buttons and with toenails like crampons. That He made us breakable indicates to me we were not intended to fall from high places onto unyielding surfaces.

There are, of course, high places and high places. I can stand on a broad mountaintop, overlooking most of the western world, without suffering acrophobia. But stick me in a chairlift twenty feet lower down on that same mountain, and my guts turn to tapioca.

Fear of flying and acrophobia seem to go hand in hand, like Famine, Pestilence, and those other guys, but oddly I have no overwhelming fear of flying. Sure, I'm nervous, and pilots with whom I'm riding have trouble landing their planes because I'm holding them in the air by willpower, but I can and do fly. Climbing cliffs, rappelling, even just riding ski lifts, however, turn me into a good imitation of my grandmother's elderberry jelly.

Acrophobia is not fun. And it's not a laughing matter. It's only human, I suppose, to laugh at some dip who is afraid of snakes or spiders or high places, especially when you aren't. For those of us who suffer from fear of heights, though, such laughter is not shared. It isn't funny to me when someone laughs as I get eight feet up a tree toward what I fondly expect to be a perfect deer-hunting perch and go instead into funk, whimpering and squinching my eyes shut like a cat that was put up the maple by the neighbor's dog.

One side effect of unreasoning fear is hyperventilation: rapid breathing that causes dizziness or unconsciousness. The cure is to breathe into a paper bag. I have a better idea—I put the paper bag over my head and imagine I'm home in bed.

Vertigo, the dizzy, disoriented feeling that comes with acrophobia, is the body's warning signal to itself that there is danger, akin to the feeling we get when we lean too far and risk losing our balance. Something tells us to pull back, straighten up. Vertigo is the body exclaiming, "You get away from the edge of that cliff or I'm gonna leave!"

Psychologists say there are only two inherited fears—that of falling and that of loud noises; all others are learned. They say that babies put on a table will shy away from the edge if they see a drop, which seems to indicate to me that babies have enormously more sense than the psychologists who put them on tables and urge them to crawl toward the edge.

Somewhere in the literature I missed the connection or lack of it between the innate fear of falling and acrophobia. It seems to be acceptable for a baby to be afraid of falling on his keister, but irrational for an adult to be afraid of falling off a mountain. Why is this? One psychologist theorized that the fear of rising and falling is evidence of a reclusive personality, one afraid of challenge, fearful of competition—plus some other stuff that wouldn't do to tell in a family magazine.

If acrophobia is inherited, why don't my kids have it? And, if it's learned, why don't they fear heights? They've seen me acting craven all their lives, yet my three oldest children are enthusiastic rock climbers, and the first four all are black-slope downhill skiers.

My wife, Marty, who tinges slightly lime in the gills when confronted with a ski lift, once climbed into a rappelling rig and loped down the sheer face of a small cliff. When they tried to get me to follow, I ran both cold sweat and for the car.

Only baby Amy, bless her chicken little heart, seems to have a bit of the old man in her . . . the groveling, terrified part over there in the corner whimpering, "I can't go up there! I won't do it!"

Some psychologists think that fear of heights masks some other fear—ranging from sexual dysfunction to fear of "falling from heights of illusory grandeur" (as one author put it). I was afraid of heights long before puberty, and my grandeur is so illusory that I wouldn't fall more than about three inches. No, I am afraid of real *heights*—high places, Way Up There.

"Contact desensitization" is what psychologists do to cure the fear of heights so their patients can make perilous climbs and break a lot of bones in falls, the way brave people do. It is a treatment with several steps or facets: 1) informing the phobic about heights; 2) observation of people clambering around on high places without falling; 3) contact with high places; 4) contact with the therapist; 5) rehearsing high jinks, so to speak; 6) and finally, Graduation Day—fun and games in high places (excluding Congress, which is a separate phobia).

The idea of contact desensitization is nothing new—it goes back to 1771, when J. W. von Goethe wrote of the value of repeated exposure to heights in treating acrophobics. This treatment, dressed up in psychojargon, appears to be about what a beginning mountain climber would do—go out with people who are experienced, watch them, have them lead the beginner through the early stages, build confidence, finally actually climb a mountain.

Another suggested cure for the high-altitude hoo-boys is use of the wrong end of binoculars. You start the victim at low altitude but make him look through the wrong end of binocs, which makes it seem higher. Or maybe you look at distant mountains the wrong way, and they look so small you immediately are contemptuous and scale them like a turpentined mountain goat. I just can't believe anyone is going to trick me out of a panic that is so deep I couldn't wade it on stilts.

Dr. Jack Sanders is a friend who is that rarity so beloved by serious mountain climbers—a climbing physician. It's desirable to have a doctor around the bivouac, especially when the bivouac is at 15,000-plus feet and frostbite, pulmonary edema, and other joys of high altitude are frolicking through camp.

But Jack has pretty well given up playing with big rocks—several climbers he knew and admired have died in falls. "Some of them were in places that weren't that tough," he says, "and I began to feel that if you pursue climbing long enough, you're asking for trouble."

Jack climbed first in the Tetons of Wyoming. He scaled the east face of Long's Peak in Colorado in the 1960s wired like a pinball machine—doing pioneer research on the effects of high altitudes on the heart. He climbed the Matterhorn, did other climbing in the French Alps, and was on an expedition that topped a previously unclimbed 18,000-foot Andean peak.

Acrophobia is not a common problem among mountain climbers. "Everyone has some fear of heights," he says. "But climbers spend a lot of time working on their climbing technique maybe ten or twelve feet off the ground. They develop technique and confidence.

"Then, when you're on a rock face," he says, "you're looking into the mountain or up, not down."

But Jack once climbed with a fellow who froze on a rock face about thirty feet off the ground. "It turned out he had had the same experience before, and I guess he was trying to beat his fear," Jack says. "But he froze, and we very carefully secured ourselves so if he fell he wouldn't take us with him, then got him lowered to the ground."

If anything, that seems to indicate the difference between a phobia and a fear. Conquering fear usually is a matter of meeting it head-on, pressing through the yips and tatters of it. But conquering a phobia is not nearly that easy.

Maybe I'm lucky even so, because acrophobia is but one phobia that can plague an outdoor type. Worst of all, I suppose, is agoraphobia, which is a fear of open spaces. Statistically, it accounts for more than half of all phobia cases. Cryophobia is a fear of ice, chionophobia, the fear of snow. Then there are entomophobia (insects), zoophobia (animals), apiphobia (bees), ornithophobia (birds), ichthyophobia (fish), the well-known ophidiophobia (snakes), nephophobia (clouds), astrapophobia (thunderstorms), limnophobia (lakes), potamophobia (rivers), gephyrophobia (crossing a bridge), cremnophobia (precipices), amathophobia (dust), nyctophobia (darkness), hylophobia (forests), and dendrophobia (trees).

Bad as that list looks, it doesn't begin to exhaust the phobic possibilities, which include pantophobia, the fear of everything.

I wouldn't worry about it overmuch, though, otherwise you might develop phobophobia, an abnormal fear of developing a phobia. As Henry David Thoreau observed in his journal 133 years ago, "Nothing is so much to be feared as fear."

NINE

CAUSE AND EFFECT

NORMAN COUSINS

Who Killed Benny Paret?

Each time a death occurs as the result of a professional boxing match, public concern is aroused over the question of whether or not this is a legitimate "sport" for civilized people. Although the following essay was written in response to the death of a boxer in 1962, it addresses the question as eloquently today as it did then. The title goes straight to the heart of the issue: Who must bear the final responsibility for these deaths? In seeking an answer to this question, Norman Cousins recalls an interview that he once had with one of the most successful fight promoters of all time. He then takes the general conclusion drawn from that interview, relates it to the specific case of Benny Paret, and places the blame accordingly.

Notice the way the author employs topic sentences to provide a sense of direction for his essay, and his use of cause and effect as a primary means of developing his argument.

(1) Sometime about 1935 or 1936 I had an interview with Mike Jacobs, the prize-fight promoter. I was a fledgling reporter at that time; my beat was education but during the vacation season I found myself on varied assignments, all the way from ship news to sports reporting. In this way I found myself sitting opposite the most powerful figure in the boxing world.

(2) There was nothing spectacular in Mr. Jacobs' manner or appearance; but when he spoke about prize fights, he was no longer a bland little man but a colossus who sounded the way Napoleon must have sounded when he reviewed a battle. You knew you were listening to Number One. His saying something made it true.

(3) We discussed what to him was the only important element in successful promoting—how to please the crowd. So far as he was concerned, there was no mystery to it. You put killers in the ring and the people filled your arena. You hire boxing artists—men who are adroit at feinting, parrying, weaving, jabbing, and dancing, but who don't pack

dynamite in their fists—and you wind up counting your empty seats. So you searched for the killers and sluggers and maulers—fellows who could hit with the force of a baseball bat.

(4) I asked Mr. Jacobs if he was speaking literally when he said people came out to see the killer.

(5) "They don't come out to see a tea party," he said evenly. "They come out to see the knockout. They come out to see a man hurt. If they think anything else, they're kidding themselves."

(6) Recently, a young man by the name of Benny Paret was killed in the ring. The killing was seen by millions; it was on television. In the twelfth round, he was hit hard in the head several times, went down, was counted out, and never came out of the coma.

(7) The Paret fight produced a flurry of investigations. Governor Rockefeller was shocked by what happened and appointed a committee to assess the responsibility. The New York State Boxing Commission decided to find out what was wrong. The District Attorney's office expressed its concern. One question that was solemnly studied in all three probes concerned the action of the referee. Did he act in time to stop the fight? Another question had to do with the role of the examining doctors who certified the physical fitness of the fighters before the bout. Still another question involved Mr. Paret's manager; did he rush his boy into the fight without adequate time to recuperate from the previous one?

(8) In short, the investigators looked into every possible cause except the real one. Benny Paret was killed because the human fist delivers enough impact, when directed against the head, to produce a massive hemorrhage in the brain. The human brain is the most delicate and complex mechanism in all creation. It has a lacework of millions of highly fragile nerve connections. Nature attempts to protect this exquisitely intricate machinery by encasing it in a hard shell. Fortunately, the shell is thick enough to withstand a great deal of pounding. Nature, however, can protect man against everything except man himself. Not every blow to the head will kill a man—but there is always the risk of concussion and damage to the brain. A prize fighter may be able to survive even repeated brain concussions and go on fighting, but the damage to his brain may be permanent.

(9) In any event, it is futile to investigate the referee's role and seek to determine whether he should have intervened to stop the fight earlier. That is not where the primary responsibility lies. The primary responsibility lies with the people who pay to see a man hurt. The referee who stops a fight too soon from the crowd's viewpoint can expect to be booed. The crowd wants the knockout; it wants to see a man stretched out on the canvas. This is the supreme moment in boxing. It is nonsense

to talk about prize fighting as a test of boxing skills. No crowd was ever brought to its feet screaming and cheering at the sight of two men beautifully dodging and weaving out of each other's jabs. The time the crowd comes alive is when a man is hit hard over the heart or the head, when his mouthpiece flies out, when the blood squirts out of his nose or eyes, when he wobbles under the attack and his pursuer continues to smash at him with pole-axe impact.

(10) Don't blame it on the referee. Don't even blame it on the fight managers. Put the blame where it belongs—on the prevailing mores that regard prize fighting as a perfectly proper enterprise and vehicle of entertainment. No one doubts that many people enjoy prize fighting and will miss it if it should be thrown out. And that is precisely the point.

QUESTIONS AND EXERCISES

VOCABULARY

1. fledgling (*paragraph* 1)
2. bland (2)
3. colossus (2)
4. adroit (3)
5. assess (7)
6. exquisitely (8)
7. intricate (8)
8. futile (9)
9. prevailing (10)
10. mores (10)

LANGUAGE AND RHETORIC

1. The main idea of this selection can be arrived at by answering the question asked in the title. Underline the sentence in each of the last two paragraphs that expresses this main idea.
2. What is the meaning of the last sentence in the essay? What is "precisely the point"?
3. The topic sentence of paragraph 3 is obviously the first sentence. What is the controlling idea?
4. The first sentence in paragraph 7 is the topic sentence. How is the paragraph developed?
5. What is the function of the first sentence in paragraph 8? Which is the topic sentence in that paragraph?
6. Once having committed himself to his subject and thesis, are there any other methods of development that Cousins might have used more effectively?

DISCUSSION AND WRITING

1. Do you agree with promoter Jacobs that most fight fans are not really interested in boxing "artists," that they want to see "killers and sluggers and maulers"? What support do you have for your position? Write a paper to illustrate it.

2. Explain what attracts you to some competitive event such as boxing or auto racing, in which someone could be seriously injured or killed. Consider whether you have any motives that you had not been conscious of previously or that you may be reluctant to face or admit. Your initial treatment of this subject in writing might most appropriately be in journal form.
3. Do you agree or disagree that "the primary responsibility [for death or injury in boxing] lies with the people who pay to see a man hurt"? Why? If you disagree, where do you think the responsibility does lie? Write an essay in which you justify your disagreement.
4. Should boxing be more rigidly controlled? If so, how? What measures would you propose and why? You may wish to "brainstorm" with others to explore possible measures as an exercise prior to writing on this topic.
5. Do you think boxing should be prohibited? Why or why not? Develop a list of reasons on both sides of the issue. Use your list as the basis for an essay defending your views.
6. Is boxing an appropriate collegiate sport or should it be limited to professionals? In an original essay, give specific reasons to support your answer.

JEWELL PARKER RHODES

The Double Whammy

Most people in recent years have been willing to grant, if not accept, the fact that at best it is tough to be a woman in a world dominated by men. If you are willing to accept that premise, try adding to it a condition of color; and imagine how doubly difficult that same world is likely to be for a woman who is black as well. Jewell Parker Rhodes establishes her identity along with her thesis in the first two sentences of this essay, and in doing so immediately illuminates the meaning of "double whammy." Having briefly noted the source of her problem as sexism and racism, she provides a series of examples to illustrate the effects, and concludes with her own strategies for dealing with the situation.

While the framework of this essay is provided by a cause and effect relationship, notice how Rhodes uses her examples to illustrate it.

(1) Business travel can be treacherous when you're female and black. Sooner or later, in neon script, the double whammy of racism and sexism hits.

(2) One morning in Saratoga, I was nibbling a cantaloupe for breakfast when a white colleague cracked a watermelon joke. "I thought y'all preferred to pick seeds," he said. A white couple at an Ivy League Club in New York mistook me for a maid and asked me to clean their room— despite the fact that my hair was neatly pinned, I carried a briefcase, and wore my "intellectual" glasses and my three-piece pinstripe suit. A

fellow professor at a convention in Detroit assumed I was a local black hooker. Why? I wasn't near a bar. On one excursion South, I eschewed a conference cafeteria lunch in favor of a hamburger diner; over relish and onions, an ancient white man offered me five dollars if I took a trip to his house: "Just for an hour." (He must have been recalling pre-inflation days.) Needless to say, my professional performance lacked luster when I delivered my paper during the afternoon conference session.

(3) Like an innocent or a fool, I began each trip with optimism, still determined that race and sex not impede my performance and acceptance. My pretensions get depressed.

(4) How potent is the subliminal irritation of being the only woman on the businessman's shuttle between New York and Washington? Of being the only minority at a professional meeting? Each trip represents for me a lesson in alienation. Yet because I'm conducting business, "networking," and trying to promote a career, I can't afford feeling alien since its engenders mistrust and withdrawal. So each trip I'm vulnerable anew.

(5) Why *can't* business travel be pleasurable? I've read all the books and articles on "how to dress for success." Wind me up and I conduct myself with adequate charm. But after following all the advice, I find myself still belittled—*and* rendered less effective—due to the emotional and psychological assaults.

(6) Articles and books don't tell you how to deal with the loneliness of being the only visible minority in a Midwestern town, or in an airport, or at a meeting. Once I walked through a community for hours and never saw another face with the slightest hint of brown. I did, however, spend my evenings being interrogated by "well-intentioned" liberals who wanted my opinion on every civil rights issue since the Civil War. Willy-nilly, I am a spokesperson for my race.

(7) Articles and books also don't tell you how to deal with sexual assaults beyond "carry a book to dinner." My rage gets dissipated only in a Howard Johnson's hotel room, alone, with room service.

(8) It becomes doubly hard to ward off sexual invitation when you feel intense loneliness because nowhere else in the conference, the hotel, or the lounge, is there anyone who in the least resembles your sex or color. One loneliness begets another. Yet ward off sexual invitations you must—since the macho, conquering male abounds at professional meetings and since men compound their sexism with racist awe regarding your color. Any nonwhite characteristics can be viewed as exotic plumes.

(9) Once, in the District of Columbia following a conference dinner, my white male colleague and escort was nearly attacked by three black youths. Only a police officer delayed their action. Do you honestly believe I was at my professional peak the next day? And there also have

been predominantly black conferences where sexist attitudes angered me so intensely I could barely function. I recall the time in Ohio when an African colleague called me in my hotel room at 1:30 in the morning so we could "discuss" improved relations between his country and mine. The rest of the night I didn't sleep.

(10) In Atlanta, I spent a whole day shunning a black male's advances. The bathroom provided my sole measure of peace. At dinner, I was enjoying my conversation with an author on my right when my ego-bruised pursuer shouted, "I'm a man too!" I groaned. I wanted to hide beneath the table. I'd forgotten that public conversation between a male and female is seen as sexual.

(11) What are the strategies for negotiating the sexist and racist trials of professional meetings? I honestly don't know. A business suit doesn't necessarily serve as armor. A book doesn't shield one from all sexual encounters. I've tried wearing makeup and no makeup. I've tried dressing up and dressing down. I've tried the schoolmarm's bun and also the thick-rimmed glasses. Still sexism abounds. Superficial transformations don't negate discrimination. About my color, I can do nothing (nor would I want to if I could).

(12) The best one can do is try to prevail with dignity. When I've been the only woman at a conference, I search for minority colleagues—shared interests and shared culture sometimes bind. When I've been the only black, I search for women—women hug you when you're down and encourage you in your work. When I've been the only black *and* the only woman, I call long distance to reach out and touch a friend.

(13) Sometimes humor helps. One year I dressed severely to compensate for my baby face. I wore high heels to compensate for my lack of height. I felt every inch the professional. Yet at the academic convention registration, I was brusquely pulled aside. "Can't you read the signs? Student registration is to the right."

(14) If they don't get you for race and sex, they get you for something else.

QUESTIONS AND EXERCISES

VOCABULARY

1. eschewed (*paragraph* 2)
2. impede (3)
3. engenders (4)
4. interrogated (6)

LANGUAGE AND RHETORIC

1. What kind of audience does this author have in mind? Point out specific evidence of your conclusion.

2. This selection originally was published with the title "When Your Sense of Humor Is Your Best Traveling Companion." Which title do you prefer and why?

3. Although there are many brief paragraphs in this essay, the writer rarely introduces a new one without having a justification. Review her practice to see if you can identify any exceptions.

4. Examine the author's use of cause and effect to develop her thesis. Show how she combines that method with examples.

5. How would you characterize the tone of this piece? What specific passages can you cite to illustrate it?

DISCUSSION AND WRITING

1. If you have ever been the object of either the racism or the sexism that the author writes about here, develop an essay of your own in which you recall such an experience and the effect that it had on you.

2. What other kinds of "whammies" are there in addition to racism and sexism? Develop a list of them and select one that is particularly important to you. Then write an essay in which you review the cause and effect relationship.

3. Much has been written about sexual harassment aside from the matter of racial prejudice. Review some of the resources on this subject in your campus library and write a paper based on your findings.

ALVIN TOFFLER

The Data Deluge

Writers in recent years have had a great deal to say about the "Information Revolution" and its effects on society; but, as Alvin Toffler notes, surprisingly little has been said about its causes. Toffler sets out to rectify that situation by taking us back in time and demonstrating the developments in commerce and industry that have been shaping a new social structure. In turn, he finds that this new society itself stimulates a demand for the Information Revolution.

Toffler makes use of an unlikely comparison in the form of an earthworm. Watch for it as you read, and see how effective you think it is.

(1) Millions of words have been written about the Information Revolution. But very little analysis has been devoted to its causes. Why are we now entering what some call the Information Age? Why not 100 years ago, or, for that matter, 100 years from now?

(2) It is, of course, always difficult to establish the causation of any great historical development, but I believe that the hidden fuel of the Information Revolution is a combustive mixture of diversity and accelerated change.

(3) Since approximately the mid-Fifties we've been experiencing the crack-up of the old industrial mass society. In scores of fields, from technology to ethnicity, we see deepening diversity—more variety of types, sizes, and models of goods and services; more varied art forms; more specialization of labor; more diverse family styles; more numerous ethnic, racial, and group identities; more varied technical processes; more special-interest newsletters and channels for electronic narrow-casting; a greater variety of corporate organizational forms, military weapons, and political-pressure groups of all stripes.

(4) Diversity is breaking out all over, and this sudden increase of heterogeneity at every level is cracking the old, familiar structures of the Industrial Age.

(5) Over the past 300 years, the Industrial Revolution gave rise to a chain of interconnected mass societies from Europe and North America to east Asia. These are societies based on mass production, mass distribution, mass education, mass media, mass entertainment, and mass political movements—not to mention weapons of mass destruction. They are societies built on a blue-collar way of life.

(6) In blue-collar societies, millions of people arise more or less at the same hour, commute to work in unison, tend the machines in sync with one another, return home, watch the same TV program as their neighbors, and turn out the lights—all in a kind of mass rhythm. People tend to dress alike, live in cookie-cutter apartments, and share the values of their next-door neighbors. In short, while this may be something of a caricature, the fact is that in all the industrial nations, from Japan at one end to Europe and the United States at the other, there was, until recently, a very high degree of what might be called "massness," or uniformity.

(7) This much-criticized homogenization of life was often attributed to technology: It was the machine that was depriving us of individualism. Indeed, thousands of novels, stories, and science-fiction scenarios assured us that the more advanced our technologies became, the more standardized and uniform we would become as people. This idea became a standard part of our intellectual equipment.

(8) The truly revolutionary fact of our time, however, is that the entire process of massification has now reversed itself. Rather than becoming more alike, we are breaking up the old mass structures and processes. A wholly different, more complex social system is arising to replace the mass society that was the social embodiment of the Industrial Age. Today's revolution is not just a matter of more or better machines; it is accompanied by a fundamental change in the underlying structure of society.

(9) Whereas throughout the industrial past the main thrust of change was toward greater homogenization, today we are rapidly moving to-

ward "heterogenization." For example, we are now moving beyond mass production to computer-based custom production. The new technologies favor diversity and short runs, rather than the long, uniform runs made necessary by precomputer industrial mechanization.

(10) In commerce, we are moving from mass marketing to market segmentation. In society, we are moving from the nuclear family as the single, socially approved model of family life to a variety of family forms. In communications, we see the once-powerful broadcast networks losing audiences, while cable and alternative media—all based on small, rather than mass, audiences—gain. We are beginning to break the grip of the mass media as we move beyond the stage of mass society.

(11) In a word, we are de-massifying the mass society. We are piecing together a more differentiated society, made up of more varied components. And that requires far more information to pulse back and forth among the components.

(12) Imagine a simple biological organism—an earthworm, for instance. It has few differentiated parts. Contrast that with a human: We have lungs and lymph glands, cortex and cornea, and thousands of other interrelated, functionally specialized parts. For all these parts to interact properly, vast amounts of "information" must flow through the body in the form of electrical pulses, chemical bursts, and hormonal secretions, each of which represents a message—so that a certain neural pulse, for example, tells the muscle to contract or the eye to dilate. These messages contain information, and tremendous amounts of information need to be routed through the body if its parts are to be synchronized or coordinated with one another.

(13) And the more specialized or diverse the parts of the body, the more information is needed to function well. There's more information flowing through our bodies than through the body of that earthworm.

(14) Now let's apply the same principle to society. If I'm right that we're moving beyond the stage of mass production, distribution, and communication—if the variety of organizational structures *is* increasing; if we *are* moving toward smaller, more numerous, more decentralized units (sometimes organized within very large organizational frameworks); if our laws *are* multiplying and our products, values, and attitudes are becoming more heterogeneous; if mass society is being replaced by a much more differentiated social order—then it takes far more information just to keep the whole emerging system in some semblance of equilibrium.

(15) In short, the heterogeneity of the new society *demands* higher levels of information exchange than did the homogeneity of a mass society. The information explosion and the new information technologies are a response to this need.

(16) Furthermore, many of the latest tools designed to help us cope

with the greater floods of essential information actually foster or facilitate still further diversification.

(17) One small example: In traditional industry, all workers are supposed to show up at the factory gate when the whistle blows—all at the same time. It is a simple system: a uniform schedule. The computer, however, facilitates the introduction of flex-time systems, that is, a great diversity of personalized schedules. Similar examples can be found in inventory control and a thousand other fields. The computer, far from being a totalitarian monster that homogenizes us, is contributing greatly to the thrust toward diversity at every level today.

(18) But diversity in the ordinary sense is only part of the story. There is another important factor as well, and that is the speed of change itself.

(19) The faster things change, the more information we need to deal with new conditions. It's really just a special case of the principle mentioned above, because change can be regarded as diversity in time. The state of being at one moment becomes different the next. And the more often that happens, the more information we need to keep on making adaptive decisions.

(20) So I see rising diversity combined with accelerated change as basic reasons why we are experiencing an information explosion. Society is evolving from earthworm to human being, as it were, at very high speeds—faster than the Agricultural Revolution of 10,000 years ago, faster than the Industrial Revolution of 300 years ago. The result: a fantastic proliferation of information on every conceivable topic and a concurrent burst of new electronic inventions for rapidly storing, coding, classifying, manipulating, and communicating information.

(21) In short, there *are* reasons for today's Information Revolution, a significant turning point in human culture.

QUESTIONS AND EXERCISES

VOCABULARY

1. narrowcasting (*paragraph* 3)
2. heterogeneity (4)
3. caricature (6)
4. proliferation (20)

LANGUAGE AND RHETORIC

1. What is the author's thesis and at what point does he first indicate it? State that thesis in your own terms.
2. How do you respond to Toffler's use of the earthworm for comparative purposes? Does it strike you as an effective rhetorical technique? Why or why not?

3. In addition to his basic method of development—cause and effect—Toffler employs several others. Identify at least two of them and show how they contribute to his purpose.

DISCUSSION AND WRITING

1. Toffler says that our mass society is breaking into a new social structure characterized by greater diversity. In paragraphs 9 and 10, he provides examples of this alleged shift. Can you think of others that would support his thesis? (Do not necessarily limit yourself to industry and commerce.)
2. Other writers have, of course, argued that recent developments in American culture have resulted in more, rather than less, of a mass social structure. Advocates of this view frequently cite the various forms of mass media— movies, broadcast television, video and audio tapes and cassettes, magazines—as largely responsible for this effect. Which view, Toffler's or this one, strikes you as closer to the truth, and why?
3. Toffler deals with the second aspect of his subject, change, in two earlier books—*Future Shock* and *The Ninth Wave*. Locate one of these volumes in your library and review it as a possible source for additional writing topics.

LEWIS THOMAS

Nuclear Winter, Again

It has taken a long time, the better part of a year, but the news seems at last to be taking hold, maybe sinking in. Thermonuclear warfare is an impossibility, and the weapons can never be used for any kind of decisive military accomplishment. This is not to say that they cannot be exploded, only that they cannot be employed by any nation on the scale needed to bring another nation to its knees. An international group of scientists has discovered that the blast and fires from even a limited nuclear attack would lift a huge, dense cloud over our earth. The cloud would bring on a Nuclear Winter, blotting out much of the sun for months, freezing much of the planet, killing almost every form of life.

This means that the destruction of weaponry, troops, cities, ports, and military command and control will have to be achieved by some other method. If nuclear weaponry is used, the nation firing off its missiles would discover that it had committed suicide. Moreover, it would bring down all the other nations in the Northern Hemisphere and, very likely, many in the Southern Hemisphere. The earth would be subjected to a permanent loss of life comparable to the mass extinction of the dinosaurs and numberless other forms of terrestrial and marine life 65 million years ago.

When I first heard the details of this discovery, late in the spring of 1983, I took it to be the greatest piece of good news to emerge from science in the whole twentieth century (a century with less than its fair share of good news up to now). Later in the year, on October 31, an international conference was convened in Washington for the explicit purpose of making the threat of Nuclear Winter as public as possible. In attendance were several hundred eminent scientists from twenty countries, representing the disciplines and subdisciplines of physics, climatology, biology, and medicine, plus various American and foreign public officials, educators, foreign policy experts, and military and arms control specialists. There were over a hundred newspaper, television, and radio journalists present. On November 1, the Washington assemblage was linked by satellite, direct and live, to a group of Soviet scientists in Moscow for a back-and-forth exchange of views.

And then, in the days and weeks that followed, the strangest of things happened: not much of anything. Some of the major national newspapers carried brief, almost perfunctory, accounts of the conference, most of them on inside pages. I do not recall hearing any mention of the affair on any of the network news programs on the next day, or indeed on any other day, with the single exception of a half-hour discussion on ABC's *Nightline* program.

A month later four Soviet scientists came to testify in Washington on the same topic in the Senate Caucus Room, together with four American counterpart scientists, at the invitation of senators Kennedy and Hatfield. They expressed their total agreement with the conclusions reached at the end of the October conference. This meeting, also unprecedented, was open to the public and attended by at least a score of media representatives. It received no notice on that evening's television news programs, and virtually none in the next day's newspapers.

Since these events, now almost a full year ago, I have been conducting an informal running poll of the friends and acquaintances I meet at random social occasions, in and out of science, a generally well informed sample of the population, attentive to the news of the day. I would estimate that around 25 percent of these people had never heard of Nuclear Winter. Late in July 1984, a paragraph in the New York *Times* stated that the President had ordered the National Oceanographic and Atmospheric Agency (NOAA) to investigate the problem and report back, next year.

The story has become more accessible in recent months. The full proceedings of the October 31, 1983, Washington conference were published in a book, out in June, entitled *The Cold and the Dark: The World After Nuclear War.* This volume contains all the available public information on Nuclear Winter as of the early part of 1984. It can be read through at one sitting, with effects that are either devastating or encouraging, depending on your point of view. Devastating if you believe that nuclear war is still possible; encouraging if you are convinced, as I am, that the weapons are now, in the flattest, most matter-of-fact military sense, *impractical*.

Most of my journalist friends have been in the devastated camp during the past year, and I think this accounts for their failure to pay the concentrated, sustained attention to this story that it has plainly merited. They have complained to me that the scenario strikes them as just another piece of bad news about nuclear bombs, not much worse than the previous news that more than one billion people will be killed outright if a nuclear war should start and that another billion will die later on. When I have tried to describe the other consequences of that opaque cloud of dust and soot—the exclusion of almost all sunlight for a period of months, which will freeze all fresh water solid and kill most plants and animals—they have their minds fixed on that figure of a billion human beings killed by blast and fire.

But now, I think and hope, things are finally different. The story is beginning to reach public awareness and concern. Numerous groups of scientists here and abroad have confirmed the general outlines of the Nuclear Winter scenario. Intensive efforts are under way to refine the details and, of greatest concern to the investigators, to determine whether the threshold of nuclear explosives—the level of nuclear blasts that would bring on the Winter—is as low as the 100 megaton range (the world's present arsenal is now around 18,000 megatons) or is, as some of them believe, still lower. The scientific academies of the non-nuclear, non-combatant nations have become increasingly worried for their own homelands. The people who seem to like nuclear missiles are starting to protest that big bombs are already obsolete anyway because of the fantastic accuracy of the new "smart" warheads; do not worry about megatons, they say, we can use neat little ones in the low kiloton range (Hiroshima was neatly taken out with only twelve kilotons). Do not worry, they say, but they are worried.

The story has been a long one, first emerging in public view almost three years ago. It began with Dr. Paul J. Crutzen, director of the Max Planck Institute in Mainz, West Germany. Crutzen had been asked to contribute an article to the Swedish Academy's journal *Ambio*, for a special issue to come out in 1982 dealing with the known physical, biological, and medical effects of a nuclear war. He had previously done work on various chemical constituents of the atmosphere, and began thinking about possible effects on the layer of ozone that shields planetary life against lethal exposure to ultraviolet light. But he had also studied the distribution of smoke over burning forests in tropical Brazil. He started work with Dr. John Birks, of the University of Colorado, and their collaboration in computer modeling experiments was the beginning of the Nuclear Winter story. The title of the Crutzen-Birks paper in *Ambio* was "The Atmosphere After a Nuclear War: Twilight at Noon."

Another group of scientists, at Cornell University and the NASA Ames Research Center in California, had been studying the effects of atmospheric dust on sunlight, based on earlier findings in the dust storms on Mars and after volcanic eruptions on Earth. They turned their attention to soot, with results that became the central topic of the Washington conference last October. Their paper is referred to as the TTAPS report, an acronym for the names of the investigators (Turco, Toon, Ackerman, Pollack, and Sagan).

As things stand today, there seems to be little or no disagreement in principle over the two reports. The questions that remain are concerned with matters of detail: What is the minimum number of megatons that might be exploded in a nuclear exchange without the risk of Nuclear Winter? How much of the cloud will drift over the Southern Hemisphere? Is there any scheme for *effective* targeting by either side that can avoid the threshold of fire and smoke?

The scientists contributing to *The Cold and the Dark* agreed, in advance of their conference, to keep their reports free of politics. This may have been a mistake. Perhaps the conference would have gained more public attention if the participants, especially the Americans and Russians, had spoken more plainly on the implications of their findings. The whole problem of nuclear disarmament has been transformed. It is no longer a deep technical puzzle to be waffled over or postponed forever by diplomats and analysts. The discoveries described in *The Cold and the Dark* mark a turning point not only in the affairs of mankind but also, in Jonathan Schell's prophetic phrase, in the fate of the earth.

Indexes

Index to Reading Selections by Subject Matter

(Most selections are listed under more than one subject.)

(A substantial number of the other reading selections also deal with this subject either directly or indirectly.)

Index to Reading Selections
by Basic Rhetorical Type

Index to Questions
on Language and Rhetoric

A 5
B 6
C 7
D 8
E 9
F 0
G 1
H 2
I 3
J 4